CAMERA MAN

CAMERA MAN

BUSTER KEATON,
THE DAWN OF CINEMA, AND THE
INVENTION OF THE TWENTIETH CENTURY

DANA STEVENS

ATRIA BOOKS

New York   London   Toronto   Sydney   New Delhi

An Imprint of Simon & Schuster, Inc.
1230 Avenue of the Americas
New York, NY 10020

First Atria Books hardcover edition January 2022

ATRIA B O O K S and colophon are trademarks of Simon & Schuster, Inc.

For information about special discounts for bulk purchases,
please contact Simon & Schuster Special Sales at 1-866-506-1949
or business@simonandschuster.com.

The Simon & Schuster Speakers Bureau can bring authors to
your live event. For more information or to book an event,
contact the Simon & Schuster Speakers Bureau at 1-866-248-3049
or visit our website at www.simonspeakers.com.

Interior design by Kyle Kabel

Manufactured in the United States of America

1   3   5   7   9   10   8   6   4   2

Library of Congress Cataloging-in-Publication Data
Names: Stevens, Dana (Film critic), author.
Title: Camera man : Buster Keaton, the dawn of cinema, and the
invention of the Twentieth Century / Dana Stevens.
Description: First Atria Books hardcover edition. | New York : Atria Books, 2022. |
Includes bibliographical references and index.
Identifiers: LCCN 2021045585 | ISBN 9781501134197 (hardcover) |
ISBN 9781501134203 (paperback) | ISBN 9781501134210 (ebook)
Subjects: LCSH: Keaton, Buster, 1895–1966. | Motion picture actors and actresses—
United States—Biography. | Motion picture producers and directors—United States—
Biography. | Silent films—United States—History and criticism. |
Motion picture industry—California—Los Angeles—History—20th century.
Classification: LCC PN2287.K4 S74 2022 | DDC 791.4302/8092 [B]—dc23/eng/20211115
LC record available at https://lccn.loc.gov/2021045585

ISBN 978-1-5011-3419-7
ISBN 978-1-5011-3421-0 (ebook)

For my paternal grandfather, David Walter Stevens,
who, like Buster, was born in 1895,
and my maternal grandmother, Shyrle Frances Hacker,
who was a chorus dancer with the Fanchon and Marco
traveling dance troupe in the early 1930s.
The history in this book is their history, too.

Contents

CONTENTS

CAMERA MAN

Introduction

I first fell for Buster Keaton twenty-five years ago, when he had just turned one hundred. It was the spring of 1996, and I was spending the year studying at the University of Strasbourg, close to the French-German border in Alsace. Nineteen ninety-five had marked the centenary of Keaton's birth, and in his honor the local *cinémathèque*, a little state-subsidized gem of a theater called the Odyssée, programmed an extended festival of his silent classics. The Odyssée was a block away from my dark basement apartment, and the student discount—again courtesy of the government's largesse—was steep, with the result that I went back to see every film multiple times.

My first sustained encounter with the character the French call "Malec"—the rubber-bodied, poker-faced cipher in a flat felt hat whom Keaton plays in nearly all his independently produced silents—marked a decisive rupture in my inner life. Who was this solemn, beautiful, perpetually airborne man? From what alternate universe, seemingly possessed of its own post-Newtonian laws of physics, had he been flung? How did he pull off such boggling feats of acrobatic prowess and comic invention, and what became of him after he sailed out of the frame? How could anyone be at once so physically agile, so right-on in his directorial instincts, and so timelessly funny?

The Odyssée had a small but excellent film library where I started spending hours a day in an attempt to learn everything I could about this gravity-defying figure. But as riveting as Keaton's life story proved to be, no degree of knowledge about it could adequately account for the mystery on display in his work. It was a maddening and seductive paradox: the more I learned about Buster Keaton, the less I understood him. When I got back to the States that summer, I continued to shortchange my dissertation by expanding my research into the period when he lived and worked, an extraordinary span of American history that stretched from the second administration of Grover Cleveland to the first and only full one of Lyndon Baines Johnson, from the year my oldest grandparent was born to the year I was.

I did, eventually, finish the dissertation and earn my degree. But over the next two and a half decades, after I left the academic job path to become a TV and then a film critic at *Slate*, I would periodically duck down some avenue or other of Keaton-related research. Thinking about him in the context of his time became, in a sense, my hobby; whenever I heard about something that took place between 1895 and 1966, I found myself trying to fit that event or phenomenon into the puzzle of his life and work. Keaton's birth and death were separated by a stretch of just seventy years, but in those years the country and the world had been profoundly reshaped by a technology born the same year he was: film. More and more I became convinced that to understand his life was to understand the history of that medium's first century.

That early phase of Keaton infatuation may have peaked one day not long after my return to the US, when, after a burger apiece and a few glasses of wine, a good friend and I decided we should each take out our notebooks and try to write a poem. Not as a competition but just because there are friends with whom drafting a poem while you polish off a bottle feels like the right thing to do. Of course my poem was about Buster, or rather it was addressed to him. It leapt from my brain to the page in as close to final form as anything I've ever written, and it went like this:

Ever wester
ever faster
Buster, hasten
your disaster.

Scale the mast and list to keening.
Buster, listen: Are you dreaming?
Are you falling? Are you flying?
Buster, cinema
is dying.

Film is falling,
time a twister,
sound unfurling
her nor'easter.

Not a whisper.
Never laughter.
Buster, thank you
for disaster.

I know we're supposed to wryly disclaim our own juvenilia, but I was far from juvenile by the time this poem was written, and I stand by those fifty words. In fact, though they were written twenty years before I started writing this book, they already contain the germ of its central idea, one that has stayed with me for decades: the image of Keaton as a human projectile hurled into the twentieth century. In order to follow the trajectory of his flight, we need to start with the year he was born.

1895

Still from L'Arroseur Arrosé (The Sprinkler Sprinkled), *one of the films shown at the Lumière brothers' first public screening in 1895.*

Our hero came from Nowhere—he wasn't going Anywhere and got kicked off Somewhere.

—Opening title card in Keaton's
1920 two-reeler, *The High Sign*

I picture Buster Keaton's entrance into history as being something akin to the no-nonsense opening of *The High Sign*. This shaggy, mildly absurdist two-reel comedy would be the first film made by the Buster Keaton Studio (though he chose to hold its release until the following year, deeming his second independent short, the now-venerated *One Week*, to be a more auspicious debut). After that jauntily existential opening title, a train hurtles across the frame from left to right—even as early as 1920, that direction of onscreen movement was shorthand for a vehicle that was outward bound, "on its way"—as our hero is flung from an open car by an unseen assailant. Has he failed to produce a ticket? Displeased a traveling companion? No matter. Scrambling to his feet and adjusting his flat hat, he sets off, luggage-less but resolute, to find his way in the dusty American railroad town into which he seems to have been chucked.

Eighteen ninety-five was quite a year to be alive in the world, let alone hurled into it from out of Nowhere. It was one of those times in history when the era that was passing and the one about to come seemed locked together like the teeth in a pair of gears, readying for the transfer of energy between them. In England that spring, with Queen Victoria entering the final stretch of her sixty-three-year reign, Oscar Wilde was convicted of "gross indecency"—a legal euphemism for a variety of gay sex acts made illegal only ten years before by the screamingly homophobic Criminal Law Amendment Act—and sentenced to two years' hard labor in Reading Gaol. In the fall in Rochester, New York, an inventor and patent lawyer by the name of George Baldwin Selden was granted the first US patent for an internal-combustion-powered automobile—though his ambitious and litigious rival Henry Ford would manage to mass-produce and market such a machine much faster than Selden ever could. Meanwhile, William Randolph Hearst, the young heir to a silver-mining fortune whose father, now a US senator, had recently given him a small San Francisco newspaper to run, made the bold move of acquiring a failing penny paper called the *New York Morning Journal*. It was the start of a multimedia conglomerate that would expand to over thirty newspapers and change the face of journalism in the coming century.

Eighteen ninety-five was also the year Guglielmo Marconi, a twenty-one-year-old Italian nobleman and scientific hobbyist experimenting on the lawn of his father's estate, first succeeded in transmitting radio waves over a considerable distance—an innovation that would soon make possible wireless telegraphy and eventually, broadcast radio and the internet.

And it was the year when, one hot night in late July, an Austrian neurologist vacationing with his family had a strange dream about a patient from which he awoke with an even stranger idea: to develop a method of analysis based on the interpretation of dreams, starting with his own.

Freud's momentous but incomprehensible dream is 1895 in its essence: not yet the twentieth century but the still-illegible sign of what it might become. Many of the public debates of that year—an unusual number of which, it seems to my perhaps overly 1895-fixated self, resonate almost unchanged into the present day—shared that quality of almost-but-not-quite modernity. It was as if the twentieth century, already in love with movement, change, and speed, were reaching back five years in time to yank the last half decade of the comparatively pokey nineteenth ahead with it.

At an agricultural and industrial exposition in Georgia in September, Booker T. Washington, a freed slave turned educator and orator who had been an early spokesman for civil rights in the postwar South, delivered a well-received speech to a mainly white audience in which he stressed the importance of a gradualist approach to integration. That speech and the unwritten social contract it implied would come to be known, with some derision, as the "Atlanta compromise" by the less conciliatory generation of Black activists to come, their own rise to prominence following in the wake of pioneer social reformer Frederick Douglass's death in February 1895. This new, more radical civil rights movement found its spokesperson in the young intellectual firebrand W. E. B. Du Bois, who became the first African American to earn a PhD from Harvard in . . . 1895.

That year, almost every sector of American life was on the brink of disorienting transformation: Technology. Entertainment. Transportation. Education. Labor practices. Race relations. Social and sexual behavior. Parenting norms. But behind these quantifiable shifts were more indefinable qualitative changes in the way whole populations of people spent time with one another and interacted with the world around them. The Victorian mind was becoming the modern one, in ways it's much easier to see and comprehend at a century and a half's distance than it must have been for anyone alive at the time. To give one example relevant to our story: the subjective experience of vision—already jarred by the advent of photography in 1839—was about to undergo an even more destabilizing shock with the arrival of theatrically projected motion pictures. And a convergence of major social and economic changes—immigration on a heretofore unseen scale, rapidly advancing industrialization, the birth of the world's first mass-produced popular culture—would help this new mode of seeing spread farther and faster than any new art form in history.

Few people in America could have seemed further removed from this maelstrom of social, technological, and cultural change than Myra Edith Cutler Keaton, who was all of eighteen years old and four foot eleven inches tall on the night of October 4, 1895, when she gave birth to her first child at the house of complete strangers in Piqua, Kansas. The house where she had the baby belonged to the town carpenter and his wife, who happened to live across the street from the church hall where Myra's husband, Joe, an acrobat and "eccentric dancer," was set to perform that night with a barely solvent traveling outfit called the "Mohawk Indian Medicine Show."[1]

Piqua was a one-stop railroad town in which neither Myra nor Joe would ever set foot again. The boy at first named Joseph Frank Keaton would pass through it once more, late in his life, on a cross-country driving trip with his third wife, Eleanor. After a five-minute inspection of the dusty main street, Buster asked if they could get back in the car and keep going. Joe claimed later that just after he and Myra left Piqua with their newborn son, a tornado wiped the town off the map entirely. Like much of what Joe said in print, this was provably untrue, a tall tale that brazenly flaunted its own falsehood.

By December 28, 1895, Myra and Joe would have moved on with their newborn to other dusty, remote towns on the prairie entertainment circuit. It was on that date that the brothers Louis and Auguste Lumière first screened the moving pictures shot on their recently patented Cinématographe machine to a paying audience. The event took place at the Salon

Indien, a basement meeting room in Paris's Grand Café. There were ten short films on the bill that night, beginning with the now-simple, then-startling *Workers Leaving the Factory* (*La Sortie des Usines Lumière à Lyon*), a series of stationary takes showing male and female workers streaming out of the Lumière family's photographic equipment factory at the sound (inaudible, of course) of the closing bell. Like all but one of the titles on the bill, *Workers Leaving the Factory* was of the genre that would dominate the first years of the industry—"actualities," or short records of real-life events, sometimes (though not in this case) restaged for the camera.

But the sixth title in that evening's lineup was *Le Jardinier* (*The Gardener*), sometimes referred to as *L'arroseur arrosé* (*The Sprinkler Sprinkled*) and often named in film histories as not just the world's first film comedy but the first filmed fictional narrative of any kind. *L'arroseur arrosé* is a forty-nine-second-long comic sketch built around the simplest of premises, a sight gag that had appeared in French newspaper cartoons. As a man waters a garden, we see a boy of maybe ten or twelve sneak up behind him and step on the hose, cutting off the stream of water. The confused gardener peers into the nozzle, cuing the boy to remove his foot so that the renewed stream catches the "sprinkler" full in the face. The sodden man then chases his young tormentor, grabs him by the collar, and administers a few firm swats on the behind before the boy scoots out of frame, pivoting at the last moment for a quick glance at whoever was behind the camera.

This primordial slapstick sketch might be seen as a far less virtuosic and less violent predecessor of the intergenerational knockabout comedy Buster and his father were about to turn into one of the most popular and controversial family acts on the early twentieth-century vaudeville circuit. The basic plot structure of *L'arroseur arrosé*—mischievous young man pulls clever prank on stern older man, catches hell for it, but still somehow wins the day by making the audience laugh—would remain the central premise of the Three Keatons' act for the seventeen-plus years that Buster served as its co-creator and unquestioned star. And in a more sophisticated form, often with the forces of nature, technology, or implacable fate taking the place of the avenging father, that same conflict would play out again and again in the films Keaton made during the prolific stretch of creative independence he enjoyed in Hollywood from 1920 until about 1929.

The ten short films shown in the Parisian café basement that night were, in essence, the Lumières' home-movie clip reel as business card, intended not as entertainment vehicles but as proofs of concept for a heretofore uncommercialized new technology. Yet the Salon Indien lineup remains spellbinding to watch well over a hundred years later. Of course, the radical novelty experienced by the program's original viewers—one of them was the then-magician and theater manager Georges Méliès, who deemed the technology an "extraordinary trick"—is lost to us now, available only via thought experiment.[2] Every person now living was born into a world already awash in moving images, and with each of the dozen decades that have passed since 1895, screens have come to inhabit our consciousness in less boundaried and more intimate ways. Glowing rectangles displaying, for the most part, images of the human body in motion beckon and jostle against each other constantly in a bid for our attention: in our houses, our offices, our cars, our public spaces, and glowing from our wrists or the palms of our hands. We live inside the world of recorded motion, and it lives inside us.

There's no way to undo the five or more generations of viewership that have made this way of seeing possible, not enough to even hypothetically reenter the minds of the sixty or so men and women who gathered on folding chairs in a café basement to watch the *arroseur* get *arrosé*, a bonneted and cranky Lumière baby (Auguste's daughter) be fed spoonfuls of porridge, or workers stream out of those factory gates into the late afternoon sun.

This is not by any means to say that what separates the Salon audience's experience from our own is simple naiveté. Members of the Lumières' educated bourgeois audience would likely have been familiar with some of the many other popular optical attractions of the time, such as Edison's

Kinetoscope. This device, already popular in arcades throughout the United States, allowed the viewer to drop a coin in a slot and peer into an individualized eyepiece to watch a strip of moving images less than a minute in duration. All the Cinématographe did differently—from the viewer's perspective, anyway—was to turn that solitary peep show into a shared public experience.

The Lumières' innovation was not in stringing still photos together to create an illusion of movement—many others had accomplished some version of that in the years since Eadweard Muybridge first documented the stages of a horse's gallop in 1878. But it was the two French brothers, already second-generation photographic innovators, who first worked out how to establish a common *space* of moviegoing. The proscenium stage familiar from centuries of theatergoing suddenly traded its dimension of depth for a flat vertical surface that, with the help of a projector, became a window on a larger-than-life simulacrum of living, breathing humanity.

An unkillable legend maintains that the Lumières' short film of a steam train pulling into La Ciotat station (which was first shown not at this December 1895 screening but at one early the next year) caused some first-time film viewers to run from the theater in fright, as if the filmed train were about to plow through the surface of the screen. This myth has been disproven many times by film scholars—there's no contemporary account that mentions anything like such a stampede—but it's easy to understand the reason for the persistence of the La Ciotat myth. If the comical image of fleeing filmgoers confused by the distinction between movies and life overstates the visual naiveté of cinema's earliest viewers, it does accurately register the symbolic violence of the rupture moving pictures were about to make in the fabric of the wider culture. They came at us with the speed and force of a moving train, and after the (pleasurable) trauma of that first filmed arrival, the distinction between the filmed world and our own would never quite be reliable again.

Even if none of those early viewers literally believed that a filmed train had the power to invade their physical space, the anecdote forcefully evokes the new medium's power to jump the tracks of representation and crash straight into the viewer's consciousness. In some of his most formally and technically ambitious works—most notably *Sherlock, Jr.*, in which, as a dreaming projectionist, he climbs inside a movie to intervene in its fictional world—Buster Keaton would revisit that imaginary torn-through screen, the place of unhealable rupture between the real world and the filmed one.

The Salon Indien lineup has an entirely different kind of destabilizing effect on the twenty-first-century watcher. For us, the effect depends not on the shock of seeing everyday life reproduced on a screen but on these first films' *dis*similarity from our daily lives, the incredible expanse of time and change that separates then from now and us from them. The Lumières' program, now easily viewable on any one of the portable Cinématographes that surround us, is moving most of all for its unpolished, unscripted specificity. As is often the case when watching very early films, it's not the event we're meant to be witnessing that draws our attention so much as the spontaneous gestures that interrupt the action. In *L'arroseur arrosé*, the young prankster's last-minute glance at the camera constitutes the first breaking of the fourth wall ever to be recorded in motion, an instant of eye contact between subject and audience that initiates a whole new era of seeing and being seen.

Another of the Salon Indien films, the forty-one-second-long *Saut à la couverture* (*Jumping on a Blanket*), features the less-than-impressive acrobatic work of a man who makes multiple failed attempts to somersault over a blanket held up, fireman-style, by group of other men in a circle. (An alternate title for this short, *A Hazing at the Firehouse*, suggests the game was some sort of manly induction ritual.) When he finally manages to pull off the trick, the jumper celebrates with a funny stiff-legged side-wise leap, as if proud to have just accomplished cinema's first successful, if unimpressive, stunt.

When I imagine the Parisians in that nightclub basement—especially Méliès, whose 1902 hit *A Trip to the Moon* may well have been among the offerings available to the seven-year-old Buster—I can't help cross-cutting their story with that of the infant born three months earlier in Piqua. Before the nineteenth century or his fifth year of life was over, he would be entertaining crowds with feats of onstage acrobatics that would put the Lumières' unnamed blanket bouncer to shame. By the end of the second decade of the twentieth century, barely yet a man, he was already beginning to take the motion-picture technology introduced by the Lumières, Thomas Edison, and others to previously unimagined (and in some ways still unequaled) creative heights. And by the end of the new century's third decade—the most prolific, artistically ambitious, and financially remunerative of his life—Keaton, still less than thirty-five years old, would already be poised on the brink of a spectacularly fast and steep fall.

The new art form of film burst out of the gate like Buster, with a velocity as unprecedented as it was unforeseeable. Accurate statistics for the rate of the industry's growth in its earliest years are hard to pin down, especially since, in the medium's first days, film prints were often sold to itinerant projectionists rather than leased by distributors, making record keeping impossible and piracy rampant (if Buster did see Méliès's *A Trip to the Moon*, it was likely a pirated American copy).

In April of 1896, Thomas Edison began showing his own films in the United States via the new projection technology of Vitascope—not an Edison invention, though he helped to patent it and marketed it under his name. That same spring the Lumière brothers took the Cinématographe on a world tour, demonstrating their marvelous innovation—an elegant wooden cube that, unlike Edison's clumsier and noisier system, not only filmed the images but developed and projected them as well—in cities as geographically distant as Brussels, London, Bombay, New York, Montreal, and Buenos Aires.

By 1899, vaudeville theaters in the United States had begun to partner with motion-picture exhibition services to integrate films into their live performance lineup. As the nineteenth century rolled into the twentieth, freestanding "nickelodeons," named for their low five-cent admission price, began popping up in towns of all sizes. These first dedicated movie venues were often converted storefronts with a few rows of chairs and a makeshift screen. The growth of the nickelodeon craze is impossible to track precisely, given that such informal businesses opened and closed faster than they could be counted. But the records of the Motion Picture Patents Company, an early trade group created to standardize the film industry, estimated that in 1910 there were around ten thousand functioning movie screens around the country, including those that featured films as a part of a larger vaudeville lineup.[3]

The motion-picture camera is a technology whose multiply authored origin has been disputed since its invention, but its birthday is traditionally, almost sentimentally, celebrated on the anniversary of that first public screening in Paris. The Lumière brothers themselves, though, had little sentiment to spare for the Cinématographe. Louis Lumière, the brother whose ingenuity had contributed the most to its creation, dismissed the newfangled gizmo as a passing fad. In fact, at some point in 1895—before the December showing at the Salon Indien, but after there had been demonstrations of the device in private settings and at industry fairs—Louis is said to have declared, according to another unverifiable cinematic legend (kept alive by, among others, Jean-Luc Godard in his screenplay for *Contempt*) that *"le cinéma est une invention sans avenir"* ("the cinema is an invention with no future").

After spending a few years promoting the entertainment system he helped create, Louis returned to his experiments in dry-plate color photography. In 1903 the brothers patented the successful Autochrome color process, the invention Louis considered their most important contribution to the medium. By the time the Second World War came around, both brothers would be devoting themselves to another kind of experiment, with Louis becoming a vocal supporter of the Mussolini regime and both brothers taking a role in the collaborationist Vichy government in Lyon.[4]

Louis Lumière's statement about the futurelessness of the art form he helped create is often quoted as an historic failure of cultural foresight. But it has a prophetic ring to it in the twenty-first century, when the future of theatrically projected cinema often does seem to be in peril as the way of seeing introduced by the Lumières makes way for other, newer forms. At any rate, I like to imagine, for the sheer symmetry of the myth, that Louis Lumière really did make that enigmatic claim about the new medium's lack of promise—and that he made it somewhere in the vicinity of October 4, 1895, when a boy who would one day prove him wrong was born in Piqua, Kansas.

PART I

THROWN

They were all talking about something. I didn't know what it was, but I knew it was good and thought it was mine—something to go with the basketball. They were calling it the twentieth century.[1]

—Buster Keaton, recalling
New Year's Eve of 1899

I

They Were Calling It the Twentieth Century

The Three Keatons, ca. 1901.
(Photo courtesy of Bob and Minako Borgen)

New Year's Eve 1899 must have felt momentous even if you weren't a four-year-old backstage at Proctor's Twenty-Third Street Theater, still buzzing from last week's Christmas gift: a big brown stitched-leather ball meant for playing an American game less than a decade old, which was just beginning to organize into professional leagues. Of course, Buster was still too young to grasp what it meant for one century to turn into the next, or for that matter what it meant that his parents—who had struggled so hard to find work in New York that winter that the three Keatons had at times gone cold and hungry—were suddenly flush enough to buy him such a lavish present.

The answer: after Joe and Myra's acrobatics-and-cornet duo act had flopped hard at Tony Pastor's continuous-vaudeville house in early December (as Joe himself would later concede in one of the columns he occasionally contributed to the *New York Dramatic Mirror*, "the act didn't go . . . 'twas bad"),[1] he had somehow wrangled them a year-end week of bookings at the prestigious Proctor's chain, earning the cash to buy the ball for his boy.

The basketball would have a long life as a Keaton prop. Just nine months later, during the family's first paid engagement as a trio at the Wonderland Theater in Wilmington, Delaware, Buster got laughs by bouncing that ball off his father's head as the old man stood downstage, holding forth on the importance of patience and gentleness to proper child rearing. ("Father *hates* to be rough," went a common opening line.) In what became the template for their act for years to come, Buster's continued interruptions—sometimes verbal, but most often taking the form of some prop-based provocation or audience-distracting piece of upstage business—would cause Joe to wheel around and witness his authority being flouted. Joe would then give both the audience and his son a more practical tutorial on day-to-day parenting by seizing the suitcase handle Myra had sewed to the back of her son's costume and flinging the boy against whatever backdrop, curtain, or piece of scenery was available.

The contrast between the roughness with which this small child was handled and the equanimity with which he seemed to spring back from every mishap provided the wellspring of the act's humor. Whatever anxiety this comic premise created in the audience—which, given the demographics of vaudeville attendance, would have included many families with children—was no incidental side effect of the merriment but part of the point. The Keatons were not just funny, they were *thrilling*, with real-time risk an essential element of the program. As a grand finale in the early years, Joe sometimes hurled Buster clear into the wings, from whence a stagehand would reappear after a few suspenseful seconds with the grinning boy in his arms: "This yours, Mr. Keaton?"[2]

Many years later, having grown too big for Joe to throw around the stage—and having learned, after many hissed paternal reminders, that the laughs got bigger when he ditched the smile—a somber teenage Buster would stand in the middle of the stage on the Keaton act's one consistent prop, a sturdy wooden table. (In the years before his son joined the act, Joe had sometimes billed himself as "The Man with the Table.") Whirling a basketball on a rubber rope over his head, Buster would approach his father's head in gradually widening arcs, first knocking off Joe's hat and, on the next revolution, clobbering the paterfamilias himself, thereby inviting whatever hair-raising act of retribution Joe proceeded to visit upon him. Another, even more patricidal variation involved Joe shaving onstage with a straight razor, whistling in blissful ignorance as Buster's whirling basketball-on-a-rope slowly approached him from behind to the audience's mounting gasps. In what must have made for an absurdist touch, Myra, a tiny woman known for her impeccably dainty Gibson Girl fashion, sometimes stood at the front of the stage playing the saxophone, serenely ignoring the melee while her son and husband courted death behind her.

Most impossible for the four-year-old Buster to comprehend was that, in some way, the century to come *would* be his, in a much more lasting way than the basketball. Though he was born five years before it officially began, Buster Keaton belonged to the twentieth century, and it to him. It was as essential in inventing him as he was in inventing it, and it's impossible to imagine either one turning out the same without the other.

For the first three decades of the new century, Buster's life as a performer and creator traced a steep and steady upward trajectory, catapulting his family from the greenhorn fringes of the entertainment industry to its topmost tiers in a remarkably short span of time. It was in late October 1900 that the just-turned-five-year-old made his first paid appearance in his parents' act, earning the Keatons an extra ten dollars a week at that Wilmington engagement. Buster's acrobatic and comic gifts were about to become so crucial to the family's reversal of fortune that, before New Year's Eve of the same year rolled around, Joe Keaton would be rounding his son's age upward by two years in a letter to the Society for the Prevention of Cruelty to Children. Joe was requesting special permission for Buster to appear onstage on the prestigious Proctor's circuit in New York State, where state law banned children under seven from performing theatrical work of any kind without a permit from the SPCC.[3]

That organization was better known in its time as the Gerry Society after its cofounder and longtime president, the powerful and controversial lawyer turned child welfare czar Elbridge T. Gerry. This prominent philanthropist and social reformer was a grandson of the founding father of the same name, a signatory of the Declaration of Independence who served as vice president under James Madison and whose skill at slicing up voting districts to his own advantage while governor of Massachusetts gave the American language the term "gerrymandering." We should pause here to learn a bit about the later Mr. Gerry and the child-protection movement he was instrumental in helping to launch, since we'll be hearing more from him and the "Gerrymen." Lord knows the Keaton family did.

2

"She Is a Little Animal, Surely"

Mary Ellen Wilson as she appeared in testimony
before the New York Supreme Court, April 9, 1874.

As the nineteenth century made way for the twentieth, ideas about what it meant to be a child were in a vertiginous state of flux, both in the realms of public policy and private behavior. Across widely disparate fields at more or less the same time—evolutionary and biological science, law, education, and the emerging science of psychology—a new model of human development was emerging. Children were coming to be seen less as their parents' economic property to dispose of or profit from as they saw fit and more as small, still-growing beings who were entitled to some degree of protection from both industrial and domestic harm.

It was in the last quarter of the nineteenth century that nearly every institution we associate with contemporary child welfare got its start: enforced restrictions on child labor; compulsory school attendance, at least up to a certain age; a juvenile justice system separate from the adult criminal courts; and child-abuse prevention organizations like Elbridge T. Gerry's Society for the Prevention of Cruelty to Children. Until 1875, the year Gerry cofounded the New York State branch of the SPCC with, as one of his partners, the creator of the American Society for the Prevention of Cruelty to Animals, "child abuse" did not yet exist as a legal concept in America. It was only with the establishment of this new private entity that the daily practice of parenting, for so long a matter of private behavior and entrenched cultural custom, became subject for the first time to legal oversight and quasi-governmental surveillance.

In many cases this new oversight was a positive, even lifesaving public good. The trial that initially led to the SPCC's founding, a case Gerry prosecuted before the New York State Supreme Court in 1874, continues to be cited as a landmark case in the history of child protection in America. Mary Ellen Wilson was a ten-year-old girl whose father, a Union soldier, had been killed in the Civil War and whose widowed mother could no longer afford the price of "boarding her out" to a caregiver while she scraped together a living. After some time spent in an orphanage, the toddler had been placed in the care of a foster couple in the rough New York neighborhood of Hell's Kitchen. Her foster mother abused and maltreated Mary Ellen systematically, confining her most of the time to a windowless locked room and, in the girl's own heartrending words to a courtroom crammed with sympathetic citizens:

> whipping and beating me almost every day. . . . I have now the black and blue marks on my head which were made by mamma, and also a cut on the left side of my forehead which was made by a pair of scissors. . . . I have no recollection of ever having been kissed by any one . . . I have never been taken on my mamma's lap and caressed or petted. I never dared to speak to anybody, because if I did I would get whipped. I do

not know for what I was whipped—mamma never said anything to me when she whipped me. I do not want to go back to live with mamma, because she beats me so.[1]

Contemporary journalistic coverage of the Mary Ellen Wilson case was both extensive and effusive, brimming with that era's deep concern with and ambivalence about the status of children. There was an enormous investment of public feeling in the little girl, who delivered her courtroom testimony—and was photographed, in a widely distributed image—in the same pitiful state in which she had been rescued the day before. She wore a ragged, long-outgrown dress, her feet bare, fresh welts still visible on her legs and a long cut (the one described in her testimony) running the length of her left forehead and cheek. An anonymously authored *New York Times* account of the trial noted that "quite a number of persons, including several ladies, were attracted to the court by the publicity which had been given to the proceedings on the previous day, all of them evidently sympathizing with the little neglected waif."

Jacob Riis, the future photographer and social activist whose influential 1890 book *How the Other Half Lives* would use the brand-new technology of flash photography to expose the squalid conditions of tenement dwellers in New York's immigrant neighborhoods, was present at the Mary Ellen Wilson trial, working as a police reporter for the *New York Tribune*. His description of the abused child's appearance in court refers to the girl by the impersonal pronoun "it," stranding Mary Ellen in a kind of limbo between little girl and dumb beast:

I was in a courtroom full of men with pale, stern looks. I saw a child brought in, carried in a horse blanket, at the sight of which men wept aloud. I saw it laid at the feet of the judge, who turned his face away; and in the stillness of that courtroom I heard a voice raised, claiming for that child the protection that men had denied it, in the name of the homeless cur of the streets.[2]

The moral contiguity between the suffering of children and that of animals—and, by implication, between the two groups' shared vulnerability to harm and entitlement to legal protection—comes up over and over in contemporary accounts of the Mary Ellen Wilson case. Etta Angell Wheeler, the Methodist missionary and social worker who first reported Mary Ellen's abuse at her foster mother's hands, did so by appealing to the Society for the Prevention of Cruelty to Animals. Wheeler made up her mind to take the case there when her niece, hearing her fret about her powerlessness to help the unfortunate child, pointed out that "she is a little animal, surely."[3]

Riis's eyewitness account of the trial ends by attributing the animal/child metaphor to Elbridge Gerry himself. Riis quotes Gerry, who had worked in the past as a lawyer for the ASPCA, as arguing on behalf of Mary Ellen's claim to at least the same rights as a domestic beast: "'The child is an animal,' he said. 'If there is no justice for it as a human being, it shall at least have the rights of the cur in the street. It shall not be abused.' And as I looked, I knew I was where the first chapter of children's rights was being written under warrant of that made for the dog . . ."[4]

The Mary Ellen Wilson case marked the beginning of a protracted public debate about the nature and limits of American society's responsibility toward the "little animals" of the human species. In the wake of the Industrial Revolution, the market economy had generated immense wealth even as the concentration of that wealth in the hands of a tiny Gilded Age elite made the country an increasingly unfit place for the most vulnerable of its citizens. For the last quarter of the nineteenth century, it was as though this long-buried secret were slowly but inexorably starting to leak through the cracks of polite society: capitalism and childhood were not compatible. Mary Ellen Wilson, wrenching as her story was, was only the photogenic (and conveniently Anglo-Saxon) poster child for a suffering juvenile underclass that had been a cause for intense social concern at least since the era of Charles Dickens. Something had to change.

The debate about what exactly that something ought to be involved a clash not only between religious and secular value systems but between old and new definitions of popular entertainment, as well as agrarian and industrial-age family structures. In the sixty-four years between the Mary Ellen Wilson trial and the passage, under FDR, of the 1938 Fair Labor Standards Act, the Progressive movement would push through significant legal reforms on behalf of children before throwing its momentum behind constitutional amendments for women's suffrage and Prohibition.

The same groups that had combined to set Mary Ellen free—a coalition of Christian social activists, muckraking journalists, and a newly empowered welfare organization that was effectively an arm of the state—would also manifest their presence as socially repressive forces over the course of the next few decades. Progressive reformers helped unionize and regulate corrupt, monopolizing industries, move children from the factory floor to the schoolhouse, and eventually earn women the franchise. But those same movements would also be behind decades of attempts to censor media of all kinds, outlaw the sale or consumption of alcohol, and otherwise inhibit the freedom of the very citizenry they aimed to uplift. The Keatons were not the only family—indeed, they were among the luckiest—to regard "the Gerries" not as liberating saviors but as menacing representatives of a senseless law, to be evaded with all possible speed, just as Buster would one day race down the center of an otherwise empty street to outrun hordes of uniform-clad tormentors in the 1922 two-reeler *Cops*.

Mary Ellen Wilson's whip- and scissors-wielding foster mother was found guilty of felony assault and battery and sentenced to a year in prison at hard labor. And in the kind of long-term happy ending that's rare in such stories, Mary Ellen herself was eventually taken in by the sister of Etta Wheeler and raised in a stable and loving home. Mary Ellen would live to the ripe age of ninety-two and prove an exemplary and caring mother to her own daughters, the eldest of whom she named Etta after her rescuer. Mary Ellen's daughters went to college, an unusual achievement among women at the turn of the century, and went on to long and successful careers as schoolteachers. They, too, would be remembered for their lifelong devotion to the well-being of children.[5]

3

"He's My Son, and I'll Break His Neck Any Way I Want To"[1]

Joe and Buster Keaton, date unknown.

Not every reform that followed in the wake of the Gerry Society's founding struck as tender a chord in the public breast as did the plight of Mary Ellen Wilson. Some poor working families who relied on their children's cotton-mill paychecks or the tips they garnered as bootblacks and newsboys failed to appreciate the nobility of Mr. Gerry's governmentally sanctioned meddling in their personal economic and parenting decisions.

There was distrust, too, of the legal gray area the Society for the Prevention of Cruelty to Children occupied, somewhere between a philanthropic mission and a policing operation. Agents from the society, nicknamed "Gerrymen," "Gerries," or simply (in an ironic slippage of meaning from the society's name) "the cruelty," were empowered by local police departments to patrol poor and immigrant neighborhoods. Their task was not just to ferret out cases of abuse or exploitation but to shoo impressionable youths away from theaters, amusement parks, penny arcades, and other forms of mass entertainment deemed dangerous to the next generation's moral fiber.

Like many Progressive causes for social reform, the child-protection movement was closely bound up at its origin with the "civilizing" values of a socially conservative white Protestant Christianity. Implicit in the project of lifting up one's fellow man was the assumption that the world he was being hoisted into should resemble, as closely as possible, that of the people doing the lifting. Denizens of the largely immigrant tenement neighborhoods where the SPCC agents plied their trade—mostly people of southern Italian, Irish-Catholic, or Eastern European Jewish origin—tended to regard the importuning officers of the society not as Etta Wheeler–style saviors but as a self-anointed Inquisition of nosy, condescending do-gooders. "The cruelty" were seen as morality cops looking for any excuse to invade poor families' privacy, threaten whatever means of livelihood they had managed to cobble together, and, in the worst-case scenario, forcibly remove their beloved—even, sometimes, when maltreated—children.

For families in the theatrical profession, where a gifted son or daughter could mean the difference between a life of comfort and one of grinding poverty, any God-given surplus of juvenile ingenuity must have seemed like a perfectly valid resource to exploit. The big-time vaudeville or "legitimate" theater circuits, whatever the rigors of the lifestyle they required (constant long-distance rail travel, the impossibility of a stable domicile or school), limited their demand on child performers to less than an hour of total onstage work per day, divided between a matinee and an evening show. And a childhood spent treading the boards, even on the smaller-time, three-show-a-day circuits, must certainly have seemed preferable to the factory floor or at-home piecework jobs that might otherwise await not just that child but his or her whole family.

It wouldn't take long for the same qualities that drew audiences to the Keatons' act—the irreverence, the potential for danger, and the sheer improvisational lunacy of the small boy's daredevil stunts—to attract the notice of the New York Society for the Prevention of Cruelty to Children. A generation after its founding in the wake of the Mary Ellen Wilson case, that group was still headed up by the now aged but still formidable Elbridge Gerry. Having chosen to make the theatrical profession one of the most visible battlegrounds in his fight to regulate child labor, he took what sometimes seemed to be a personal interest in preventing this particular underage star and his arrogant, rule-averse father from appearing onstage anywhere in New York State, home to the nation's most prestigious and best-paying vaudeville venues.

An 1876 law following hard on the heels of the Mary Ellen Wilson case banned employing any child under the age of sixteen for the purpose of "singing, playing on musical instruments, rope or wire walking, dancing, begging or peddling, or as a gymnast, contortionist, rider or acrobat, in any place whatsoever."[2] Children under the age of seven were forbidden to appear onstage in any professional capacity—hence Joe's casual hiking up of Buster's age in that first letter to the Gerry Society. Minors between the ages of seven and sixteen could appear in speaking roles with a special permit from the society, as long as they refrained from singing, dancing, or performing any sort of stunts, acrobatics, or other physically dangerous work.

Concern with the physical safety of the Three Keatons' juvenile star was an issue that came up constantly during Buster's childhood, in part because of the society's monomaniacal dedication to shutting down the act and in part because of Joe's P. T. Barnum–worthy skills as a marketer of his firstborn. The Three Keatons were known around the circuits as, in Buster's later description, "the roughest act that was ever in the history of the stage."[3] Over the years they mastered the art of toning down the act's violence for the week's first matinee, when they knew the Gerries

were likely to be sniffing around, then spending the week ramping back
up to the level of mayhem their audiences expected and preferred. But
after Joe deliberately thumbed his nose at the Gerries by bringing not
only twelve-year-old Buster but his two much younger siblings onstage
for a benefit performance in Brooklyn, the Society banned the Keatons
from performing on any New York stage for two years.

Not only in his memoir but in radio, television, and print interviews
throughout his life, Keaton recounted stories of his family's narrow escapes
from do-gooding Gerry agents in a tone of amused pride, as if remembering his screen characters' ingenious flights from their own pursuers,
the buzz-killing enforcers of an abstract law. True to the Huck Finn type
of his childhood stage persona, the older Keaton continued to regard
authority as an obstacle to find ever smarter and funnier ways around,
under, or over. Chuckling over the Three Keatons' legal scrapes in 1960,
he describes the letter-of-the-law loophole that got the Keatons out of
one Gerry Society charge: "Our lawyer beat them in court by pointing
out that the law barred children only from performing on a high or low
wire, a trapeze, bicycle, and the like. There was not one word that made
it illegal for my father to display me on the stage as a human mop or to
kick me in the face."[4]

Viviana Zelizer writes in her classic sociological study *Pricing the
Priceless Child: The Changing Social Value of Children* that the question
of where child performers belonged in the ranks of employed minors
"triggered one of the most highly publicized and controversial defini-
tional battles" of the entire child-labor reform movement.[5] The total
number of minors employed in stage work at the turn of the century
was negligible in comparison to the armies of mistreated and poorly
paid children working in textile mills, mines, garment factories, and
other industrial jobs. Yet the issue of children onstage took on outsized
symbolic importance in the period's debates about the proper nature of
and limits on child labor.

Benjamin Barr Lindsey, a Progressive judge and child-labor activist
who was instrumental in establishing a separate court system for juveniles,

supported the work of children on the stage, noting that it was "the only question concerning child labor that has threatened any division of opinion" among reform advocates. For Lindsey, the distinction between stage and factory labor was a meaningful one. He had no problem with individual states licensing minors to appear onstage, as long as "the performances of such child shall be considered a part of its training and education. This recognizes the work of the willing, talented stage child as different from that mere drudgery of the unwilling and unprotected factory child."[6]

Writing in the *North American Review* in 1890, Elbridge Gerry refused to recognize any such distinction. He bemoaned the plight of "child-slaves of the stage" who "but for the present human provisions of the law, would be subjected to a bondage more terrible and oppressive than the children of Israel ever endured." Gerry's condemnation of the practice shows the Victorian ideas about class and gender that underlay his organization's attempt to ban children from the stage:

> Again, the associations are bad for the children. In the spectacular plays alluded to they are constantly brought into contact with persons about whose morality or virtue the less said the better. Constantly exhibiting in such troupes, the girls soon lose all modesty and become bold, forward and impudent. When they arrive at the limit-age of the law, they have usually entered on the downward path and end in low dance-houses, concert saloons and the early grave. . . . The boys, unfitted by their idle life for useful work, find employment for a time in the lowest class of theatres, and end by becoming thieves or tramps.[7]

Why did the questions raised by juvenile performance strike such a nerve around the turn of the century, pitting theatrical families like the Keatons against the "cruelty" agents who sought to break up their acts and dividing even committed child-welfare advocates into bitterly opposed factions? And what must it have been like to be an underaged professional performer in the late nineteenth and early twentieth centuries, tasked with embodying the Victorian ideal of childhood in sentimental dramas like *Little Lord Fauntleroy* and *Uncle Tom's Cabin* even as one's own formative years were given over not to the Progressive ideals of protection, education, and leisure but to nonstop travel and daily labor?

In trying to understand not just the work and life of Buster Keaton but the world into which he was born—to understand him through that world, and that world through him—I keep returning to the now-insoluble riddle of his persona as a child performer. Why is it that trying to reconstruct the particular content and audience appeal of the act he and Joe built together over the course of Buster's seventeen years as a juvenile slapstick prodigy feels like a meaningful pursuit, half a century after Keaton's death and not many fewer decades since the youngest person to have witnessed one of those ephemeral sketches must also have passed from the earth?

Some part of it must be simply regret at having missed the chance to see the child Buster in performance: the melancholy of temporally bound existence, of having to occupy a fixed place in history and experience all of the past only through the fragmentary records left by others. I want to witness Buster, Joe, and Myra (and, for the brief period when they were less-than-successfully brought into the act, Harry and Louise) doing whatever their Keaton thing was onstage—not via the archive-augmented time machine of imagination but live and in person, preferably without any foreknowledge of who that airborne kid would grow up to be. I want to know what their act looked, sounded, and moved like as they amused and startled jostling, sweaty crowds in a gaslit (or, by the Three Keatons' second decade on the boards, likely electricity-fueled) theater.

If I could go back in time and see the Three Keatons, I'm fairly certain I would laugh, because there's no entertainer in the world who can make me do that more reliably and more helplessly than the adult Buster on film. But is it possible I might also be moved to cry, or yell "Stop!" or march backstage after the show and give Joe a piece of my mind, as the legendary actress Sarah Bernhardt is supposed, probably apocryphally, to have done after one Three Keatons performance? Given the shifting meaning of childhood at the time, this range of reactions must have coexisted within one audience, and indeed within individual members of it. When people went back year after year to see that poker-faced, rubber-bodied little boy get hurled around the stage and somehow, miraculously, survive, what was the miracle they were trying to enact?

4

"The Locomotive of Juveniles"

Buster, circa 1901.

To understand what set the Three Keatons apart in a turn-of-the-century entertainment market glutted with child stars and family acts, it's instructive to look at the intense response Buster engendered in turn-of-the-century audiences. "Keep your eye on the kid," Joe instructed the vaudeville world in an advertising tagline that ran through the 1901 season. But when you read through contemporary coverage of the Three Keatons, the admonition seems superfluous. One gets the sense that, when Buster was onstage, audiences had their work cut out for them keeping an eye on anything else. As a fellow performer wrote in the autograph book Buster carried with him for other acts on the bill to sign, he was "the locomotive of juveniles," the fastest-rising child star on the vaudeville circuit.

During Christmas week of 1900, when he would have just turned five and had been a part of the act for around two months, Buster is mentioned only as "assist[ing]" in his parents' act at the Grand Opera House in Nashville. Exactly six months later, in late June 1901, the *Atlanta Constitution* identifies him as "the star of the Keaton aggregation of three." By October of that same year, on his first tour of the Western Orpheum theater circuit, the newly six-year-old Buster, the "tiny comedian" who is the only member of "the Keaton combination" mentioned by name, is said by the *San Francisco Call* to "[live] up to his name as a laughmaker"—suggesting that, less than a year into his stage career, Buster's reputation from the East Coast already preceded him on the West.

Even a cursory glance through mentions of Buster in the turn-of-the-century press makes one thing clear: he shot to the top ranks of a crowded field with astonishing speed. In January 1902, just over a year past his stage debut, the Richmond, Virginia, *Times* placed the six-year-old Buster "at the top of the class of youngsters seen at the Bijou, and there have been some of the best at the popular Broad Street house." A few weeks later the Three Keatons were on the bill at Tony Pastor's, one of New York's premier vaudeville venues (though Pastor, himself a former child prodigy, preferred to call it a "variety theater," mocking the term *vaudeville* as "sissy and Frenchified"). By September of that year, the Scranton *Republican* noted that "the Three Keatons . . . who are the top-liners in the New York vaudeville houses, have created much merriment this week at Dixie's theatre. Buster is acknowledged to be the brightest young acrobat on the stage today, and the act of the Keatons is one that provides constant mirth."

By the time Buster was seven, he started to crop up in vaudeville coverage as a standard of comparison for other underage comedians. A write-up of a 1902 bill on which the Three Keatons did not appear remarked that the mother-and-son act of Lillian and Shorty De Witt "kept the house in good humor for twenty minutes. 'Shorty' is nearly as funny as little 'Buster' Keaton." And by the age of eight Buster was sometimes cited as one of the few saving graces on an otherwise subpar bill, the kind of performer that made even the most jaded critic sit up and take notice.

A 1903 review in the *Washington Times* yawned that "polite vaudeville at Chase's this week is largely veneer and little substance." The family acrobatic troupe the Great Martinettis, who topped the bill, were skilled enough, but "few novelties figure in their act." The "performance elephants put in their second week"—the anonymous critic's sigh of lassitude can be heard at a distance of 118 years—"and are an interesting feature to those who have not seen their performance." Louise Dresser—the renowned singer and legitimate-stage actress who would serve as the namesake for Buster's future little sister—"has a pleasing contralto voice, but her selections are not happy. Her original parody songs, illustrated with screen pictures, might be improved somewhat."

But that ho-hum night at Chase's did have its moments. "Buster Keaton, of the Keaton eccentric comedy trio, is the latest in child performers, and deserves favorable mention. In the role of an Irish comedian he poses, jokes, sings, imitates prominent performers with the gusto of a veteran and the added interest of an infant phenomenon."

That last phrase may ring oddly in modern ears, especially when used to describe a child of seven who was already a veteran of the stage. Whether this languid unnamed critic fully realized it or not, he was invoking a long and contested tradition in theatrical history by using the words "infant phenomenon" to describe the boy who made him laugh that otherwise too-polite night at Chase's. How contested that tradition was can be seen in the fact that, a few months earlier, an equally pro-Buster critic in St. Louis had used a very similar formulation to insist that it *didn't* apply to the three Keatons' popular human cannonball. This second writer makes clear his distaste for onstage child prodigies as a category by contrasting the "unnatural" precocity the term implies with the "sprightly" and "roguish" energy of Buster.

> The Three Keatons are the laughing hit of the bill. Buster Keaton is unusually clever. He is not an infant prodigy but a healthy, roguish child,

with a sprightly dash that is irresistible. Without appearing unnatural, he manages to keep the audience laughing from entrance to exit.

Buster's status in the performance milieu of his time—the child star as prop, as projectile, as the personal belonging of a father who employs him as a household cleaning tool, and yet also, paradoxically, as a "natural" creative performer with an admirable mastery of his craft from a very early age—only begins to make sense when you take a longer perspective on the nineteenth-century stage. Both in England and America, that stage was a place that had already gone through several generations of sensationally popular child performers by the time Buster was getting his earliest laughs.

Sometimes these juvenile celebrities were acting prodigies playing classical roles written for adults, like the English sensation Master William Betty, who made his debut in 1803 at age eleven playing the lead in Voltaire's *Zair*. He went on to play adult Shakespearean roles to wild acclaim, and became so popular that his appearances on the London stage caused stampedes and riots. Other times children were cast as characters near their own age, either in all-juvenile companies or in popular cross-generational entertainments based on bestselling children's books like *Peter Pan* or *Alice in Wonderland*.

The fad for child actors in the nineteenth and early twentieth centuries found its ideological source in the Romantic notion of childhood as a separate and sacred time of life, a fleeting inner Eden where, in William Wordsworth's phrase, "the child is father to the man." But the ubiquity of child performers also provoked ambivalent feelings in audiences. At the height of the Master Betty craze in 1904–5, Wordsworth wrote of the boy, whom he had never seen onstage, that "I think of him, I scarce know why, with melancholy feelings. . . . When I think of him tears often start into my eyes, and I am sure I could not see him on the stage without weeping or deep sadness." Long before the organized child-welfare movement had begun, observers of children working onstage recognized that the young performers tasked with embodying the ideal state of "nature" were often leading unnatural and sometimes unhealthy lives.

A generation later, Charles Dickens's serial novel *Nicholas Nickleby* featured a pitiful child performer who was billed by her exploitive father, the manager of a traveling theater troupe, as the "Infant Phenomenon." The stunted and singularly untalented Miss Ninetta Crummles, as the book's omniscient third-person narrator dryly observes, had remained "precisely the same age . . . for five good years. But she had been kept up every night, and put on an unlimited allowance of gin-and-water from infancy, to prevent her growing tall." The disquiet that accompanied early nineteenth-century sensations like Master Betty had, by the 1830s, become a cause for social reform.

It's not quite correct to say that the early nineteenth-century fashion for young performing prodigies was later followed by a reformist backlash. Rather, the two things—the public demand for "infant phenomena" to marvel over and the public fear that there was something pitiable and wrong about these unnatural specimens of childhood—coexisted and informed each other from the start.

By the time Buster was taking his first paid public falls at the turn of the century, watching talented children onstage was a cultural thrill that came with a built-in moral twinge, even when those children weren't being flung into scenery or the rib cages of hecklers by their strapping fathers. The awareness that "the cruelty" was liable to shut down the show must have added to the audience's frisson of mingled guilt, pleasure, and suspense—the precise mix of affects Joe and Buster's father-son knockabout act also specialized in eliciting. This conflicted cultural, legal, and psychological space, where children were at once fragile treasures to be protected, market commodities to be exploited, and private property to be disposed of at their parents' will, was the world into which Buster found himself thrown.

5

A Little Hell-Raising Huck Finn

Buster on the cover of the New York Dramatic Mirror, *1908.*

The reason managers approved of my being featured was because I was unique, being at that time the only little hell-raising Huck Finn type boy in vaudeville. The parents of the others presented their boys as cute and charming Little Lord Fauntleroys. The girls were Dolly Dimples types with long golden curls.

—Buster Keaton to Charles Samuels,
in his 1960 as-told-to autobiography
My Wonderful World of Slapstick

The older Keaton's mordant observation on the narrow range of "types" available to turn-of-the-century child performers is both vindicated and complicated by research. Popular theater in the late nineteenth and early twentieth centuries was indeed awash in velvet-knickered Fauntleroys and simpering, pin-curled fairy princesses—as well as in audiences that, young and old alike, couldn't seem to get enough of such sentimental and idealized versions of middle-class white childhood. Indeed, while Myra Keaton was in confinement with her third child, Louise, in 1906 (a second, Harry "Jingles" Keaton, had been born in 1904), a mortified Buster spent a season playing melodramatic children's roles with a New England stock company, including a velvet-suited and corkscrew-wigged Little Lord Fauntleroy. But there were all sorts of other popular child-centric acts that either appeared on bills with the Keatons or competed for their audience in rival theater chains.

Mayme Remington and her Pickaninnies, who frequently shared bills with the Keatons around the turn of the century, were a touring company of singing, dancing Black children introduced and "managed" onstage by a glamorously dressed white woman—a stock genre at the time, though in some variations the mistress of ceremonies also sang, danced, and/or wore blackface. A reviewer of Remington's act remarks that the leading lady "doesn't do much herself, except wear dazzling costumes and manage the act. The 'pics' are dark-skinned dominoes of dance."[1]

Vaudeville divas like Sophie Tucker, Nora Bayes, Louise Dresser, and Eva Tanguay all traveled at one point or another with teams of "picks," and talented young Black performers commonly used the position as a launchpad. One child in Mamie's troupe in the 1890s was Bill "Bojangles" Robinson, who would grow up to become a legendary tap dancer and the highest-paid African American entertainer in the first half of the twentieth century. The historian Robin Bernstein has defined the figure of the "pickaninny"—a ubiquitous motif in turn-of-the-century entertainment, advertising, and pop iconography—by three essential qualities. Pickaninnies were children, they were Black, and—worth noting in the context of Buster's frequent billing as the "boy who couldn't be damaged"—they were always depicted as being cheerfully, not solemnly, impervious to pain or harm.[2] But unlike the Three Keatons, pick acts rarely featured knockabout violence. Rather, they focused on the sex appeal of the troupe's leader and the irrepressible cheer and skill of her dancing charges. Such routines sustained a delicate balance of race, gender, age, and power differentials that allowed an attractive white woman to share a stage with young Black males. The picks' status as implacably happy, well-"managed" children spared the act from accusations of sexual or racial impropriety.

The Keatons also sometimes shared bills with family circus acts from Europe and Asia whose skills had been passed down for generations. As an adult Buster would recall mastering the many circus skills he would use throughout his career—juggling, wire-walking, trick cycling—by observing and imitating such acts behind the scenes. And then there were the more conventional family acts, warmer and less edgy than the Keatons', like the Seven Little Foys, a meticulously father-coached sibling set who danced their way onstage in a descending line from eldest to youngest, told jokes, sang songs, and engaged in some light insult comedy.

The older Buster's demurral notwithstanding, his child self must have stood out in more ways than just the mischievous "type" he embodied onstage. From the days of his first appearances with his parents' act, his uncanny gifts were the object of a particular kind of commentary and speculation in the vaudeville press. It isn't just, as we've seen, that critics and audiences immediately responded to Buster, laughing at his pratfalls and gasping in shock at the breakneck risks he took. It's that their appreciation had a certain double-edged quality: from the beginning they experienced him as both an accomplished, adult-level performer *and* a "natural," freely playing child. In his effortlessly airborne body, nature and art seemed to coexist without opposition. As a reviewer noted in the

New York Dramatic Mirror when Buster had just turned eight, "'Buster' does not give the impression of having been taught."

When Buster was only five, the *New York Clipper* marveled that "the tiny comedian is perfectly at ease in his work, natural, finished and artistic." Descriptions of the Keatons' act, whether from critics or contemporaries, invariably stress not only Buster's precocious athleticism and high degree of technical polish but the "ease of manner" and "natural talent" that authenticate his status as a lovable, spontaneous child. He is described not as a well-trained team member or cute sidekick—on the contrary, from early on it is Myra and Joe who are framed as his "support." Buster is an independent laugh-getting agent and the act's primary generator of new material. "The house is in a constant uproar while he is on the stage," observed the *New York Dramatic Mirror* in 1902, "as he has a knack of giving the audience frequent surprises."

The next year in Cincinnati, eight-year-old Buster was again identified as the act's driving creative force: "The three Keatons are again with us and are funnier than ever. This is made possible through the fact that the memorable 'Buster' has failed to stand still, but has gone on adding clever things to his stock." This degree of innovation was not universal in vaudeville, as is made clear by the presence on the same bill of two acts—a Hebrew dialect comedian and an animal act identified as "Captain Webb's sea lions"—that were singled out for their failure to offer a new "stock of goods," though the reviewer admitted that the sea lions "are always so good that the old round seems new."

A whole subgenre of Buster coverage in local papers—much of it, no doubt, either planted or shaped by Joe—focused on the boy's status as both performer *and* child, insisting on his unaffected playfulness and curiosity as well as his virtuosic skill. Often these stories included some sort of suspense narrative involving a threat to the boy's physical safety, resolving in an assurance that everything would be all right. When Buster was eight, the Louisville, Kentucky, *Courier-Journal*, apparently having a slow week, ran a two-part story over the course of several days involving his purchase of a toy train from a local shop. On his way back to his parents' dressing room with this prize, Buster was allegedly almost crushed by a steamroller he had stepped into the street to examine. ("Inquisitiveness Gives Lad a Severe Fright," reads the delightful headline.) When a bystander "saw the lad's peril and shouted to him," Buster "jumped into the street and disappeared behind a car before the engineer of the roller knew what had happened."

Whether or not this brush with death happened as described, the resemblance of the steamroller encounter to one of the countless vehicle-based stunts in Keaton's future films is unmistakable. After assuring readers that "there were no serious injuries," the anonymous narrator of the incident closes by linking Buster's survival to his performance skills: "the rough-and-tumble work of 'Buster' on the stage was probably responsible for his salvation."

A separate item in the same paper that week marveled at the boy's enjoyment of his new toy, contrasting his childlike instinct for play with his status as a vaudeville veteran—in which guise he is no longer described as a child but a "midget."

> For four years this midget has been on the stage. It has the same fascination for him that it does for his seniors of the footlights. And yet for all that, the little fellow is a boy. While waiting his "turn" the lad may be seen playing among the stands and settings behind the scenes. He yesterday purchased a toy train of cars that gives him the same pleasure it would give a boy who has his own nursery.

The most curious of the Buster-as-real-boy write-ups I've come across appeared in the *Indianapolis Star* in 1903, just a week after the supposed steamroller near-disaster. "'Buster' Keaton Mixes with Boys and Has Fun," reads the headline, and the piece records an afternoon of play shared by the eight-year-old and a group of local children who ambush him outside his hotel and run with him through the streets of town. Eventually Buster and another boy wind up in an impromptu velocipede race, which Buster is on the point of winning when—in another image straight from a Keaton movie chase—he crashes into "a large dog that was prancing about the street" and goes "heading to the pavement."

The author seems at pains to remind us of the dual nature of Buster as a performing child: he is both an exemplar of youth at its most "natural" and a kind of stunted adult. "So clever is the little fellow in his monologue that there are many who believe him to be a dwarf," writes the anonymous reporter, "but such is not the case. He is a light-hearted child, like any other boy when away from the theater, and the small people who live in the neighborhood will miss him greatly when he departs." After assuring readers that "there were no serious injuries" from the bike crash, the author describes how Buster himself blurred the distinction between child's play and entertainment by "giving part of his monologue" after the aborted bike race, as though to make up for the interrupted spectacle. The item ends on a rueful note, contrasting Buster's life on the road with the rooted small-town happiness of the local children: "He has been on the stage since he was a little fellow, and his greatest delight is to make a stop of a few days in some town and get a chance to mix with other boys of his age and participate in their unrestrained joys."

Whatever mixture of truth, authorial embroidery, and Joe-engineered PR went into these Buster-the-real-boy stories, their existence reveals something about the way he was experienced and treated as a child performer, the mix of awe and affection he inspired in audiences and journalists alike. Buster's dual status as both a prodigy and a "natural" child—as a "boy who couldn't be damaged" and a regular hell-raising kid whose curiosity and penchant for risk-taking left him *especially* vulnerable to physical harm—seemed some-how to resolve whatever anxiety viewers might have felt about the violence of the Three Keatons' act. They could laugh at his apparent endangerment as if he really were the human rubber ball he seemed onstage to be. The Romantic and Victorian fascination with prodigious and exceptional chil-dren was beginning to bang up against a new understanding of childhood as a fragile and precious time of life, to be walled off from exploitation and social harm. One of the more public staging grounds of that conflict around the turn of the twentieth century was the body of Buster Keaton.

6

The Boy Who Couldn't Be Damaged

*The Three Keatons' business letterhead with
photos and drawings of scenes from their act, ca. 1901.*

As little as you are
As big as you get
Bear in mind always
Your pa's with you yet.

> —Ad copy in verse for the
> Three Keatons' act, contributed
> by fellow vaudevillian Frank Milton
> of the Four Miltons

One of Joe's oft-repeated tall tales sketched a spiral of escalating calamities straight out of a future Keaton film. As the legend has it, a toddler-aged Buster, left in the care of a boardinghouse proprietress one afternoon while his parents were off doing their hitch kicks and cornet solos, lost his right fingertip to the first joint by poking it into a metal laundry wringer. Later that same day, wandering around, presumably, with a bandage on the freshly severed digit, Buster threw a brick at a peach tree in an attempt to dislodge a piece of fruit, only to knock himself out when the poorly aimed missile landed on his head. (The sprinkler sprinkled!) Still later—after, one hopes, an extra-long nap—the boy was picked up by a passing cyclone that deposited him, entirely unharmed, in the street a few blocks away.

The clothes-wringer story is verifiable, and not only because the missing fingertip can be spotted in nearly every one of Keaton's movies. In March 1899 the Kinsley, Kansas, *Graphic* reported that "the little Keaton boy, who has been appearing on the stage here with the medicine show, had the end of one finger taken off by putting it in the cogs of Mrs. Wolgamot's wringer."[1] But that first part of Joe's tall tale also rings true for the characterological glimpse it provides of a very young but not yet performing Buster, already mechanically curious, physically daring, and prone to trouble. The layering on of the peach-tree mishap and the cyclone, though—not to mention the temporal compression of all this action into a single afternoon—places us firmly in the realm of Joe Keaton mythmaking.

True or not, Joe's fanciful boasts would take root in Buster's dreams. The image of a mounting spiral of cataclysmic events through which a still, small figure persists, unharmed, at the center became Keaton's idée fixe. He would revisit it in a decade's worth of intricate action sequences in which every chase, gag, or stunt must be topped by the next, ascending skyward in a figurative and sometimes literal whirlwind of disaster. This spiral-shaped structure finds its most sophisticated expression in the grand crescendo of climate-related disasters that ends Keaton's last independent feature, *Steamboat Bill, Jr.* But some version of it can be found in nearly every one of his films of the 1920s—a period so prolific, creative, and personally tumultuous that it constituted, in a way, the *how-did-he-survive-it?* whirlwind at the center of Keaton's own life.

The toddler action serial of Joe's fancies seems in some deep way to have informed his son's later screen persona. The hapless but game baby at the eye of Joe's anecdotal cyclone is a direct antecedent of the stalwart creature who gazes out at us from every one of Keaton's silent films (and into the lens of nearly every still camera he ever faced in his private life): Buster the unbreakable, the unfaze-able, forever poised at the edge of disaster yet providentially and inexplicably always somehow *safe.*

Young Buster's comic gifts aside, how did he and Joe manage to score seventeen-plus years of success with their ever-evolving enactment of a peculiar fantasy of limitless and downside-free parental violence? The family scrapbook Myra kept for years, full of undated clippings that are mostly trade ads for the Three Keatons' act, is equally full of braggadocio about the beatings this youngster could take. As Joe boasted in one long-running ad, his marvelous firstborn was "The Boy Who Can't Be Damaged." Another tagline for the act stressed Buster's utility as a household object, designating him "The Human Mop," while a third explicitly compared the boy's treatment to that of the lucky ticket buyer: "You think you were treated roughly as a kid? Wait till you see how they handle Buster."

Sometimes, as with the whimsical copy Joe wrote and encouraged fellow vaudevillians to contribute for the family's weekly trade-paper ads, the father's pride in the skills of his firstborn was palpable. "Wanted: A funnier kidlet comedian than Buster. Oh, what's the use?" began one affectionate ad from 1903, unattributed and thus likely written by Joe. But sometimes his extreme publicity stunts could be strangely hostile, even infanticidal in tone.

In a weird open letter published in the vaudeville trade papers and addressed to the "German-American Staff of Physicians and Surgeons'

Institute"[2] (perhaps intended as a sort of paid product placement, though no specific remedy is endorsed), Joe gave an unsettlingly graphic description of a near-death medical experience Buster had supposedly undergone. With macabre glee, Joe detailed the state of his child's "bloated" stomach and "fleshless" limbs, averring that "there never seemed to be one little chance for saving his life." In fact, despite multiple local and state inquests in which Buster was asked to take off his shirt and examined for signs of abuse, he was by all accounts a remarkably healthy child who almost never had to miss work for reasons of physical incapacitation. One rare exception: the time when Joe misjudged the height of a kick to his preteen son's head, knocking him out cold for eighteen hours.

Joe was not above staging the abduction of his own baby for a headline. In 1906 he paid a prop man at a Portland, Maine, theater to make off temporarily with Buster's younger brother Harry "Jingles" Keaton, then a year and a half old, just so a prominent news item would run in the local paper to remind everyone the Keatons were in town. A few years later, Joe penned a studiedly breezy *Variety* column about the family's one-week run at London's Palace Theater. Joe began by describing getting in trouble with the authorities on their transatlantic voyage, who were unamused when he jokingly tried to auction off little Louise, then two, to the highest bidder.

Later in the same column Joe recounted how, after the Keatons' first few performances in England, he was called to the office of Alfred Butt, the legendary music hall impresario who had invited them to play the Palace. "'Is that your son or an adopted one?'" demanded Butt. Keaton told him that Buster was indeed his biological child. "'My word,'" replied Butt. "'I imagined he was an adopted boy and you didn't give a damn what you did to him.'"[3] (In a sign that times have changed in some ways for the better, no one in the chain of custody of this anecdote—including Buster, who retells it in nearly identical words to his first biographer—questioned the premise that an adopted child might or should earn differential treatment from a parent's "own.")

Incensed at the suggestion that his treatment of Buster was anything less than idyllically paternal, Joe booked passage on the first boat back to the United States after their one-week run was over, cutting short the family's long-awaited first European tour. Playing the continent represented a conventional victory lap for American vaudeville acts at the top of their game. Joe's old friend Harry Houdini had done it years before, as had W. C. Fields, the singer Sophie Tucker, and many more of the Three Keatons' contemporaries on the big-time circuits. But going abroad, the proudly jingoistic Joe asserts in his editorial, had never appealed to him in the first place: he only agreed to the trip because of "the brimming tears in Buster's eyes."[4]

Like everything Joe published, this account of the Palace engagement seems to have undergone copious embellishment. But brimming tears or no, it seems likely that Buster would have taken the cancellation of his first-ever trip overseas hard. He had just turned thirteen, never an age for taking disappointments lightly, and had been rocketing to the top of his field since age five, for most of that time serving as the chief creative force behind the act's infinite variations on its naughty son/angry dad premise.

By his mid-teens Buster began to tire of this routine as he grew too big to throw, Joe came onstage ever drunker and more aggressive, and their exchanges devolved into something more nakedly akin to creative self-defense: two full-grown men whacking each other with brooms as the house orchestra sawed out Verdi's "Anvil Chorus." If there's anything descriptions of these late routines suggest, it's a live-action version of a Warner Bros. cartoon, coyote and roadrunner locked in their senseless yet eternal zero-sum game.

Though it's difficult to tell just when the Keatons' act began to tilt from daring to dangerous, the slide seems to have begun sometime after the England trip. Joe's worsening alcoholism, hair-trigger temper, and tendency to settle scores in front of a live audience began to sour his relationships with managers and bookers. Buster, for his part, was also growing restless and resentful as his father got harder to work out new material with. Press notices remarked on the changes taking place in the act during this ungainly phase. In 1912 a reviewer in the *New York Dramatic Mirror*, long a cheering section for the Keatons, tartly observed that "it is not an enlivening spectacle to see two grown persons in support of a lad of sixteen," adding that Buster "should make an effort to put more enthusiasm into his work."[5] Three years later, the Fort Wayne, Indiana, *Journal-Gazette* remembered when "Daddy Keaton could throw Buster around livelier than a political candidate can throw the bull." That is, until Buster "failed to run true to his mother's belief and grew up like any other boy." We would seem to be in familiar territory here; the disappointing adolescence of the youthful prodigy, the awkward post-adorable age that's marked the decline of many a modern-day child star.

And yet, this same item continued, "Buster's increase in bulk has not been his only gain. He has grown considerable gray matter under his hair and thinks of new stunts, trick novelties, etc., to include in the performance. . . . As a result no two performances by this combination ever are alike and that's what worries Father Keaton, trying to keep Buster outguessed."[6] This image—of a bright young man chafing at the family act's constraints, outgrowing his father's skill level by leaps of magnitude, and trying out new material even in a relative collaborative vacuum— flashes forward to the spring of 1917 in Roscoe Arbuckle's New York movie studio. There, newly freed from the constraints of daily live performance and paired with a young and inventive comedian who was as much his partner as his mentor, Buster's "gray matter" would be tested by the challenges of an entirely new medium—one he would not only adapt to right away but, almost as quickly, find ways to reinvent. He entered the movies already flying.

7

"Make *Me* Laugh, Keaton"

Martin Beck, date unknown.

In the spring of 1916, not long after Buster turned twenty, came the mundane yet momentous event one biographer dubbed "the Providence furniture massacre"—the trigger of a cascade of Joe misbehaviors that would abruptly put an end to the Keatons' decade-and-a-half-long run at the top of their profession.[1] Enraged when a Rhode Island theater manager docked the act's pay for having broken some of the house's rickety old prop chairs in the course of a weeklong run, Joe methodically trashed the theater's entire stock of stage furnishings, including a costly French sofa. This scorched-earth act of vengeance suggests Joe may have been

half-consciously looking for a way to commit professional suicide. It was
the kind of self-destructive gesture Buster would repeat years later in the
depths of his worst years at MGM.

The following week Joe had a decisive run-in with the powerful
impresario Martin Beck, the former promoter of both Harry Houdini
and W. C. Fields, who now ran the prestigious Orpheum theater circuit.
Beck, a volatile, demanding, and highly cultured man, had been beefing
with Joe for well over a decade, and the vaudeville gossip circuit was robust
enough that by the time the Keatons arrived at Beck's Palace Theater in
New York, Beck was well aware of the swath of destruction Joe had just
cut through Providence.

After moving the Keatons to the insulting spot of first act on the bill,
Beck stood in the wings during a matinee and sarcastically challenged Joe
to "make *me* laugh, Keaton." Joe left the stage then and there—leaving
Buster to vamp awkwardly with recitations and songs—and proceeded
to chase Beck out of the theater and down Forty-Seventh Street at top
speed, until he lost him in a crowd several blocks away. ("It was a good
thing," the older Buster would observe of Beck's narrow escape from his
father. "He'd have killed him for sure.")[2]

By way of revenge, Beck ordered the Keatons to cut their precisely
timed act down to twelve minutes—a request they protested by coming
onstage with an alarm clock and abruptly deserting the audience at the
twelve-minute mark. The following season Joe found himself and his
family demoted to the second-class, three-show-a-day Pantages circuit, a
humiliating comedown for an act of the Keatons' reputation and caliber.

The next few months spent on the small-time boards, taking long
train rides between western states to do more work for less pay, were a
depressing and downwardly mobile time for the Keaton clan, the first
major reversal of professional fortune they'd suffered since the revelation of Buster's gifts had lifted his parents out of poverty seventeen years
before. Louise and Harry "Jingles" Keaton, aged nine and eleven, were
now attending boarding school in Michigan, not far from the family's

beloved summer cottage at the actors' colony Joe and Myra had helped start in the lakeside town of Muskegon.[3] Harry and Louise were enjoying material advantages their breadwinning sibling never had: education and a steady place to live. But it's easy to imagine these two preteens, whose attempted integration into the act years before had foundered on their lack of either interest or talent, feeling superfluous and lonely on being ejected from the well-oiled performing and touring machine their parents and older brother had comprised since before they were born.

For an act as physically depleting as the Keatons', the difference between doing two and three shows a day was immense. Joe in particular was drastically less fit to perform his trademark hitch kicks and high jumps than back when he was younger and soberer. But the new schedule was also brutal on Buster and Myra—not least because, as Buster would confide to his first biographer four decades later, "Joe was abusing her too."

Mother and son seem to have grown closer during this grim Pantages period, or maybe the mounting crisis of Joe's addiction simply forced them to acknowledge their interdependency in a way that was atypical for the family's close-to-the-vest emotional style. Buster talked about Myra infrequently in comparison to Joe, though she played a much larger role in his adult life. There were only a few standard Myra stories, most of them involving her unflappable temperament, fondness for hand-rolled cigarettes, and fanatical dedication to backstage pinochle. But she looms large in his account of this painful transition: the great California abandonment of early 1917, when Myra and Buster conferred behind the carousing patriarch's back and agreed to hop a train from Los Angeles to Muskegon without even leaving Joe a note.

Ultimately, Buster insisted, the choice was Myra's more than his: "We were on the train from Oakland to Los Angeles when she said to me, Buster, God help me, I can't take any more." In the course of a life marked by passivity both in personal and business relationships, Buster would be faced with a few such decisive moments, and often—sometimes, though not this time, to his own detriment—he would leave the decision-making to someone else. "Except for Myra," he admits, in an acknowledgment of this lifelong character trait, "I guess I'd have gone on taking it."[4] Joe wouldn't learn of their desertion until, emerging from his latest bender, he took a train down to their next booking in Los Angeles and failed to find his wife and son, or their trunks, waiting at the stage door. Instead there was only his own trunk and the same scuffed wood table he had started with, back before Buster was born.

With the same seriousness of purpose he would later invest in his movies' technical and comedic innovation, Buster seems to have cared about the reputation and quality of the family knockabout act. It was disappointment at its decline and concern for his professional future, as well as fear for his mother's and his own physical safety, that led him to agree to break up the act that fateful day on the train.

Keaton's description of the act's waning years in conversation with his first biographer, Rudi Blesh, is dry and understated in tone but frankly appalling in content. He mentions, for example, the increasingly trans-actional nature of his and his father's onstage displays of violence, "those lickings onstage for things that had happened before. No more private spankings." Not that Buster couldn't give back as well as he got: "Finally I'd get sore and we'd start trading."

Joe, in Buster's words, began to transform into a different man, "mad most of the time, and could look at you as if he don't know you." The cause was not difficult to guess: "When I smelled whiskey across the stage, I got braced." The routine with the whirling basketball seems to have developed in part out of Buster's instinct for self-protection during this period: "That's when I had to fasten a rubber rope onto that old basketball of mine and keep swinging it around like a hammer thrower to keep him off me."

A conversation Buster recalls having with his mother around this time reveals Myra at her most philosophical. "'Joe's not punishing you,'" she tells her son, to which he responds—in a flash of vulnerability rare in the annals of Keaton interviews—"It *feels* like it." But Myra insists, again in Buster's retelling: "'No, he's not mad at you or anyone else. It's old Father

Time he'd like to get his hands on. Man or woman,' she said, 'some can take getting old, some can't.'"[5] Coming from a woman who was herself getting beaten—and who was about to effectively end the marriage in which she'd spent more than half her life, though Myra and Joe would never officially divorce—this was a wise and fair assessment, maybe fairer than Joe deserved.

Buster's account of the act's final days ends with an uncharacteristically introspective riff about his and Joe's father-son comic chemistry at its height, beginning with a recognition of his father's fallibility and even pathos.

> Yet you have to say, "Poor son of a bitch, fighting something he'd never catch up with!" But sweet Jesus, our act! What a beautiful thing it had been. That beautiful timing we had—beautiful to see, beautiful to do. The sound of the laughs, solid, right where you knew they would be . . . but look at what happened, standing up and bopping each other like a cheap film. It couldn't last that way.[6]

By that point in his life, of course, Buster would have known he was talking about more than one beautiful career brought down by drinking, bad choices, and the relentless march of Father Time. In this burst of nostalgia for the dysfunctional magic that was the Three Keatons' act, I can hear Buster's love for his father, just as I hear his love for Myra in the story of their conversation on the train. But just as plain is his love for the work they did together, their shared investment, over the course of many years, in refining the art of getting laughs. Though he would never consider himself an "artist"—would, in fact, poke dry fun throughout his life at any comedian who did—Keaton would always be motivated by this goal at the cost of all others. He was an atrociously terrible businessman, an indifferent celebrity, and, until late in his life, a dilatory husband and father at best. Nearly the whole of his prodigious intellectual and physical energy was channeled into the drive to create work that was "beautiful to see, beautiful to do," to hear those laughs right where he knew they would be.

But in the spring of 1917 Buster needed to figure out a way to work without the only comedy partner he had ever known. With what must have been dizzying suddenness, he found himself cut loose from the family act—although not from the financial obligation to support his family into the indefinite future. Joe had hurled him offstage for the last time, and there was no stagehand waiting in the wings to catch him. What was waiting instead was the medium that had been born alongside him and had grown up with him all his life: the movies.

PART II

FLYING

My God, in those days, when we made movies, we ate, slept and dreamed 'em.[1]

—Buster Keaton

8

Speed Mania in the Kingdom of Shadows

The State-Lake Theatre in Chicago, ca. 1921.

In 1917, the year Buster Keaton met Roscoe Arbuckle and began his life in film, *Theatre* magazine ran an article titled "Speed Mania Afflicts Vaudeville," written by a journalist and former vaudeville performer with the euphonious name of Nellie Revell. According to Revell, "vaudeville audiences demand speed and action, and the more they get, the more they want. Motion pictures have given people the habit of enjoying themselves via the eye. At a glance they can comprehend a situation that it would take many words to unfold." Adducing a recent stage sketch called "Supper for Two" as evidence that "the vaudeville playlet is in decline," she lamented that the piece "is practically a photoplay."[1]

Cinema's displacement of theater as the nation's most popular and influential form of mass entertainment took approximately a generation, a span of time that happened to coincide with Buster Keaton's first twenty or so years of life. During those decades the relationship between the two forms was both familial and antagonistic—a complex intergenerational rivalry not unlike like the on- and offstage struggle between Buster and Joe. The earliest films were often fragments of stage plays, and the first place many Americans saw moving images was in a theater as a part—usually the last part—of a vaudeville lineup. Around 1905 came the first dedicated movie venues, mostly converted storefronts with a makeshift screen and as many seats as would fit, where a program of short films played continuously throughout the day for a five-cent entrance fee.

But even the nickelodeon boom, which lasted until the advent of purpose-built movie theaters around 1915, didn't sever the close ties between film and vaudeville. Throughout Buster's early childhood most bills he played on included an act devoted to the demonstration of some type of motion-picture projection device. These machines were marketed as attractions in themselves under a variety of poetic product names that, like the Lumières' "Cinématographe," combined the Greek or Latin terms for "movement" or "life" with suffixes having to do with seeing or writing. They were life-lookers, movement-writers, and ghost-seers: the Vitascope, the Biograph, the Projectiscope, the Phantiscope.

The name for the images these mechanisms projected also remained in flux for the medium's first decade. They could be phantograms, kinetograms, cineographs, photo dramas, or, to use Revell's term, "photoplays." That word was just beginning to fall out of fashion when she employed it, having peaked in the previous year; it would live on as the name of a seminal celebrity magazine. Since around 1910 "movies" had begun to take over as the most common English term for the flickering shapes that the Russian novelist Maxim Gorky, on first observing the Cinématographe at work, had described as "vague but sinister" dispatches from "the Kingdom of Shadows."[2]

As audiences grew used to the novelty of film technology, the brand name of the machine that showed the pictures began to be replaced by descriptions of the pictures themselves. A few weeks after the assassination of President William McKinley in 1901 the Keatons shared a San Francisco bill with Edison's Biograph, which was said to present "moving pictures of the late President's funeral." Two years later, a trade ad for an evening of "polite vaudeville" in Washington, DC, offered audiences the chance to feed Lockhart's Performing Elephants, see singer Louise Dresser, comedian Jack Norworth and the Three Keatons ("including funny little 'Buster'"), watch Hale and Francis's "hoop rolling extraordinary," and last but not least witness "motion views of a real fire."

But the practice of titling movies was becoming the industry standard as the form graduated from a technological novelty to a new and uniquely transfixing form of narrative entertainment. A *Washington Times* write-up of that same 1903 bill mentions "the motion pictures of A *Midnight Rescue*, which is said to be the most thrilling fire scene ever portrayed in this way." So in two different contexts during a single run, A *Midnight Rescue*—which seems likely to be an alternate title for Edwin S. Porter's popular 1903 rescue drama *Life of an American Fireman*—is described as both a series of "views" and a "scene," suspended between the more culturally legible categories of still photography and live theater.

This evidence of overlapping nomenclature—the same reel of film seen in the same theater on the same run, presented in one place with a flat description of its subject and in another as a *movie* in our modern sense of the word, complete with a title and the promise of thrills—hints at how quickly the new medium was evolving. Before we could turn into the nation of transfixed movement-lookers we were about to become (and remain to this day), Americans first had to figure out what movies were and how to watch them. We had to apprehend these "galloping tintypes" at once as optical, narrative, social, and economic experiences—and in each of those realms, motion-picture technology brought huge and irrevocable change.

What did critics like Nellie Revell have against the movies? Their complaints echo the charges brought against each new entertainment and information technology that has come since: radio, television, the internet. In a process seen as akin to contagion ("speed mania *afflicts* vaudeville"), the fast pace and kinetic intensity of those first one- and two-reel films was said to be increasing the velocity of life itself, training young minds to expect ever more stimulation from an increasingly omnipresent media environment.

Nearly everywhere you look in early film criticism, the medium is characterized above all by its speed. In *The Art of the Moving Picture*, a 1914 book that's often cited as the first book-length work of film criticism, the poet Vachel Lindsay deplores "the incipient or rampant *speed-mania* in every American," using the exact term Revell would employ two years later. In the disorienting blur of the films Lindsay classifies as "Action Pictures," "the story goes at the highest possible speed to be still considered credible." In such films, he laments, "people are but types, swiftly moved chessmen."[3]

The sense of acceleration movies brought with them wasn't always cast in a negative light, but there was an ambient concern about the social change this emerging art form might bring in its wake. "The nickelodeon," writes Lucy France Pierce in *World Today* magazine in 1908,

> is more varied than any other type of amusement. It presents its lessons more graphically, more stupendously, reproducing in heroic action life itself without the limitations of art. It is evident that so far-reaching and commanding an institution among the masses may work irreparable evil or boundless good.[4]

By 1911, the anonymous authors of a Chicago police commission report are more explicit in their account of the depredations of public cinemas: "Many liberties are taken with young girls within the theater during the performance when the place is in total or semi-darkness. Boys and men slyly embrace the girls nearest them and offer certain indignities."[5] In nearly the same language that would be used a few years later by critics of the enclosed automobile, those who distrusted the changes the new medium was bringing characterized the interior of the movie theater as a licentious and potentially degrading place.

From both an aesthetic and social point of view movies remained suspect commodities until the second decade of the twentieth century, when they began to acquire enough prestige to attract more middle-class viewers. The popularity of movies also began to give rise to secondary industries like film criticism, fan magazines, and purpose-built movie theaters whose comfort and glamour drew a tonier audience than the nickelodeons of old. In those same years, a host of changes—the emergence of the feature-length film, the establishment of a stable economy of film production and distribution, the rise of the star system, the codification of basic film grammar—would make the moment of Keaton's entry into the industry especially propitious.

The stretch of Keaton's life that begins in 1917 and ends in 1929— that run of years he spent both in front of and behind the camera, at liberty to film whatever insane feats his mind could dream up and his body could execute, while the country around him went through one of its most violently transformational eras—is both the most exciting and the most daunting to write about. In evoking his childhood on the vaudeville stage I could assume, however clumsily, the guise of a cultural historian. All those performances, the whirling of basketball on rope and hurling of boy through pasteboard drop, are lost to time. Our best hope is to reconstruct them using contemporary descriptions or latter-day recollections.

But starting with *The Butcher Boy*, the two-reel short in which Keaton first appeared opposite Arbuckle, the films serve as their own artifacts. After decades of diligent rediscovery, restoration, and preservation, they're as easily available as they've ever been. Which means that this book's task now becomes as much critical as historical; in addition to considering his life in the context of its time, I must consider his movies in the context of both.

It's easy now to classify all of Keaton's silent output as slapstick comedy. But looking back from an era in which genres have grown ever more clearly defined, not to say calcified, what's remarkable is how many of our current cinematic forms he worked in and helped to create. Sure, his movies are packed with gags and stunts and chases and falls, each more audacious than the last. But while maintaining that commitment to high-density comic action, he also made romantic comedies like the all-time classic two-reel short *One Week*. He made topical spoofs like *Three Ages*, which parodied D. W. Griffith's gigantic white elephant *Intolerance*, or *The Frozen North*, which sent up the sentimental western star William S. Hart so skillfully that Hart, a friend of Keaton's, held a grudge against him for years afterward. ("You can't spoof a bum act, only a good one," Keaton insisted, and Hart eventually came around.) He made a Civil War epic, *The General*; a boxing picture, *Battling Butler*; and a maritime adventure, *The Navigator*. He made special-effects extravaganzas (*The Playhouse, Sherlock, Jr.*), period romances (*Our Hospitality*), and a heartwarming father-son reconciliation story (*Steamboat Bill, Jr.*)

This genre experimentation didn't spring from some desire on Keaton's part to build his résumé or, God forbid, to expand his artistic range. Right into old age he insisted that all he was out for was a laugh. The breadth of his output over those dozen or so years was the natural result of being a consummate craftsperson and a singularly gifted entertainer at a time when the new medium was at its most malleable. His curiosity and ambition grew to fit what the movies were becoming, and the form, in turn, expanded to make space for what he could do.

The decade that began in 1917 marks a sweet spot between the DIY experimentation of film's early years and the mass industrialization that would come in with synchronized sound. In fact, with the exception of the addition of sound, "the movies" as we still think of them now were fairly well in place by the time Keaton first set foot in Arbuckle's Comique

Studio. They had an agreed-upon name, a stylistic grammar that was more or less universally comprehended, stable financing and distribution channels, and an increasingly respectable if still uneasy social status. But film was still an undiscovered country, up for grabs as a technology and as an art form.

9

Pancakes at Childs

Childs restaurant interior, ca. 1920.

The way the story is usually told—and in Keaton lore this story, in whatever variant, is *always* told—Buster and Roscoe began making movies together the day they met. Over the course of that same day, if you believe the tale in its most condensed version, Keaton would also be introduced to his first wife, decide to leave the stage behind for motion pictures, and learn to take apart and reassemble a film camera.

It was in New York in late March 1917, a few months after Buster and Myra had abandoned Joe in California while he was on a bender, breaking up the Three Keatons' act for good. Joe had taken a few weeks to sober up and trail his wife and son by train to Jingles' Jungle, the family's nickname for their Muskegon summer cottage. In this flimsy structure

without heat or indoor plumbing, Joe would spend the remainder of
that winter alone and shivering, at least according to Buster's account.
"There was enough money in the bank account," Buster recalled in his
autobiography, in a tone at once solicitous of his father's well-being and
dryly dismissive of his material privations. "Pop wasn't going to die in
Muskegon of either hunger or loneliness. Knowing him, I was sure he
wouldn't die of remorse either."[1]

Myra was staying with relations in Detroit while Harry and Louise stayed
on in boarding school near Muskegon. And for the first time since Myra
Cutler had run off to elope with Joe Keaton in 1893, no one in the household
was bringing in a cent. The whole rickety contraption that was the Keaton
family—an alcoholic father, an abused mother, two expensive-to-educate
siblings, and no fit abode for any of them to live—now rested on Buster's
back. It was up to him to reinvent his career in a way that could support
his family, use his unique comic and acrobatic talents, and, if he was lucky,
move beyond the constraints of the father-and-son roughhouse act he and
Joe had been riffing on for the past seventeen years.

Not that finding work was a problem once Buster's train pulled into
New York. The day he arrived he signed a contract with the powerful
theatrical agent Max Hart to appear as a "single" (solo act) in the Passing
Show of 1917, a yearly Broadway musical revue at the Shuberts' Winter
Garden. Joining that show would have been a logical career move for
Buster, a better-paid step up from his long-held spot as vaudeville's peri-
patetic boy wonder. The Passing Show often acted as a showcase for rising
talent. The following year it would feature a brother-and-sister dance act
from vaudeville, Fred and Adele Astaire, of whom Adele was considered
the superior dancer and bigger stage personality, though it was her perfectionist younger brother who took charge of the choreography. A slightly
more risqué competitor to the Ziegfeld Follies, the Passing Show was
known for its sendups of the previous season's popular entertainments, a
form perfectly suited to Buster's gift for mimicry.

Still, Buster awoke that March morning feeling uneasy. For one thing,
the papers were full of news about America's inevitable entry into the war

in Europe—a momentous possibility that impinged on the consciousness of the serenely apolitical Buster mainly as the awareness he might soon be called up to serve, as indeed happened in 1919. More pressing at the moment was the matter that, with rehearsals for the Passing Show set to begin in just days, he had no idea how to structure a fifteen-minute-long solo turn without his father to torment and be tormented by. How would he create conflict or a beginning, middle, and end without an onstage adversary? With no one there to throw him, how would he fall?

With these questions weighing on his mind, Buster went into a Childs restaurant and ordered a stack of pancakes. This detail appears only in the account of the day he gave to biographer Rudi Blesh, but amid the conflicting versions of this much-mythologized story its specificity and randomness have the ring of truth. At key turning points in our lives it's not unusual to recall the last meal we ate before everything changed—and anyway, it's hard to see what rhetorical advantage would be gained from falsely claiming you did something so ordinary as have breakfast at Childs.[2]

Childs was one of America's, and therefore the world's, first restaurant chains. It lasted from 1889, when the first location was founded in lower Manhattan by the brothers Samuel and William Childs, until the early 1960s, when the last straggling outposts were absorbed by a fast-food franchising giant that still operates Wendy's, Taco Bells, and other chains across swaths of Manhattan. Like Keaton, the Childs chain would enjoy its biggest boom years in the 1920s, when the country, flush with cash and in constant motion, wanted everything on the double. At its height the franchise extended to more than 125 branches in the United States and Canada.

The Coney Island Childs, built in 1923, was a high-volume dining emporium that served simple, inexpensive food to families and large groups visiting the shore. This location, a stucco-clad fantasia of a building covered in maritime-themed bas-reliefs, enjoyed such success that it led to what we would now call a rebranding of the whole Childs empire. The chain became known for its distinctive architecture, with the brothers hiring a top design firm to create Spanish Revival–style buildings adorned with nautical motifs and other playful touches.

By the mid-1920s the Childs restaurant chain, like the movie industry, was constructing whimsically ornate branded palaces everywhere it could afford to. You can still find Childs buildings here and there in New York City with the help of online walking tours. When you spot the elegant curve of a Deco-style glass window above the awning of a T.G.I. Friday's in Midtown, or pass a pizza joint in Queens ringed with an incongruously graceful pattern of interlocking seahorses, it's like a bracing draft of marine air, a reminder that New Yorkers, whether we feel it most days or not, are an island people.[3]

But back in the 1910s the chain's distinctive look connoted not whimsy or seafaring adventure but modernity, cleanliness, and efficiency. The Childs of that era was known for its simple white-tiled lunchrooms staffed with white-clad waitresses, a modern touch in an era when male waiters were still the norm. "Griddle cakes" of several kinds—rye, cornmeal, buckwheat—were a Childs specialty, often cooked on a griddle in a window facing the street to attract customers. The draw was not only the smell of sizzling flapjacks but the pristine yet discreetly erotic appeal of the young women turning them, as this description from *Time* magazine makes clear: "In the windows, immaculate young ladies flip purest battercakes to the attraction, the invitation, of passersby."[4]

In the 1936 short *Grand Slam Opera*, the best of the low-budget "cheater" films Keaton made with the Poverty Row studio Columbia in his down-and-out years, he would stage a scene around a pretty girl flipping pancakes in the window of an unnamed restaurant. Annoyed with his moony ogling, she flips a cake directly onto the plate-glass window between them, obscuring his face.

Being a waitress at Childs required extensive training. Demure behavior was expected, and no "diner slang" allowed. The job paid better than most service jobs for women at the time, though the girls were required to purchase and launder their own starched white shirtwaists, and were charged in full for any crockery they broke or bills their customers skipped out on. These women, most of them young and foreign born, served cheap, wholesome meals to a working- and middle-class clientele.[5]

The rise of the Childs chain at the turn of the century was part of that era's broader quest for reinvention, anonymity, mobility, and novelty. The locations' familiar white-tiled neutrality was like the blank slate of a movie screen, a backdrop against which all sorts of urban encounters might happen. And in the popular culture of the twentieth century, Childs frequently served as an actual backdrop. In 1935 E. B. White wrote a poem in the *New Yorker* about witnessing a subtle flirtation between a Childs customer and a waitress. After demurely observing the proper service protocol, the white-clad server glances back with a "modest smile," "quick as the passing of summer rain."[6]

Richard Rodgers and Lorenz Hart included a lyric about the chain in their popular 1925 song "Manhattan," characterizing it as a place to be stylishly, even romantically broke: "We'll go to Yonkers / Where true love conquers / In the wilds / And starve together, dear, in Childs." Almost a quarter century later, Betty Comden and Adolph Green name-checked the franchise in a song for the 1953 musical *Wonderful Town*. The song's heroine, an aspiring actress from Alabama, arrives in New York with "repertoire ready / Chekhov's and Shakespeare's and Wilde's / Now, they watch her flipping flapjacks at Childs." As late as 1968, in the opening shots of the movie *The Odd Couple*, a neon-lit Childs can be clearly seen on one corner as a distraught Jack Lemmon makes his way through the streets of Manhattan at night.

What variety of flapjack Buster chose that day in 1917 has been lost to history, but at any rate, as he recalled to Blesh, he was too preoccupied to eat. He paid his ten-cent bill—fifteen, if he also ordered a cup of coffee—and made his way back into the street, where he ran almost immediately into Lou Anger, a former vaudeville comic by then working as a studio manager for Roscoe Arbuckle. Had Buster ever seen a movie being made, Lou asked? He had not. Well then, why didn't he come along and visit the set of Arbuckle's first independently produced film, *The Butcher Boy*, then in preparation for its first day of shooting?

The notoriously unloquacious Buster only had about three or four standard anecdotes he told over and over in interviews, and the encounter that would follow was one of them. If you believe the most condensed version of the story, in the day to come he was about to be introduced to his best friend, his wife-to-be, and the art form that would change his life, and whose history he would help to shape. But when I think of that late March morning, suspended between two eras in Buster's history and the country's, it's the visit to Childs I imagine: the uneaten pancakes, the newspapers with war in the headlines, the floating shapes of the waitresses in their starched white dresses. I wonder if one of them noticed the handsome young man with the worried face as she cleared away his untouched plate, and broke protocol by smiling.

10

Comique

Buster, Roscoe Arbuckle, and Al St. John, ca. 1917.

The building that housed Roscoe Arbuckle's Comique Studios, a squat redbrick rectangle on East Forty-Eighth Street in Manhattan, was torn down in 2012 to make room for the UN mission of the Republic of Singapore. Not that there would have been a strong argument to make to the New York Landmarks Commission in favor of preserving an undistinguished structure, originally a warehouse, that for a while in the late teens housed a trio of small movie production companies. But back in 1917, Joseph Schenck, the up-and-coming producer and film mogul who owned and ran all three studios, must have been pleased to find an affordable location with just the right disposition of space for the family business he planned to launch.

The block at that time would have been dark and a little dodgy, wedged between the derelict East River waterfront and the shadow of the elevated tracks on Second Avenue. But Joe Schenck knew a good real estate deal when he saw one. He grew up in a tenement on the Lower East Side with seven brothers and sisters, a child of Russian Jews who had arrived with the great wave of immigration that began in the 1880s. He and his younger brother Nick had gone from working at a pharmacy to operating a concession stand at the uptown end of a Manhattan trolley line, finally becoming the co-owners of two successful amusement parks.

In 1907 Marcus Loew, the head of a chain of vaudeville theaters, took the smaller park off the brothers' hands and made them his partners in a business aptly named Consolidated Enterprises. Loew's aim was to buy up as many vaudeville and movie venues as possible, extending the concept of franchising from restaurant and theater chains to motion-picture houses. By 1917 Nick was in charge of more than one hundred Loew-owned theaters nationwide, while Joe's interests—personal as well as financial— had begun to turn to the production side of this booming new business.[1]

The first two floors of the building on East Forty-Eighth Street were occupied by a pair of studios founded for and named after the famous Talmadge sisters, Norma and Constance. Norma and Joe had been married just a few months before—he was thirty-nine to her twenty-two—and he had already set up both sisters with their own dedicated production companies.

The Talmadge sisters had grown up in even more straitened circumstances than the Schenck brothers. Their mother, Margaret "Peg" Talmadge, had been abandoned by her alcoholic and jobless husband when the girls were still tiny—according to some accounts he walked out on Christmas morning, though Peg's stories had a way of layering on the schmaltz. Peg had brought up her daughters as a single mother in Brooklyn, taking in washing and selling cosmetics to get by, at least until her girls hit adolescence and revealed themselves as beauties. (This was something of a surprise given Peg's own physiognomy, which might be tactfully described as "plain.") Peg had vicarious artistic ambitions—she had always wanted to become a great painter, as she explains in her bonkers 1924 memoir, *The Talmadge Sisters*. These ambitions, combined with her eminent financial pragmatism, made her one of the earliest and most formidable of Hollywood stage mothers, presiding over and reveling in every moment of her daughters' success.

Norma, the eldest, was a stately brunette with a noble profile who had gotten her start as a teenager modeling for "song slides," the projected photos that often accompanied live singalongs in variety shows. When she caught Joe's eye as a contract player at the Triangle Film studio, Norma was around twenty. She and Constance, known to the family as "Dutch" for her Dutch-girl-style blond bob, were finding their way in the film business, but they would attain a whole new level of stardom once Joe took charge of their careers. A *Photoplay* magazine poll in 1920 named Norma the most popular actress in America, with her sister a distant second.

Though Norma's Roman-bust features and the elaborate costume dramas that were among her specialties have gone out of fashion, she was both hugely successful and critically praised in her time, considered to be the more beautiful as well as the more "serious" of the acting Talmadges. In 1923 the powerful celebrity columnist Adela Rogers St. Johns named her "one of the leading dramatic actresses of the silversheet."[2] Schenck — who would go on to a long life as a Hollywood Svengali, helping to shape Marilyn Monroe's early career in the context of their on-again, off-again sexual relationship — had a keen sense for his young wife's market appeal, especially among female audiences. No one looked better than Norma Talmadge swathed in brocade, gripping the back of a Louis XIV chair as she gazed after a departing lover.

Constance, the youngest sister, stood directly opposite Norma on the spectrum of Hollywood female types of the day. She was a gangly comedienne with the insolent pout and athletic slouch of a Jazz Age "flapper," years before that term passed into everyday parlance. The typical Constance Talmadge vehicle was a mildly naughty farce involving mistaken identities and romantic entanglements, often with a story and intertitles by the sisters' good friend Anita Loos.

But Constance's most enduring performance would turn out to be as the "Mountain Girl," the incongruously modern tomboy heroine of the ancient-Babylon plotline in D. W. Griffith's ponderous transhistorical epic *Intolerance*. This refreshingly unmythologized creature, as opposed to virtually every other woman in the three-plus-hour-long movie, is neither a cradle-rocking symbol of the eternal feminine nor an exoticized temptress but a rough-and-tumble country lass who enjoys snacking on raw green onions. When a Babylonian masher tries to make time with the Mountain Girl, she rolls her eyes and slithers free of his reach as though they were seated in the back of a Model T Ford rather than beneath a three-hundred-foot-tall replica of a Mesopotamian city gate. Perhaps because of this perennially modern quality, Constance is the Talmadge whose screen presence has weathered the best. Unfortunately, most of the eighty or so films she made are now lost.

The building's third floor was devoted to soundstages for Joe's newest investment, Comique Studio (pronounced, with a would-be Gallic flair, "cuh-MEEK-ee"), where Arbuckle was brought on to make two-reel comedies with his own production company after Joe's offer of creative independence lured him away from Mack Sennett's Keystone. Finally there was the company's business office, also staffed by family. Natalie, the middle Talmadge sister, worked as the secretary and accountant for Joe's companies, helping to balance the books and answer her sisters' voluminous fan mail. Known to the family, and later to Buster, as "Nat" or "Nate," Natalie was smaller, shyer, and, by the standards of her time, less attractive than her two glamorous siblings. She was also the most educated of the Talmadges, having taken a course in stenography and bookkeeping.

Natalie did sometimes appear in her sisters' films in bit parts, at least up until her marriage to Buster in the spring of 1921. The role she was assigned was often that of a frumpy spinster in need of a makeover to land a man. In *The Love Expert* (1920), Constance's character confiscates her glasses and bobs her hair while she sleeps. To modern tastes the petite, fine-featured Nate might well be deemed the prettiest of the three, but onscreen her deep-set eyes and serious face seemed to recede into the shadow of her sisters' showier beauty. She would appear a handful of times in her husband's films, most notably as the antebellum love interest in *Our Hospitality* (1923), but in his lineup of leading ladies she is among the least expressive. Any attempt to plumb the mystery of Natalie Talmadge—who she was, what she saw in Buster or he in her, what went on in the black box of their eleven-year marriage—by watching her scattered appearances on film is bound to founder in frustration. She never aspired to be an actress, only a sister or wife doing her part to help out with the family business, and her onscreen presence is accordingly opaque.

The Talmadges and the Schencks are two entirely distinct balls of wax, both due for fuller treatment later on. For the moment it's enough to know that these two powerful show business families were present from Buster's first day at Comique. He had grown up in a family-run business, albeit a much smaller one, where the only product on sale was the live performance he and his parents re-created on stage twice per day. From his first day at Comique he was involved in a whole different enterprise: no longer the featured star of an ever-changing live act but one member of a team creating mass-produced entertainment that could be copied and distributed all over the world.

The building on East Forty-Eighth Street was a kind of multi-use entertainment factory. Norma and Constance provided the tragedy, light romance, and celebrity-magazine fodder, while Joe signed the checks and Natalie signed the autographed portraits mailed out to fans in her sisters' names. The role of Arbuckle's company was to turn out six to eight two-reel comedies a year. (A reel of film lasted about ten minutes; "two-reeler" was the standard term for a twenty-minute short.) To a man like Schenck with an eye on the future, Arbuckle, a three-in-one deal who directed and edited his own films, represented a rapidly appreciating parcel of show business real estate. Except for the megastar Charlie Chaplin, who had recently signed a one-year contract with the Mutual Film Corporation for the record-breaking sum of $670,000 (around $17 million in today's dollars), the spherical, angel-faced "Fatty" was the most famous film comedian in the world.

The top female contender for that title was Roscoe's former screen partner and sometime director Mabel Normand. She had also just launched her own production company, backed by her former Keystone producer and ex-boyfriend Mack Sennett. It was all the rage for a while in the late teens to set promising creator-stars up with their own independent studios, as producers began to realize that what drew audiences into movie houses had less to do with story content or production value than with the familiar faces of specific, beloved performers. Joe must have figured that Arbuckle's reputation for crowd-pleasing slapstick would be a sure-fire hook to get audiences into the theater for Norma's and Constance's luxuriant feature-length spectacles.

It was into this stacked hive of industry on Forty-Eighth Street—with cameras cranking, costume racks rolling, carpenters building and breaking down sets just out of frame, possibly a live musician or two playing to set the mood for the girls' romantic scenes—that Buster and Lou Anger walked that March day in 1917, having crossed paths on Broadway after Buster's uneaten breakfast at Childs. Or it might have been the next day; the existence of an entry in Keaton's 1917 datebook noting the studio's street address indicates that at least some time elapsed between encounter and visit.

Whenever it happened, Anger's storied encounter with Keaton may have been less a chance meeting than a deliberate act of headhunting. After all it was Lou, representing Joe Schenck, who had poached Arbuckle from the notoriously tightfisted Sennett a few months before, sneaking his way past the guards on the Keystone lot to lure the rotund comedian from California to New York with an irresistible offer: $1,000 a week for three years, with complete creative control over his projects and the possibility of a raise to $1 million a year if his films proved successful. He might even, Arbuckle was told, eventually star in his own features, an as-yet rare distinction for a comedian. Even Chaplin—who along with Normand had played a villain in the first feature-length comedy, *Tillie's*

Punctured Romance, in 1914—had not yet starred in a full-length movie of his own direction.[3]

Anger's encounter with the newly unemployed Buster might have had both professional and personal motives. For the whole of Buster's life up to that point, and for quite a bit of it still to come, work and personal life existed in a state of near-complete overlap. He and Lou were longtime colleagues, the Keatons having traveled the same vaudeville circuits as Anger and his wife, Sophye Bernard. Lou had been a middlingly success-ful "Dutch" dialect comedian, specializing in broad ethnic humor about malapropism-prone German immigrants, while Sophye was a popular songstress and sheet-music cover model known, after the title of her biggest hit, as "the Poor Butterfly Girl." Lou had sixteen years on Buster, and while he may not have been a show business *macher* on the level of the Schenck brothers, he was by all evidence a seasoned professional with an eye for rising talent.[4]

Having heard via the vaudeville rumor mill about the Keaton family's truncated last season on the Pantages circuit, Lou would no doubt have inquired after the welfare of Joe, Myra, Harry, and Louise. Buster, to judge by the degree of emotional openness he displayed in later interviews, would have supplied whatever polite but unforthcoming answer moved the conversation along the quickest, and talk would soon have turned to work. On learning that Buster had just signed with the Shuberts to appear in the Passing Show, Lou would naturally have seen fit to divulge that he was now managing Arbuckle in a just-launched studio venture. The possibility of a job offer would have been mutually understood, whether or not it was stated outright.

Whatever the circumstances of their encounter, Buster's consistent framing of the meet-up with Lou as pure luck—and his telescoping of the events that followed into a single, providential day—gets at an important psychic truth about his and Roscoe's working relationship: from the day they met and filmed a scene together, it was *as if* they had been brought together by a benevolent turn of fate. Their partnership, which soon became a close friendship, developed uncannily fast, and their complementary energy was plain from the minute the camera rolled. Within weeks Arbuckle seems to have entrusted virtually every aspect of production to his young sidekick. Buster described this sped-up apprenticeship with typical verbal economy over four decades later: "Arbuckle was his own director, and I'd only been with him probably about three pictures when I was his assistant director. In other words, I was sittin' alongside the camera when he was doin' the scene. And he taught me the cutting room also because he was his own cutter."[5]

The day Lou brought Buster in and introduced him around, Arbuckle was setting up to shoot his first independent short for Schenck, *The Butcher Boy*. In two somewhat disjointed reels, it tells the story of a lovelorn general-store employee (Arbuckle) who gets into a series of dry goods–related scrapes and then, in an only obliquely related second half, finds himself infiltrating an all-girls' boarding school in Mary Pickford–esque drag, complete with cascading blond ringlets, lace bloomers, and a frilly white parasol. Dressed as a girl, Roscoe could poke fun at the craze for plucky prepubescent heroines played by grown women (Pickford, at twenty-five, had just played an eleven-year-old in *The Poor Little Rich Girl*) while also demonstrating his formidable flair for skipping and simpering.

Buster would do his share of cross-dressing in the Comique years, too, transforming as needed into an exotic odalisque or a blushing bride. Using drag as a story device allowed the shorts to stray into mildly risqué territory while remaining irreproachably family friendly. Like the vaudeville-era Keaton, Arbuckle was a particular favorite with child audiences, and he valued his role as a juvenile entertainer: "I cater to the kids," he told the film columnist Kitty Kelly in 1915.

At first Buster resisted Roscoe's invitation to throw together a costume and get in on the day's filming; he was only there, he said, to observe. But whether it was at Roscoe's prodding or simply a result of Buster's own lifelong drive to explore and refine whatever comic material he encountered, he soon found himself on the general-store set, suited up in some baggy farmer's overalls, a pair of absurdly long "slapshoes," and the flat gray porkpie hat that would become his longest-lived sartorial trademark. In his very first scene on film, that now-unmistakable piece of headgear appears not just as a costume element but as a key prop. Roscoe's grocery-clerk character nonchalantly uses it as a receptacle for a bucketful of molasses, setting off a sequence of stickiness-based gags.

The inspired mayhem that developed on set that day, and the more solitary inspiration of the night that followed, when Buster asked permission to take the camera back to the theatrical boardinghouse where he was lodging so he could disassemble it and put it back together in time for the next day's shoot, have passed into film history legend. But however indistinct the details may have become over a hundred years of retelling, the story's denouement remains consistent and plausible. The morning after his first encounter with filmmaking, Buster returned to his agent's office and asked if it was too late to tear up his newly signed contract with the Passing Show. After spending one day in front of and one night inside a motion-picture camera, he knew, for the first time in the last few restless and troubled years, exactly where he wanted to be.

II

Roscoe

Roscoe Arbuckle directing, date unknown.

N o one who loved him called him "Fatty" (with the exception, naturally, of his fans). He was Roscoe to his friends and to the three women he would marry in his forty-six years on earth. But Arbuckle was a man who generated nicknames everywhere he went, a testament to the respect and affection he inspired in cast and crew mates. Buster, eight years his junior, sometimes addressed him as "Chief." Other pet names did invoke Roscoe's size, if in more idiosyncratic and less cruel ways than "Fatty." His frequent onscreen partner and sometime director at Keystone, Mabel Normand, called him "Big Otto" after an elephant in the menagerie of producer Bud Selig, the man who had gotten Arbuckle started in films. To his fellow Keystone Cop Fred Mace, he was "Crab"—a name whose origin is unknown but which suited Arbuckle's physiognomy: a broad, convex middle (said, in Roscoe's case, to be solid muscle) conveyed through the world by incongruously nimble limbs. Charlie Murray, another Keystone-era collaborator and fellow vaudeville veteran, always referred to Arbuckle as "my child the Fat," which captures both the actor's girth and his some-times unsettling air of permanent boyishness.

In Mack Sennett's rollicking if unreliable memoir, *King of Comedy*, the eccentric producer recalls that on their first meeting, Arbuckle, skipping up the Keystone Studio steps "as lightly as Fred Astaire," told him, "Name's Arbuckle, Roscoe Arbuckle. Call me Fatty!"[1] That detail alone is enough to prove that Sennett and Arbuckle were never friends. "Fatty" was the character Roscoe played onscreen, a childlike yet occasionally lascivious merrymaker with a pronounced penchant for cross-dressing. (Arbuckle's feminine alter ego was popular enough to have starred in a Keystone one-reeler of her own, the Arbuckle-directed *Miss Fatty's Seaside Lovers*, in 1915.) "Fatty" was also the name in the title that sold the picture, one of the first proper names in film history with the power to do so—even if Normand did beat him there by two years.

As early as 1913 Arbuckle was gaining a following in one-reel comedies like *Fatty Joins the Force* and *Fatty's Day Off*. By 1914 he was acting as his own director in such delightfully titled two-reelers as *Fatty's Magic Pants*, *Fatty's Tintype Tangle*, and *Fickle Fatty's Fall*. In 1915–16 he and the tiny, vivacious Normand became an unlikely but massively popular onscreen couple, teaming up in a series of co-branded "Fatty and Mabel" shorts; these were also, for the most part, directed by Arbuckle, with increasing sophistication and skill.

But as far as his jovial screen persona had taken him in life, Roscoe would never have introduced himself that way. If you watch his films with care, you can see that none of the other characters address him as "Fatty." Read Mabel's lips as she calls out for her missing sweetheart in *Fatty and Mabel's Simple Life*, and they unmistakably form the word "Roscoe." He avoided gags built around his weight (getting stuck in doors, breaking furniture) and appears never to have chosen "Fatty" as a performance name: it was simply a schoolyard taunt that stuck, and then sold. When new acquaintances used it, his first wife, Minta Durfee, recalled, he would reply evenly, "I've got a name, you know."[2]

A century on, the idea of a schoolyard taunt like "Fatty" doubling as a professional identifier makes us flinch, or at least it should. Even if "Fat Amy"—the self-christened a cappella queen Rebel Wilson plays in the *Pitch Perfect* films—is in her way still wringing laughs from the stigma that gave rise to Roscoe's nickname, at least that character's moniker is a self-assumed choice, and the actress's own name isn't replaced in both credits and title by a mocking epithet. The casual submergence of Roscoe Arbuckle's identity into "Fatty" is one of many unfortunate aspects of his passage from world fame to a vague historical infamy.

Today most people who have heard of Roscoe at all probably think of him first as "Fatty Arbuckle," now the brand name not of a beloved funmaker but of a lurid Jazz Age scandal: the death of the young actress Virginia Rappe after a party in his San Francisco hotel suite in 1921. When his name comes up in the popular media—usually in connection with some current celebrity scandal or inaccurate #MeToo analogy—he's generally "Fatty" first and Roscoe second, if at all, and the crucial detail of his legal innocence often goes unmentioned. It may be a petty indignity next to being falsely remembered as a rapist and murderer, but if you care at all about Roscoe—and watching his surviving films or reading about his short, sad life, it's hard not to—hearing him called by a name he was known to have hated adds an extra sting.

Even the appellation he was given at birth, Roscoe Conkling Arbuckle, contains an embedded insult; his identity springs from a primal act of rejection. William Goodrich Arbuckle, a sod farmer eking out a living near Smith Centre, Kansas, despised the youngest of his five children from the day the boy was born in March 1887. The newborn weighed in at nearly fourteen pounds; according to family lore, complications from the delivery would be what killed his mother, Mary, twelve years later, though her real cause of death is unknown. William, a man of slight build whose wife was also petite, refused to believe this gargantuan baby could be his. Out of spite he insisted the child be named after Roscoe Conkling, a New York senator whose radical pro-civil-rights positions he scorned.

William, who like Buster's father drank too much and got violent when he did, abandoned the family soon after relocating them to Southern California when Roscoe was still a toddler. Roscoe's siblings were old enough to leave home by then, and he spent his early childhood as the only child of a poor single mother. William played very little part in his son's life until shortly after his wife's death in 1899, when he remarried— to another woman named Mary, with six children of her own. When the grieving twelve-year-old took a train to San Jose to move in with his estranged father, he found William had skipped town without leaving an address. Finally, reluctantly, Roscoe's father did allow him space under his roof, but he subjected the boy to a nonstop stream of physical and psychological abuse, with William's unabated disgust at Roscoe's size as an ongoing theme.

In an interview from the time of the 1921 Arbuckle scandal, when tabloid reporters would talk to anyone even remotely connected to the case, the second Mary tells a self-flattering but illuminating story about saving Roscoe's life as "his father was choking him and beating his head against a tree." Any sympathy she might have earned for this act dissipates when, elsewhere in the same interview, she allows that, though his father regularly beat him, her "aggravatingly lazy" stepson "often deserved it."

Roscoe made his theatrical debut the same year Buster was born, filling in for another child actor in a stock company production. Later, the teenage Roscoe built a reputation not for comedy but for the delicate tenor voice in which he warbled sentimental parlor songs to accompany the illustrated "song slide" projections—part paintings, part tinted photographs, sometimes including lyrics for an audience sing-along—that alternated with movies in variety lineups.

After the theater owner and future picture-palace impresario Sid Grauman discovered him in 1903, Roscoe joined the company at Grauman's

Unique Theater in San Francisco. In 1906, when much of that city, including the Unique, was destroyed in the Great San Francisco Earthquake, Roscoe took his act on the Pantages vaudeville circuit, the same small-time western chain where, a decade later, the Three Keatons would spend a season in exile after Joe's disastrous feud with Martin Beck. According to one unverifiable legend, the opera star Enrico Caruso—that turn-of-the-century symbol of European high culture, whose concert Will Rogers boasted of skipping out on during his honeymoon to catch the far livelier Three Keatons—took young Roscoe aside to scold him for wasting his gifts on the variety stage instead of saving his voice for opera.

By the time he met Buster at Comique, Roscoe, then thirty to Keaton's twenty-one, had racked up a whole lifetime's worth of experience in many performance genres. He had visited remote Alaskan trading outposts with a theatrical stock company, joined a veteran comedy duo on a tour of the upper western circuit (dubbed the "death trail" for its long distances between gigs), and toured East Asia singing and performing comic operas, including the title role in Gilbert and Sullivan's *The Mikado*, with his first wife and stage partner, Minta Durfee.

Roscoe's start in movies came in 1909 at the Selig Polyscope Company, Southern California's first permanent movie studio. (Long after its film-production wing shuttered in 1918, it lingered on as a zoo that supplied animal talent to Hollywood productions. Denizens of the Selig zoo, besides Roscoe's pachyderm nicknamesake Big Otto, included Leo, the twice-roaring lion in MGM's long-standing company logo.) Unfortunately none of the films Arbuckle made in the year or so he spent with Selig survives. He and Minta spent the first half of the 1910s moving up the ranks at Keystone alongside Roscoe's nephew Al St. John, a lanky acrobat and trick bicyclist who would become a core member of the Comique company.

When Joe Schenck lured Roscoe away from Sennett with a deal so sweet it included a Rolls-Royce Silver Ghost touring car—as the saying at Keystone went, "get your start with Sennett, get rich someplace else"—Al came along with him and Minta didn't. The causality of this decision

remains unclear: Did Roscoe, as Minta claimed in one late-in-life interview, betray her trust by promising her a place at Comique that never
materialized, instigating their separation? Or was their breakup already
in progress, leading Minta to instead choose to stay in Los Angeles and
costar opposite her good friend Mabel Normand—by far the most famous
and powerful woman in comedy—at Mabel's newly created independent
studio? Either way, by early 1917 Minta and Roscoe were on different
paths, remaining man and wife in name only until he remarried in 1925.

In the tumultuous year preceding Comique's launch, Arbuckle had
also survived a brief but debilitating bout of morphine addiction. After
surgery for an infected carbuncle on his leg, he got hooked on the drug
and was able to kick the habit only after a grueling stay in a rehabilita-
tion sanitarium—a locale he reimagined as the "No Hope Sanitarium"
in the macabre Comique short *Good Night, Nurse!*, featuring Buster as
a doctor in a suspiciously bloodstained smock. Though their marriage
was dissolving, Minta stood by Roscoe through his recovery, as she would
through his three very public manslaughter trials in 1921–22. She spoke
of him with fondness for the rest of her life, which ended in 1975 after
seven decades of acting on stage, screen, and television.

Having come of age on the fringes of the vaudeville industry in the
same years the Three Keatons spent near its top, Roscoe must surely have
been familiar with their act. If so he would no doubt have appreciated
the young Buster's flair for comic invention. They shared an affinity for
bits of business that doubled as virtuoso displays of prowess. Like Keaton,
Arbuckle loved to alternate broad sight gags—falls, fights, chases—with
a display of next-level fine motor skills. Both men could juggle, balance,
catch, and throw with astounding ease. Both had phenomenal aim. One of
Arbuckle's go-to moves was to take off his hat, toss it behind him without
a glance, and have it land perfectly on a hat rack some distance away, a
gag Keaton copies in *Sherlock, Jr.*

Roscoe's characters—often cooks, mechanics, soda jerks, or other service workers in prop-rich environments—were forever flipping pancakes,
butchering pig carcasses, mixing drinks, and changing tires in novel and

amusing ways. Another Arbuckle specialty was a sleight-of-hand trick in which he rolled a cigarette, popped it in his mouth, and lit it in one quick, continuous gesture. This bit had been used by earlier stage and screen comics, most famously Roscoe's older cousin Macklyn Arbuckle, but never with more dexterity and grace.

Arbuckle's and Keaton's uses of facial expression couldn't have been more distinct. Roscoe's broad features were in constant motion, and he liked to break the fourth wall to establish a teasing complicity with his audience, sometimes triangulating with the spectator to discreetly mock another character: *Can you believe this guy?* Buster's secret weapon — even in the early Comique days, when his characters occasionally laughed, smiled, or cried — was his self-contained stillness, the sense that his interiority resided somewhere beyond the camera's reach. But there was a kinship in their approach, a shared respect for the well-turned comic detail, that made them born collaborators.

Like most Americans in the 1910s, Keaton went to the movies a lot, and would in the natural course of things have been familiar with the cherubic visage of "Fatty." As a teenager itching to move beyond his and Joe's increasingly dysfunctional father-son routine, Buster might well have taken notice of the largest yet most surprisingly agile member of the Keystone Cops, that chaotic pack of bumblers whose ranks also briefly included Charlie Chaplin, Harold Lloyd, Al St. John, Charley Chase, and virtually every future silent comedy star except for Keaton himself.

Even if he missed Arbuckle's few appearances as a Cop, Buster would certainly have been aware of the subsequent emergence of "Fatty" as a Keystone staple and one of the first name-brand movie stars, his round, beaming face and too-small derby hat almost as universally recognizable as the Little Tramp's mustache, baggy pants, and cane. (A legend, probably invented wholesale by the cheerfully mendacious Keystone publicity department, holds that the trousers Chaplin first commandeered when putting together a costume for the character belonged to Arbuckle.)

After Chaplin's highly publicized departure in 1914 to make his own films for the short-lived Essanay Studio, Arbuckle's profile and creative power on the Keystone lot continued to grow. Over the next two years he would star in dozens of one- and two-reel comedies, often directing himself. The jewel in the crown of Arbuckle's Keystone period was the 1915–16 "Fatty and Mabel" series, a run of hit two-reelers, nearly all directed by Arbuckle, that paired his clownish bulk with Normand's Edwardian-valentine beauty. Usually the two played a couple, sometimes courting, sometimes already married.

Domestic life tended to be treated with a smirk in the anarchic and unsentimental Keystone universe. To be married was to be henpecked, harangued, unjustly deprived of other female companionship (male randiness being a first principle of Keystoneworld), and worst of all forced to endure the presence of one's mother-in-law, a fate "Fatty" endured in many a Keystone short. (The real-life Roscoe, hungry for family life since the early loss of his mother, was close to Minta's mother, whose home they shared in their first years of marriage.) The Fatty and Mabel comedies replaced that cynical—not to mention sexist—view of gender relations with a warmer, more hopeful portrait of romantic love.

Arbuckle and Normand were friendly offscreen, and they made a curious kind of sense together as an onscreen couple: both were athletic, flirtatious, physically fearless, and heedlessly impulsive. They could be childlike, but they were never infantile in the manner of, say, Mary Pickford, who played juvenile parts well into her thirties. Their onscreen connection was wholesome but not sexless, even if desire could be suggested only via playful sublimation. Finding Mabel's bloomers suspended from his clothesline in *Fatty and Mabel's Wash Day*, Roscoe gives them an oh-you-naughty-girl spank. In *Fatty and Mabel's Simple Life*, set like many of their shorts on a farm, she milks a cow and squirts a stream of milk in his eye.

The exasperated but lasting affection these characters showed for each other moved domestic comedy in a new direction, closer to what we would call romantic comedy. Two of their later Arbuckle-directed collaborations, *That Little Band of Gold* (1915) and *He Did and He Didn't* (1916), even explore the ambivalence and disappointment of both partners in a marriage, without mocking either of the spouses or the institution itself. They're worldly and frank in a way American sex comedy would not be again until the pre-Code 1930s.

Arbuckle and Normand's last and probably best film together, *Fatty and Mabel Adrift* (1916), is packed with innovative directorial touches that create a distinctly un-Keystone-like mood of scenic beauty and lyrical tenderness. As Roscoe leans down to kiss Mabel good night (udder-based foreplay notwithstanding, the two still sleep in separate beds), Arbuckle frames the shot to show not his profile but the shadow it casts on the wall. Later, thrown into silhouette by the setting sun, he throws a stick for his trusty Staffordshire terrier—Roscoe and Minta's real-life pet Luke, one of the first canine movie stars, who appeared in over a dozen films with Roscoe and, later, Buster as well. In the big action finale, the couple's hilltop house, which has been flooded out of spite by Roscoe's romantic rival Al St. John, floats out to sea with them still in it. The image of the house-turned-boat gestures toward the surrealism and grand-scale bravado of later Keaton classics like *One Week* and *Steamboat Bill, Jr.* It's obvious, watching the still-impressive twenty minutes of filmmaking that is *Fatty and Mabel Adrift*, that Arbuckle was ready to find more to do on both sides of the camera.

The Roscoe whom Buster met in spring 1917, then, was a creatively ambitious, financially successful, and almost unprecedentedly famous young man. He was also a recovering addict and child abuse survivor who had just broken up with his wife of eight years. He was powerful and fragile, generous and temperamental, high-spirited and melancholy, hardworking and hard-partying. He seemed to have a limitless future ahead of him in the booming new business of movies. His run of good luck had just four years to go.

12

Brooms

Buster Keaton, 1921.

K eaton's first scene on film, an improvised take in *The Butcher Boy*, is
played alone. As an overall-clad customer at a rustic general store, he
pauses in front of a barrel of brooms. After choosing two and subjecting
them to an obscure series of maneuvers—plucking out the straws of one,
dropping another to the ground and kicking it up neatly into his hand—he
tosses them both back in the bin with nonchalantly precise aim. At this
point in his life Buster knew from brooms; for the past few years he and
Joe had been using them as a key prop in their act. In addition to their
mutual whacking routine timed to "The Anvil Chorus," father and son

had developed a simple but audience-pleasing bit in which they labored to free a broom handle stuck in a hole that had been pre-drilled into the stage.

The brooms he inspects in *The Butcher Boy* never come into play again in that film, though *The Rough House*, the next short he made with Arbuckle, did contain a short broom battle. But there is something fitting about Buster's first filmed appearance involving the examination and rejection of a favored Three Keatons prop. It's how he would spend the next few years at Comique: picking over the routines of his past, rejecting some and reworking others, choosing who he was going to be as a solo performer. In those same years, the movie industry was also reinventing itself.

What makes the Keaton of the Arbuckle years fascinating to watch — once you get past his mind-bending acrobatic skill and knee-buckling good looks — is the relative permeability of his persona. After a childhood spent as a poker-faced projectile, he seems to have welcomed the chance to explore a wider range of expression. In his first months at Comique, as his role behind the scenes grew from apprentice to assistant to codirector, Keaton played third-banana roles to Al St. John's second: he was the delivery boy, the waiter, the saloon keeper, the farmhand. But far from resenting the demotion to forty-dollar-a-week bit player in a troupe after a lifetime spent headlining a family act in top vaudeville houses, he seems to have thrown himself into his new job with a will. He invested those supporting parts with deft touches of character humor and never missed an opportunity to wedge in a spectacular stunt or fall. Since his character was seldom at the center of the film's story, he often appeared in cutaway shots, reacting to his surroundings or to whatever dilemma "Fatty" found himself in. This brief respite from centrality gave Keaton the chance to simply *be* onscreen in ways he never could in his own films, where his body, always in motion, often in peril, was always at the crux of the action.

Of the fourteen surviving Comique shorts in which Keaton appears (only one, 1918's A *Country Hero*, remains lost), *Coney Island*, shot on location on a busy day in Luna Park in 1917, may be the one in which his character displays the widest emotional range. In the first scene he shimmies up a pole to watch a Mardi Gras parade, laughs, and tries to applaud—causing him to lose his grip on the pole and fall onto his date for the day (Alice Mann). Buster also weeps theatrically to the camera when the girl deserts him at the entrance to a boardwalk ride called the Witching Waves. Later he laughs some more, doubling over in mirth at the plight of poor Roscoe, whom Buster has just inadvertently knocked down with a giant mallet at a "test-your-strength" booth. In the second reel, feeling his oats in a brand-new lifeguard uniform, Buster executes an impeccable standing backflip, for no other apparent reason than because he can. He even preens for a beat or two afterward, puffing up his chest before exiting the frame in an attitude of manly resolve.

Once he inherited Arbuckle's production company and began making films under his own name in 1920, Keaton would never indulge in such narratively unmotivated hamming. But the Comique shorts, with their loose, patched-together structure, leave room for these bursts of meaning-free exuberance: they're collections of comic and acrobatic bits rather than through-composed stories. As such, they represent a bridge between the "cinema of attractions"—the term, from the film historian Tom Gunning, covers the whole range of gag films, trick films, historical reenactments, and nonfiction "actualities" that dominated the medium's first decade—and the narratively driven, tonally homogeneous "classical Hollywood style" that many scholars mark as beginning in 1917, just as Keaton was entering the business.

Histories of film comedy tend to give short shrift to the Comique years, treating them either as an apprenticeship period for Keaton or a tragic swan song for Arbuckle, whose career would be cut short by his involvement in the Virginia Rappe scandal in 1921. It's possible, too, that the crude and sometimes shocking racism and sexism that crop up in the Comique shorts make them hard for audiences to reencounter now.

Some critics even at the time complained about the taste boundaries these movies transgressed, though what bothered them has little to do with the parts that trouble us. It's not the gore on Buster's surgical smock in *Good Night, Nurse!* we object to but the sight of Roscoe, Buster, and Al shooting at the feet of a Black bar patron to make him dance for them in the western spoof *Out West,* or Roscoe filling a perfume-counter spritzer with chloroform so he can steal a kiss from a female customer in *His Wedding Night.*

The Comiques combine such cruelly retrograde "jokes" with an at times avant-garde degree of filmic innovation. They swing freely, some-times in the same scene, between savage cynicism and an almost pastoral sweetness. Watching them, you can sense the social tensions of their era with a directness that the smooth surface of the "classical Hollywood style" would soon render impossible.

The 1910s were a time of disruptive transition, the adolescence of the film industry. In under a decade, movies went from one-reel curiosities viewed in storefront nickelodeons to feature-length prestige productions screened in swank picture palaces. Everything about the new medium was in question: how long movies should be, who should control their means of creation and distribution, how much the public should know about the stars who appeared in them, whether the state ought to have any role in regulating their content.

Outside the theater things were just as tumultuous. Though the social apartheid of the Jim Crow era was still in full effect, Black American art forms were beginning to make their mark on popular culture, including the modish new music first recorded in 1917 by a band of white musi-cians under the name "jass." The "New Woman," a more or less notional creature when the term was first coined in the 1890s, was making her presence concretely felt, entering the workforce in unheard-of numbers and demanding the right to vote. Complex new technologies—the auto-mobile, the telephone, the wireless radio—were being mass-produced and marketed as consumer goods, changing the way people socialized, communicated, and moved through the world. We think of the early twenty-first century as a period when the pace of life is accelerating faster than usual, but next to the changes in American life that took place between 1910 and 1920, our era is positively languid.

The Comique shorts come out of that atmosphere of velocity and tumult. They are weird documents, feverishly energetic and cheerfully perverse, a mix of vestiges of the era that was passing (vaudeville, the cinema of attractions, the frenetic slapstick of the Keystone shorts) and hints of the age of mass-produced technological spectacle to come. Their sophistication and their shagginess are two sides of the same coin: they're inventive in part because the young team behind them is gifted and adventurous, and in part because no one involved seems quite sure what a twenty-minute film comedy is supposed to be.

Oh Doctor! is an off-putting 1917 Comique in which Buster plays the spoiled young son of Roscoe's character, a wealthy physician bored with domestic life. It's an atypical release from the company in several ways. Instead of his usual buoyant working-class rascal, Roscoe's character is a bourgeois cad, a successful but unhappily married man not unlike the protagonist of his self-directed Keystone short *He Did and He Didn't* (1916). The plot of *Oh Doctor!*—which has Arbuckle's discontented Dr. I. O. Dine sneaking out on his wife and child to dally with a vamp who's secretly conspiring to rob him—harks back to the gleefully amoral universe of earlier Keystone films. Not only does Roscoe's character gamble, drink, and chase women but he wallops his unfortunate son with as much enthusiasm as frequency. The film's sympathy remains throughout with the doctor, who's presented, unconvincingly, as an endearing roué.

The choice to cast the twenty-one-year-old Buster as a young child, complete with short pants and boater hat, lends the whole of *Oh, Doctor!* a surreal and slightly sick quality. The father-son slapstick harks back to the Keatons' old routine, but for the fact that Buster's juvenile stage persona, a stoic imp impervious to both the laws of physics and his father's blows, would have wanted nothing to do with the sniveling brat of *Oh, Doctor!*, who howls theatrically every time he falls down. The built-in uncanniness of watching a grown man play a child is compounded by the irony of seeing this particular man, so recently emerged from such a public and prolonged childhood, at once returned to it. What's worse, the child he plays is stripped of the quality that set Buster's stage persona apart and made the violence of the act not just bearable but funny: his capacity to endure.

James L. Neibaur, the author of an indispensable survey of the Comique collaborations, writes that the Buster of *Oh, Doctor!* "appears to enjoy camping it up in such an uninhibited fashion."[1] But this performance has always struck me as a rare example of Keaton struggling to locate the humor in a role. Economy of gesture and expression are so crucial to his way of getting laughs that, when adopting the maximalist style of a Keystone player, he loses his comic center. Like the bumbling "Elmer" character he would play in those awful early talkies at MGM, Keaton's *Oh, Doctor!* character is antithetical to who he was as a performer. The contract he implicitly makes with his audience—that he will dazzle us, confound us, make us laugh or gasp once per second, but never let us past the opaque screen of his face—depends on a foundation of infinite reserve. Keaton was known to be a ready and frequent laugher in real life, the deviser of elaborate technology-assisted practical jokes. But when he laughs in the Comique shorts the effect is that of candid footage inserted into the movie, as if he had broken character to express his pleasure in the moment of filming. When he wails in outraged self-pity the effect is even odder, as if he were simulating a state of mind he'd never really felt.

The sour domestic comedy of *Oh, Doctor!* plays to neither Roscoe's nor Buster's strengths. The critic at *Variety* wondered politely if the film might be "an experiment," though he allowed the audience seemed to like it just fine. But in the best of the Comique-era shorts—*The Bell Boy, Moonshine, Good Night, Nurse!*—Arbuckle and Keaton function as a true comic team, their contrasting sizes and temperaments part of a stage and screen tradition that long predated Laurel and Hardy. The dynamic between their characters varied, but it often included an element of mock hierarchy that played as a spoof of their real-life boss-employee relationship. Buster's character, one rung inferior in rank to Roscoe's, would comport himself with awed deference whenever the "chief" was in sight, saluting crisply and pivoting on his heel in military fashion, even if their shared task was not to save the world for democracy but to mop floors and schlep trunks in a hotel whose lobby sign promised "third-class service for first-class prices."

The Comique films include moments of technical experimentation that prefigure some of Keaton's later in-camera miracles. The most impressive of these is the long take in *Moonshine* (1918) when a single car is shown to contain at least fifty men, a team of revenue agents in pursuit of a bootlegging ring. Buster, as the loyal second-in-command, soberly ushers the troops out and lines them up in rows as the familiar circus gag stretches on and on and on, longer than would be imaginable for even the most expertly stuffed of clown cars. It's a moment that gets a laugh not just for its visual silliness—with Buster's matter-of-fact demeanor belying the physical impossibility unfolding before his eyes—but also for the filmmakers' cheeky use of technology to push an old joke as far as it will go.

This ambitious trick shot is a cinema-of-attractions moment if there ever was one, stopping the narrative in its tracks for the sheer fun of wowing the audience. Keaton enjoyed describing how the effect was achieved: first he had the cameraman, part-time aviation daredevil George Peters, mask half the lens to film a continuous stream of extras entering the car on one side and exiting the other. They then rewound the film, masked the other side and filmed the empty vehicle.[2]

The techniques of multiple exposure and lens masking were nothing new. When Buster was just three years old, he might have caught Georges Méliès's one-minute trick film *The Four Troublesome Heads*. In this 1898 special-effects blockbuster Méliès, at that time better known as an illusionist and magic-theater owner than as a creator of film fantasies, appears to remove his own head three times in a row before sitting down to strum a banjo and sing a quartet with the newly separated appendages. Later, D. W. Griffith's groundbreaking cameraman G. W. "Billy" Bitzer used masking not as a trick effect but as a narrative device: irising in and out of scenes, for example, or indicating characters' thoughts by superposing a floating image next to their heads. But visual wizardry at the level of the *Moonshine* stunt was rare in comedy, and hard to find anywhere with the degree of perfectionism and technical innovation Keaton brought to it. Given Arbuckle's general lack of interest in camera effects and the free hand he gave Keaton by this point in their collaboration, it's safe to assume that *Moonshine*'s clown-car gag was Keaton's brainchild.

In his own 1921 short *The Playhouse*, Keaton would take the masking-and-rewinding technique to a higher plane, multiplying his own image many times over to play the crew, cast, and audience of an entire vaudeville show, including a conductor and orchestra, a minstrel troupe, and a trained monkey. By that time, though—in the classical Hollywood style that was becoming the industry standard—the visual stunt would be integrated into the story, as the impossible theater full of Busters turns out in the second reel to be only a dream of the real, solitary Buster, a stagehand who's fallen asleep on a backstage set.

The Comique shorts feature many such moments, effectively sketches of ideas that Keaton would later develop in their full form. *Moonshine* starts with a fight scene atop a moving train that contains the germ of his locomotive-chasing masterpiece *The General*, while the charming *Backstage* features a theater set that falls around Roscoe, framing him in the window opening—a gag that would return first in Buster's 1920 solo debut, *One Week*, and later on a grand scale in the spectacular falling-housefront scene in *Steamboat Bill, Jr.* But the best moments in the films Buster and Roscoe made together are the ones that *couldn't* occur in a solo Keaton film, bursts of camaraderie and free-associative play that would clash with the mature Keaton's singleness of focus, not to mention his character's essential solitude.

In many cases these scenes involve dynamics that might be called comic contamination. Buster, observing the physical behavior of another character, falls into a mimetic trance, transforming briefly and as if unconsciously into the other actor's double. In *The Cook* (1918), he plays a waiter who becomes entranced with the "Egyptian"-style contortions of a hired dancer. As the dancer contorts her body into stark geometric shapes Buster first follows, then elaborates on her movements, gradually getting so caught up in the routine that upon returning to the kitchen to fetch his next order he's still furiously striking hieratic poses. His movements exercise a similarly hypnotic effect on Roscoe, who's moved to assemble a Cleopatra costume from kitchen utensils and enact a suicide scene with a string of link sausages serving as impromptu asp.

Pop-culture Egyptophilia was riding one of its recurring waves of faddishness in the wake of the 1917 megahit *Cleopatra*, which starred the scandalously near-nude Theda Bara, the first movie star to be dubbed a "vamp." That film, like most of Bara's once wildly popular work, is now lost but for a few seconds of fragments. The 1917 *Cleopatra* is among the most sought-after of all lost silent films—a canon that, remember, includes about 75 percent of all movies made in that era—for the glimpse it would offer of both the changing sexual mores of the mid-teens and Bara's short-lived but intense appeal. But given Buster's childhood subspecialty in impersonating his famous contemporaries, it's easy to imagine that the broadly tragic style he and Roscoe spoof in *The Cook* might be drawn from Bara's now-irretrievable performance, making *The Cook* a living link to the missing *Cleopatra*.

A scene between Buster and Al St. John in *Moonshine* takes the game of unconscious mimicry still further. After getting drawn into a kind of face-making contest in which he attempts to match and top Al's ever-more-grotesque expressions, Buster abruptly devolves into an ape. Loping with a chimpanzee's hunched gait to a nearby tree, he swings from a branch to scratch himself, then climbs to the top with the ease and grace of a forest-dwelling primate. The action in this scene was sped up slightly by undercranking the camera, but even viewed at a more naturalistic speed, Keaton's athleticism and skill at self-transformation are startling. St. John, an able acrobat with the mobile features and string-bean frame of a young Jim Carrey, also turns into an ape to chase Buster up the tree, but it's hard to keep your eye on his ascending form next to the clean lines and economical movements of the small figure next to him.

My favorite two-way improvisation in the Comique films happens between Buster and Roscoe in one of the crown jewels of the company's output, the scabrously weird *Good Night, Nurse!* (1918). Buster, as the abovementioned bloody-smocked doctor, finds himself in a hallway with

Roscoe, who, in a bid to escape the sanitarium where he's been sent to dry out, has donned a full nurse's getup complete with starched pinafore, curly wig, and pasted-on beauty mark. The effect, as ever when Roscoe became the character known as "Miss Fatty," is oddly fetching, and Buster's character soon engages the zaftig lass in a prolonged flirtation. In fact, their exchange of coy glances and gestures goes on at such length that, as with the shot of the car full of men in *Moonshine*, the duration becomes the joke. Roscoe shyly twists a finger against a door frame, then peers up at Buster, suggestively nibbling the same finger. Buster, appearing to suppress a character-breaking laugh, diligently copies the movements, but overdoes them by so far that any implied eroticism becomes pure absurdity. He wraps an arm around his head to stuff all five fingers in his mouth, then engages in a mad rush of finger-twisting and door-frame-fondling, shooting besotted glances at Roscoe all the while. Soon the two are lolling their way down opposite sides of the hall, lovingly caressing the wooden wainscoting.

The hallway scene in *Good Night, Nurse!* lasts for a solid two minutes, punctuated by several sensational Keaton falls, and it may be the best example on film of Roscoe and Buster's riffing off each other in real time, with no other actors present and no props but a pair of walls. Given a stock comic situation—the then mildly naughty joke of a cross-dressed man flirting with another man who takes him for a woman—they draw it out for so long that the scene becomes a parody of the act of heterosexual flirting, with all its sly innuendo and faux-naif misdirection. The misogyny and homophobia that so often attended gender-bending scenarios in movies of the 1910s and after are nowhere in sight, so complete is Roscoe's enjoyment of his feminine alter ego and Buster's investment in impressing the comely nurse. Just as Keaton transformed into an Egyptian dancer or a tree-scaling ape to suit his circumstances, so the two of them become, instantly and effortlessly, what they pretend to be; for a moment the truth of the sketch takes over and the larger plot about a runaway patient and his dubiously competent doctor is forgotten. Watching the *Good Night, Nurse!* flirtation scene, it's easy to sense Roscoe and Buster's real-life friendship, their pleasure in collaboration and respect for one another's comedic choices. They make us laugh by trying, and nearly succeeding, to crack each other up.

Had Roscoe's career and life not gone as they did after the death of Virginia Rappe, maybe he and Keaton would have teamed up again. Or they might have gone their own way as solo comedians while continuing to influence each other as filmmakers, watching and learning from each other's work. But things did go the way they did, and the fourteen films they made together at Comique mark the extent of their collaboration.

The story of what happened to (not *between* but *to*) Roscoe Arbuckle and Virginia Rappe in 1921 has been embedded in rumor and myth for so long that, as recently as the #MeToo reckoning of the late 2010s, the case was still being cited, without details or context, as an example of sexual assault and violence from Hollywood's early years. In fact, Arbuckle's three trials for the rape and manslaughter of Rappe, a model, actress, and fashion influencer once voted "the best dressed girl in pictures," stemmed from a tragic series of events in which neither rape nor killing played any part. Though the precise circumstances of Rappe's death remain murky to this day, that much seems clear.

After a day of heavy drinking at a Labor Day party in Arbuckle's suite at the St. Francis Hotel in San Francisco—a party Keaton had been invited to but declined to attend—Rappe grew agitated, vomited, and finally passed out. After the hotel doctor was summoned and declared that she was merely drunk, Roscoe rented a separate room for her and left her there to sleep it off. Four days later, after the comedian had returned to Los Angeles in his brand-new custom-built Pierce Arrow, Rappe died in a sanatorium of peritonitis resulting from a ruptured bladder.

A friend who had come with her to the party—a woman named Bambina Maude Delmont, who had a history of extortion and fraud—told reporters that Rappe's last words had been "He did it. I know he did it." Delmont never testified in court, but a corroborating story was told by two other women who had been present. Both later admitted on the stand that they had been pressured by the prosecution to commit perjury.

The three trials that unfolded over the next year, the first two ending in hung juries, changed the history of the film industry and effectively ended Arbuckle's career. In the midst of a massive scandal eagerly fanned by William Randolph Hearst's tabloid empire, the US postmaster Will Hays was summoned from Washington, DC, to Hollywood to root out what was seen as widespread immorality. The production code he helped put in place would become the chief organ of self-censorship in the film industry for the next forty-plus years.

At the end of the third trial Arbuckle was acquitted of all charges, with the jury issuing an unusual statement of apology to the defendant: "Acquittal is not enough for Roscoe Arbuckle," it began. "We feel that a great injustice has been done him. . . . There was not the slightest proof adduced to connect him in any way with the commission of a crime." But Roscoe's career and his spirit had been broken. Hays banned him from appearing onscreen after the scandal but ruled that he could work behind the camera under an assumed name. The pseudonym he chose, which he would use until his death in 1934, was William Goodrich—the first and middle name of the father who had beaten and insulted him since early childhood. In a glimpse of the dark-humored streak the two friends shared offscreen, Buster claimed to have proposed the variant "Will B. Goode."

Buster and Roscoe did *try* to work together one more time. In 1924—after the three trials and the too-late acquittal, after Arbuckle had been blacklisted and stigmatized by a suddenly scandal-wary Hollywood—Keaton would invite his former "chief" to serve as codirector on the technically challenging feature *Sherlock, Jr.* But after only days on the *Sherlock* set Roscoe became hard to work with. More than forty years later, Buster still used the present tense in describing what must have been a painful experience: "He's now so irritable and impatient that he loses his temper easily. He screams at people and gets flushed and mad. . . . He hadn't recovered from those trials, of being accused of murder and nearly convicted. In other words, it made a nervous wreck out of him."[3] The aborted collaboration would end their working relationship but not their friendship. Buster continued to set aside a portion of his salary to help out the struggling Roscoe for the remaining nine years of the latter's life.

For a few years at the end of the teens, though, the two were inseparable both onscreen and off, especially after Schenck moved the Comique company from New York to the recently incorporated beachside town of Long Beach, California. There they had the space and light to invent wilder stunts and more elaborate chases than the cramped space and dicey weather of New York City had allowed. Shooting *Moonshine* in the foothills of the San Bernardino Mountains, they breathed fresh mountain air that Keaton, in his as-told-to autobiography four decades later, would compare to wine. (That often-cited flight of poetic diction has always struck me as distinctly un-Keatonian. His cowriter Charles Samuels may have distilled it from Buster's general descriptions of that time, but the idyllic spirit it captures seems broadly accurate.)

Until Buster was sent to the French front in 1919 to serve in an entertainers' unit in the last phase of America's involvement in World War I, he had little on his mind but courting pretty girls (among them frequent Comique leading lady Alice Lake), supporting his parents (who had come west to move in with him, Keatons being Keatons), and making as big an audience as possible laugh as hard as possible. The last part, though he threw his whole self into it, was easy. By the time he went into the movies at age twenty-one, he had already been doing it for more than three-quarters of his life.

13

Mabel at the Wheel

Mabel Normand filming Molly O *in 1921.*

During the same years as Keaton was entering motion pictures, a phenomenon was taking place in the business that would not become visible—or, at any rate, be considered worthy of notice—for about a hundred years. More precisely, a trend that had characterized the medium's first two decades was in steep decline. Women, who until around 1916 had wielded a degree of power in the film industry unmatched to the present day, were vanishing from the high places they had occupied and being shunted into the narrow space they would be allotted for the rest of the twentieth century and into our own. For that short span of time, though—the same years Buster was growing up as a child phenomenon in vaudeville—what now seems like a shockingly high number of women held positions of real creative power in the world of film. This is not to say that the industry's gender balance was anywhere near equitable. As a cutting-edge technology with mass moneymaking potential, the new medium remained predominantly the province of men. But a higher percentage of American movies were directed by women in 1916 than has been true in any year since, a bracing reminder that gender discrimination in the film industry is about as old as the Model T Ford and, unlike that long-obsolete vehicle, still rolling.

A telling of the film history that might have been would start with Alice Guy, the French filmmaker who began as a secretary at Paris's Gaumont studio in 1896. She was only twenty-five when she made her first film two years later, a whimsical fantasy called *The Cabbage Fairy* that was one of the first-ever filmed narratives and also, at a running time of almost one minute, one of the longest movies yet made. In 1910 Guy moved to Long Island to launch the Solax film company with her husband and collaborator, Herbert Blaché, who would direct Buster in *The Saphead* in 1920. By then Guy had directed hundreds of movies, including one of the world's first multi-reel features, a four-reel dramatization of the life of Christ.

A few years later Lois Weber, the American director and screenwriter who spearheaded the "uplift" movement, became the most successful female filmmaker in early Hollywood and one of the first directors of any sex to receive billing above the title. Weber's films, with titles like *Too Wise Wives*, *Where Are My Children?*, and *The Hand That Rocks the Cradle*, were social-issue melodramas that lent middle-class respectability to such taboo topics as birth control, divorce, and "white slavery," a genteelly racist euphemism for enforced prostitution.

Then there was the "serial queen" craze. For a while in the mid-1910s every production company seemed to have its own fearlessly athletic female star: Pearl White at Pathé Frères, Kathlyn Williams at Selig Polyscope, Helen Holmes at Kalem. These prototypical New Women, often using their own first names as their characters', chased would-be robbers on horse-back or leapt from motorcycles onto the sides of moving trains. Holmes, in real life the daughter of a railway clerk, played an indomitable railroad telegraph operator in the long-running serial *The Hazards of Helen*, also serving as the films' producer, writer, stuntwoman, and animal trainer. In 1916 she told an interviewer that

> if a photoplay actress wants to achieve real thrills, she must write them into the scenario herself. And the reason is odd: nearly all scenario-writers and authors for the films are men; and men usually won't provide for a girl things to do that they wouldn't do themselves. So if I want real thrilly action, I ask permission to write it in myself.[1]

Holmes's serials, many of them directed by her husband, J. P. McGowan, remain "thrilly" to this day, not least because, in most of the episodes that survive, our heroine Helen pursues her dual passions of railway telegraphy and bad-guy-walloping with nary a romantic subplot in sight. Holmes may not match Keaton in acrobatic virtuosity, but she's every bit his equal for sheer physical courage: Watch her ride a motorcycle at top speed off a high bridge in *The Wild Engine* or dangle over a railroad trestle to land on the roof of a moving train in *The Escape on the Fast Freight*.

The most powerful woman in Hollywood in the 1910s was unquestionably Mary Pickford, a one-woman media conglomerate who rose from a rough childhood spent touring the country in juvenile dramatic roles to become, by 1916, the highest-paid performer in all of show business. Barely over five feet tall, with a round, angelic face, a childlike frame, and a dense mass of pale-gold sausage curls, she was adored by audiences with a fervency that's hard to comprehend in our celebrity-sated era. *Photoplay* critic Julian Johnson, whose long-lived "Impressions" column was a poetic tribute to the charms of a different actor or actress each month, compared Pickford to "dawn over a daisy-filled meadow; the spirit of spring imprisoned in a woman's body; the first child in the world."[2] But Pickford's appeal also lay in the implacable force of will she manifested both onscreen and off. To further quote the besotted Johnson, her "luminous tenderness" was contained within "a steel band of gutter ferocity."[3] A colleague of Johnson's at *Photoplay*, the splendidly named gossip columnist Delight Evans, answered his florid tribute with a simpler formulation: "But one does not understand Mary Pickford. One loves her."[4]

Many of Pickford's films deliberately play on her trademark mix of childlike sweetness and iron tenacity; one of her most acclaimed, *Stella Maris*, divides her into two separate characters, a cossetted beauty and a plain, desperately poor orphan, via the technique of split screen. Pickford's fame was so meteoric and her bargaining skill so legendary that she changed the balance of labor relations in the industry, helping to initiate the era of the movie star as free agent. In 1916, a few months after Charlie Chaplin signed a record-breaking contract with the Mutual Film Corporation for $670,000 a year, Pickford walked into Adolph Zukor's office at Paramount and demanded the same salary, plus half the profits from her films, over which she was to have full creative control. Her total yearly take at Paramount was over $1 million, or around $18 million in today's money.[5]

When she left her first husband, actor Owen Moore, for the swashbuckling action star Douglas Fairbanks, also married at the time, Pickford not only escaped the public censure that generally followed divorce but also reigned on uncontested as America's first cinematic sweetheart. The couple's Beverly Hills mansion, grandly dubbed Pickfair, became an obligatory American stopover for everyone from visiting foreign royalty to Mr. and Mrs. Albert Einstein, and was always open to Fairbanks's best friend Charlie Chaplin. In 1919 the three of them, along with D. W. Griffith, would form United Artists, originally a film distributor designed to break the major studios' grip on the market by releasing movies from the creators' independently financed companies.

United Artists provided an early model of what independent distribution and production might look like, even as the studio system was congealing into place. UA released some of the most acclaimed pictures of the silent era, including Pickford's *Sparrows*, Fairbanks's *Robin Hood*,

Rudolph Valentino's *The Son of the Sheik*, and, after Joe Schenck was made chairman of the company's board in 1924, the last three independent features of Buster Keaton. Pickford's massive popularity and formidable bargaining skill, as well as her close association with some of the industry's most powerful men, allowed her to remain a formidable force in the film industry well after the careers of most of her 1910s colleagues had flamed out.

Any one of these women, and many others — among them the Russian theater legend turned avant-garde lesbian impresario Alla Nazimova and the writing-directing-acting-producing comedy powerhouse Fay Tincher, promisingly described in a 1918 press release as "a merciless autocrat when she directs men's activities"! — would merit her own chapter in a fuller account.[6] But when I think of the female talent that was draining from the film business just as Keaton was entering it, the face that comes to mind first is Mabel Normand's, that cameo-ready oval with huge dark eyes, a nervous smile, and the mobile features of a born comedienne who, if things had gone differently in her life and in the industry, might have had a life as long and a filmography as lasting as Keaton's, Chaplin's, or Lloyd's.

Normand came as close as any woman in silent comedy to achieving that degree of success and creative freedom. To watch her films now — the majority have been lost, but dozens still survive and are widely available — is to ache for the future she might have had. But in her thirty-eight years on earth — over half of them spent in the motion-picture business — she got a fair bit done. She was the first star, male or female, to have their name appear in the title of their films, the first actress to serve as her own director, and among the first film performers to start their own self-named production companies. According to a Sennett-generated legend, Normand was also the first film comedian to throw a pie in someone's face, though hurled pastries played a relatively small part in the Keystone joke repertoire, and at any rate too many silent films are now lost to verify any such claim. In her own time, Normand was sometimes called "the female Chaplin"; her more widespread nickname, "our Mabel," gives a ion she inspired in her fans. In a 1915 poll she was chosen as the top female comedy star, with Chaplin as her male counterpart and Mary Pickford as the favored "leading actress."

Back before movie actors were credited by name, the teenage Normand had become known as "Vitagraph Betty" for the character she played in a hit series of one-reelers for that company beginning around 1911: *The Indiscretions of Betty, Betty Becomes a Maid, How Betty Won.* The boy-crazy, practical-joke-loving Betty delighted audiences, but some critics found her a tad earthy. Her cross-dressing antics in *The Troublesome Secretaries* (1911) drew a comment from one reviewer that though "attractive Mabel Normand as Betty is extremely funny," he wished she had not been "so free in her hugging and kissing, but had been more refined and dainty."[7]

After her time at Vitagraph, Mabel spent a couple of years working for D. W. Griffith at Biograph, where Mack Sennett was then running the studio's comedy arm. In addition to starring in a series of action-packed and mildly racy one-reelers for Sennett (*The Diving Girl, The Fatal Chocolate, The Fickle Spaniard, Dash Through the Clouds, Hot Stuff, Oh, Those Eyes!*), Normand appeared in five melodramas under Griffith's direction. Often she was cast as the sultry brunette antithesis of the more ethereal blond heroines the director preferred. In *The Mender of Nets* Mabel played a tragic temptress who steals the love interest of the ever-saintly Mary Pickford. But Griffith, never a filmmaker known for his sense of humor, disliked the impetuous and impertinent Normand. She had been known to mock the director behind his back on set and to spur other actresses, among them Lillian Gish's unsaintly sister Dorothy, into rowdy behavior like going drinking after hours.[8]

In 1912 Sennett and Normand, by then involved in real life as well as the movie business, had left Biograph to launch Keystone, an independent all-comedy studio in the thinly settled Los Angeles suburb of Edendale. Over the next five years they churned out hundreds of rough-and-tumble two-reel comedies with a revolving stock company of actors. Performers who launched their careers at Keystone included not just future slapstick greats like Chaplin, Arbuckle, Harold Lloyd, and Harry Langdon but also cartoon-faced character comics with durable audience appeal: Fred Mace with his perpetually exasperated eyebrows, Ford Sterling with his square beard and sputtering rage-takes, and good old rubber-limbed Al St. John, who after the Comique years with his uncle Roscoe would costar in a long-running western comedy serial as a bearded cowboy sidekick named Fuzzy Q. Jones. Other silent stars who got their start at Keystone were the future sex symbol Gloria Swanson and the popular eccentric comedienne Louise Fazenda, whose pigtailed and gingham-clad rube character was forever getting played by a succession of slick city cads.

All these talents passed through Keystone on their way to other things. But Mabel, the only female member of the company present at its founding along with Sennett, Sterling, and Mace, was Keystone's public face. She was also, crucially for the studio's early success, its public body. Her athletic curves caused a sensation when she appeared in *The Water Nymph* (1912), sheathed in one of the skintight full-body bathing suits known as Kellerman suits after the vaudeville swimming sensation Annette Kellerman. Mabel could swim and dive like a seal, and did her own stunts in countless water-based pratfalls. Her early aquatic feats made her the first in the venerable tradition of Sennett's "bathing beauties," who could be relied upon to periodically interrupt the movies' action with their narratively unmotivated ball games played in racy-for-the-day beach getups.

Sennett sometimes appeared in his own films, usually as an ungainly oaf. He was a colorful and eccentric figure, an Irish-Catholic immigrant from rural Quebec known for conducting studio business from the huge marble-and-silver bathtub he had installed in his office.[9] Sennett was a masterful public relations mythmaker and a keen spotter of new talent, even if he was too cheap to hold on to his strongest performers for long. But it was Mabel's mischievous, incandescent persona that served as both Keystone's chief artistic asset and its main marketing draw. In 1915 Julian Johnson—the same *Photoplay* critic who rapturously praised business whiz Mary Pickford's childlike freshness—described Mabel as "a kiss that explodes in a laugh; cherry bonbons in a clown's cap; sharing a cream puff from your best girl; a slap from a perfumed hand; the sugar on the Keystone grapefruit."[10] But behind the camera as well as in front of it, Mabel's role went beyond mere sweetening.

"Director" as a job title meant something less defined on a 1910s movie set than it does in our auteur-focused age. As we've seen, Keaton and Arbuckle more or less traded off directorial responsibilities depending on who was in front of the camera. Slapstick comedy "direction" also overlapped with what would now be called screenwriting, given that shooting scripts weren't used at all for most early two-reelers. Sennett sometimes wrote up rough prose treatments of the story lines of upcoming films, but for the most part comedies in the teens were something you made by taking a camera to a free outdoor location, working out ideas for gags and chases, then building a plot around them and shooting until you lost the light. Recalling his apprenticeship at Keystone, Chaplin wrote: "All we needed was a park bench, a bucket of whitewash, and Mabel Normand."[11]

Even at the Buster Keaton Studio a few years later, written scripts would be nonexistent, though Keaton meticulously planned out the set design, action sequences, and general story line with his production crew and gag-writing team. But at Keystone two-reelers were churned out in a hurtling rush, often incorporating real-life events like car races or world's fairs, with Sennett cutting every budgetary corner. Keystone casts and crews were not above sneaking onto the sets of other films in production to shoot a scene or two. Normand remembered Thomas Ince, the celebrated producer of grand-scale westerns, yelling at Sennett through a bullhorn to "get those infernal clowns off my set!"[12] Actors had to hustle and improvise to set their performances apart from the mayhem that swirled around them, as first Arbuckle and then Chaplin managed to do.

By the mid-teens, dramatic narrative film had become a "respectable" art form that drew increasingly middle-class audiences and was beginning to be seen as an author's medium. This shift corresponded with the rise of the feature-length film, tied to the emergence of name-brand dramatic directors like D. W. Griffith, Lois Weber, and Cecil B. DeMille. But the de facto director of an early two-reel comedy was often the star, the performer whose rhythms set the film's pace and who had the best sense of how to use the camera to capture his or her comic choices.

Mabel came to film not from vaudeville or the dramatic stage but, like her friend Norma Talmadge, from the world of modeling and advertisement. As a young teenager she had posed for influential fashion illustrators like Charles Dana Gibson and James Montgomery Flagg, embodying the "Gibson Girl" type in all her bicycle-riding, taboo-breaking, suffrage-demanding glory. Mabel's photographed, painted, or drawn image had sold Coca-Cola, dress patterns, luggage, and lingerie. By the time she made an impression as Vitagraph Betty she was already a master at deploying the power of her pretty, protean face. But Mabel had higher artistic aspirations as well. Born into a working-class French-Irish family on Staten Island, she had grown up with dreams of becoming an illustrator and had begun modeling to pay for art classes. Later, when she was rich enough to order frocks from Paris by the dozens and drive a car with a custom makeup table that folded down from the dashboard, she would travel with a full-time French tutor in her entourage and stock her home library with volumes by fashionable thinkers like Nietzsche and Freud.[13]

In late 1913, the trade papers announced that "Mabel Normand, leading woman with Keystone, will hereafter direct every picture in which she appears. Madame Blaché has been the only woman director for some time, but she now has a rival in Mabel who will both act and direct."[14] There's a healthy dose of Sennett braggadocio in that statement. As we've seen, Alice Guy-Blaché was far from the only woman holding the reins behind the camera in this era; in fact one of Lois Weber's most innovative early one-reelers, *Suspense*, was released that same year, and both Pearl White and Helen Holmes had begun assembling the companies that would launch them as producers of their own action serials.

Still, there was considerable novelty in the fact of a twenty-one-year-old movie star, famous for her fearless diving stunts and the dark, expressive eyes one columnist described as "luminous orbs," directing herself onscreen.[15] Given how loose the division of labor on a film set was at the time, it's hard to know exactly how much authorial power Normand had in the hundreds of films in which she appears. She is credited as sole director on around sixteen titles, and gets codirecting credit on a dozen more. But knowing how free a hand Sennett gave her in the studio's day-to-day operations up until around 1915, it's likely she had extensive input on any film she appeared in and some she didn't.

Arbuckle told a reporter visiting the set of one of his productions that "Mabel alone is good for a dozen new suggestions in every picture."[16] Later in the same profile Normand drove the reporter to the ferry, volunteering the information that she had directed any number of Keystone films (including some of Chaplin's first onscreen appearances) and adding that she needed to hurry back to the studio to go over that day's rushes with Arbuckle. This evidence of Normand's creative clout at the studio notwithstanding, the article concludes on the image of the smitten writer bidding a reluctant goodbye to the "pretty little star," still hoping to convince her to accompany him back on the ferryboat.

A story about one of Normand's early collaborations with Chaplin at Keystone offers a telling snapshot of how and why women's power in the industry waned after the mid-teens. The title of the two-reeler in question was, appropriately enough, *Mabel at the Wheel* (1914). In it Normand's character, the girlfriend of a race car driver, winds up commandeering his car to win a race in his stead when he's kidnapped by a gang of villains led by Chaplin.

As the project began, Normand was set to be the film's sole director. Chaplin, new to films and only two months into what would turn out to be a year-long stay at Keystone, had not yet committed to the "tramp" persona that would make his fortune, though he had played a similarly costumed character in two of his earlier outings, *Mabel's Strange Predicament* (also directed by Normand) and *Kid Auto Races at Venice*. In *Mabel at the Wheel* he plays a blustering bad guy plainly copied from the stock character of Keystone cofounder Ford Sterling, who had recently left the company and whom Chaplin had been hired in part to replace.

Sennett had lured the twenty-four-year-old stage comic into the movies after seeing him perform with Fred Karno's touring pantomime troupe. By the time of *Mabel at the Wheel*, Chaplin had already worked under several male directors at Keystone and had clashed with at least two of them. One was Henry "Pathé" Lehrman, a journeyman figure in the lore of early Hollywood, the opportunistic boyfriend of Arbuckle's alleged murder victim Virginia Rappe. A photo survives of Lehrman with hands on hips, glaring at Chaplin with undisguised antipathy as the latter, in costume as the Tramp, observes a scene from behind the camera. The other was a veteran director named George Nichols, who later played Mabel's father in a string of early 1920s features. Nichols had disliked his experience with Chaplin enough that, in the comedian's own words, "he went to Sennett saying I was a son of a bitch to work with."[17]

Only weeks into his time at Keystone, Chaplin was already gaining a reputation for his slowness on set and his perfectionist hardheadedness about doing things his way. These were qualities that would only intensify once Chaplin began making his own movies. Chaplin's reputation for foot-dragging was something that Keaton, chained for life to the two-shows-a-day vaudeville work ethic of his youth, sometimes spoke of in interviews with dry irony. Asked in 1958 about his early impressions of Chaplin, he replied, "I was in love with him, same as everybody else."[18] But "following *The [Great] Dictator*," Keaton continued, "was when he got good and lazy. By the time he'd decide on a subject and make it, it was three years later or something like that."[19] For Keaton, who by 1958 had not had the chance to make a movie his own way for thirty years, the idea of having the resources to do so and throwing the opportunity away must have rankled.

At any rate, on the set of *Mabel at the Wheel* Chaplin came up against an obstacle he could not surmount: the humiliation of being directed by a woman, and a young, pretty, and unusually powerful one at that. For a scene in which his character sprayed the racetrack with water to slow down Mabel's speeding car, Chaplin suggested a bit of business with the hose: What if he were to step on it by mistake, examine the nozzle to see what the problem was, and then spray himself full in the face?

As any half-competent film historian will recognize—and as Mabel, who had by then made dozens of comedies, surely understood—this was quite literally the oldest joke in the business, having been used by the Lumière brothers in 1895 in that first-ever piece of recorded slapstick, *L'arroseur arrosé*. When Mabel rejected Chaplin's idea—"We have no time! We have no time! Do as you're told!" she cried, according to a lengthy and unwittingly self-incriminating anecdote in Chaplin's autobiography—the studio's new hire sat down on the curb and refused to work, shutting down production for the rest of the day.

Telling the story fifty years later, Chaplin recalls with unabated resentment that taking orders from his more experienced costar "nettled me, for, charming as Mabel was, I doubted her competence as a director." To be rushed by a male authority figure was one thing; only a page earlier, Chaplin had described Nichols rejecting his ideas with the identical phrase: "We have no time, no time!" But to hear those words from the mouth of a twenty-one-year-old woman playing opposite him as a spunky ingénue—and one who in the end defeats and spurns his own unsympathetic character? "That was enough," writes Chaplin simply. He told her as much in so many words: "I'm sorry, Miss Normand, I will not do what I'm told. I don't think you are competent to tell me what to do." After the day's shoot wrapped early, the crew, loyal to Mabel, was furious: "One or two extras, Mabel told me afterwards, wanted to slug me, but she stopped them from doing so," recalls Chaplin, providing evidence of her fair treatment of him even as he looks for an opportunity to pout. Back at the studio that night, while the comedian was removing his greasepaint, Sennett burst in and read him the riot act, taking Mabel's side: "You'll do what you're told or get out."

Chaplin rode the streetcar home that night with a fellow Keystoner, speculating fretfully about the firing they both assumed was imminent. But the next day when Chaplin got to the studio, Sennett was conciliatory, encouraging him to "swallow his pride and help out," including doing his best to get along with Mabel. (To add insult to injury, their conversation was conducted in Mabel's dressing room, which was empty at the time because, writes Chaplin, "she was in the projection-room looking at the rushes"—as directors will do.) Though Chaplin professed "the greatest respect and admiration for Miss Normand," he did not apologize for his treatment of her the previous day, nor did he hesitate to reiterate to his new boss (and Mabel's then-fiancé!) his doubts about her basic competence—based only, he assured Sennett, on her extreme youth. (Normand was three years younger than Chaplin, and had about five years' experience in filmmaking to his none.)[20]

Chaplin's telling of this story implies that the reins of the film in production were handed over to him by Sennett then and there, and also that he negotiated the right to direct himself in his next picture on the spot. In fact, Sennett himself seems to have taken over the direction of *Mabel at the Wheel*, sharing onscreen credit with Normand, and for the next several films she made with Chaplin she continued to be credited as either the director or codirector. But though Chaplin's framing of the story (like much of his autobiography) may err in the direction of self-aggrandizement, his larger point stands. By the time Mack took over *Mabel at the Wheel*, Mabel's real-life turn in the driver's seat was almost up, while Chaplin's was just beginning.

After a number of successful directorial outings, some on her own and some in collaboration with Sennett, Chaplin, Arbuckle, or Nichols, Mabel would receive her last behind-the-camera credit around a year later, on the also-appropriately-titled *Mabel Lost and Won*. By 1916 she was telling a *Picture Play* reporter—the same one who clung to the hope she would skip out on work to join him on the ferry—that she had once been a Keystone director herself, but now preferred to focus on acting.[21]

Whether or not the conversation between Chaplin and Sennett in Mabel's dressing room really happened as Chaplin describes it, his recollection of the *Mabel at the Wheel* incident—which takes up three solid pages of his autobiography!—shows how and why the film industry began closing its top ranks off to women just as it became clear this new business was shaping up to be big business. In a pithier example of the same phenomenon, Sennett's memoir erases the incident completely.

Speaking of *Mabel at the Wheel*, he recalls simply, "I directed that one, and Mabel Normand acted in it."[22]

Sennett's newfound patience with Chaplin, it turned out, had an economic motive. The morning after Chaplin's and Mabel's on-set row, Mack had received a telegram from the moneymen in the studio's New York office, pressuring him to keep the Chaplin product coming, as the studio's new acquisition was becoming a box-office draw. Other companies would soon come sniffing for Chaplin, and by the end of that year he would sign the first in a series of ever more lucrative independent contracts.[23]

In a long serial interview given to *Liberty Magazine* in 1928, two years after she had retired from pictures, and published after her death in 1930, Normand describes working with Chaplin in terms almost identical to those Keaton would use in recalling his process with Arbuckle: "We reciprocated. I would direct Charlie in his scenes, and he would direct me in mine."[24] But if Arbuckle and Keaton had a relationship in which the pupil quickly became his mentor's equal, Normand and Chaplin had one in which the student effectively usurped the teacher's place in the middle of an early lesson and got her demoted, while the principal (Sennett) nodded tacit approval. You could argue that Chaplin's innate gifts were so ready to flower at that moment that further apprenticeship was unnecessary. But you might also maintain that in 1914, Normand's gifts were at an equally crucial place in their development, and that undermining this young female director's authority on set and in private with her producer/boyfriend was one of the most damaging things a rising star of the company could do. The reciprocity of relationship taken for granted in a partnership between two men was simply not guaranteed in the same professional relationship across genders.

In justifying his kneecapping of Normand to his reader and himself, Chaplin strikes a half-apologetic if gratingly condescending note: "I also was susceptible to her charm and beauty and secretly had a soft spot in my heart for her, but this was my work."[25] Fifty-plus years after those words were written and more than one hundred since Mabel was disrespected on her own set, the obvious comeback still presents itself: What about *her* work? How might film history have been different if, after an apprenticeship with D. W. Griffith and a long collaborative relationship with both Sennett and Arbuckle, Mabel Normand had gotten the chance to direct and star in exactly the films she wanted to make, with the cast, crew, and stories she chose, the way every male comedian of her stature in her generation got to do?

That this never happened is not solely the fault of an increasingly patriarchal system of power transmission within the film industry. There was also Normand's own chronically ill body, presented in the press as continually beset by vague maladies, while behind the scenes she struggled with the chronic tuberculosis that would kill her at age thirty-seven and with an addiction to both alcohol and the opium-laced cough syrup she referred to as "my goop."[26] There may have been other drugs in the mix as well; it's impossible now to conclude whether years of persistent tabloid innuendo about the "inside dope" on Mabel's fragile physical condition had any basis in fact. But there's no doubt that in her later roles, after a stint at a convalescent farm, she seems altered, her face thin and drawn, her movements stiffer and more cautious.

Something else seems to have happened to shake Normand's power at Keystone between 1914 and 1916, when her name dropped off the directing roster and became associated with leading lady–hood alone. According to a much-retold and possibly apocryphal story—albeit one recounted in credible detail sixty years later by Mabel's costar and close friend Minta Durfee, the first Mrs. Roscoe Arbuckle—one afternoon in mid-1915, only weeks before her long-scheduled wedding to Sennett was set to take place, Mabel walked in on Mack in flagrante delicto with the newly hired bathing beauty (and Mabel's friend) Mae Busch. In the melee that ensued Normand sustained a serious blow to the head, allegedly after Busch flung a vase in her direction.[27]

Sennett's blustering as-told-to autobiography offers a heavily sanitized version of this tale, in which he and an unnamed actress were simply having dinner to discuss her upcoming role and Mabel, misunderstanding, stormed out and faked an injury afterward, going so far as to come to set the next day with her arm in a sling. The gossip columnist Adela Rogers St. Johns, as given to fabrication as she was fixated on her subjects' suffering, wrote in her memoir that she, Mabel, and others were having dinner at a seaside restaurant when the actress, distraught over Mack's cheating, attempted suicide by throwing herself off the Santa Monica Pier.[28]

Whoever's story, if anyone's, is true, Normand did suffer a head injury that year serious enough to put her in the hospital for several weeks, while the press hyperventilated as if in training for the decade of Mabel Normand scandals still ahead. "Mabel Normand Fighting Death," blared a story in the Los Angeles Herald that attributed the wound to an unspecified on-set accident.[29] (To contextualize the drama of that headline, it's worth noting that only weeks earlier Photoplayers Weekly had run a story headlined "Octopus Seizes Mabel Normand.")[30] The studio put out a cover story: while filming a wedding scene with Roscoe, Normand had been hit in the head with a thrown boot.[31] To add to the confusion, in an interview a year after the mysterious incident Normand appeared to make light of the whole affair, explaining that her hospitalization had been the result of an on-set accident in which "Roscoe sat on [her] head by mistake."[32]

The proliferation of contradictory stories combined with Normand's coy deflection make it seem likely that whatever took place was something both she and the studio wanted to keep under wraps. At any rate, this period marks the end of Normand's and Sennett's romantic involvement, which as both acknowledged was rocky to begin with. Sennett continued as her producer at Keystone until 1918 and returned to making films with her in the early twenties, but the severing of that romantic connection may have handicapped Normand in her rise in the film world, just as earlier female creators, including Lois Weber and Alice Guy, had at first found their professional fortunes tied to those of their producer husbands and business partners.

Then came Normand's peripheral involvement with a series of film industry scandals in the early 1920s. Though she had nothing to do with the 1921 hotel party that led to Arbuckle's downfall, her longtime onscreen partnership with the beloved comic associated her in the public's mind with the unwholesome off-camera doings of Hollywood funmakers. Less than a year later came the killing of the director William Desmond Taylor, a friend of Normand's whom, by pure chance, she had visited at home on the evening of his (still-unsolved) murder, leaving only minutes before a neighbor overheard the shot that killed him. In 1924, with the Taylor murder still being combed over by a sensation-hungry press, she was back in the tabloids when her chauffeur shot the oil-tycoon heir Courtland Dines after a long day of partying at which Mabel, Dines, and Chaplin's leading lady Edna Purviance were all present. Even though the second shooting was nonfatal and Normand was cleared of all wrongdoing in both cases, the Taylor and Dines scandals dominated headlines for months and permanently stained her reputation.

Just like Keaton, Normand was often her own worst enemy, as self-destructive and impractical as she was gifted and driven. But unlike him she was not protected by the system that began to emerge in the mid-teens, which allowed stars like Arbuckle and Chaplin (and, in a rare feminine exception, Pickford) to act as free agents determining their own projects and salaries. Normand's self-named company, formed in 1916, would make only a single film, *Mickey*. That feature sat on the shelf for nearly two years because of financing problems and production delays. But when *Mickey* finally did come out, it was a surprise hit, the top-grossing film of 1918. In a wave of popularity reminiscent of the "Chaplinitis" craze of 1915–16, *Mickey* hats, dresses, and dolls flew off the shelves as young female audiences flocked to identify with Mabel's rags-to-riches tomboy heroine. This being the days before licensing or product tie-in campaigns, the studio saw no profit from these ventures; even as *Mickey* played to packed houses and inspired a hit song of the same name, the Mabel Normand Feature Film Company was closing down.[33]

Sennett never quite got the hang of structuring a feature-length film, and *Mickey* plays like a series of two-reelers placed end to end, some more effective and original than others. But Normand's presence — rambunctious, goofy, mercurial, uncontainable — runs through the indifferent action and tepid romance like a silver thread. As if in an unintended metaphor for the star's own life, the story is built around other characters' attempts to limit and constrain her character's freedom. In one of several climactic scenes, the dauntless Mickey poses as a male jockey to ride a racehorse to a near-spectacular finish—until, tellingly, she falls off her horse just short of the finish line, necessitating a rescue from a huge crowd of onlookers that includes her father and her most ardent (and ultimately victorious) suitor.

Watching this scene it struck me that the crowd rushing to care for the helpless Mickey serves as a proxy for the audience. Normand was the Marilyn Monroe of the early silent era, the funny, tragic, evanescent woman a whole generation of viewers longed to step through the screen and rescue. During the last few months of her life in late 1929, spent mostly in a TB sanitarium, some radio shows signed off every night by wishing her good health.[34]

Normand's career was far from over when she stopped taking a credited role behind the scenes. But from the mid-teens onward she fashioned herself a movie star, an object of the camera's gaze rather than a guider of it. After *Mickey*, she signed with an up-and-coming producer named Samuel Goldfish (soon to change his name to the more dignified Goldwyn, later of Metro-Goldwyn-Mayer) to make a string of forgettable comedies in between posing for studio glamour shots. According to some unverifiable rumors, she also may have gotten pregnant by Goldwyn, resulting in either an abortion or a late-term miscarriage; at any rate, the fact that her new producer was in constant pursuit of Normand is documented in several sources.[35]

Her last feature film was 1923's *The Extra Girl*, directed by Sennett in a late-career attempt to remake himself as a director of sensitive romantic comedies. Its story, perhaps more than in any film Normand made, stands as an ironic commentary on her short-circuited career and life. In what was essentially a remake of the 1913 Keystone one-reeler *Mabel's Dramatic Career*—Mack loved nothing if not recycling old material—she played an ordinary girl who longed to go to Hollywood and get her start in the movies. In *Mabel's Dramatic Career* the fictional Mabel, a lowly scullery maid, had been successful at turning herself into a version of the real-life star, much to the chagrin of her spurned country-boy suitor (played by Sennett). Ten years later, *The Extra Girl* ends on a less triumphant note: after struggling behind the scenes as a wardrobe assistant, Normand's character finally gives up her dreams to marry her childhood sweetheart. The last scene jumps ahead to show her as a contented young mother, watching an old screen test of herself on a home projector with her husband and child. As the film ends, she cradles her toddler in her arms as a title card reads, "Darling, hearing him call me 'mother' makes me happier than any career ever could."

Mabel continued working well into the 1920s, ending her career making two-reelers at the Hal Roach studios, home of Laurel and Hardy and the Little Rascals. Of the films that survive from this period, at least one, *Should Men Walk Home?*, is quite good, even if her deteriorated physical state is detectable under the clown-white makeup she adopted in this period. But as Normand's sporty Gibson Girl persona was replaced in popular taste by the sleeker, more jaded flapper type, demand for her particular brand of charm decreased. Her last released film, the now-lost short *One Hour Married*, came in 1927. The following year, increasingly impaired by both tuberculosis and dependence on alcohol, she impulsively married her former *Mickey* costar Lew Cody, who was a good friend of Buster Keaton's and a fellow full-time drinker.

The pallbearers at Normand's funeral in early 1930, including Cody, Sennett, Griffith, Chaplin, and Arbuckle, were a lineup of fellow luminaries from the silent era that had just passed. (Keaton was there, too, among thousands of other mourners; "not since Valentino's funeral has there been such a throng," reported the *Los Angeles Examiner*.)[36] All of them—even the disgraced Arbuckle, whose career had been cut short by scandal when he was just thirty-four, and who would die of heart failure at forty-six—got longer lives and more chances at self-reinvention than she did.

In that long 1928 interview for *Liberty Magazine*—a conversation that was as candid as it was, in all likelihood, because Normand knew she was running out of time—she described her first memory of Mack Sennett at Biograph in far less romantic terms than those he would use in speaking of her for the remainder of his long life. The second sentence of his autobiography, written almost forty years after their breakup, reads, "Once upon a time I was bewitched by an actress who ate ice cream for breakfast"; in the book to follow, he returns again and again to his regrets about never having set up housekeeping with the elusive Normand, at one point observing that "maybe I wanted to marry a wife and not an actress."

For her part, Normand, opening up to the film journalist and future Warner Bros. animator Sidney Sutherland two years before her death, seems less focused on romantic than professional regrets. She recalls how on her first day on a Griffith film set she found herself in costume as a page, "holding up the train of a noblewoman: My silk-clad legs embarrassed me, and while I was rehearsing I noticed a stocky, red-faced Irishman leaning against the wall, looking at me and grinning." When she looked back after shooting the scene, Mack was gone. "I remembered his face, though, and years later I made a tremendous fortune for that Irishman."[37]

14

Famous Players in Famous Plays

Rosalind Byrne and Buster Keaton in Seven Chances, *1925.*

Nineteen twenty, the year Buster Keaton began his career as an inde-pendent filmmaker, was a pivotal year in American history, a date after which, in both concrete and intangible ways, nothing would be the same. Two weeks after the century rang in its third decade with what must have been an epic New Year's Eve, the whole United States went dry. The stroke of midnight on January 16 marked the beginning of the enforcement of the Eighteenth Amendment, which had been voted into law the previous year. In the short term, the enactment of Prohibition did little more than make it marginally harder and more expensive to acquire alcohol of a suddenly much lower quality (unless you had the money to import the good stuff, as Buster very soon would). But the most pernicious effect of the ban was to encourage, if not abet, the rise of organized crime networks by handing the racketeers full control over a precious and reliably popular commodity.

A little more than eight months later, Tennessee's foot-dragging passage of the Nineteenth Amendment granted women the right to vote after a suffrage battle that had been grinding on for at least seven decades. The back-to-back passage of these two amendments was no accident: the growing power of women in public life had fueled the temperance movement since the turn of the century, as the states approved partial suffrage laws one by one. By the time the Nineteenth Amendment was passed, many states already had some form of law on the books allowing their female citizens (the mere phrase must have struck many Americans at the time, including some women, as a comical oxymoron) to participate in local and sometimes national elections.

Of the two amendments, it was the Nineteenth that would have more impact on the rest of the decade to come. Frederick Lewis Allen, the long-time editor in chief of *Vanity Fair* and a popular social historian, opened his 1931 bestseller *Only Yesterday*, a survey of the social changes brought about by the previous decade, with a vignette of an average middle-class couple, Mr. and Mrs. Smith, as they get ready for their day one morning in 1919. The first details Allen sees fit to provide in this deft sketch of shifting mores have to do with what the lady is wearing. "She comes to breakfast in a suit, the skirt of which — rather tight at the ankles — hangs just six inches from the ground. . . . Mrs. Smith may use powder, but she draws the line at paint." Allen goes on at some length about Mrs. Smith's attire, even speculating about her likely undergarments: an "envelope chemise" and a petticoat with "thick ruffles" designed to make it plain that "she was not disposed to make herself more boyish in form than ample nature intended."[1]

This change in the culture's popular feminine ideal — from the respectable Victorian "angel of the household" to the brash, sensation-seeking "flapper" — was maybe the single most visible transformation in a feverishly transformative decade. In his debut novel, *This Side of*

Paradise—published in 1920!—F. Scott Fitzgerald offered a precise distillation of this shift even as it was getting under way: "the 'belle' had become the 'flirt,' the 'flirt' had become the 'baby vamp.' "[2] Keaton's short *The Scarecrow*, made in the summer of 1920, features an unusually topical intertitle that references the Nineteenth Amendment: "I don't care how she votes, I'm going to marry her!"

The arc from belle to vamp can be traced in the films Keaton made over the course of the decade, as his characters' love objects went from the demure young bride played by Sybil Seely in his first independent release, *One Week* (1920), to the worldly, hard-drinking single actress embodied by Dorothy Sebastian (Keaton's longtime real-life mistress) in his last film of the decade, *Spite Marriage* (1929). Though his marriage to Natalie Talmadge rose and fell in the years between those films, it isn't likely that Keaton's personal beliefs about the social status of women changed much during that stretch of time, or ever. Having grown up with a mother who not only spent her life on the traveling vaudeville circuit but rolled her own cigarettes, played cards into the wee hours, and nipped whisky straight from the bottle, Keaton had no patience for the D. W. Griffith cult of unspoiled female purity. He parodied Griffith in his first feature, *Three Ages*, and once nominated the director's favored heroine, Lillian Gish, as an example of an ideal candidate for a pie in the face, her style of prim femininity being especially vulnerable to a pastry-smeared takedown.

Still less did Keaton care about advancing the cause of women's rights, or any other cause for that matter. But even movies that show little interest in their female characters' social freedom or lack of it—which is to say, most movies made in the 1920s—can't help but reflect the conditions of their time. If Buster's romantic foils gain in sophistication and autonomy over the course of the 1920s, it's a phenomenon largely independent of his design; it's simply that the world changed around him, expanding the range of acceptable behavior for women in movies and in public life.

In *Seven Chances* (1925), Buster's character must find a woman to marry by seven o'clock in order to inherit the sum willed to him by a deceased relative. At a country club, after being turned down by several acquaintances, he gets a chilly rejection from a hat-check girl (Rosalind Byrne) with a deadpan stare to match his own. She's decked out in high flapper style in a shingled black bob, a drop-waist black dress with ruffled collar, and a hip-grazing rope of beads. Byrne's hard-edged chic comes with an unflinchingly modern gaze reminiscent of Louise Brooks, though when *Seven Chances* was released, Brooks, a dancer and Ziegfeld Follies showgirl, had yet to appear in her first film role. After Buster's hat has been returned and the tip gingerly proffered, the two lock eyes for a moment. But before he can pop the question—which, as she knows from prior observation of his sorry plight, will be not just "Wanna go out sometime?" but "Will you marry me?"—she responds with a brief but unambiguous shake of the head: not a chance, Buster.

It's a tiny moment in a film Keaton considered one of his lesser efforts, but a valuable snapshot of how much gender relations had already changed in the five years since women got the vote. The hat-check girl with the drop-dead "nope" may not have been written into the movie as an exemplar of New Womanhood, but she had a job, autonomy over her own romantic choices, and the self-possession to turn down a masher without cracking a smile. Keaton's earlier films usually contained some version of the formal courting call he pays at the start of *Our Hospitality*: a forbidding father or lineup of large brothers are appealed to for approval, and often the lady herself denies Buster her affections until he can "make good" in some business or military venture. In less than seven seconds the hat-check scene in *Seven Chances* illustrates a more modern tradition: not a chivalric ritual but a failed pickup.

The first year of the new decade saw other changes besides the move from wet to dry and from suffragettes to citizens. In January Babe Ruth was traded from the Boston Red Sox to the New York Yankees, who paid the most money ever offered for a player, initiating the cult of the sports superstar that continues to this day. In Indianapolis that spring the first game of the Negro National League was played, thanks largely to the organizing efforts of a Black pitcher-turned-manager-turned-baseball-executive named Rube Foster. The NNL, which would endure until Jackie Rob-inson integrated the sport in 1947, was both a response to the Jim Crow social policies of the time and a symptom of them. The creation of an all-Black professional league gave promising athletes of color a place to practice their sport, but also built a ceiling of success above which they could never rise.[3]

Radio technology, up to then mainly used for telegraphy and military communications, was first marketed to home consumers in the spring of 1920. An electrical engineer and inventor at the Westinghouse Company in Pittsburgh, Frank Conrad, had already become the nation's first evening music broadcaster, playing records on his own living room Victrola into a homemade radio receiver two nights a week for the enjoyment of local wireless enthusiasts. Observing how many people eagerly tuned in to this jury-rigged amateur broadcast, Conrad's boss had the idea of creating more on-air programming as an excuse to sell radios. By that November the "talking box" was popular enough that the results of the 1920 presidential election, which put Warren G. Harding in office, were the first ever to be broadcast.[4] Over the next few years the soon-to-be-ubiquitous home radio would transmit to the nation that landslide election's dispiriting results, as the Harding administration foundered in a series of corruption and graft scandals of which Teapot Dome is now the best remembered, if far from the most appalling.

The American Civil Liberties Union held its first meeting in 1920, as did the League of Nations, President Woodrow Wilson's doomed proj-ect for a pacifist world government. And only two years after the end of the war Wilson had first resisted, then thrown the country into with an eleventh-hour rush of patriotism, political violence manifested itself in a then-new and by now hideously familiar form. On Wall Street on September 16 — a warm and cloudless late summer day, not unlike a Manhattan morning eighty-one Septembers later — a horse-drawn wagon parked outside the headquarters of the J. P. Morgan Bank exploded in a gigantic fireball. The wagon, whose driver had disappeared before the bomb went off, was packed to the roof with dynamite.

The final death toll would come to thirty-eight people and one horse, with hundreds more passersby and bank employees injured: the first large-scale terrorist incident on US soil. This tragedy was paired perhaps too hastily in the public mind with a series of mail bombings and attempted assassinations that had taken place the year before. The resulting crackdown by what was then known as the Bureau of Investigation set off the first Red Scare, a period of intense public paranoia about domestic terrorism that eventually led to the creation of the modern FBI under J. Edgar Hoover.[5]

Keaton incorporated elements from the Wall Street bombing and its aftermath into his 1922 two-reeler *Cops*: An anarchist lobs a bomb from a rooftop just as Buster, driving a broken-down horse and wagon, finds himself riding through a police parade. The unwitting Buster, noting the explosive device on the seat next to him, uses its burning fuse to light his cigarette. He then tosses the bomb aside, nonfatally charring a squadron of cops, falsely identifying himself as the terrorist, and setting off the surreal grand chase that ends the movie.

As usual when Keaton borrows from real-life occurrences, no social satire or political commentary seems intended. He's neither condemning anarchist violence nor protesting police overreach, simply mining an event in the headlines for its comic possibilities. *Cops* may not offer explicit commentary on the Wall Street bombing two years before — it's hard to think of an example, on film or in life, of Keaton offering explicit commentary on much of anything — but it unquestionably takes place in a world already scarred by that incident. In 1922 the image of an "anarchist" — a type signified by raggedy clothes and vaguely Italianate facial hair — throwing a bomb off a roof was a broadly legible sign of public disorder, as well as a handy symbol for the chaotic moral universe where Buster's hero makes his uneasy home. The cosmos of *Cops* is a place of random injustice and meaningless violence, where valor, industry, and even true love go unrewarded. This is almost certainly the funniest movie ever to open on a shot of its hero behind bars and end on his implied suicide, as Buster's willing self-surrender to the mob of furious policemen is followed by an image of a porkpie-hat-topped tombstone.

Of all the superb two-reel comedies Keaton produced between 1920 and his first feature-length film three years later, *Cops* is the most modern, in the specialized meaning that word would later take on to describe the post–World War I moment in American and European culture. Keaton's modernism—brash in ambition but melancholy in tone—is that of his fellow 1890s babies F. Scott Fitzgerald and Hart Crane, who both made spectacular literary debuts in 1920. Like those writers (whom he almost certainly never read), Keaton was formally innovative, inclined to puncture social pretension, and given to making art that was, in a uniquely 1920s way, sardonic and romantic at once.

Keaton doesn't immediately jump to mind as a member of the "lost generation" (the phrase, originally Gertrude Stein's, was quickly taken up and popularized by Ernest Hemingway). And he himself would surely have resisted any such taxonomy, being allergic to self-pity and introspection in equal measure. But his peculiar vision of the world, as seen in the shimmering strand of silent films he made between 1920 and 1928, was formed during the same slice of history as that of American artists like Fitzgerald, Hemingway, Stein, Dorothy Parker, William Faulkner, Robert Benchley, e. e. cummings, Duke Ellington, Cole Porter, Bessie Smith, and Martha Graham, all born in the 1890s. Outside the United States, Keaton's generational compatriots included Antonin Artaud, Joan Miró, Bertolt Brecht, Tamara de Lempicka, Luis Buñuel, and Walter Benjamin.

Such a list is worth compiling not just to note what a deep bench of brilliant iconoclasts the turn of the century produced but because seeing Keaton and these artists as members of the same generation helps to explain why his films often seem to resonate with ideas and whole artistic movements their creator couldn't possibly have known about at the time, and almost certainly would not have cared about if he did. The pervasive sense of anxiety and dislocation, of the need to reinvent the world from the ground up, that groups like the Surrealists or the Bloomsbury authors sought to express in images and words, the human mop-turned-filmmaker expressed in the comic movement of his body and the placement of the camera that recorded it.

Keaton was a highly intelligent but formally uneducated man whose reading diet didn't extend much further than the daily paper, with an occasional glance at the trades. Yet a century later it's clear at a glance that his work was in conversation with, to take just one often-used example, that of Franz Kafka, whose Keatonesque fables about the tragic absurdity of modern life under the omniscient eye of the state were still years away from their first English translation when Buster's wagon driver wandered into that police parade.

In a showstopping montage of trick shots in *Sherlock, Jr.* (1924), Keaton's hero, a film projectionist who's fallen asleep on the job, climbs into the frame of a movie in progress. As the movie he's entered cuts from one landscape to another, he's suddenly stranded on a rock amid pounding surf. Diving in, he finds himself landing headfirst in a snowbank, which transforms in its turn into a bench in an elegant garden. This dizzying demonstration of the power of film editing seems to predict the not-yet-made work of the Soviet director Dziga Vertov, whose avant-garde documentaries used montage to explore how motion-picture technology was changing human perception.

The more you immerse yourself in the 1920s, a period of enormous creative dynamism but also of teeth-rattling instability, the more a single insight seems to animate nearly all the art and popular culture of that age: that the world is a dangerous and unpredictable place, and in it each of us is alone. The mass extinction caused by the Great War and the even more lethal global influenza epidemic of 1918 would have been enough to explain this ambient pessimism, before even factoring in the rapid urbanization of a once-rural America, the resulting steep decline in traditional religious practice, and the continual upending of long-held social customs that accompanied those events.

The third decade of the twentieth century kicked off in a mood of nihilistic low-grade mania. If no other certitude remained but the sheer sensory data of material existence, then young men and women just reaching adulthood would be damned if they weren't going to enjoy their material existences to the hilt. Ann Douglas's book *Terrible Honesty*, a gloriously readable history of the culture of New York City in this period, succinctly captures the tenets by which young people of the era, to a more or less conscious degree, lived their lives.

> This culture billed itself as irreverent if not irreligious, the first such in American annals, alert to questions of honesty but hostile to all moralizing. The tone might be as dark as Parker's bitter *bons mots* and Bessie Smith's grief-and-rage struck blues or as lighthearted as Eubie Blake's piano rags and Fitzgerald's happiest harlequinades, but the primary ethos of all the urban moderns was accuracy, precision and perfect pitch and timing. It was an ethos the white moderns labeled "terrible honesty." (The phrase was Raymond Chandler's.)"[6]

As Douglas's book explores, Black culture of the time had its own distinct expression of the prevailing irreverent mood. While also intent on remaking their world, the Black moderns were, on the whole, more optimistic and less fashionably depraved than their white counterparts. Langston Hughes, Zora Neale Hurston, Josephine Baker, and Louis Armstrong, all born near the turn of the century, evinced a hopefulness and humanism in their art that, however shadowed by past suffering, looked forward to a freer and fairer future. The Great Migration from the rural South to northern cities that had begun in the mid-teens was well under way by 1920, leading to newly dense concentrations of young Black talent in the cities of the North and Midwest. What felt vital and world-renewing to African American creators in the 1920s was not modish alienation—a spiritual luxury they had no interest in affording—but an embrace of both their own long-denigrated cultural traditions and a new kind of urban cosmopolitanism, with its melting-pot promises of global belonging.

What changes the decade ahead might hold were of little concern to Buster Keaton as he returned from ten months of army service in the spring of 1919.[7] What he wanted, once the hearing loss he had incurred from an ear infection had been treated with less than full success at a veterans' hospital, was to get back to the life he'd left behind. Filling out a draft form, he had identified "home" as Muskegon. Jingles' Jungle may have been the most permanent address available to the family at the time, but it was California, where the Comique Company awaited his return, that was now Buster's home and would remain so for the rest of his life. After the army sent him as far as Muskegon, he spent a few days with his parents before continuing alone by train to Los Angeles.

To Buster, who throughout his life depended on others—his producers, business managers, and wives—to take care of the everyday practicalities of life, Joe Schenck was both a benevolent father figure and a personal ego ideal. When he and Norma threw a party, Schenck liked to grill steaks to order for his guests, an uncommonly hands-on approach to hosting in a time when Hollywood bigwigs had live-in cooks and butlers. A few years later, when Keaton had made it big enough to entertain in grand style, he would adopt his brother-in-law's grilling tradition.[8]

Even after both his filmmaking career and his marriage to Natalie Talmadge went south, Keaton talked about his first benefactor with the utmost respect and refused to hear a word against him. When James Karen, a younger actor who befriended Buster late in life, once spoke his mind about how angry stories of Schenck's exploitive behavior toward his friend made him, Keaton rose and quietly left the room. Like the other Joe who loomed large over Buster's life, Schenck would forever remain, in his former protégé's eyes, the generous paterfamilias he had once been.

Keaton's deep sense of filial loyalty applied as well to Arbuckle, who was more like the older brother he had never had than a father. After Keaton's return from the war, at least two film companies made him offers to come work for them for $1,000 a week, but he refused, preferring to finish out his $250-a-week contract with Comique. This decision might well have been based on professional ambition as well as fraternal feeling. There were already rumblings that Roscoe would soon be offered a contract to direct and star in his own feature-length comedies for Paramount, the fast-growing film company that now served as distributor for Schenck's stable of independent studios. If Buster stuck around, he must have known, he stood a very good chance of inheriting Comique from Arbuckle, as indeed happened early in 1920.

Feature-length comedies were still a novelty, though the multi-reel drama had become standard since the success of *Birth of a Nation* in the mid-teens. Chaplin had appeared in the first comedy feature, the Sennett-directed *Tillie's Punctured Romance*, but had not yet directed one himself, and despite the popularity of that 1914 hit (costarring Mabel Normand in a rare villainess role), long-form laughter had not really caught on even five years later. There was no pressing reason for comedies to get longer. Theater managers needed two-reel offerings to run before the featured picture, and canny executives like Paramount's Adolph Zukor were beginning to sell their films only in indivisible bundles, a practice known as "block booking" and deplored by theater operators. Zukor's tireless quest to vertically integrate the movie industry would become the subject of a decades-long antitrust fight before the practice of block booking was outlawed by the 1948 Supreme Court decision *United States v. Paramount*.

In 1920, though, Zukor—a former furrier with middlebrow taste in movies but a matchless sense for the future of the business—was doing pretty well with his dream of founding a single super-company that would control the production, distribution, and theatrical projection of its own output, collecting profits at every point along the chain. "Automatic Vaudeville" had been the name of the storefront entertainment arcade off Union Square that Zukor had opened with a fellow fur merchant back in 1903, when the medium was still a nickel novelty. For the rest of his very long life—he died at age 103 in 1976, remaining at least the nominal head of his beloved business to the end—the paradox built into that phrase would describe what Zukor was best at doing: shaping the audience for an older art form into an audience that would be ready and willing to line up for the next one.

One of Zukor's earliest big enterprises as a producer was to bring *Queen Elizabeth* (1912), a prestigious French feature starring the stage legend Sarah Bernhardt, to the United States for a grand premiere at

Broadway's Lyceum Theater, followed by a nationwide "roadshow" tour with reserved-only seating. *Queen Elizabeth*, at about forty minutes the longest film to be shown in the United States up to that time, is not a good movie, either by current standards or those of its day. The talky palace intrigue of the play it's adapted from, *Les Amours de la Reine Elisabeth*, translates clumsily to the silent screen. The takes are long and the camera placement proscenium-like, making the viewer feel far from the action. Most remarkably, Bernhardt's fabled stage presence somehow fails to register on film; watched now, her acting seems to confirm the widespread and usually incorrect stereotype of silent film acting as melodramatic posing. It's also possible that Bernhardt was simply tired and ill: when *Queen Elizabeth* was made she was sixty-eight and walked at times with a cane, a setback that did not impede her from continuing to play romantic parts. A few years later, her right leg would be amputated after a fall suffered during a performance. Bernhardt's age and infirmity made her an odd fit for the story's central *amour fou*, even if in real life she was in fact involved with her forty-years-younger costar, the lanky Dutch heartthrob Lou Tellegen. In all, *Queen Elizabeth*'s stilted and stagy style befitted the name of the French company that had gone broke before finishing it, allowing Zukor to step in to complete the film: L'Histrionic.

But the quality of the film aside, importing *Queen Elizabeth* to the United States was a brilliant move on Zukor's part. The national tour earned him a tidy sum that he would soon use to start buying up the rights to the films of young independent producers like Schenck. More significantly for the future of the medium, the stateside success of Bernhardt's roadshow tour was enough to convince other studio executives that feature-length movies could turn a profit. *Queen Elizabeth*'s stodginess might even be seen as integral to Zukor's grand plan. With its big-name theatrical star and European stage pedigree, the film exemplified his model for what movies needed to attract the middle-class audiences who still held the medium in disrepute. This approach was summed up in the admirably straightforward slogan of the first production company Zukor founded, essentially a baited hook dangled before those members of the educated middle and upper class who styled themselves stage-over-screen holdouts: "Famous Players in Famous Plays."

Not long after, Famous Players merged with the independent concern of the former Broadway producer Jesse Lasky. Soon after that, Famous Players–Lasky would be absorbed by the Paramount distribution company to form the gigantic entertainment entity still known as Paramount, the oldest Hollywood studio currently in operation. The "famous plays" part dropped away as it began to become clear that writing for the silent screen was a new and entirely separate art from adapting work from the stage. But Zukor had been prescient about the first half. In the dawning age of mass-marketed celebrity, "famous players" were what was going to count. The company that could attract, retain, promote, and invent its own stars was the company that would last.[9]

In 1919 the famous player Zukor wanted to attract was Roscoe Arbuckle, whose name and face, like Chaplin's, had near-universal marquee appeal, but who unlike Chaplin had a reputation for delivering his comedies on budget and on time. Zukor offered him $3,000 a week, on top of the $1,500 Schenck was already paying him; as Keaton biographer Tom Dardis explains the transaction, Schenck was in essence leasing his biggest star to Paramount, where Arbuckle would have the resources to make longer and more technically sophisticated movies than at a mom-and-pop two-reeler shop like Comique. Including the 25 percent of his films' profits he was promised, Arbuckle stood to make nearly a million dollars a year, becoming one of the highest-paid film stars in the world.[10]

In 1920, mom-and-pop-style filmmaking suited the former Three Keatons headliner just fine. When Schenck not only offered him the Comique company—now to be renamed the Buster Keaton Studio—but threw in a newly purchased studio and backlot that had previously been used by Chaplin, Keaton was thrilled to accept. Schenck's description of the job was simple: the company was to turn out eight two-reel comedies a year, to be released through Marcus Loew's new distribution company, Metro Pictures. Keaton could handpick his own crew, from cameraman to production designer to gag writers and carpenters, and keep them at his disposal year-round, so that when a wild new idea needed exploring or a complicated set needed building, the crew was there to execute the director's vision. Keaton did not yet know, though Schenck may have already suspected, that this model of small-scale, creator-driven independent filmmaking would not remain sustainable much longer.

15

Home, Made

Sybil Seely and Keaton in One Week, *1920.*

Somewhere in between his return from army service in the spring of 1919 and the filming of *One Week*, his first release as an independent filmmaker, in the middle of the following year, Keaton must have caught the industrial short *Home Made*, produced by the Ford Motor Company. Though he never cited this undistinguished one-reeler as an influence—he may well not have remembered seeing it—*One Week* appears to take its story structure and a few of its key images from *Home Made*, a resemblance first pointed out by the seminal silent film historian Kevin Brownlow.

   In both films, a young couple builds—or, less entertainingly, supervises the building of—a mail-order kit home while a hand tears pages off a calendar, tracking the progress of the house under construction. *Home Made* ends with the bride and groom descending a narrow set of church steps under a cascade of rice and old shoes; *One Week* opens on the same image, almost identically composed and framed. A heart carved on a tree with the lovers' initials in the Ford film becomes, in Keaton's remix, a pair of linked hearts painted on the house's clapboard siding. These similarities leave little doubt that a four-minute reel of what we would now call branded advertorial content must have been one of the scraps Keaton gathered from the world around him to create *One Week*, a twenty-minute arc of domestic disaster that's among his most perfectly realized films, as well as the most hopeful and romantic movie this characterological pessimist ever made.

Keaton certainly would have had ample opportunity to see *Home Made*, and many other Ford shorts, in the normal course of being a moviegoer in the late teens. Since 1913, in addition to running the world's largest automobile factory, Henry Ford had been funding what became for a time the world's largest motion-picture business. By 1919 his company was spending $600,000 a year—something like $10 million in today's dollars—on the production and distribution of nonfiction one- and two-reel films to be shown, alongside newsreels and short comedies like *One Week*, before the full-length feature. Ford-produced shorts, often focused on technological innovations within the company or in other industries of mass production, reached wide audiences in the United States and overseas. By the time Keaton would have seen *Home Made*, the popularity of the Ford shorts was at its peak and about to begin a steep decline.

At first these short films had been provided free of charge to theater owners, their only advertising pitch a line in not-that-small print at the bottom of each title card: "Distributed by the Ford Motor Company." But in 1920, hoping to offset production costs, Ford began charging theaters a dollar a week. In protest, many managers refused to show his reels. Viewership dropped much more sharply a few months later when the Michigan newspaper Ford had recently acquired, the *Dearborn Independent*, began serially publishing the virulently anti-Semitic hoax text *The Protocols of the Elders of Zion*.

As it would turn out, Ford was just warming up as an anti-Semite. He would spend much of the 1920s disseminating more such rabid hate literature. An anti-Semitic pamphlet series called *The International Jew*, based on a weekly column attributed to Ford in the *Independent*, was freely available at company dealerships nationwide. Ford would soon become a hero of the young Adolf Hitler, who kept a framed photo of Ford on his desk and wrote of him admiringly in *Mein Kampf*.

The disproportionately Jewish ranks of the nation's movie and vaudeville theater owners were understandably less than thrilled to be asked to pay for the privilege of running advertising for such a man. Within months, before the *Independent*'s serialization of the *Protocols* had even finished running, the number of theaters nationwide showing Ford shorts had dropped from 5,200 to around 1,300. By late 1921 Ford's in-theater programming was discontinued, though the company's production unit continued to make nonfiction shorts for distribution at schools, churches, and other institutions.[1]

Ford sometimes took an executive producer credit, but he had little personal involvement in the product his film division churned out, though he did occasionally permit camera crews to film his personal exploits: playing with his son, the future auto magnate Edsel Ford, on the mansion lawn, or going camping with the likes of Thomas Edison and Teddy Roosevelt. To the extent Ford industrial shorts reflect any ideology at all, it's the sunny dogma of economic and technological progress. Many of them, like *Home Made*, combine documentary and reenactment to showcase either the convenience of some new labor-saving device or the orderly utopia of a working factory floor. The true star of *Home Made* is the house, whose origin story we accompany from the log-milling stage onward while only intermittently tracking the rather dull romance of its occupants-to-be. *Home Made* is a celebration not of companionate marriage but of mail-order houses.

These were exactly the kind of up-to-date gadgets that appealed to Keaton's fascination with new technologies and mechanical tinkering.

And like so many other quintessentially twentieth-century innovations, kit homes had sprung into being in synch with his lifetime. Sears, Roebuck, the first company to ship precut building materials by rail beginning in (say it with me now) 1895, started selling whole disassembled dwellings in 1908, from the cut-to-order lumber and flooring down to the nails, paint, trim, and window sashes—but not the bricks or other masonry, which could be acquired from local merchants as part of the package, presumably because they were too heavy to ship. The kits were delivered by boxcar, making them particularly popular in parts of the country easily accessible by rail. (It's easy to imagine that, in a childhood spent riding those same rails, Keaton must have witnessed more than one such shipment reaching its destination.) Usually, as seen in the Ford documentary, the kits were assembled by a locally hired crew over a period of weeks or months—not, as in *One Week*, by the frazzled owners themselves in a single seven-day stretch. And depending on the size and design of the house in question, the materials could take up as much as two full boxcars, a far cry from the single large crate Buster and his bride in *One Week* (Sybil Seely) receive as a wedding gift from a never-seen "Uncle Mike."

The mail-order home business was just entering its heyday when it came into Keaton's sights as potential gag fodder. In 1919, the year *Home Made* was released, the first Sears Modern Homes sales office opened up in Akron, Ohio. Before long the company had offices in nine different cities, where prospective buyers could compare floor plans and view scale models of the latest designs, a transaction that's somewhat stiffly dramatized in the Ford short. Since 1911 Sears had also made financing available for both the houses and the lots they were built on, making the company a proto-mortgage lender decades before the creation of government-subsidized lenders like Fannie Mae.[2]

Though Sears came to dominate the market in mail-order homes, other companies also thrived in the early decades of the century, including Aladdin (named after the genie who builds his master a palace overnight) and Sterling Homes (the company featured, with prominent brand-name placement, in *Home Made*). But after the financing part of the business fell away during the Great Depression, kit-home sales plummeted. The Sears Modern Home catalog would continue to be printed through 1940, but the market for build-them-yourself houses peaked during roughly the same years as the silent film era and came to almost as abrupt a halt.

The fad for kit homes was only one part of a nationwide real estate boom—some economists would call it a bubble—that lasted the whole of the 1920s. This decade-long rise in housing starts was fueled by a strong postwar economy, a soaring stock market, and the continued movement of the population from country to city, including but not limited to the first Great Migration of southern Blacks to northern factory cities. The extension of railway lines and the increasing ubiquity of distance-shortening devices like the automobile and the telephone were changing where and how Americans lived. As rural dwellers moved into cities, family farms on those cities' outskirts were being sold and divided into lots for development. Meanwhile in city centers the population was getting ever denser, leading to a rise in skyscraper construction and a corresponding spike in real estate speculation.

Kit homes, with their mobility, ease of construction, and ability to be customized to individual consumer tastes, represented a new conception of "home" for the generation born around the turn of the century. Instead of hoping to inherit the family farm as their parents might have, a young couple in 1920 might aspire to pick out and oversee the construction of their own off-the-shelf dream home, a product whose existence was made possible by the same developments in industrial production and cross-country rail service that had caused them to leave the farm in the first place.

The most popular kit-home models were modest middle-class dwellings, often built in sturdy bungalow shapes with deep, pillared porches—not innovative in design but modern by dint of their very existence as factory-produced, mail-ordered consumer goods. The Sears catalog copy for the company's perennial bestseller the Winona, a one-story, five-room model that remained in the pages of the catalog for twenty-seven straight years, presents it as neither a bargain nor a luxury but as an everyday commodity, unpretentious yet up-to-date: "The Winona bungalow is a popular American cottage home" whose wide eaves and full porch "give it a pleasing appearance from either perspective."

The house under construction in *One Week*, a two-story clapboard number with a narrow porch running the length of its front wall, pleases from pretty much no perspective, but its big reveal on the third day of construction does get a reliable laugh. Far from progressing with Ford-style efficiency from mill to work site to home sweet home, the *One Week* house, a product of the fictional "Portable Home Co.," is doomed from the start by the vagaries of love and fate. Buster's romantic rival, Handy Hank (played by a hulking, sepulchral-faced actor who goes unnamed in the credits and has never been identified) tricks the newlyweds by switching the numbers on two boxes of precut lumber. The resulting structure makes the cabinet of Dr. Caligari look Grecian in its symmetry.

One outer wall slants sideways at a forty-five-degree angle; an upstairs door opens onto thin air, setting up a spectacular two-story fall onto a flat back that put Buster on bed rest, slathered in horse liniment, for the remainder of the shooting day. The roof is both too small for the house and sits the wrong way atop it, like a poorly fitted hat. The whole cursed thing is forever falling apart, springing leaks and, in the delirious penultimate set piece, spinning on its axis like a carnival ride, expelling its own inhabitants as they try to throw a housewarming party during a hurricane.

The house in *Home Made* was shown to have all the characteristics a Ford-produced infomercial would be expected to promise: solidity, symmetry, affordability, ease of construction, even the fundamental capacity to stay in one place and accumulate value as a piece of real estate. Buster and Sybil's hopelessly cockeyed abode, on the other hand, operates as a centripetal force of destruction, dispersion, and loss. Even the ground the *One Week* house stands on turns out to be tenuous, its status as private property uncertain. Late in the film a man in a straw hat (is he a fellow homesteader? a developer?) arrives to inform Buster and Sybil that the sign demarcating their lot is upside down: they've been building not at

99 Apple Street, the lot so kindly purchased for them by Uncle Mike, but at 66.

In a metaphor that's so baked into the story there's no need for a title card to spell it out, building a home together turns out to be, like marriage, a laughably insuperable challenge and a daily-renewed reminder of the absurdity of human striving. The structure Buster and Sybil hammer together with such innocently unjustified hope seems to actively thwart their efforts to construct, furnish and inhabit it. It's as if the house is striving to revert to the state of being mere lumber, a condition it finally attains in the transcendent last scene. Take twenty minutes to watch *One Week* now if you never have, because the description that follows spoils the closing gag, which Keaton pointed to late in life as an example of his pet method: "I always wanted an audience to outguess me, and then I'd double-cross them sometimes."[3]

As they attempt to roll the ramshackle dwelling to its designated lot on wheels crudely fashioned from barrels—a setup for a superb sight gag involving the nailing of their car to the house—Buster and Sybil find themselves stalled halfway across the railroad tracks in the path of an oncoming train. After a few frantic seconds of pushing, they give up on moving the house out of the way in time and jump off the tracks to save themselves, eyes shielded from the coming destruction. The train roars past—as it turns out, on a track parallel to the one the house is stuck on, sparing it from harm. The lovers heave a mutual sigh of relief just as a second train tears in from the other direction and smashes their house (and the car nailed to it) to smithereens. With the blank resignation of the newly unburdened, the couple joins hands and walks off down the tracks, Buster briefly returning to leave a "For Sale" sign and the assembly instructions on the heap of splintered wood.

One Week is a still-single young man's optimistic dream of what a life built in common might be like, and yet also a startlingly wise vision of marriage as the shared endurance of endless, cyclic disaster. It certainly shows a more mature view of love than Keaton brought to either of his first two marriages. A high-quality copy of this short should be given to

every newlywed couple as a housewarming gift—a less extravagant offering than Uncle Mike's ready-to-build house, maybe, but more portable
and less likely to disappoint. *One Week* is a valentine, a mitzvah, and a
design for living.

Yet for all its romantic optimism, *One Week* stands alongside *Cops*,
made the following year, as one of the great early expressions of Keaton's
deep streak of fatalism. The worlds into which these films' protagonists
are thrown are absurd, incomprehensible, even cruel. Why can't the lead
couple of *One Week* catch a break as they try with such ardent enthusiasm
to build and inhabit their new kit home? Why must the inadvertently
lawbreaking hero of *Cops* be hunted down by an entire city's police force,
then rejected by the girl for whose sake he got into all that trouble in the
first place? *One Week* and *Cops*, made two years apart, can be seen as
companion pieces with opposing theories of the abyss. One proposes love
as a potential, if fragile, bulwark against the universal principle of entropy,
while the other more bleakly posits Buster, and by extension all of us, as
constitutionally and irrevocably alone. It's only Buster's undaunted per-
severance in the face of chaos—matched, in *One Week*, by Sybil's—that
lends the universe of these films moral meaning.

One Week was Keaton's first release as a solo director but not the first
film to be released by the just-launched Buster Keaton Studio. That was
The High Sign, the scruffy two-reeler mentioned at the beginning of this
book, with Buster as a drifter thrown off a train in a town where he must
find his way on his own. The character he would go on to play in most
of his films—a resourceful loner in pursuit of a girl who either scorns his
advances or lays down conditions for him to win her—is much closer to
the protagonist of *The High Sign* than to the uxorious householder of *One
Week*. But it's easy to see why Keaton chose, over Joe Schenck's objections,
to shelve *The High Sign* for a year and kick off his solo career with *One
Week* instead. While brilliantly funny, *The High Sign* doesn't feel new
to Keaton or to film comedy. Its proto-Surrealist prop gags hark back to
the early Arbuckle collaborations, the ones that veered freely between

storytelling and extranarrative riffs: a painted hook on a wall somehow serves to hang up a hat. An unfolding newspaper keeps opening up and up until Buster's whole body is engulfed by a page of newsprint the size of a bedsheet. *The High Sign* still bears an allegiance to the "cinema of attractions" of the medium's early days, and owes the same debt to vaudeville and trick photography. In the space of twenty minutes Keaton strings together a dog trick, two sharpshooting displays, and an ingenious chase through a trapdoor-rigged house, filmed in cross section to resemble a four-panel comic strip in motion.

In *One Week*, though, story and action are fully integrated. Every gag is in service of the central conflict, with Buster and Sybil on one side and their obstinately unbuildable house on the other. The home at its heart may be unstable, but *One Week* is as solidly constructed as the battered table Joe Keaton hauled from gig to gig for the length of Buster's childhood. It's as perfect a first film as any director ever made (though calling it Keaton's debut is something of a cheat, given that he had been codirecting with Arbuckle for three years and creating twenty-minute comedy sketches for far longer than that), and it makes an implicit promise to the audience for the next near-decade of independent Keaton productions to come: However inhospitable the circumstances, we know Buster will keep trying his dammedest to build the best house or boat or car or train—above all, the best movie—he possibly can.

One Week's maddeningly uninhabitable house is only the first in a long line of frustrating Keaton dwellings. In his shorts *The Electric House* and *The Haunted House*, painstakingly tricked-out homes—one rigged with labor-saving modern gadgets, the other with fake ghosts and skeletons— appear to turn on their occupants. In the 1923 feature *Our Hospitality*, a southern family's home becomes a trap when Buster's character, visiting his girl (Natalie Talmadge, by then married to Buster and pregnant with their second son), realizes that her family and his are foes in a generations-long feud. The young lady's father, the patriarch of the opposing clan (frequent Keaton heavy Joe Roberts), reminds his bloodthirsty sons that southern etiquette forbids killing a guest under their own roof, so Buster's challenge becomes to stay in the house as long as possible till he can devise an escape.

In *The General*, too, Buster's character finds himself hiding out in a house behind enemy lines, this time to rescue his girl (Marion Mack), who has been taken prisoner by Union soldiers. And in his last independently produced feature, *Steamboat Bill, Jr.* (1927), the climactic action sequence consists of nothing but the destruction by hurricane of a succession of formerly stable shelters: a prison, a hospital, and the two-story house whose entire façade collapses onto Keaton, leaving him framed in a narrow window opening. That gag, now perhaps the best-remembered single image of Keaton's career, was three movies old by then but still developing, growing in scale each time. In *Back Stage*, one of the last Arbuckle-Keaton collaborations, Roscoe gets framed by a falling piece of scenery with a cutout window, while in *One Week* a wall on a hinge does an unexpected 180-degree pivot, framing Buster on the ground and hoisting the formerly earthbound Sybil high in the air.

For Keaton, every potential home is a space of danger and transformation; no façade stays standing for long. Structures that seem to offer shelter and physical safety reveal themselves to be nothing but heaps of wood on their way to becoming splinters. The ephemerality of the built world reveals the foundational homelessness of Buster's character, whose defining trait is his ability to move through chaos while remaining miraculously unperturbed. This is the central joke of the Three Keatons' act projected on a cosmic scale: the boy who couldn't be damaged, winged into the backdrop not by his father but by weather, physics, history, and fate. The universe his films posit, however playful and imaginative, is also frighteningly unstable.

The kit home of *One Week* is the earliest and most benevolent expression of a recurrent theme in Keaton's work: that no man-made object should be regarded as permanent or trustworthy. Not only buildings but cars, trains, boats, whole railway bridges show themselves to be as flimsy and perishable as theatrical scenery. In several movies set in backstage environments, what appears to be a "real" interior space is suddenly taken apart by stagehands, revealing the room to have been a set all along.

Keaton may not have remembered seeing the nondescript *Home Made*, but the film he wove together using fragments of it deftly parodies the staunch industrial-age optimism of the source material. Uncle Mike's generosity notwithstanding ("Wish you joy," ends his note to the newlyweds—would that we all had such an uncle!), his wedding gift turns out to be a curse. The kit home's resolute failure to cohere into a viable living space is what initiates the newlyweds into the fallen world of double-crossing rivals and untrustworthy assembly instructions, of disappointment and loss and plain old bad luck. But the couple's undimmed devotion as they walk into the horizon at movie's end hints at the possibility of hope and even happiness in an insecure world.

Keaton would make many more films structured around female love interests, returning over and over to plots that required his initially passive character to attempt heroic feats to win the heart, or ensure the physical safety, of his beloved. But *One Week* is one of very few in which the woman is Buster's true partner in the comic action. A rare Keaton two-hander, *One Week* could only soar the way it does with a costar who was Buster's match in energy and fearlessness. In hiring Sybil Seely—who probably got the job more because she was available, affordable, and attractive than for her experience or specific performing skills—the newly launched Buster Keaton Studio lucked out.

Seely was a recruit from the ranks of Mack Sennett's Bathing Beauties, then twenty to Buster's twenty-five, with a wavy dark bob, a mischievous expression, and a livelier, more athletic screen presence than most of Keaton's female costars, who sometimes tended toward the phlegmatic. She was born Sybil Travilla on the second day of the new century, the next to last in a family of seven children. After their father, a former saloonkeeper turned respectable tire merchant, died suddenly in 1905, three of Sybil's older brothers, already known in their seaside hometown on Santa Catalina Island as champion swimmers, helped support the family by diving for coins thrown by passing tourists off boats.

By the early teens the Travilla brothers were touring the United States and Europe as a vaudeville act, doing underwater stunts in a large glass tank with their trained seal, Winks. On the small western circuits they traveled they would have been unlikely to cross paths with a big-time act like the Three Keatons, but the Travillas did well enough to support their mother and young siblings. A 1912 Sacramento bill wryly summed up their act, which ended with Winks and the three young men sitting down to an underwater meal: "The Travilla Brothers exploit a seal with a human brain. It will remain a mystery until the post-mortem is performed whether their claim is correct or not, but at all events it is an animal that at least thinks that it thinks."

Given how crucial Winks was to the Travilla family's survival in a difficult time, it seems more than plausible, as the silent film blogger Lea Stans has suggested, that the aquatic mammal may have inspired Sybil's performing name, sometimes spelled in credits as "Sealy." In her earliest roles with Keystone in the late teens, she often went by the name Sibye Trevilla; she can be seen cavorting in group beach scenes, dancing in translucent "Grecian" robes or posing on a fur rug in one of the mildly racy publicity shots the Bathing Beauties did to advertise upcoming Sennett titles. When she bursts into an impromptu dance in Keaton's *The Scarecrow*, clambers from one moving car to another in *One Week*, or balances gracefully on Buster's shoulders in a jokey set photo, Seely shows evidence of having a background in dance or acrobatics, but it's not known whether she had any formal training.[4]

When she played a bride in *One Week*, Sybil really was newly married, having walked down the aisle a few months earlier with Jules Furthman, a newspaper reporter turned successful Hollywood screenwriter. Furthman is credited on an astonishing number of classic studio-era scripts: *Shanghai Express*, *Blonde Venus*, *Morocco*, *Only Angels Have Wings*, *Body and Soul*, *The Maltese Falcon*, *To Have and Have Not*, *The Big Sleep*, *Mutiny on the Bounty*, and *Rio Bravo* are among the over two hundred movies he wrote or cowrote over a four-decade career that included collaborations with Josef von Sternberg, John Ford, Howard Hawks, Jacques Tourneur, and Dorothy Arzner.

Sybil would make four more two-reelers with Keaton—*The Scarecrow,* *Convict* 13, *The Boat,* and *The Frozen North*—before leaving show business to devote herself to raising the only child she and Furthman had together, Jules Jr.[5] Of all the actresses who played opposite Keaton, she is the best remembered and a longtime fan favorite, even though her time as his semiregular leading lady lasted less than two years. But because so little of her life was led in public, it's hard to know more about Sybil than the basic biographical details: her life story emerges mainly in the margins of coverage of her more famous brothers, husband, and short-term costar. An undated gag photo of Sybil and Jules Sr. shows her lying supine on the grass as he stands above her in jodhpurs and boots, leaning on a prop rifle, one foot lightly balanced on her stomach: a game hunter and his prey. The choice of pose now seems gruesomely comic in its literalization of patriarchal power. But there's a sweetness to this snapshot as well, a spirit of consensual playacting that's absent from the stiff publicity photos Buster and Natalie would pose for after their marriage.

Sybil and Jules stayed together until his death in 1966, the same year as Buster's and twenty-two years before her own. Their life together was not without struggle and sorrow: Jules Jr. was born with a developmental disability whose nature is hard to determine, given the stigma that surrounded such conditions at the time. It's possible that the extra care her son needed was what kept Sybil from returning to acting—or maybe, like many women at the time, she simply regarded marriage and motherhood as the natural end of a career. At any rate, the Furthmans appear to have cared for their son and each other, and to have arrived early on at a place of domestic stability and marital well-being that Keaton would take twenty more years to find in his own life. All three Furthmans are buried together in a section of Glendale's Forest Lawn cemetery called the "Garden of Everlasting Peace"; their markers identify them simply as "Beloved Wife and Mother," "Beloved Husband and Father," and "Beloved Son."

By the mid-1930s, while Buster was enduring his worst years of alcoholism and underemployment, Sybil and Jules were living on a sprawling stretch of still-unsettled land in Culver City, raising their son, collecting modern art and rare books, and constructing seven greenhouses for the cultivation of prize orchids, a passion they shared.

The Furthman mansion is still inhabited, and photos of its interior and exterior can be found online. Its airy open-flow plan and the modern, asymmetrical curve of its central iron staircase suggest a life of culture, leisure, and play—a far cry from the disaster-prone kit home of *One Week*. The real-life Sybil had ascended, as Buster would for a few short years, into a real estate category beyond the highest-end offering of the Sears Modern Homes catalog. The housing market and the movie business were bursting into bloom at the same time, and the result of their cross-pollination was that rare orchid, the Hollywood estate. These would become places for the newly rich and unprecedentedly famous to display their wealth, taste, and personal beauty, for their fans to dream of visiting or living themselves one day, and for the increasingly powerful celebrity press to bring occupants and gawkers together.

16

Rice, Shoes, and Real Estate

Norma Talmadge, Natalie Talmadge, Keaton, and Constance Talmadge on Natalie and Buster's wedding day, 1921.

Only two years after *One Week* and less than a year into his own first marriage, Keaton made *My Wife's Relations*, a satirical short that paints the institution of marriage in a decidedly grimmer light. Through a series of bureaucratic mix-ups and linguistic misunderstandings, Buster's character finds himself wed to a complete stranger, a woman twice his size who lives in a cramped apartment with an extended family as large, intimidating, and violence-prone as the lady herself. The bride is played with implacable ferocity by the Irish-born character actress Kate Price, who would go on to success as a similarly broad type in the ethnic comedy series *The Cohens and Kellys*.

My Wife's Relations is saved from being offensive to modern audiences—barely—by the charisma of Price's performance and the relative benignity of its humor: Buster's ill-mannered new wife and in-laws are affectionately ribbed rather than cruelly mocked. But the view the film takes of domestic life is markedly sour, especially coming from a twenty-six-year-old married for less than a year. As the fictional Buster and his bride lie side by side in twin beds, each pretends to be asleep in order to land furtive blows on the other, culminating in her breaking a large ceramic pitcher on his head.

Feuding couples and uncouth in-laws were stock comic tropes of the time, and the roughhouse humor of *My Wife's Relations*—in which the "relations" who crowd Buster's domestic space are burly but easily fooled men—has little to do with the matriarchal mini-society that was the Talmadge family. But it wasn't uncommon for Keaton to use his life for inspiration: witness the many, many films in which he has it out with his father or a fatherlike authority figure. Perhaps the disaffected tone of *My Wife's Relations* is evidence that the real-life Buster was beginning to chafe at the constraints of life in sometimes smothering proximity to the extended Talmadge clan.

Buster and Natalie were married on May 31, 1921, in a small family ceremony at Joe Schenck and Norma Talmadge's summer house in Bayside, Queens, a neighborhood then still remote enough that the *New York Times* announcement of the ceremony called it "a quiet country wedding." Natalie's bridesmaid was the novelist and screenwriter Anita Loos, who had befriended the sisters while writing a series of light romances for Constance to star in. (It was later said that Loos based much of the dialogue of Dorothy, the bluntly pragmatic gold-digger in her 1925 bestseller *Gentlemen Prefer Blondes*, on the sometimes unintentional bons mots of Peg Talmadge, mother of the bride.) Keaton's best man was the actor Ward Crane, who a few years later would play his rangy nemesis in *Sherlock, Jr.*

The elder Keatons, who had by then sold Jingles' Jungle and were living, siblings and all, with Buster in Los Angeles, skipped the wedding. This might have been because the cross-country train trip seemed arduous, though if anyone had the habit of long-distance rail travel it was the Keaton family. Or it might have been because they sensed that, like their son, they were liable to be treated with a vague air of condescension by the richer and more culturally aspirational Talmadges. Buster was successful and beginning to be famous, but he was no Joe Schenck; in Peg's mind, an established movie mogul far outranked a rising slapstick clown in the husband-material hierarchy.

Photos of the wedding party, like many publicity shots that would be taken of Natalie and Buster over the eleven years their marriage lasted, have a Zelig-like quality: the blank-faced groom might have been pasted in from a different album. In a shot of him surrounded on all sides by Talmadge sisters, he actually appears to roll his eyes. Natalie's face in this photo is also blank, if less affectedly so, but the movie star sisters who flank them are beaming.

In later publicity stills, and in front of a movie camera as the heroine of Keaton's 1923 feature *Our Hospitality*, Natalie tends to project the recessive quality of someone who dislikes being photographed. A 1922 gag photo of her with Buster in the film magazine *Photoplay* mines comic-strip clichés about henpecked husbands and hectoring wives: while Natalie half-heartedly wields a prop rolling pin, Buster sits beside her, his legs elegantly crossed and one ankle shackled to a ball and chain, fixing the camera with that same look of opaque blankness. His lack of expression—the default mask he assumed in any picture he knew was being taken from about the age of six onward—is a part of the intended joke; this time around, unlike in the wedding portraits, it's a performance that suits the occasion.

In *The Talmadge Sisters*, Peg's heavily fictionalized 1924 account of her daughters' rise from Brooklyn obscurity to Hollywood fame, she describes the wedding ceremony in terms that recall that carefree first shot of *One Week*: "Natalie was married outdoors with the sunshine streaming down on bright faces and bright flowers, and she departed amidst a perfect bombardment of rice, old shoes, kisses, hugs, admonitions and congratulations." Peg freely admitted to mixed feelings upon the marriage of her middle child, not, she insisted, because she regarded the groom as unworthy but because she was bereft at the prospect of losing the daughter she had nicknamed her "home girl."[1]

Peg and Natalie had been living together on the East Coast while the other sisters continued their work at Schenck's Forty-Eighth Street studios, with Natalie doing secretarial work for the company and playing bit parts when needed. When Natalie took a train cross-country with Buster to set up housekeeping—a trip that would serve as their honeymoon, since he had a shooting schedule to return to at his own studio—the rest of the Talmadges at first stayed behind. But after Natalie's pregnancy was announced later that year, the Talmadges packed up their no doubt enormous wardrobes and moved to Hollywood, husbands, production companies, and all.

Buster and Natalie's domestic life got off to a very different start than that of the doughty newlyweds of *One Week*. They were more materially advantaged, to be sure—a rising movie star and the sister of two already famous ones—but also more encumbered by domestic complications than the fictional Buster and Sybil, who seem to have no family beyond the mysteriously benevolent Uncle Mike. Buster had spent most of his life sharing close and transitory quarters with his parents and siblings. After marrying Natalie, he found himself in uneasy transition between show business vagrancy and the search for a stable home. The boy who had grown up between railway sleeper cars and theatrical boardinghouses would spend the next thirty-five years looking for a place to settle that was less damage-prone than the cursed kit house of *One Week*.

For the first few months of their marriage, he and Natalie crowded into the bungalow Buster had rented for the Keaton family the previous year. But once the Talmadge contingent moved west, Buster and Natalie took a larger house in the once exclusive but, by the early 1920s, somewhat down-at-the-heels neighborhood of Westmoreland Place. They needed a place big enough to accommodate Norma, Constance, and Peg, who were spending more time with Natalie than at their own far posher digs, especially after the birth in 1922 of Joseph Keaton III. The baby was quickly nicknamed "Jimmy" by Natalie. After her divorce from Buster in 1932, she would legally change their oldest son's name to James Talmadge, symbolically erasing every trace of the man she by then despised.

The Westmoreland Place house may no longer have had a fashionable address, but it was no *One Week* kit home, either. The entire third floor was given over to a formal ballroom, where Constance liked taking her bicycle out for a spin. This house's elegant Tudor-style exterior can be seen in Keaton's 1922 short *The Electric House*, where it "plays" the fancy private home his character is hired to rig with a variety of pointless yet ingenious modern conveniences. Buster's onscreen alter ego may have been a humble journeyman struggling to electrify a house for his wealthy boss, but in real life he was the one looking to upgrade his living quarters.

Buster and Natalie lived in four different houses over the course of their first four years together, moving steadily westward as the growing settlement often called "the film colony" extended itself over Beverly Hills, a stretch of former lima bean fields between Benedict Canyon and the sea. Like many investors in real estate in the 1920s, Keaton did some rapid trading up, especially considering the poor head for business he would display a few years later in his dealings with MGM. He first purchased a house with a loan from Joe Schenck and resold it ten months later for a tidy profit. With the proceeds from that sale he bought another house, lived there for a short time, and flipped that, too. Somewhere along the way, he got Myra and his siblings settled in a modest but comfortable four-bedroom place on Victoria Avenue in the Wilshire district. (In less flush times, starting in 1941, he and his third wife, Eleanor, would return to live there with them for more than fifteen years.) Joe, by this time, was more or less permanently installed at the Continental Hotel, a hangout for old theatrical types where he could kibitz to his heart's content, and where Buster paid the monthly bill. Amid all this upwardly mobile chaos Natalie had a second son, Robert, in 1924.

Sometime shortly after the baby's birth, Buster was unceremoniously exiled to his own separate bedroom. As he told the story in later years, this was a decision presented to him by the Talmadge family as a whole; having decided to stop at two children, Natalie was quite simply done with sex, and her mother and sisters supported her in withdrawing from that part of the marriage, though the sisters were sexually active both in and outside their marriages.

The only source we have for this anecdote is Buster, who spoke in euphemistic but frank terms with interviewers about the businesslike nature of his conversations on the subject with the immovable Peg Talmadge. As he described it, he made it clear to her that while he would not throw his money away on a mistress or embarrass Natalie by conducting his affairs in public, he had no intention of giving up that part of his life for good. The truth of what drove the couple apart was no doubt far more complicated than his version of the story lets on, but the mere fact that he was negotiating the future of his conjugal sex life with his mother-in-law suggests the degree to which, as in *My Wife's Relations*, marriage was for him at that time as much a transaction between family units as it was a union of two individuals.[2]

While financially profitable, the fast turnover in living situations during the early years of the Keaton-Talmadge marriage was ultimately in the service of what Keaton identifies in his autobiography as "an old vaudevillian's yearning for a stable home."[3] (He's talking there not about himself but about his childhood friend Lex Neal, an Actors' Colony pal from Muskegon days whom Buster brought west in the 1920s to work as a gag writer. Buster's own yearnings were not a subject for discussion.) Not long after their second son was born, Buster secretly had built and furnished a new house as a surprise for Natalie. This was a spacious three-bedroom spread with a swimming pool in an unglamorous but comfortable stretch of a new development known as the Beverly Hills Flats, where their neighbors would have included not marquee movie names but a doctor, a bookstore owner, and an old couple who owned an orange grove.

Keaton describes at some length in his autobiography, and later in conversation with his first biographer, how he drove Natalie to the property, announced with pride that it was theirs, and offered her a walk-through, only to be chagrined when she turned down the offering on sight. In Nate's eyes, the house was too modest in scale for the kind of life she intended to lead as the wife of a movie star. As she pointed out during their tour, it lacked even the space for servants' quarters or a live-in governess—amenities that Buster had been unaware his young family would soon be requiring.

This story comes to us only through Buster's retelling, and is usually adduced as evidence of Natalie's acquisitiveness and social climbing. But seen through the lens of our modern understanding of marriage—or even the view of companionate homemaking in *One Week*—the choice to single-handedly create a complete furnished home for a family of four without consulting one's partner is a strange one. If nothing else, the story of the rejected house offers a snapshot of the state of their marriage four years in: the dream of creating an idyllic love nest was still in full force, but neither partner was sharing their version of that dream with the other.

Buster's response to Nate's objections was to promptly sell the house to MGM fixer Eddie Mannix and his wife, Bernice, who would live there for the next decade, and start construction on the palatial home that would come to be known as the Italian Villa. This twenty-room, ten-thousand-square-foot mansion, built on a sloping three-acre lot directly behind the Beverly Hills Hotel, was one of the grand estates of silent-era Hollywood. True, it was not as vast or elaborate as several other movie star homes within walking distance: Rudolph Valentino's six-acre horse ranch, Falcon's Lair; Harold Lloyd's soon-to-be-built Greenacres, a forty-five-thousand-square-foot mansion built on fifteen acres, with its own nine-hole golf course and child's amusement park; or Douglas Fairbanks and Mary Pickford's palatial Pickfair, a former hunting lodge that Fairbanks had converted into a twenty-five-room home for his new bride, with a lawn so big it once served as a landing pad for the Goodyear blimp. But the Keatons' place stood out among this lineup, not for its square footage or degree of luxury but for its tasteful design and top-of-the-line construction. In contrast, Charlie Chaplin's nearby spread became known as the Breakaway House because, rumor had it, the mansion had been hastily built by his studio carpenters with an eye to appearance rather than durability.

The Italian Villa, like any Keaton creation, was crafted down to the last detail. Built in a fashionable mix of Italian, Spanish, and Moorish styles known as Mediterranean Revival, it was codesigned by Buster and architect Gene Verge, Sr., with input and landscaping help from Buster's longtime technical director Fred Gabourie. The house's central feature was a grand tiered back garden that descended four levels of marble steps to a thirty-foot swimming pool. Two levels of gracefully arched loggia overlooked the grounds, giving the whole spread the feel of a Renaissance palazzo.

There were whimsical touches: the master bathroom in Natalie's wing had a custom-sized sink and toilet to match her petite frame. In the yard, a miniature model of the house served as a playroom for the Keatons' two sons. A small sunroom with a black-and-white-tiled "tango floor" referenced the popularity of tango-dancing heartthrob Rudolph Valentino, a Beverly Hills neighbor who died around the time the house was completed. (In Billy Wilder's *Sunset Boulevard*—a 1950 black comedy about silent-era excess that features Buster in a tiny but unforgettable cameo—Gloria Swanson's Norma Desmond proudly displays her own tiled dance floor, declaring that "Valentino said there's nothing like tile for a tango!")[4]

By the time the Keatons moved into the Italian Villa in 1926, Buster was at the height of his success, making two features a year and earning the then-extravagant salary of $3,000 a week. (However, in an ominous sign for the financial future, he owned not a single share in his own production company. The shareholders were Joe Schenck, his brother Nick—now running the business side of MGM—Buster's Comique-era manager and old vaudeville pal Lou Anger, and the songwriter Irving Berlin.) Every Sunday, if Buster and Natalie were in town, they hosted big outdoor parties where Keaton, as perfectionistic about entertaining guests as he was about entertaining fans, grilled English-cut lamb chops and steaks to order as guests splashed in the pool or fished in the mechanically operated trout stream. The actress Louise Brooks, who knew the Keatons socially during this period, keenly sized up the fantastical atmosphere at the Villa to biographer Tom Dardis in a 1977 letter: "Buster's whole life then was a movie . . . his house was a set, the swimming pool was a set, the barbecue pit was a set."

Brooks's movie-set metaphor would become literal in *Parlor, Bedroom and Bath*, a 1931 MGM talkie filmed in part at the Italian Villa. An early scene has Buster's character, a humble poster-hanger in love with an unattainable heiress, attempting to flee from her (in real life, his) palatial home. He dives out a second-floor bedroom window to shimmy down an Italianate arched wall, then leads a gang of pursuers on a chase down those cypress-lined marble steps, into and out of the swimming pool, and around the impeccably kept grounds. Keaton is at "home" in these early scenes, but he has never looked so out of place, nor so desperate to escape.

Parlor, Bedroom and Bath is not the worst sound film Keaton made at MGM, but like all of them it's plenty bad enough, a flimsy sex farce with a contrived plot, long stretches of achingly stiff dialogue, and only the most fleeting opportunities for comic action. The director was Edward Sedgwick, who had been teamed with Keaton since the latter arrived at MGM, sometimes to excellent effect, as with the two silent films they essentially codirected, *The Cameraman* and *Spite Marriage*. But by 1931 Keaton's hand had been removed from the creative tiller entirely, and even the able Sedgwick (who would go on to direct Harold Lloyd and Laurel and Hardy) is hamstrung by the limitations of the project, a creaky remake of a now-lost 1920 film that was itself based on a 1917 stage play.

Very few comic or directorial choices in *Parlor, Bedroom and Bath* appear to have made by Keaton, but there is a wan reprise midway through of the last gag from *One Week*: those two trains tearing in from opposite directions, this time first sparing and then destroying not a house but a snazzy two-tone convertible. But in this version, the characters struggling to move the car off the tracks—Buster's Reggie and Joan Peers's Nita— aren't newlyweds or lovers, only slight acquaintances who've been set up on a fake date to make their respective sweethearts jealous. When they walk away from the wreckage, it's not with the bittersweet resignation of a young couple starting again from scratch but with the numb relief of two strangers who have survived a traffic accident.

By the time he was filming *Parlor, Bedroom and Bath*, Buster spent most nights not at the Villa but at the studio bungalow he called Keaton's Kennel, often with female company. His promise to Peg to be discreet about his affairs had proved impossible to keep. In 1931 there had been a nasty incident with an MGM bit player who showed up at the door of the Kennel demanding money, the implication being that she would otherwise reveal their affair. When he ordered her out, she brandished a pair of shears, there was a scuffle, and MGM had to scramble to create a not-very-credible cover story. Natalie put up with that and many more affairs besides, but by the summer of 1932 she had had enough. She arranged with a detective and her sister Constance to catch Buster asleep with a girl on the yacht he'd bought for his wife and named the *Natalie*—although as he later told it, he and the girl were both so drunk that night that nothing had happened between them.

After filing for divorce and packing the boys off to military boarding school, Natalie put the Italian Villa on the market, where it sat for more than a year, the Great Depression having put a serious dent in even the high-end housing market. It eventually sold to Fanchon Wolff Simon, one-half of the brother-and-sister dance team Fanchon and Marco; later it would belong to or be leased by a series of stars including Cary Grant, Marlene Dietrich, Jean Gabin, and James Mason. The Villa would figure into Keaton's life again decades later, when he knocked on the Masons' door in search of old film prints he had left behind in a shed on the property. But Buster's time as the designer and occupant of his own Hollywood dream palace—a role he had never aspired to himself but that, once cast in, he played to the hilt—was less than seven years total, and almost uninterruptedly unhappy.

In 1956, several career phases, two wives, and many addresses later, Keaton would sell the rights to his life story to Paramount for $50,000, the equivalent of nearly half a million dollars in today's currency. The resulting biopic, starring Donald O'Connor as Keaton, was both a wildly inaccurate account of its subject's life and a terrible movie, but the proceeds were enough to buy Buster and Eleanor Keaton a comfortable ranch house on an acre and a half of land in the San Fernando Valley town of Woodland Hills—the place they would live for the remainder of his life. They were both painfully aware, Eleanor said later, that *The Buster Keaton Story* stunk, but they were grateful to it for establishing them in the kind of quiet country spread Buster had long dreamed of, a place he would proceed to rig out like the "electric houses" of movies past. By way of congratulations, Sybil Travilla Furthman sent the Keatons a box of orchids from her and her husband's by then extensive network of greenhouses. I like to think of this gift as a late housewarming present for the poor doomed kit home of *One Week*, that cursed heap of lumber that took thirty-six years to be properly rebuilt.

17

The Shadow Stage

Norma Talmadge on the cover of Picture-Play *magazine, 1922.*

When the 1920s began, film was still being written about mostly as if it were a supplement to live theater, even though the vaudeville business had already started to lose much of its young talent pool to the movies. In the same years Keaton was setting up shop as an independent filmmaker, film criticism as we know it emerged from a matrix of other forms of writing about the medium, some familiar from earlier modes of cultural commentary, others as new as the technology that gave rise to them.

The theatrical press took its sweet time catching up with just how popular movies were getting. For the first decade and a half of the medium's

existence, the default tone of most writing on film toggled between prig-
gish alarmism and wry disdain. Until around 1910, discussions of film
in the popular press usually had more to do with its effects on public
morals than its potential as an art form. And for people in the theater
industry—critics and performers alike—the advent of film represented
an aesthetic threat as well as an economic one.

A few chapters back we heard the writer and ex–vaudeville performer
Nellie Revell in 1917 decrying the "speed mania" that had been afflicting
the stage ever since the advent of the motion picture. Not long before that,
with the worldwide craze of "Chaplinitis" at its peak, a theater critic at
a publication as august as *Harpers Weekly* felt comfortable boasting that
"of [Chaplin's] drollness I am not fit to judge, never having seen him, nor
indeed any motion pictures soever, which is a great distinction in itself."[1]

But just two months later, that same magazine ran an influential one-
page essay by the celebrated stage actress Minnie Maddern Fiske, who
billed herself, Victorian-style, under the name Mrs. Fiske. Fiske ran her
own theater company with her husband, Harrison Grey Fiske, as her
producer and manager. She was known for her ultra-restrained onstage
style—she liked to deliver key speeches standing with her back to the
audience—for first bringing Henrik Ibsen's proto-feminist modern dramas
to American audiences, and for her company's open defiance of the powerful syndicate that controlled the nation's theaters. The notion that the
advent of silent film, with its infinite reproducibility and transnational
reach, might have had a hand in Chaplin's rise to global fame seems not
to have occurred to the performance-centric Fiske. Instead, the actress
explicitly tied the comedian's unprecedented celebrity to theatrical virtues that predate the motion-picture era: "The critic knows his secret. It
is the old, familiar secret of inexhaustible imagination, governed by the
unfailing precision of a perfect technique."[2]

The issue of *Harpers* that included Mrs. Fiske's essay also ran, on
the facing page, a reprint of an article from *Motion Picture Magazine* by
theater critic Charles Grau. This lighthearted column kicked off by flatly
contradicting the actress's claim that Chaplin was being appreciated by

a growing cohort of "cultured, artistic people": "Theaterdom, which in modern times includes the movies, still regards the exploits of Charlie Chaplin as a gigantic hoax."[3] But the focus of Grau's piece was not the validity of Chaplin's art; it was the size of his salary.

A few months earlier the comedian had negotiated the most lucrative contract in the history of the medium. Chaplin's Mutual contract was the result of a bidding war among at least six film companies for the services of the Little Tramp. The $670,000-a-year figure he negotiated with the help of his older brother and business manager Sydney was so astronomical that for months it remained the subject of gobsmacked press coverage. Many commentators adopted the tongue-in-cheek tone of Grau's article, turning the very excess of Charlie's income into a meta-joke: "The idea that the funniest man in all the world, who only very recently was appearing in the flesh on the vaudeville stage at a weekly salary of $100, is to receive now a weekly pay of $13,500 is so funny that Broadway refuses to accept the proposition seriously."

The tension between these two facing pages of Chaplin commentary — one focused on the new medium's potential artistic merit, the other on the transformative effect movie money was having on the entertainment landscape — dominated the first two and a half decades of writing on film. It seems noteworthy that the issue of *Harpers Weekly* that ran this Chaplin debate in May 1916 was the venerable magazine's second-to-last. *Harpers Weekly* closed up shop just a week later, having been around since 1857, when a group of pro-Union journalists began publishing it under the lofty subtitle "a Journal of Civilization." A full twenty years after the first projection of Edison's moving pictures at Koster and Bial's Music Hall in New York — a program of dancing girls and pounding waves described in the *New York Times* the next day as "singularly real and wonderfully exhilarating" — the question of whether the new art form yet belonged under the heading of "civilization" was still undecided.

As far back as early 1907, a much younger publication than *Harpers Weekly*, the then two-year-old theatrical trade paper *Variety*, had published an announcement that "commencing with the current issue, reviews of new moving picture series presented in the vaudeville theatres of New York and Chicago will appear in this department." That same day *Variety* ran a pair of what are sometimes called the first American movie reviews: paragraph-long descriptions of Pathé's *An Exciting Honeymoon* and the Edison company's *Life of a Cowboy*, both signed by the paper's founding editor, Sime Silverman. The tone of these items is mainly descriptive, with only brief forays into evaluative language. *Life of a Cowboy*, directed by the veteran Edwin S. Porter, is "a long and interesting moving picture" at thirteen minutes. Silverman sums up a busy plot involving a stagecoach holdup, a trick lariat demonstration, and a "tragic finale" in which a young Native American girl shoots a "bad man" creeping up on the lover of the white heroine, before ending on a comparison that shows how deep a debt moviegoing still owed to the medium of theater: "The series is so melodramatic in treatment that it acted on the audience like a vivid play."[4]

Film in the early twentieth century still fell somewhere in between a novelty to be gawked at for its own sake and a transparent storytelling medium that audiences could identify with as they would a stage play. A century-plus later, watching moving images edited into narrative form (and editing them ourselves on palm-sized devices) has become such a universal human activity that it's theater, with its large dramatic gestures and fixed spectatorial perspective, that native screen-gazers have to learn to see. But for decades after its emergence, cinema struggled to be seen as anything more than a technological curiosity or a threat to public morals.

Just as film was steadily colonizing the spaces once devoted to theater— to Keaton's dismay, his favorite New York vaudeville house, Hammerstein's Victoria, switched over to an all-movie format in 1915—so movie coverage, whether in the form of reviews, morally alarmist essays, trade-paper gossip, or celebrity profiles, first appeared in publications created to cover the stage. As the movie industry grew in scale and importance, its coverage in the press split into a few major categories. There were reviews and film-related features in the general interest press, trade papers created especially for the industry, and specialized photo- and gossip-filled magazines for fans. The growing division of labor between writer and publicist would soon require entertainment journalists to build relationships with press representatives and stars. But in the frontier days of the medium, often one person simply did both jobs at once.

The *Motion Picture Story Magazine*, generally regarded as the first periodical directed at film fans rather than at the industry, debuted in 1911. For the first few years of its existence, even after the name was shortened to *Motion Picture Magazine* in 1914, it would be devoted almost entirely to short stories fleshed out from the scenarios of current films. A typical early issue might contain a dozen or more complete pieces of what we would now call fan fiction, illustrated with stills from the movies in question, along with half a dozen poems devoted to moving-picture themes. The back of the book was for reader contests and polls ("Who is your favorite picture player?"), write-in Q&A columns, and articles on the social aspects of moviegoing. In the table of contents for the August 1911 issue, a reflection on "The Religious Possibilities of the Motion Picture" serenely rubs elbows with "The Cash Prize Contest."[5]

A poem that appeared in the same magazine the following year marked the first appearance in print of future fan-magazine fixture Gladys Hall, who would write soft-focus celebrity profiles and a widely syndicated column about the Hollywood scene over the next six decades. In this bit of verse, entitled "Fetterless," Hall praises the young art in fulsome, almost spiritual terms, as if to defend it from the accusations of triviality and sinfulness that had dogged it since its earliest years:

> The lurid desert, tropical; abysmal grandeur of the snow,
> Life moving, regal in the courts, or squalor-stricken 'mid the low,
> War's clarion cry—the calm of peace—may be yours at the Photoshow.
>
> Love, trapped in dress of centuries gone, knights and their dames of fair
>   conceit,
> And deeds of lion-hearted men who know no fear, brook no defeat;
> Life, many-colored, vari-hued upon the Motion Picture sheet.

You who seek rest in bigger things—who weary for a broader way,

You who are heart-sick, sore distrest from petty trials of the day,

May sound the depths of all mankind at God's own gift, the Photoplay.[6]

But the *Motion Picture Story Magazine*'s most popular feature, and one that would be replicated in many fan magazines to come, was the Answer Man column, a multi-page section whose anonymous author fielded questions sent in by curious picture fans around the country. The term "picture fan" was itself a coinage of the *Motion Picture Story Magazine*; "fan" had been in use for followers of baseball since the 1800s, and after expanding into a more general name for aficionados of sports and theater, was first proposed as a word for movie lovers in the magazine's pages in 1911.

As the twentieth century's second decade got underway, many movie actors were growing famous enough to build their own mobile fan followings, to the initial dismay of producers who preferred to keep stars' identities secret and their salaries low. Until the use of onscreen credits became common in the mid-teens, if a certain actor or actress caught your fancy, the only way to identify him or her was to write in to your favorite publication's "answer man" and to keep buying issues of the magazine until your question got a reply. This was a cozy arrangement both for magazine publishers and for film studios, who soon realized that keeping their stars' names secret would be much less lucrative in the long run than allowing them to build a loyal fan base.

The original *Motion Picture Story* "answer man," who never used a byline, was in fact a woman, Elizabeth M. Heinemann. Most of the questions she fielded came from people seeking either to identify actors from recent pictures or to track the movement of players from one film company to another. Gossip about stars' private lives was explicitly discouraged. An early column laid out the ground rules in a stern header: "Information about the matrimonial alliances of the players and other purely personal matters will not be answered. *Questions concerning the marriages of players will be completely ignored.*"

The Answer Man reminded his (her) readers that not every studio had yet lifted the ban on revealing actors' identities: "No questions can be answered relating to the identity of the Biograph players." A letter writer identified as "Miss D. B." was scolded for breaching this last rule: "The pretty light-haired Biograph player has no name. None of the Biograph players have. You ask that, and then tell us that you are a constant reader!"

To scan these columns at a century's remove is to see modern celebrity culture in embryonic form. The short, decontextualized bursts of information dispensed by the Answer Man read for all the world like posts on a message board, or tweets. There's no particular reason we should care more than a century later that "Brown Eyes" once needed to know that "Olive Golden was the sister in *Tess of the Storm Country*," or to share in Mrs. G. K. from Brooklyn's maternal disappointment upon learning that "something more than prettiness is demanded of a Motion Picture baby actress." But the vectors of fantasy and desire that circulate through the Answer Man columns retain their power to fascinate.

Before the relationship between mass-produced entertainment and mass media had settled into a fixed pattern, with publishers, film studios, and advertisers working in tandem to entertain audiences while relieving them of their cash, movie magazines were a place for fans to satisfy their curiosity about the new medium and push the boundaries of what they were allowed to know about the figures who transfixed them onscreen. To write to the Answer Man, especially about topics that were officially forbidden, was to help shape the future of movie coverage and indirectly of the motion-picture industry.

Launching later in the same year as *Motion Picture Story* was the lavishly illustrated *Photoplay*, long-reigning queen of the Hollywood fan magazines. It continued to be published weekly until 1980, by which point it had merged with other publications to form *Photoplay and TV Mirror* and was as likely to feature a cover story on the lead actresses of *Dallas* as on the film stars of the day. Handsomely designed and packed with full-page studio portraits, *Photoplay* split the difference between fan-pleasing gossip and studio-pleasing gauziness. Its worldly and well-connected editor,

James R. Quirk, had no qualms about sharing the marital status of the stars: a 1915 cover line cheerily promised that an article within would clarify "who's married to whom." In that same issue, a Q&A column similar to *Motion Picture Story*'s (if less sprawling in scope) informed an inquisitive reader that Mary Pickford was indeed the wife of the actor Owen Moore, though the author drew the line at revealing the couple's religious affiliation: "What difference does it really make what their religion is?"

Five years later, when Pickford divorced Moore to marry the swashbuckling action star Douglas Fairbanks—who for his part left his wife and young son, the future actor Douglas Fairbanks Jr.—*Photoplay* was instrumental in presenting the story in such a way as to shield the two stars from scandal. Far from being framed as a sordid double infidelity, the "Pickford-Fairbanks wooing" was proclaimed "one of the greatest love stories of all time": "It is high time the film of their narrative is tinted with the sentimental blue of eventide that so long has been lacking." *Photoplay*'s tint job worked, and Doug and Mary reigned as the undisputed royal couple of Hollywood throughout the 1920s.

Like *Motion Picture Story*, *Photoplay* featured short fiction, but in addition to padding out the plots of current movies, its stories sometimes took place at the intersection of Hollywood fantasy and everyday life. A common plot line involved some sort of romantic intrigue between a film actor and an ordinary mortal, either for the purposes of vicarious wish fulfillment or, just as often, to deromanticize the apparent specialness of those involved in the picture business. One such story in the October 1923 issue of *Photoplay*, "The Stuffed Shirt," made mention of Keaton in a way that shows how stars populated the imaginations of fans, not only as romantic ideals (a role in which slapstick comedians were seldom cast) but as models for social behavior.

The heroine, an ordinary girl called Norma Lawrence, falls for an actor named William B. Gaites, "the screen's most masculine personality." When he calls on her to go walking for their first date, he brings along a "big brute of a police dog" who will soon become crucial to the story, explaining, "No motion picture actor can claim to have arrived until he owns a police dog, Buster Keaton says, so I finally got one." When his dog attacks a stranger's dog in the street, endangering its life, the faux-rugged screen personality is revealed as a sniveling coward when he shrinks away from breaking up the fight.[7]

It was true that Keaton then owned just such a dog, a German shepherd named Captain that Constance Talmadge had given him as a wedding present, and who often appeared with his owner in publicity shots. I haven't been able to find anyplace where Keaton declares police-dog ownership a prerequisite for stardom. But the comedian's glancing cameo in a work of fiction intended for movie-mad women (the target demographic of magazines like *Photoplay*) tells us something about the way fan magazines served both to prop up the personas of popular performers and to encourage audience identification. Just as the reader of the story is invited to imagine herself in the place of the protagonist, the fictional William Gaites aspires to real star status by imitating the manly pet ownership of Buster Keaton. Like the "Answer Man" write-in columns, the film magazine fiction of the teens and twenties provides a glimpse into the hall of mirrors that was early movie fandom. Moving pictures had become more than a thrilling novelty. They were invading hearts and minds, changing popular notions of how to live and whom to love.

Photoplay was important to the developing film industry as more than a repository for the questions and fantasies of fans. It was also one of the first magazines to feature something like genuine criticism alongside the studio-approved puffery. "The Shadow Stage," a recurring column beginning in the mid-teens, offered capsule reviews of current movies that didn't hesitate to pan those the critic deemed to be real dogs. Cecil B. DeMille's *The Golden Bed* (1923) came in for a drubbing: "A lavishly stupid spectacle. A pearl onion in a platinum setting." Theda Bara in the much-hyped, and now lost, *Cleopatra* (1917) was "brazen in a ponderous manner." A 1924 comedy called *Mile-a-Minute Morgan* "might have been worse, but it doesn't seem possible."

Even stars like Mary Pickford, adoringly profiled in issue after issue, were not immune to critique if their latest effort was deemed a disappointment. Only months after *Photoplay* celebrated the Pickford-Fairbanks marriage as "the story of filmdom's greatest romance, with a real-life moonlight fadeout," the former theater critic Burns Mantle, writing in "The Shadow Stage," noted that in Pickford's latest drama, the aptly titled *Suds*, "the pathos . . . is laid on a bit thick."

But this early *Photoplay* feature still lacked some crucial features of movie criticism as it's now practiced: contextual analysis and a unitary authorial voice. The blurbs in the "Shadow Stage" section were very short, often allowing space for only a single line of evaluation after the cast list and basic plot line were laid out. They evaluated movies only in relation to other movies, not to politics or the larger cultural scene. And the column's authorship was collective: in some issues it was the magazine's editor in chief James Quirk who wrote the copy, in others his coeditor Julian Johnson, the ex-drama critic Burns Mantle, the gossip maven Adela Rogers St. Johns, or some anonymous combination of these contributors and others. The notion of a single critic with a recognizable style and point of view, associated with a single popular publication—especially one not exclusively dedicated to film—only started to take shape around 1920. If we can say Buster Keaton was born along with the movies, there is also a case to be made that the birth of film criticism as we know it coincided more or less exactly with the start of his solo filmmaking career.

18

Battle-Scarred Risibilities

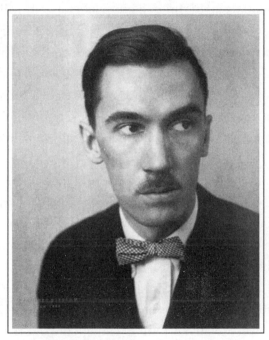

Robert Sherwood, 1925.

One of Keaton's earliest and most enthusiastic critical champions was Robert Sherwood at *Life*, then in its first incarnation as a satirical humor magazine rather than the general-interest photojournalism weekly it became after *Time* publisher Henry Luce bought it in 1936. Sherwood was a ubiquitous figure in the intellectual, cultural, and political life of the 1920s, '30s, and '40s, a six-foot-seven World War I combat veteran who went from Algonquin Round Table wit and film critic about town to Pulitzer Prize–winning playwright, presidential speechwriter and adviser, and Oscar-winning screenwriter. In the mid-1920s he also tried, briefly and unsuccessfully, to write a scenario for a Buster Keaton comedy—but we'll get there in a bit.

Bob Sherwood joined the staff of *Life* in 1920, when he was only twenty-four (a year younger than Buster). He was the pampered son of a cultured and well-off New York family and had been expelled from Harvard for spending all his time staging elaborate satirical revues rather than attending classes. But he had also already lived through a shattering experience that would shape the rest of his life. While he was serving at the French front with the Canadian Black Watch regiment—the US military had rejected him on the basis of his height—he was first hospitalized for exposure to tear gas and soon after sent on a mission through no-man's-land, where, still physically and mentally impaired from the gas inhalation, he fell into a German booby trap. It was a story he sometimes embellished after the war to make the circumstances sound slightly more heroic, but the reality was bad enough: the trap was a pit lined with sharp stakes and filled with barbed wire where Sherwood incurred painful leg wounds that, combined with lingering heart damage from the chemical attack, earned him an early release in 1917.

Compared to the paralyzed and badly burned soldiers he saw being treated alongside him during his months-long recovery in England, Sherwood's injuries were relatively minor. Though the injuries that sent him home eventually healed, he sustained permanent physical and psychic damage—for the rest of his life he would suffer from attacks of tic douloureux, a painful nervous condition of the face that worsened as he aged.

The brutality and senseless death Sherwood witnessed at the front never ceased to inform his work. His great subject, whether as a critic, dramatist, biographer, or political speechwriter, would remain the moral paradox of war: its unspeakable cost, its grotesque absurdity, and its occasional tragic necessity. In the words of his biographer Harriet Hyman Alonso, Sherwood went to war a "starry-eyed patriot" and came back a committed pacifist. But that commitment, fierce as it was, would shift in the years between the two world wars. By the time he began writing speeches for President Franklin Roosevelt in the late 1930s, Sherwood believed in the moral urgency of engaging in the fight against fascism as passionately as he had argued for the cause of peace in the 1920s.[1]

Sherwood's first job in publishing was as an editorial assistant at *Vanity Fair*. There he met the slightly older (but still very young) Dorothy Parker and Robert Benchley, who took a shine to the shy but sharp-witted Bob and began inviting him to their near-daily alcohol-fueled lunches at the Algonquin, a midtown hotel whose name soon became associated with their particular brand of rapid-fire repartee. All three of the friends lost their jobs in 1920 after a dispute with management: when they complained about low wages, a memorandum was circulated forbidding employees to discuss their salaries. Sherwood, Parker, and Benchley promptly made signs to wear around their necks detailing their exact rates of pay.

Parker went freelance, eventually moving to Hollywood to write screenplays, while Benchley spun his unique brand of absurdist humor into a long career as a *Life* theater critic, a *New Yorker* wag, a stage monologist, and, with the coming of the talkies, a film personality. Sherwood pursued a career path none of his wisecracking lunch mates could have predicted, going from magazine journalist to Broadway dramatist to wartime information officer. For the next eight years at *Life*, the last three as the magazine's editor in chief as well as its movie reviewer, he earned the title one colleague would bestow on him: "the dean of American film criticism."

Though his weekly column was titled "The Silent Drama," Sherwood wrote just as often about comedy, and from his earliest days at the magazine he made a point of championing Keaton's work. This was the case even though Buster was then still making two-reel shorts, a form not generally afforded close critical attention. The critic's first-ever mention of the comedian acknowledges this when he includes *One Week* in a 1920 roundup of "the short and frivolous films which have succeeded in tickling our battle-scarred risibilities."[2]

Late in 1921 Sherwood published a list of the ten best pictures of that year, a critical tradition that was already familiar enough for him to ironize about it: "Ten seems to have been designated by unwritten law as the official number of best pictures that can be produced in one year, and one never hears of the 'five best' or the 'twenty best.'"[3] Among the ten he chose—including Chaplin's debut feature *The Kid*, the Rudolph Valentino–starring World War I epic *The Four Horsemen of the Apocalypse*, and the Anita Loos–scripted Constance Talmadge vehicle *A Woman's Place*—the only short film included was *One Week*. It was also the only title on the list that had in fact been released in 1920, a discrepancy that speaks to the drawn-out release schedules of the era, but also to Sherwood's willingness to bend the rules out of fondness for Keaton's comedy.

When Keaton did break into features in 1923 with *Three Ages*, a spoof of D. W. Griffith's transhistorical epic *Intolerance*, Sherwood's praise remained lavish, even for a movie now regarded as one of Keaton's weaker features. Sherwood, never a fan of Griffith's sentimental pomposity, used Keaton's sendup as an excuse to get in a dig at the master: "*Three Ages*, in which Buster Keaton tumbles through the Cro-Magnon period, the Roman era and the present day, is just about as incoherent as *Intolerance* and about fifty times as funny." His *Three Ages* review ends with an allusion to world politics that hints at his future work as a playwright and presidential speechwriter, and also pushes film criticism in a new direction as he brings events outside the theater to bear on his experience inside it:

> Buster Keaton is one of the few genuinely funny men of our time. . . .
> He has helped to keep this much-molested human race in good humor,
> at a time when it has nothing but high taxes, United States Senators,
> coal strikes, banana shortages, wrong numbers and Signor Mussolini to
> think about.[4]

The Playhouse, a 1922 short in which Keaton used cutting-edge camera trickery to create the illusion of a vaudeville theater where he played every role including the audience, brought out Sherwood's speculative side. "If ever we want to punish our very unborn offspring severely," his review begins, "we shall tell him, or her—or them, that he (she, they) cannot go to see Buster Keaton. Then we shall go out and kick ourself for being an unmerciful parent."[5]

Sherwood's particular appreciation of the scene in which Buster takes the place of a trained ape he's accidentally let out of its cage demonstrates his attunement to the nuances of Keaton's mimicry. Though Buster's incarnation of the primate is "more sophisticated than his brother of the Borneo jungle," writes Sherwood, the comedian "nevertheless carries on the simian tradition of light-hearted whimsicality and delicate buffoonery with a touching fidelity and sincerity. Detail upon detail, he has built up a consummate monument of characterization that is a fitting tribute to his great understanding of, and broad sympathy for, a humble people."[6]

Sherwood often treated Lloyd and Keaton as neck-and-neck rivals in the race for second place to Chaplin, even if he had a personal soft spot for Keaton's bracing pessimism. On one occasion he ran identically worded side-by-side rave reviews of Lloyd's and Keaton's latest releases, changing only the proper names and movie titles, as if to drive home the point that the two stars were, to his eye, equally worthy of esteem.

But above and beyond all such comparisons ran Sherwood's profound esteem for silent comedy itself. His write-up of *The Paleface*, a 1922 Keaton short whose use of white actors in Native American "redface" now makes it tough to watch, becomes less a review of a particular movie than a meditation on the possibilities of the form:

> It is strange that silent drama should have reached its highest level in the comic field. Here, and here alone, it is pre-eminent. Nothing that is being produced in literature or in the drama is as funny as a good Chaplin, Lloyd or Keaton comedy. The efforts of these three young men approximate art more closely than anything else that the movies have offered.

Sherwood's *The Best Moving Pictures of 1922–23* was a sort of glorified top-ten list in book form, intended to be the first volume of an annual tradition, though only one such collection was ever published. All the films mentioned in the main body of the book were of feature length, so Keaton, whose first feature, *Three Ages*, wasn't released until late 1923, didn't make it into the official roundup. But Sherwood had a special place in his heart for the logic-free absurdity of the two-reel comedy short, and in a coda devoted specifically to such pictures, he mentioned Keaton before all others:

> Among the comedians, of whom there are a great number, the undisputed leader has been Buster Keaton. He has taken the place held first by Charlie Chaplin and subsequently by Harold Lloyd—both of whom are now definitely committed to a policy of feature pictures. Keaton, whose incredibly solemn visage is not the least effective of his comic attributes, has made a number of pictures this year that have been distinctly and individually his own. In collaboration with his director, Eddie Cline, he has produced "The Paleface," "The Frozen North," "Cops" and "My Wife's Relations"—all of which were glorious examples of divine nonsense.

Sherwood was the first critic to note that the former vaudeville knockabout, until recently known best as an Arbuckle sidekick, was bringing something unique to film comedy. "Buster Keaton is a distinct asset to the movies," he wrote in a 1922 column that rounded up three Keaton shorts: *The Frozen North, The Electric House,* and *His Wife's Relations.* "He can attract people who would never think of going to a picture palace to see anyone else. Moreover, he can impress a weary world with the vitally important fact that life, after all, is a foolishly inconsequential affair."

The critic's admiration for Keaton was such that he grew protective when other performers horned in on material that, to his mind, belonged to the poker-faced comic. Though he adored Douglas Fairbanks in action-adventure mode—he called *The Three Musketeers* "everybody's dream of what a movie should be, come true"—Sherwood was unimpressed by Fairbanks's 1921 venture into slapstick, *The Nut.* His review allowed that "it is unquestionably amusing—in an idiotic way," but declared it "an awful drop from *The Mark of Zorro*" and concluded that "Fairbanks has no right to do this sort of thing, which constitutes an actual incursion into Buster Keaton's territory." When he noticed Keaton engaging in similar poaching, Sherwood did not hesitate to point it out. His one-line review of *The Haunted House,* a short that came out the same year as *The Nut,* notes that "Buster Keaton borrows some tricks from other comedians which are not quite as good as his own."

Sherwood would not have been the critic he was if he were not able to respond negatively to the work of even his most beloved auteurs. What is striking about the Keaton features that failed to win him over is that they are among those today considered the filmmaker's best. When *The Navigator,* the biggest commercial success of Keaton's independent career and the film he often cited as his own favorite, came out in 1926, Sherwood's response was lukewarm. "Some day," he wrote, "Buster Keaton will gain a capability for sustained effort — and then we, who are called upon to attend all the major movie events, shall see the funniest comedy in history." He allowed that *The Navigator's* story, which strands Buster's incompetent millionaire Rollo Treadway on an abandoned ship with an equally feckless love interest (Kathryn McGuire), made room for "some gloriously comic material," but regretted that the good stuff had to exist alongside "some that is just plain stupid."

Sherwood's problem with *The Navigator* was mainly structural. The comedian, he said, "has developed his points with amazing ingenuity, but he has not been able to figure out the shortest distance between them." The evolving playwright and the evolving filmmaker had diverging ideas of what story structure should be. Was a well-crafted narrative to be valued for its clarity of theme, as would be the case with the verbally deft comedies of ideas that later made Sherwood a Pulitzer Prize–winning playwright, or for its ingenuity at combining spectacle, character, and action, a skill Keaton had by then been honing for over twenty years?

For all his reservations about *The Navigator's* quite literally drifting plot line, Sherwood recommends the movie as a whole to his readers, assuring them they will "have occasion to be devoutly grateful for the laughs that it affords. Still," he concludes, "I can't help wishing that Buster

Keaton possessed the architectural skill of that shrewd craftsman, Harold Lloyd." The review ends with a concession that "Buster Keaton, in his own right, is twice as funny as Harold Lloyd." But according to Sherwood "it is Lloyd that has the brains; and brains are still of vast importance, even in the movie business."

To a twenty-first-century viewer it is puzzling to understand how *The Navigator*, with its meticulously timed chase across multiple decks of a football-field-sized ocean liner, its groundbreaking underwater photography sequence, and its many ingenious prop gags, could be construed as in need of a brain transplant from Harold Lloyd or anyone else. But it is true that Lloyd tended to pack his films with more plot and character than the minimalist, action-focused Keaton.

Not long after *The Navigator*'s release, Keaton prevailed on Sherwood to write a scenario for his next picture. Keaton may have always maintained that he was indifferent to critics—"this critic likes you and this one don't, so that's that," he shrugged to one interviewer late in life—but he indicates in his memoir that he was familiar enough with Sherwood's work to sense their affinity. Sherwood's "perceptive and amusing film reviews," he told his ghostwriter Charles Samuels, showed that the critic had "a true comedy mind."

In the spring of 1925 a short *Variety* item announced that "Buster Keaton's next feature will be adapted from an original story by Robert Sherwood which the comedian acquired on his recent trip East." The working title, according to the *Los Angeles Times*, was *The Skyscraper*, and the movie was to be "built along new comedy lines."

What path those lines might have traced will never be known, because Sherwood's script was never finished. The concept he pitched sounds like a landlubbing twist on *The Navigator*, the very film he had just dismissed in his column as substandard Keaton. In *The Skyscraper*, Buster's character, the elevator operator on a sixty-story high-rise under construction, was to be stranded on the roof of the still-skeletal structure with the daughter of the building's architect after a workers' strike shut off all power. Like the seafaring couple in *The Navigator*, the pair would be forced to set up housekeeping in an inhospitable environment while looking for a means of escape.

Sherwood spent his two-week summer vacation that year working on the story with Keaton and his old vaudeville compatriot and newly hired gag writer Lex Neal, but they were unable to devise a clever way to end the film that would both sustain the suspense of the setup and avoid a deus ex machina rescue. (As Sherwood may well have pointed out in their story meetings, *The Navigator* ends on just such an unlikely resolution, with a submarine happening to surface beneath Buster and his girl in the nick of time to save them from drowning.)

The way Keaton described it, the problem had to do with a mismatch between Sherwood's cerebral style and the comedic intuition that usually guided the studio's writing team: "From time to time we brought famous and talented writers from New York. I do not recall a single one of those novelists, magazine writers, and Broadway playwrights who was able to write the sort of material we needed." Keaton's main writing partners up to that point, the comedy veterans Joseph Mitchell, Clyde Bruckman, and Jean Havez, had been, as he approvingly put it, "not word guys at all."

This wasn't quite accurate—Bruckman had gotten his start as a newspaper sportswriter and would later write sound comedies for Laurel and Hardy—but the point was clear. What made for a successful "writer" of silent comedy was a gift for bypassing language to craft a story that relied as completely as possible on the movement of bodies and objects through space. Keaton often told interviewers in the 1920s that the "scripts" for his studio's films could easily fit on a postcard, and if that card were lost it would be no great matter. And in the 1970s, after Buster was gone, Louise Keaton described to biographer Tom Dardis how her brother would spend hours moving silently through the house, absorbed in the mental composition he called his "writin'."

Sherwood understood and could describe the signature kineticism of Keaton's style as well as any writer ever has, but analysis, however astute, is a far cry from creation. The critic went home to New York that summer without having solved the conundrum of *The Skyscraper*'s ending, but neither he nor Keaton held their failed collaboration against the other. An older Buster told the story of seeing Sherwood, by then a speechwriter for President Roosevelt, stride past him in the lobby of London's Dorchester Hotel in 1940. Out of the corner of his mouth he muttered, "Stop worrying, Buster, I'll get you down off that building yet!"

It wasn't until the release of *The General*, the 1927 Civil War comedy that today is considered Keaton's crowning achievement and regularly named to lists of the best films of all time, that Sherwood had a response to a Keaton release that was not just negative (as were most of *The General*'s contemporary reviews) but actively repulsed. The fact that this dark comedy showed several explicit or implied deaths on the field of battle horrified the man who nine years earlier had survived chemical warfare and witnessed up close the death of several close comrades and an untold number of Germans.

Although Sherwood allowed that "the ingenuity displayed by Buster Keaton in keeping these possibly tedious chases alive is little short of incredible," and that he would rather watch *The General*, or Harold Lloyd's also disappointing concurrent release *The Kid Brother*, than "ninety-eight one-hundredths of the films that fate and the nature of my job force me to view," he was harsh in his condemnation of the movie's depiction of war. Keaton, he said, "has . . . displayed woefully bad judgment in deciding just where and when to stop . . . many of his gags at the end of the picture are in such gruesomely bad taste that the sympathetic spectator is inclined to look the other way."[7]

Sherwood must have taken offense at two moments in particular: the late scene where Buster's character's repeated attempts to brandish his sword finally send the blade flying from its hilt, conveniently dispatching a nearby Union sniper; and the sensational climactic shot of a locomotive crashing through a burning bridge into the river below, presumably killing anyone on board. "Someone should have told Buster that it is difficult to derive laughter from the sight of men being killed in battle," the *Life* critic wrote, in a sincere and polemical tone far removed from his usual urbane irony.

Sherwood was far from the only critic to scold the onetime pratfaller upon *The General*'s release. The reviewer at the *Akron Beacon-Journal*, Howard Wolf, agreed in strikingly similar wording that "Buster needs to be talked to." But Wolf's objection had nothing to do with *The General*'s comic representation of bloodshed. "Ever since the critics told Chaplin he was an artist," the Ohio reviewer complained, "the other buffoons and zanies of the celluloid have been fired by ambition." Why, he wondered, couldn't Keaton return to the "uproarious horseplay, pie throwing and comedy falls" of his earlier years?[8]

In point of fact, no pies were ever hurled in the course of an original Keaton production, but Wolf's point was clear: the attempt to combine comedy, action, and historical drama in a grand-scale period piece like *The General* was an unseemly overreach. Keaton should give up on expensive train chases and get back to his "stuffed clubs, blowtorches and boxing gloves full of horseshoes."

Sherwood's *General* pan is more complicated than the wish to reclaim some slapstick Eden, but he too expresses doubts about Keaton's "vaulting ambitions" and the "pretentious proportions" of the story. "He appears to be attempting to enter the 'epic' class," notes the *Life* critic with distaste. "Epic," for the bombast-allergic Sherwood, tended to be a word used only in parodic contexts. In a 1923 column titled "Historical Events," he gave a potted history of the cinema that listed 1895 as the year the "first movie critic coined the phrase 'screen-epic'" and 1920 as the one when "critics fear that supply of 'screen-epics' will be exhausted," with every milestone in between (the move from shorts to features, the release of Griffith's *Birth of a Nation*, and, later, his *Intolerance*) serving as an excuse for a repeated satirical chorus of the word.

As if to twist the knife, Sherwood concludes his review of *The General* by favorably mentioning a different recent Civil War comedy, noting that Keaton's train-chasing epic is "not nearly so good as Raymond Griffith's . . . *Hands Up!*" That now nearly forgotten 1926 hit featured the suave silk-top-hatted Griffith as a Confederate spy pursued militarily by Union officers and romantically by two pretty sisters. *Hands Up!* included two attempted executions and at least one casually comic onscreen death, incidents of war-related violence that seem not to have gotten in the way of Sherwood deeming the movie "darned funny." This may be because *Hands Up!* was an imaginary caper that took place on the periphery of the historical war, while *The General* took its story from a real-life occurrence involving real bloodshed. In fact, the historical event was far bloodier than in Keaton's retelling. The ten Confederate soldiers who conspired to hijack a train to slow the progress of the Union army (in the film, the sides are reversed) were all sentenced to death by hanging.

Sherwood's intense antipathy to *The General* is more than a one-off exception to the critic's long-standing fondness for Keaton's work. His distaste for the film is as much a matter of morals as of aesthetics. The element of *The General* that made Bob, a "sympathetic spectator," have to "look the other way" was *The General*'s use of comic violence in the service of an essentially apolitical story. Keaton's character, Johnnie Gray, is a southern railroad engineer who tries and fails to enlist in the Confederate army not out of patriotic duty but in order to impress the girl he loves, the poetically named Annabelle Lee (Marion Mack).

When Johnnie sets off in pursuit of the Union spies who have hijacked his beloved train, it's not in defense of the Confederacy's property but his own. The only thing he cares more about than Annabelle, as we learn from an early shot of him lovingly brushing a speck of dust off the engine, is that train, the "General" of the title. In one of the most memorable sequences Johnnie scrambles across the top of the train as it hurtles past fields full of soldiers on horseback riding into battle. He's so focused on keeping the wood-burning engine stocked with fuel that he's oblivious to the historic events unfolding around him. It was the idea of Buster placing himself outside history that was unacceptable to Sherwood, both as a veteran and as the politically engaged writer he was becoming.

The General was released in February 1927, just weeks before the opening of Sherwood's first Broadway hit, *The Road to Rome*. In this comedy set during the Punic Wars, a Roman noblewoman seduces the Carthaginian general Hannibal, then spends the night convincing him of the futility of warfare, ultimately halting his advance on the city. It is a combination of mildly racy sex farce and earnest pacifist tract that, while it now reads as dated, was utterly plausible as a crowd-pleaser and conversation-starter in the late 1920s, when the generation formed by World War I was just growing mature enough to reflect on the war's meaning.

Even before Sherwood turned to playwriting, the representation of war had been one of his chief critical obsessions. If a war film succeeded in his eyes, he praised it to the heavens. Rex Ingram's *The Four Horsemen of the Apocalypse*, the World War I saga that launched the career of Rudolph Valentino, was a "living, breathing answer to those who still refuse to take motion pictures seriously. Its production lifts the silent drama to an artistic plane that it has never touched before." Above all, it was the movie's commitment to a staunch antiwar stance that, for Sherwood, made it a film that "deserves—more than any other picture play that the war inspired—to be handed down to generations yet unborn, that they may see the horror and futility of the whole bloody mess." Conversely, the moment Sherwood detected any trace of jingoism, mawkishness, or, as he saw in *The General*'s case, failure to treat war with the moral seriousness it deserved, his scorn was withering. The 1927 wartime romance *Lilac Time* was "a fairly stupid epic" (that word again) costarring Gary Cooper and "an impish and over-strenuous Colleen Moore." The lavishly produced historical sagas of D. W. Griffith and Cecil B. DeMille were no more than "grandiose posturings."

When Chaplin's World War I–themed short *Shoulder Arms* was brought back for a revival run in 1922, Sherwood proclaimed it "the greatest comedy in movie history." This beloved 1918 hit was neither pro- nor antiwar but simply the portrait of a klutzy new conscript adjusting to life in the trenches; its supremely silly climax involves Charlie's clueless soldier making his way across no-man's-land camouflaged as a tree.

Shoulder Arms also contains battle scenes with implied offscreen deaths; while manning a machine gun in the trenches, Charlie keeps a running tally of victims on the chalkboard next to him. Yet Sherwood raised none of the moral objections that he had to *The General*. To him the film's one

"unutterably tragic" scene was not a death in combat but "the delivery of
the mail in the front line, when everyone gets a letter but Charlie."

Inevitably, his hyperbolic praise of the Chaplin short brought up the
two comedians to whom Chaplin was most often compared, then as now:
"Harold Lloyd and Buster Keaton are remarkably good; but there never
can be question of Chaplin's supremacy. He is the one real genius of
the lot." And harking back to the by then hoary debate about Chaplin's
status as a serious artist, Sherwood ends his review on the proposal that
the question be put to rest for good: "Anyone who can conscientiously
deny that this is art deserves to be housed in an institution."

The Robert Sherwood of the late 1920s was struggling with his relationship to war, not just as a film critic and budding playwright but as a
veteran and an American citizen. His life over the next two and a half
decades dramatized that struggle for the world to see. His plays in the
decade to come, like *Idiot's Delight*, *Abe Lincoln in Illinois*, and *There
Shall Be No Night*—all three of which won Pulitzers—told stories of at
first isolationist characters who slowly and painfully come to recognize
the necessity of engagement.

Sherwood's emotionally candid diaries showed him walking the same
line as he weighed his visceral disgust for war against his despair at the
rise of global fascism. While writing his play *Idiot's Delight* he considered
revising a character who was an arms trader to make him more sympathetic, then reconsidered after reading a callous quote from a real-life
munitions profiteer. "I believe that such people are the arch villains of
mortal creation," he wrote in 1936. "Such men are sons of bitches and
should so be represented."

After the successful nationwide tour of the anti-isolationist drama
There Shall Be No Night, Sherwood was approached by Harry Hopkins,
a close adviser to President Franklin Roosevelt. (Sherwood later wrote a
book about the working relationship between the two, a nine-hundred-
plus-page tome that won him his fourth and last Pulitzer Prize, this time
in the category of biography.) Hopkins had been eyeing Sherwood as a
potential speechwriter for the president's war mobilization effort.

Over the next few years, Sherwood grew close to Roosevelt and Hopkins, often living in the White House for extended periods as the three men collaborated on the language for the president's public addresses, radio announcements, and fireside chats. After the United States entered the war in 1941, Sherwood's role changed. America, he argued, needed a war propaganda department to combat the virulent Nazi disinformation machine. His impassioned case for a government body capable of launching a multimedia "peace offensive" against the Axis powers resulted in the founding of the Foreign Information Service, where Sherwood remained until the end of the war, helping, among other initiatives, to create the worldwide network of government-funded radio stations known as the Voice of America.

After the war, Sherwood reinvented himself yet again when he adapted a novella by a World War II correspondent—the interweaving stories of three returning soldiers, originally written in blank verse—into the screenplay for William Wyler's film *The Best Years of Our Lives*. That now-classic drama was a blockbuster hit, the highest-grossing film of 1946, and won seven Oscars, including one for Sherwood's script.

The Best Years of Our Lives has proven to be the most famous thing Bob Sherwood ever wrote, assuming he was telling the truth when he insisted that the enduring phrases associated with Roosevelt's wartime speeches—"a date which will live in infamy," etc.—came from the pen of the president himself. Wyler's film appears regularly on lists of the greatest American movies, and almost inevitably on those devoted to the best war films. The flaws Sherwood had been so quick to find in war-themed movies as a critic—cheap sentimentality, hollow patriotism, or the flippant lack of moral seriousness he objected to in *The General*—are nowhere to be found in this quiet, emotionally astute drama with its undercurrent of savage humor about the promised economic and technical wonders of the atomic age.

Sherwood died of a heart attack in 1955, aged only fifty-nine. He spent the last decade of his life in an uneasy relationship with the congealing hostilities of the Cold War. As his biographer put it, "after World War II,

Bob was politically confused." He publicly denounced the Hollywood blacklist and wrote a letter to President Eisenhower protesting Senator Joseph McCarthy's persecution of his contemporaries in the theater and film world after *The Best Years of Our Lives* was placed, absurdly, on a list of communist-sympathizing works. But Sherwood also wrote an anti-communist movie, the 1953 drama *Man on a Tightrope*, for the director Elia Kazan, who had alienated many of those same industry colleagues when he went before the committee to name names.

Bob's brand of romantic humanitarian idealism was ill suited to the chilly realpolitik of the arms-race era, and his writing late in life some-times floundered, sounding programmatic or hectoring where he had once displayed a light comic touch. But he never stopped defending free speech or lending his voice to initiatives for a system of world government, which he saw as the only way to forestall more global disasters like the two wars he had weathered. In the late 1940s he collaborated with Eleanor Roosevelt on the wording of the preamble for the United Nations' first Declaration of Human Rights.

Looking over the sweep of Sherwood's career, with its steady stream of prestigious awards and growing political and cultural influence, it would be easy to dismiss his *Life* magazine reviews of the 1920s as ephemeral fluff, a charge that is often leveled at culture criticism of any age. But his writing on Keaton, usually amounting to no more than a few hundred words at a time, includes some of the keenest observations made to date about that much-analyzed comedian.

Sherwood's film writing of the 1920s is, in a way, the prose equivalent of Keaton's comedy from the same era: playful, nimble, and buoyant, curious about new technology, allergic to pretense and sentiment. Like Keaton making the most of a prop, he seems interested in exploring what this new gadget of film criticism can do. During his eight years as *Life*'s weekly critic, Sherwood's unsnobbish enthusiasm for the new medium did much to break down the barrier between the old guard and the new. By the time he left the magazine in 1928, the year of King Vidor's *The Crowd*, Carl Theodor Dreyer's *The Passion of Joan of Arc*, and Keaton's

Steamboat Bill, Jr., no one was seriously arguing that movies could not be works of art.

Sherwood's last review of a Keaton film as *Life's* weekly critic was of *The Cameraman* in the fall of 1928. Like his write-up of *Steamboat Bill, Jr.* earlier that year, it was a typical Sherwood-on-Keaton rave. He described the scene where Buster, alone in Yankee Stadium, mimes a game with himself in the roles of pitcher, batter, and fielder as "beautiful and true and infinitely touching," "typical of Buster Keaton at his best."[9] But this review was also noteworthy for sharing column space with Sherwood's assessment of a very different current release: an Al Jolson musical titled *The Singing Fool*, which, after expressing some mild reservations, the critic deemed "the supreme triumph, to date, of the talkie."

A year after *The Jazz Singer* and a year before the stock market crash, Hollywood was in a convulsive period of transition. Theater managers around the country were frantically rewiring their houses for sound, and long-standing careers were being upended as new ones were set into motion. *The Cameraman*, the first and best film of Keaton's MGM period—and one of the last movies in which he had any share of creative control—still struck Sherwood as superior to the best that sound technology had to offer. "The talkies are progressing rapidly," he wrote in closing, "but it will be a long time before they can produce comedies that reach the old silent standard."[10] But time was exactly what silent films, and Keaton as an independent filmmaker, were fast running out of. Within a year he would appear in his last silent movie, *Spite Marriage*, and thereafter be subsumed into the MGM factory system, where he was no longer the creator of his own material, just another performer to be plugged into whatever script his bosses saw fit.

Sherwood did write about Keaton again, in a short blurb for the trade paper *Film Daily*. "Screen Comedian Out of His Element," reads the understated headline of Bob's 116-word burial of *Free and Easy*, the 1930 musical that marked the beginning of Buster's truly dark days at MGM. Sherwood was by then more focused on the Broadway stage and the troubling developments in Europe than on the business of Hollywood, and he seems unaware, as most fans must have been, that his pet comedian had signed away his freedom. As usual, Sherwood's reading of Keaton was dead-on. "Buster Keaton," he writes, "trying to imitate a standard musical-comedy clown, is no longer Buster Keaton and no longer funny."

Warming to his theme, he restates a favorite leitmotif from his *Life* column: that "it is in the field of comedy that the motion picture has reached its highest peaks of artistry and also of individuality." Given that distinction, he asks, "why . . . should a member of this mighty trio"—the trio of course being Chaplin, Lloyd, and Keaton, Sherwood's long-standing comic pantheon—"consider it necessary to wear musical comedy costumes and sing silly songs for the getting of a laugh?"[11]

It seems likely that Buster's life was by then in enough disarray—his marriage to Natalie crumbling, his drinking increasing, his legendary work ethic for the first time in his life starting to slacken—that he would have missed this small blurb in a trade daily. I hope so, because it's sad to imagine him, at a low point in his life, reading a devastating pan from the man who had once tried to rescue him from atop a skyscraper. But even if Buster did come across the item, I doubt he would have taken it personally. Keaton may not have been a "word guy," or have had much truck with the political struggles that defined Sherwood's life. But as one professional to another he must have sensed that a film critic, like a filmmaker, can only do their job well by telling the truth.

19

One for You, One for Me

The $42,000 train wreck in The General.

*T*he General* was considered an expensive bomb when it came out in early 1927. People went to see it, but in nowhere near the numbers they had gone a few years before to see *The Navigator*, another transportation-themed Keaton passion project. Not every critic objected to the film on the moral grounds that Robert Sherwood had in *Life*. But most reviewers converged on the opinion of the *New York Times*'s Mordaunt Hall, a reliable marker of consensus taste, that *The General* was "by no means so good as Mr. Keaton's previous efforts."[1] Today, Hall's complaint that "his vehicle might be described as a mixture of cast iron and jelly" reads more like praise than a putdown; it's the fact that *The General*'s trains seem more flexible and stunt-ready than your average speeding hunks of metal that makes the movie's action so pleasurable to watch.

The film's plot is almost mathematical in its symmetry: A train chase moves in one direction up to the midpoint, then reverses course as the pursuer becomes the pursued. Gags and stunts from the first half recur with variations in the second. This structure strikes modern viewers as elegantly simple, but it was seen by audiences in its day as monotonous. "Its principal comedy scene is built on that elementary bit, the chase, and you can't continue a fight for almost an hour and expect results," grumbled *Variety*. "There are some corking gags in the picture, but as they are all a part of the chase they are overshadowed."[2] Keaton fans accustomed to rapid-fire visual jokes may also have been confused to find his latest more of an action thriller than a comedy. Like the Three Keatons' old stage act, *The General* sought to elicit gasps as often as it did laughs.

The *Brooklyn Daily Eagle* published a rare rave, marveling that "hardly a foot of celluloid is ground out of the camera but the stoical comedian hasn't some amazing new trick to pull out of his sleeve to the renewed pleasure of the audience."[3] But most write-ups took the cooler tone of this wry headline from the *Los Angeles Daily Times*: "*The General* Has Moments of Fun and Locomotive Is Really Great Actor."[4] The *New York Daily Mirror*, the entertainment trade paper where Joe Keaton had once published embellished anecdotes about the Five Keatons' mishaps riding the rails, admonished Joe's now-grown son in a fittingly paternalistic tone to "pull yourself together, Buster. That's all."[5]

Critics also ironized about the movie's lavish budget, advance word of which had made it down the West Coast during filming. "No one denies his expenditure of a great deal of money in working to achieve an exceptional entertainment," read a small *Los Angeles Times* item dryly headlined "Opinions Vary." "And the picture is exceptional in every respect except for the small amount of mirth it creates." Even critics who praised *The General*'s virtues mentioned its budget: the *Brooklyn Daily Eagle* writer allowed that "Buster Keaton has made a financial faux pas, perhaps," but insisted that "it is this humble reviewer's opinion that it was worth all it cost and more."

The General has been called "the *Heaven's Gate* of the '20s."[6] There's some hyperbole in the comparison: Keaton's budget overruns never approached the scale of Michael Cimino's 1980 white elephant of a western, nor did his movie's poor returns at the box office threaten to bring down all of United Artists. But taking a longer film-historical view, the analogy holds up. Like *Heaven's Gate, The General* was less a cause than a symptom of the end of a certain way of making movies. The independent production model that for ten years had allowed Buster the freedom to make exactly the movies he wanted, first at Comique and then at his own self-named studio, was collapsing under its own weight.

Keaton was hardly the only profligate visionary of the silent era: the Austrian émigré Erich von Stroheim, whose original (now lost) cut of his 1924 masterpiece *Greed* ran to nearly eight hours, was a far more flagrant example of that phenomenon. But the move toward a corporatized studio system came about for systemic reasons that were larger than the choices of any one filmmaker. It was simply more efficient and profitable for a large studio to churn out and market its own entertainment product—what today we would call "content"—than it was for a small-scale shop like Keaton's to recoup the investment of an individual producer.

For Joe Schenck, *The General* represented little more than his clever but impractical brother-in-law's costly folly, and a sign that things needed to change in their producing partnership. The film's so-so box-office take didn't even begin to recoup its cost. The climactic train crash shot alone had cost $42,000, or more than $650,000 in today's dollars; an entire 215-foot-long trestle bridge had been built for that scene just for the purpose of being destroyed.[7] Although the incomplete records from the medium's early days make it hard to know for sure, that fifteen-second-long take of a locomotive falling through a burning bridge into a river was probably the most expensive single shot in silent film history.

The production of *The General* marked the high point of, and would put an end to, Buster's preferred approach to running a film set. Never again would he get that much money or that much freedom to make a movie exactly the way he wanted. Clyde Bruckman, Keaton's longtime gag writer and the credited codirector on *The General*, described the Keaton team's relaxed but focused way of working in glowing terms almost thirty years later:

> Buster was a guy you worked with—not *for*. Oh sure, it's a cliché, like the happy family. But try it some time. . . . Harold Lloyd was wonderful to me. So was Bill [W. C.] Fields. But with Bus you belonged.[8]

A high level of performance was expected, certainly; among the rare times the conflict-averse Buster snapped was when a cast or crew member seemed to be slacking on the job. But a Keaton set was generally a congenial workplace, with breaks between afternoon setups for games of cards or an inning or two of idea-generating baseball.

It was a managerial style that came naturally to the former star of a traveling family act. In Buster's mind, during the years the Buster Keaton Studio was in operation he was running a company, not in the business sense of the word—it was Schenck who took care of that end—but the theatrical one. Writers like Bruckman, Eddie Cline, and Jean Havez, cameramen like Elgin Lessley and Dev Jennings, and the ever-ingenious production designer Fred Gabourie had worked with Keaton faithfully (although not exclusively) for years, conceiving and executing complex projects from the ground up. Their job was to think up fantastical new sets, gags, and action sequences; Joe Schenck's job was to pay for it.

The rotating house of *One Week* was an early prototype for a succession of ever more elaborate sets, props, and stunts. The custom-built period train of *Our Hospitality*, the underwater photography sequence in *The Navigator*, that spectacular burning bridge: the major set pieces from Keaton's independent period are all expressions of the collective creativity of his team. If those falling housefronts and avalanches of papier-mâché boulders seem to have emerged straight from the Buster character's unconscious, it is because the real-life Buster was able to devise and create exactly the effects he envisioned with a crew of highly skilled craftsmen who trusted his intuition and got his sense of humor. Often, in fact, it was a trusted member of his inner circle who came up with the key idea or image for a film. Bruckman gave Keaton a copy of the Civil War memoir that inspired *The General*. Lessley, always up for a technical challenge, suggested *Sherlock, Jr.*'s central image of a projectionist who dreams his way inside a movie screen. Gabourie discovered a massive freight ship about to be auctioned off for parts and immediately called his boss, insisting Keaton lease the craft sight unseen and build *The Navigator* around it.

In another way of life inherited from Buster's theatrical past, the cast of a Keaton comedy often included one or more members of his real-life family. Natalie and the one-year-old Joseph Jr. (billed as "Buster Keaton Jr.") appeared in *Our Hospitality*, Joe Keaton the elder played a series of small roles including an angry Union officer in *The General*, and Louise was sometimes on hand to serve as the stand-in or stunt double to Buster's leading lady.

The filming of *The General* had taken place in the summer of 1926 in Cottage Grove, Oregon, where the terrain was deemed sufficiently scenic and the train tracks in good enough shape to stand in for the Civil War–era South. The cast's and crew's families were invited to accompany them on the shoot, and their presence turned the small Pacific Northwest lumber town into a buzzing Hollywood colony in exile. Far from being regarded as interlopers, *The General*'s cast and crew were warmly received by the Cottage Grove natives. People drove in from neighboring towns to observe the filming, Buster played charity baseball games with the Lions Club team in nearby Eugene, and the residents of Cottage Grove threw dances and picnics for the visitors from Hollywood. One crew member married a local girl in an impromptu ceremony arranged by Keaton and other members of the company in the lobby of their hotel.

Extras were hired from among the locals, the tiny main street was dressed with Civil War–era building façades, and around five hundred troops from the Oregon National Guard were brought in to play members of the Confederate and Union armies. As Buster recalled to an interviewer in the early 1960s, "I housed the men for a week in tourist cars given to us by the Union Pacific . . . and put 'em in blue uniforms and bring 'em goin' from right to left, and take 'em out, put 'em in gray uniforms, bring 'em goin' from left to right."[9]

The *Cottage Grove Sentinel* reported almost daily, and sometimes multiple times per day, on developments related to the *General* shoot. The day the collapsing-bridge shot was filmed after extensive scouting, construction, and preparation, thousands of onlookers were on hand to watch. "After the engine had taken its pretty spill," reported the *Sentinel*, "taut nerves of those handling the production were greatly relieved and Buster himself was happy as a kid."[10] The town's goodwill toward the *General* crew continued even after sparks from one of the train's engines caused a forest fire that the crew had to stop filming to help put out. After the flames were extinguished, the air was too smoky to continue filming, and production was shut down for six weeks.

For the second Oregon shoot, in the name of efficiency, Buster had the cast and crew's families stay at home. But *The General* continued to be his baby, with a generous portion of its budget dedicated to re-creating historical details to a degree of authenticity unusual at the time. That level of care has paid off in the film's long-term reputation. Stills from *The General* are often compared to Mathew Brady photographs of the Civil War, even by viewers unaware that Buster and the crew started the production process by poring over those very images.

Up until the mid-1920s, Joe Schenck's mini-empire of independent studios had been among Hollywood's most successful examples of how large-scale movie production could work outside the corporate studio system. But starting around 1925, few of the films released by any of Schenck's companies were turning a meaningful profit. The early Hollywood model of the individual producer as patron was giving way to the factory-style model of the studio. These changes would not torpedo Buster's life until the coming of sound two years later. But after the economic fiasco of *The General*, Keaton was under pressure from Schenck to make a box-office hit. The tacit understanding as they chose his next project was "one for you, one for me": no more brainstorming crazy stunts on the fly on remote location shoots that had to be rescheduled around forest fires. Whatever Buster did next needed to be crowd-pleasing, reasonably budgeted, and above all, profitable.

The project he ended up with, *College*, was the safest of bets in the fall of 1927. Comedies set in the world of higher education were then, to use a slang term that might well have appeared in one of them, the berries. Just two years before, Harold Lloyd's *The Freshman* had been a huge box-office hit. It would prove to be the single most successful film of Lloyd's career and one of the top-grossing comedies of the 1920s.

By the time *The Freshman* came along, the "college movie" was already familiar enough to constitute a cliché worth sending up. That movie opens with Lloyd's protagonist, Harold Lamb, posing in front of a mirror next to a poster of his idol Lester Laurel, star of the movie *The College Hero*. (At the time the title was fictional, but two years later, with the campus-movie craze still raging, Columbia Pictures would release a film by that very name.) Harold's dearest hope is that, once he enrolls at the also-fictional Tate University, he will achieve the popularity of the letter-sweatered paragon who beams down from the poster.

A few years later, after both Lloyd's and Keaton's college-themed movies had come out, Robert Sherwood, ever the keen observer of pop culture trends of his time, dryly noted the inescapability of movies set on sports-mad coed campuses. In a 1928 column he provided a list of clichés of the genre, almost all of which appear in some form in both *The Freshman* and *College*: the "puny, bespectacled grind" who proves himself to be one of the "rough and worthy he-men of the silent drama"; the presence of "crabby old professors who pretend to abominate football" (*College*'s version of this character is played by the diminutive, sour-faced character actor Snitz Edwards, who had several memorable roles in Keaton films); and the "melodramatic home team win in the last minute of play."

Everything college-related was in vogue throughout the 1920s, from intercollegiate football—until the 1950s, a far more popular sport than the professional version—to the eccentric fashions associated with campus life. Some of these show up on characters in *College*: felt beanies with panels in school colors, plus-four knickers, letterman sweaters. Although he never dons one in *College*—probably because his character is meant to be of modest means—Keaton is pictured in the promotional poster, drawn by the quintessential Jazz Age cartoonist John Held Jr., wearing one of the more extravagant campus looks of the time: a floor-length raccoon coat. One year later, in *Steamboat Bill, Jr.*, Buster's character starts off the movie dressed as an over-the-top parody of a pretentious college dandy, complete with beret, pencil mustache, and ukulele.

Not only in film and fashion but in popular literature, college life in the 1920s was inescapable. F. Scott Fitzgerald's first novel, *This Side of Paradise*, published to wild success in 1920, tells the largely autobiographical story of a middle-class midwestern boy's fascination and eventual disillusionment with the campus culture of Princeton. In 1924, Percy Marks, a college English instructor, published the bestselling novel *The Plastic Age*, a dishy tell-all about sexual shenanigans on campus. The next year the film version launched the career of the arch-flapper Clara Bow. A series of bestselling novels and comic strips featured a character named Frank Merriwell, an impossibly clean-cut college student who excelled at every sport. Just after contemplating his screen idol at the beginning of *The Freshman*, Lloyd's aspiring big man on campus settles down to leaf through a stack of books that includes a Frank Merriwell novel.

In a multimedia feedback loop, the movies, books, and fashion spreads that glamorized campus life became marketing opportunities for the idea of college itself. Red Grange, the legendary University of Illinois quarterback, played a college star in a hit 1926 film, *One Minute to Play*. *Motion Picture* magazine's write-up of *The Plastic Age* (1925) describes the getup of Gilbert Roland's caddish antihero in language indistinguishable from fashion copy: "the English sport jacket, the plus-four knickers, the ivory cigaret [*sic*] holder, and best of all, that savoir-faire air that the girls love."

College girls, too, inspired all sorts of fashion crazes, some overlapping with the archetype of the flapper: cloche hats, middy sailor blouses, and long sweaters over daring knee-length tennis skirts. The popular image of a college youth, male or female, was of someone socially sophisticated, mad for sports, and in many cases (though not in Lloyd's or Keaton's) more sexually adventurous than their old-fashioned peers. In *College* and *The Freshman*, as in most Jazz Age representations of campus life, the dull notion of attending classes or studying played virtually no part at all.

There were material reasons for the prevalence of higher education as a theme in mass entertainment. The post–World War I economic boom and a soaring stock market had created enough surplus wealth for college to start to seem like an achievable rite of passage even for families that had never considered it before. Over the course of the 1920s college enrollment in the United States rose by 84 percent, reaching a million students for the first time in history. Formerly single-sex institutions were going coeducational in growing numbers, and the notion of a young woman seeking a college degree was no longer a novelty in itself, even if the careers she could seek after graduation were still limited to female-coded professions like teaching, nursing, or secretarial work. As industrial and communications technology grew more complex, there was a demand for more specialized white-collar workers than ever before. Even agriculture was becoming a technical field that required a degree, if you wanted to do anything more than keep up the family farm.[11]

Demographically, too, the timing of the college craze makes perfect sense. The generation that came of age in the 1920s was the first to be shaped by the Progressive-era reforms that kept children in school up to a certain age by law. Buster had grown up surrounded by these social changes and was acutely aware of them; after all, the push for universal compulsory education was part of the same children's rights movement that had given rise to the Keaton family's longtime nemesis, the Gerry Society. But as the chief earner in a family of traveling entertainers, Buster never personally benefited from those reforms. As we've seen, the Keatons regarded the child-protecting "Gerries" primarily as a pack of bureaucratic pests.

If the story the older Keaton often told about having spent a total of one day in school in his life was exaggerated, it was not by much. The demands of a two-show-a-day vaudeville schedule, combined with Joe and

Myra's constitutional indifference to both state authority and middle-class norms, meant that their eldest son lived a life almost completely without formal education. (His younger siblings, by contrast, were sent to boarding school with the money he earned, though they never went beyond high school.) An older Buster sometimes told interviewers that, given a chance at higher education, he would have liked to study civil engineering. But he proposed this alternate life path without conveying regret or a sense of lack. Rather, there was an implied pride in his status as autodidact. In his own way, he must have known, he *had* become a master engineer, one whose materials included not just steel, wood, and electrical circuits but celluloid, light, the passage of time, and the movement of human bodies, especially his own.

In all of Keaton's greatest films the Buster character enacts a process of self-education, moving from an initial state of passivity in the midst of chaos toward an at least partial (if never stable) sense of mastery over his world. The idea of Buster in a classroom, much less in the role of the timid, conformist grind he plays in *College*, just does not make sense. His way of learning, knowing, and being in the world is essentially anti-institutional. This mismatch accounts in part for why *College* is one of Keaton's weakest films and almost certainly his worst feature. More than any of Keaton's independently produced silents, *College* plays now like a vehicle he settled on for commercial reasons rather than a creation that sprang from his and his crew's imagination.

When *College* was filmed, Buster was thirty-one, the same age as Harold Lloyd when he made *The Freshman*. Although both men were in top physical condition and looked young for their age, they had also both clearly aged out of the role of a boy in his late teens. But more crucially, the material simply seems to have held little interest for Keaton. Just the opposite was true for Lloyd. He had left high school a few credits shy of graduation to pursue a career in Hollywood. But in the years since, he had served a long and dogged apprenticeship in the comedy factories of Mack Sennett and Hal Roach. He spent the 1910s creating a series of unsuccessful characters—Willie Work, Lonesome Luke—who copied

Charlie Chaplin's tricks as diligently as Harold Lamb emulates the jaunty catchphrase and "nice-to-meet-you" jig of his screen idol. Lloyd's aspirational, try-hard "glasses character," as he came to call the screen persona he finally landed on around 1917, was perfectly suited to a campus setting, and *The Freshman* remains one of his funniest and most inventive features.

College, by contrast, feels like nothing more or less than the half of the "one for me, one for you" bargain it represented between Keaton and Schenck. Buster's usual team had dispersed: his longtime gag writer Jean Havez had just died, and other stalwart collaborators—Elgin Lessley, Clyde Bruckman—had been loaned out to other studios. For the first time Buster was working with both a codirector, James Horne, and a writer, Carl Harbaugh, who were not trusted members of his inner circle but ringers supplied by the company. Keaton seldom spoke ill of people he had worked with, but in a 1965 interview he had choice words for his *College* collaborators: "James Horne was absolutely useless to me. . . . I don't know why we had him, because I practically did *College.*"[12] Harbaugh, a writer and actor who played an unsympathetic supporting role in *College,* came in for more detailed criticism: "He wasn't a good gag man, he wasn't a good title writer, he wasn't a good story constructionist . . . but I had to put somebody's name up, and he was on salary with us."[13]

College also marked the first time Buster's longtime publicity agent Harry Brand received onscreen credit as a movie's "supervisor." Schenck's addition of this credit to the opening titles without Keaton's knowledge caused a rare flareup between the brothers-in-law. Buster's problem was not with the sharing of credit; though he was for all practical purposes the director (and editor) of all his independently made films, he frequently used a codirector's name either alongside or in place of his own. But the notion of Schenck installing Brand as an embedded company spy to keep watch over production costs must have rankled with Buster, especially after the freedom he had experienced making *The General.*

College contains its share of big laughs, but its predictable story proceeds via a series of sketch-like vignettes, rather than the dramatically integrated plot arcs of Keaton's more personal films. The hero's motivation is even flimsier than in the many other Keaton films where the leading lady sets arbitrary conditions on her affections. And the central conceit—that Buster's character, Ronald, is a dull bookworm completely unversed in sports—is belied by the dazzling athleticism he displays in the movie's central sequence.

In this twelve-minute-long set piece, Ronald visits a near-empty stadium during track-and-field practice in order to try and fail miserably at a series of events: the long jump, the hurdle, the discus, the shotput, the javelin, the pole vault. The humor of the sequence comes in large part from the gap between Ronald's supposed incompetence and Buster's self-evident mastery. Sure, it's hard to clear a set of ten closely spaced hurdles without knocking over a single one; it's arguably harder still to leap over the same obstacles, topple one after the other with clocklike timing, then clear the very last one in a short, self-satisfied hop.

The track-and-field sequence is mesmerizing to watch for the physical prowess displayed not just by Keaton but by the multiple Olympic athletes who were cast to show viewers how the event in question was *meant* to be done. (One of them, the 1924 gold medalist Lee Barnes, doubles for Buster in a pole-vaulting shot later in *College*, the only time Keaton is known to have used a stunt double in his silent-era career.) But this extended demonstration of Ronald's athletic ineptitude isn't exactly *funny*—at least not in the manner of the action scenes of great Keaton films that weave laughs and thrills together as the hero scrambles to resolve some intractable high-stakes dilemma. Instead, the track-and-field sequence works as an isolated bit that hardly advances the film's story at all, except to further prove that Ronald is an unathletic schlemiel teased by his jock classmates. Ironically for a film so focused on games, what *College* lacks is a sense of freedom, playfulness, and risk—at least until the startlingly dark finale.

It all starts off formulaically enough: After Ronald leads the school crew team to a surprise victory as their indomitable if clueless coxswain, he finds himself dashing across campus to rescue his love object, Mary (Anne Cornwall), who's being held prisoner in her dorm room by the bullying Jeff (Harold Goodwin). Perhaps to avoid any un-family-friendly suggestion of intended sexual assault, the intertitles go out of their way to establish that Jeff's motive is to get Mary kicked out of school for having a boy in her room so that the two of them will be free to . . . marry. On the race to his sweetheart's dorm, Ronald's love miraculously endows him with all the athletic skills he once lacked as he hurdles hedges, long-jumps over a lilypond and finally, with well-disguised stunt help from Lee Barnes, yanks up a stake from a clothesline in order to pole-vault through Mary's second-story window. Once inside, he hurls everything handy at the offending Jeff: a phonograph record becomes a discus, a floor lamp a javelin. After the villain flees under this onslaught, the couple skips off to the campus chapel to be married.

This is exactly where most silent romantic comedies would have ended, and many of Buster's did. But *College* concludes on a ten-second-long montage of scenes from the couple's future life together: In the first, he reads the paper as she sews, while their children play in the background. Dissolve to Ronald and Mary in age makeup as an old couple by the fire. As she knits, he takes his pipe out of his mouth, appearing to speak to her sharply—there's no intertitle, but Buster's manner conveys a cranky old man's irritation. A final dissolve reveals the morbid punch line: two adjacent blank headstones.

The three-shot closing montage of *College* represents the harshest version of a type of parodic ending Keaton had used at least twice before. *Cops* concludes on an animated image of a porkpie hat perched on a lone tombstone—the suggestion being that Buster's character, rejected by his girl, has willingly sacrificed himself to the angry police mob he spent the whole movie trying to outrun. And the 1922 short *The Black-smith* ends not on the hero's death but on a visual pun that gently tweaks the cliché of the happy ending. After Buster and his girl escape their pursuers by hopping on the back of a passing train, a title card tells us, "Many a honeymoon express has ended thusly." The train carrying the lovers then appears to crash off a bridge, as if in a sneak preview of *The General*'s budget-busting shot four years later. But in a bit of classic Keaton misdirection, this apparent tragic derailment turns out to involve only a miniature train in a child's nursery. Buster, now a father with a bathrobe and pipe, replaces the toy on the tracks as his wife sews beside him in the nursery. Yawning, he then blocks our view of this cozy scene by pulling down a window shade inscribed with the words "The End." Is that yawn intended as a sign of paternal contentment or of boredom? Either way, *The Blacksmith* subverts the romantic-comedy formula by going one scene beyond the usual wedding finale to hint at the potentially humdrum reality of domestic life.

College's three-shot closing montage combines these images of disenchantment and death into an incongruously downbeat coda. The best-case scenario for this sweet young couple is a long and not too happy life together, followed by an eternity of side-by-side anonymity. This savage poke at romantic convention was presumably Buster's way of smuggling in a protest against the conventional movie he had just made to please Joe Schenck and the Keaton Studio's stockholders. And whether he was conscious of the parallels or not, the ending also can't help but seem like a bulletin from his marriage to Natalie circa 1927.

Six years after their wedding the Keatons were at last installed, with two small sons, on the impossibly lavish grounds of the Italian Villa. They had achieved the picture-postcard version of heterosexual Hollywood bliss—in fact, tinted photographs of their house appeared on real picture postcards for the tourist trade—yet they were by all accounts sexually and emotionally estranged. The separate bedroom Buster had been exiled to in 1924 had become a whole separate wing. The Keatons of the mid-1920s barely shared a life in common: He spent his days on the studio lot or on location, returned home for a quick dinner, and then left to play cards and drink with his friends into the night. Except for the Sunday barbecues they continued to host by the pool, Buster was largely absent from the grand estate whose creation he had so meticulously engineered for his wife. For her part, Natalie, perhaps tired of being known as the mousy younger sister of the glamorous Talmadges, was gaining a reputation as one of the movie colony's most extravagant shoppers. According to rumor, she spent something like $900 a week—more than $14,000 in today's dollars—on clothes. ("Who's the best dresser in Hollywood?" went the joke. "Buster Keaton, because he dresses Natalie.") Their sons later remembered an early childhood where day-to-day affection came mainly from nurses, governesses, and two doting, childless movie-star aunts.

College is a lesser Keaton film for many reasons, the most depressing of which we're about to discuss. But that casually existential "life's a bitch and then you die" finale is a bracing dash of vinegar on the movie's relative blandness, a ghoulish memento mori to cap off a plot that otherwise hews cautiously to the period formulas of the campus comedy. Keaton's vision of marriage as the first stop on a sped-up train ride to the grave is a prime example, if in a grimmer register than the comedian's usual, of the stoic philosophy that Robert Sherwood saw in all his work: "the vitally important fact that life, after all, is a foolishly inconsequential affair."

20

The "Darkie Shuffle"

Bert Williams, 1921.

Although the anti-romantic ending of *College* is memorably bleak, by far the hardest part of the movie to watch going on a hundred years later is the three-minute-long scene Buster plays in blackface, masquerading as a waiter in a restaurant with an all-"colored" staff. This hardly marks the only time an independent Keaton production resorted to racial humor. The 1921 short *The Playhouse*, an experiment in multiple-exposure cinematography, includes among its many vaudeville acts a minstrel troupe with Keaton playing all nine parts. *Neighbors*, from the same year, has

Buster's face being half-blackened by a spilled bucket of paint, leading to a gag in which some white cops mistake him for a Black man they're chasing and threaten to arrest him until he turns his head, revealing his face's white side. And *Seven Chances* (1925), the Keaton feature with the highest number of individual race-based gags, has a few variations on a joke in which Buster's character, racing against the clock to find a bride in time to inherit a family fortune, approaches a woman only to realize that her ethnicity (Black or, in one case, Jewish) renders her off-limits as a potential mate.

There are other such moments in the Keaton oeuvre, if for the most part mercifully short ones. The film historian Daniel Moews, author of an exhaustive analysis of Keaton's silent features, counted eighteen separate instances of jokes related to skin color or ethnicity over the course of all his independent films of the 1920s. Buster Keaton was ahead of his time in many ways, but when it came to the ambient cultural racism of the Jim Crow era, he was unfortunately very much a product of it.[1]

Unpleasant as it is to sit through now, the "colored waiter" scene in *College* warrants a modern-day rewatch more than the throwaway gags in other Keaton films where people of color or whites in black- or redface appear for the sake of some broad ethnic joke or other. The mini-drama the *College* restaurant scene enacts, of a white man trying and failing to pass himself off as Black in a segregated public setting, is the longest and most involved instance of race-based humor to be found in a Keaton film, and in ways of which its creator was surely not aware, it speaks volumes about the representation of race on stage and screen in the early twentieth century.

To set up the scene: Early on, it's established that the bookish Ronald is the only son of a doting single mother (nicely played in a few scenes by Florence Turner, who twenty years before had gained fame as the original, pre–Mabel Normand "Vitagraph Girl"). They are a family of modest means, but when his mother frets about the cost of sending him to college, Ronald assures her he can work his way through with odd jobs, "just as other boys do." This exchange sets up two unconnected vignettes that show the hapless Ronald flaming out on his first day at a new job.

In the first, he tries and fails to copy the stylings of a skilled soda jerk, soda fountains with implement-juggling servers being another youth sensation of the day. This short scene makes for some amusing prop comedy as Ronald bungles order after order, dousing the customers and himself in jets of soda water between pitiful attempts to crack an egg one-handed or toss scoops of ice cream in graceful arcs through the air. But it's with Ronald's second botched job attempt, as a waiter at a restaurant seeking "colored" help, that Keaton veers into uncomfortable racial humor.

The action of the restaurant scene centers around a pair of swinging doors that separate the kitchen, a space reserved for the all-Black staff, from the dining room full of white customers. As the busy servers pass each other on their way through the doors—one labeled "in," one "out"—the crash that seems inevitable keeps getting delayed in an intricate choreography of precarious tea trays and almost-spilled bowls of soup. Buster/Ronald, his face and hands darkened to a disquieting shade of flat shoe-polish black, charges through the doors with more confidence than he twirled the utensils at the soda fountain. One near-collision even gives the chance to show off a neat trick from vaudeville days that he had never done before on film: the "teacup roll," a somersault executed while holding a full cup of liquid without spilling a drop. But it is his character's shifting social status on either side of the doors that becomes the scene's structuring joke.

In the kitchen, Ronald is surrounded by Black workers who at first seem oblivious to his ruse. A middle-aged female cook makes moony eyes at him, while a younger male dishwasher watches their interaction warily.[2] The point of this encounter was to stoke the audience's presumed anxiety about miscegenation by raising the laughable yet threatening (or laughable *because* threatening) prospect of a young white man—a college student, yet—being flirted with by an older Black female kitchen worker. As with most instances of race-based humor in Keaton—with one salient exception being the "savage" Black cannibals Buster and his girl encounter near the end of *The Navigator*—the point of the joke is not to show individual characters of color in a negative light; rather, it is to demonstrate the incongruity of the Buster character's presence in their context.

Black bodies in Keaton films are often markers of a social boundary that his character—usually a member of the striving middle class, though he sub-specialized in pampered rich dimwits—cannot cross. He may start off the film excluded from his heroine's good graces, his father's respect, or the right to enlist in the army, but the Buster character always benefits from a baseline of freedom and social mobility that people of color, in his movies as in the outside world, lack.

But in the restaurant scene in *College*, Buster-as-Ronald's racial disguise inhibits that freedom. Emerging from the kitchen into the restaurant's dining room, he encounters a fresh set of problems as he must convince the white customers, among them his unrequited crush and her bullying suitor, that he is the real thing: a Black man employed in the kind of menial job that, when done right, should make him invisible to them.

In one of those perverse flights of illogic that mark the white imagination of the Jim Crow era, passing as Black is shown to be easier to pull off in the company of actual Black people than in the white-dominated space of the dining room. Ronald's romantic rival immediately suspects something is amiss with the server who nervously attends his table. Sensing that his disguise is insufficient, Ronald doubles down on the ruse by returning to the kitchen in a peculiar hunched, arm-swinging gait—a stylized version of the "darkie shuffle" that would have been familiar to audiences from generations of minstrel shows and productions of *Uncle Tom's Cabin*. It is one of dozens of moments in Keaton films when a performance tradition he absorbed as a child comes to life again in the movement of his body, although in most cases those moments bring with them a sense of felicitous rediscovery rather than pain and shame.

Growing up, Keaton would have seen countless stock minstrel characters on the stage. Most of them were still played by white men in blackface, as they had been since the tradition of minstrel performance began in the 1830s. But by the turn of the century some were represented by performers of African descent who wore burnt cork themselves. The most famous of these, and the one I suspect Keaton is channeling in the *College* restaurant scene, was the legendary Bahamian American comedian and singer Bert Williams.

Williams, born in Nassau in 1874 and brought to the United States by his parents at age eleven, was among the first performers to integrate the Broadway stage. In 1903 he costarred in the all-Black musical *In Dahomey* alongside his performing partner, the African American dancer and comedian George Walker. In 1910 Williams, working as a solo act, became the first Black featured performer in the Ziegfeld Follies. When some of his white costars threatened to quit in protest, the impresario Florenz Ziegfeld is said to have responded, "Go if you want to. I can replace every one of you, except the man you want me to fire."[3]

Williams was a major star from around the turn of the century until his death in 1922, and is now considered one of the first great "crossover" artists of the twentieth century. He made some of the top-selling records of the 1910s and performed on the same big-time vaudeville bills as many white acts, including the Three Keatons.

Williams's signature persona, though usually performed in blackface, was no crude stereotype but an original and complex character, albeit one derived from a familiar minstrel tradition. In his early days touring as one-half the team of Williams and Walker, the tall and ungainly Williams played a "Jim Crow" type, a lumbering foil to Walker's smaller, snappier "Zip Coon."[4] The fast-talking Walker was always coming up with outlandish moneymaking schemes, while Williams played his slow-witted, shambling sidekick. When Walker died of complications of syphilis in 1911 after a long decline, Williams had to refashion this comic persona into the star of a solo act.

The "Jonah Man," like the Old Testament prophet who gave him his name, was a dolorous figure, an Everyman seemingly conspired against by fate. In a too-small dress suit, a top hat, and slapshoes not unlike those worn by knockabout comedians like Buster and Joe, he told shaggy-dog stories that were sometimes set to catchy tunes and sometimes presented as spoken comic interludes Williams called "lies." These were sharply observed tales of work and family, laced with topical jokes about pop culture and Prohibition. Williams's songs often sprang from painful experiences rooted in Black life, but the pain was expressed in general enough and funny enough terms that many white audiences could relate. "I'm Gonna Quit Saturday" is sung from the point of view of a working man unconvincingly declaring that this time his boss's exploitation has gone too far. The narrator of "Ten Little Bottles" amasses a tidy stash of black-market moonshine, then counts down in dismay as it disappears a bottle at a time, doled out to importuning relatives, nosy neighbors, and thirsty local cops.

Williams's signature song was "Nobody," a song he admitted to growing sick of singing by the end of his life, though his audiences never tired of hearing it. With music by Williams and words by his frequent collaborator, the Black composer Alex Rogers, it was a plaintive lament about poverty and loneliness that, in the move from verse to chorus, suddenly changes tones to become a defiant protest of the singer's powerless position.

When life seems full of clouds and rain
And I am full of nothin' but pain
Who soothes my thumpin', bumpin' brain?
Nobody

When winter comes with snow and sleet
And I with hunger and cold feet,
Who says "Here's twenty-five cents, go ahead and get somethin' to eat?"
Nobody

Oh, I ain't never done nothin' to nobody
I ain't never done nothin' to nobody, no time
So until I get something from somebody, sometime
I'll never do nothin' for nobody, no time.

The opening title for Keaton's first-produced independent film *The High Sign*—"Our Hero came from Nowhere—he wasn't going Anywhere and got kicked off Somewhere"—seems to owe something of its existential tone to Williams's mournful but wryly funny hit. Still, there are key differences between Williams's luckless protagonist and Keaton's blank slate of a hero. Explicit references to material privation and loneliness figure much more prominently in the world of Williams's down-on-his-luck Jonah Man than in that of the typical Buster character. Keaton's protagonists often start off in a state of exclusion, whether from their beloved's good graces or from some aspect of the social order that surrounds them: enlistment in the army (*The General*), success in a business venture (*Cops*), or access to an inherited fortune (*Seven Chances*). But they are seldom shown as experiencing genuine poverty ("hunger and cold feet") or complete abandonment. A Keaton hero's struggles are typically those of the white middle class, having to do with upward mobility and romantic fulfillment rather than day-to-day survival. And an act of passive resistance like the one Williams suggests in the chorus of "Nobody"—"I'll never do nothing for nobody, no time"—would be completely out of place in a Keaton plot line, where it is the protagonist's commitment to action and engagement that eventually earns him in a place in his world.

Bert Williams was a far cry from a protest singer. In fact, some fans of color who had thrilled to his success in all-Black musicals like *In Dahomey* decried his move to the Ziegfeld Follies, an otherwise all-white show performed before segregated audiences, and criticized him for continuing to wear blackface even after it began to fall out of favor among the younger, more progressive generation of Black artists associated with the "New Negro" movement of the 1920s. The minstrel tradition dating back to pre–Civil War years would remain in full force on stage and screen for most of the twentieth century, even if, by the 1920s, many African American groups, including artists of the Harlem Renaissance, had begun to speak out against the practice. "Corking up" for individual songs set in an idyllic prewar South would remain a staple of Hollywood musicals through the 1950s, and persist at private white social gatherings long after that.

But Williams's art nonetheless drew deeply from his experience as a person of color and an immigrant. Out of costume he was not a drawling southern "darkie" but a light-skinned man of mixed race with a West Indian accent, so the act of blacking up, putting a kinky-haired wig over his naturally wavy hair, and speaking in dialect was also a way to mask the ambiguity of his own racial presentation. In an essay he wrote for the *American Magazine* in 1918, Williams discusses the effect of this transformation on his growth as an actor without directly touching on the subject of race: "It was not until I was able to see myself as another person," he writes, "that my sense of humor developed."[5]

Keaton profoundly admired Williams. In a 1958 interview he identified him as one of his top two favorite stage comedians, placing him in the company of the revered Spanish clown Marceline, a great favorite of child audiences during his decade-long residency at the New York Hippodrome starting in 1905. Speaking to another interviewer in 1960, Keaton again cited Williams as a "pet" from his early days, mentioning him alongside a series of white vaudevillians who performed in blackface:

> Now I go in for blackface comedians. My pet was Bert Williams, who was actually a colored man, but used to put burnt cork on, black up . . . the same as Moran and Mack, or Lew Dockstader, Frank Tinney; we had some great blackface comedians. We've lost them completely.

Although he mentions that Williams was set apart from the three white acts by being "a colored man," Keaton's nostalgia for the form does not seem to distinguish between two very different modes of performance. To him, a person of color "blacking up" is the same as a white comedian masquerading as an excluded racial other.

His interlocutor Herbert Feinstein, a San Francisco–based broadcast journalist and professor of English literature, goes on to press his subject at some length about why minstrelsy might have fallen out of favor in the decades since. He asks whether Keaton can see why a servile and dimwitted Black character like Stepin Fetchit, the performing name assumed by the actor Lincoln Perry, "might be used by some anti-Negro groups to say this is what the Negro is." Without disputing that negative stereotypes might have such an effect, Keaton's even-keeled response demonstrates the same race-blind neutrality as his earlier statement about his nostalgia for blackface comedy: "Well, that's the wrong way to look at it from the theatrical viewpoint, because you've got stupid people in every walk of life and in every country."[6]

In his extended exchange with Feinstein about the waning of ethnic comedy in the post-vaudeville era, Keaton seems unable or unwilling to distinguish between the painful cultural meaning of blackface and the relative benignity of the other styles of ethnic humor with which he grew up, from the stereotypical "Irish" getups he and his father wore in the early days of their act to what he recalls, with proprietary affection, as "my pets: my German comedians, my Jewish comedians, and Italian." This blindness to the deeper and uglier inequities that reinforced the practice of blackface comports with moments in Keaton's work like the restaurant scene in *College*, which mine racial difference for laughs while remaining oblivious to the brutal social conditions that permit the scene's "humor" to work.

Reading about the impression Bert Williams made on audiences of his day, it is obvious what Keaton must have admired as a child, watching the older man's performances "from a theatrical viewpoint." Like the silent comic-to-be, Williams was renowned for his extreme economy of movement. The critic and journalist Heywood Broun, a longtime fan, described Williams's stage presence in a tribute written after his death in 1922: "a tall man, his face clownishly blackened with burnt cork, who stood still in the center of the stage and used no gesture which traveled more than six inches."

Williams himself notes his tendency to occupy only a small space on the stage in the abovementioned *American Magazine* essay. He attributes his use of stillness to a need to find the place on the stage where his voice, which he regarded as his weakest attribute as a performer, would best carry:

I study carefully the acoustics of each theater I appear in. There is always
one particular spot on the stage from which the voice carries better. . . . I
make it my business to find that spot, and once I find it I stick to it like a
postage stamp. People have sometimes observed that I practice unusual
economy of motion. . . . It is to spare my voice and not my legs that I
stand still while delivering a song.[7]

In 1903 the *New York Times* described Williams's star power in his
Broadway breakthrough *In Dahomey* with words that suggest the kind of
influence Williams might later have had on a young comedian watching
him perform from the wings. Only eight at the time of *In Dahomey*'s premiere, Buster would likely not have had a chance to see Williams onstage
until a few years later, after his self-reinvention as a solo act. But even
in his early incarnation, Williams's shambling comic character seems to
have gotten laughs with methods we would now call Keatonesque, when
in fact maybe it was Keaton who was Williams-esque all along.

> Williams, in particular, had electric connections with the risibilities of
> the audience. He is of a serious, depressed turn of countenance; dull, but
> possessing the deep wisdom of his kind; slow and grotesquely awkward
> in his movements. He holds a face for minutes at a time, seemingly, and
> when he alters it, bringing [*sic*] a laugh by the least movement . . . He
> has the genius of the comedy in full measure.[8]

The *Times*'s unsigned review of *In Dahomey* may bubble over with
praise for the whole production, but it can't escape the biases of the
day in its condescension toward Williams. The comedian is praised for
his masterful timing in the same breath that he's pronounced "slow,"
"grotesquely awkward," and "dull." Rather than actual intelligence, he's
granted only the "deep wisdom of his kind." The (presumably white)
writer's genuine admiration for Williams's comic brilliance is inextricable
from the language of racial otherness used to praise it. This description
also effaces the distinction between actor and character, when in fact

the Jonah Man's slow-thinking "dullness," like his countrified speech, was a carefully cultivated element of Williams's stage persona. In private life the actor, though his education went no further than high school, was extremely well-read, spending a portion of his lavish income on an extensive home library for his Harlem apartment.

The performance of race at the turn of the twentieth century was a wild patchwork of imitations and borrowings, as evidenced by the fact, noted further on in the same *Times* review of *In Dahomey*, that one member of the all-Black cast played a character "made over into a Chinaman." (To give a sense of how pervasive such ethnic stereotyping was at the time: a quick scan of the same page of theater coverage yields the headline "Jap Jugglers Who Mystify" and the description of a new musical satire called *The Sultan of Sulu*.) Twenty years later, the artists of the Harlem Renaissance would shun Williams's embrace of the burnt-cork tradition as a demeaning throwback. But around the turn of the century he was a pioneering figure, one of the first Black artists to find grand-scale commercial success in two entertainment media at once: the variety stage and the recording industry.

Reams of great scholarship have been written on the relationship between Black and white art in the Jim Crow era, an ambivalent knot of love and hate, imitation and repudiation. Buster Keaton's history with Bert Williams is only one small example of that complex cultural encounter in action, but it is an illustrative one. When Williams's name came up in conversations about Buster's childhood memories, Buster always seemed, in his laconic way, to empathize with the obstacles this older Black comedian had faced as an early integrator of the show business industry. Yet as evidenced by scenes like the one in *College*, that admiration and empathy never translated to understanding Williams's difficulties as a part of the same system that had made Buster an unqualified success beginning around age five.

In his memoir, Buster relates the story of his father running into Williams—like Joe, a sometime problem drinker—at a Boston saloon while the two were appearing on the same vaudeville bill. Joe asked

Williams to join him at his end of the bar. Williams, gesturing to indicate that he was sitting in the "colored" section, said, "I don't think that would be a good idea, Mr. Joe," so Joe crossed to Bert's side of the bar to drink with him there. (Note that, even in a story told to highlight Joe's racial tolerance, the white man still gets called "Mr. Joe" while addressing "Bert" by his first name without an honorific.)[9]

The professional admiration between Williams and Keaton appears to have cut both ways. When the Three Keatons made their 1909 trip to London to perform at the Palace, one feature of the act was Buster's Bert Williams impression, specifically a performance of the song "Somebody Lied," a spin-off of "Nobody" that had been a hit for Williams several years before. According to Keaton's account, Williams even rewrote the song's lyrics to suit the needs of a thirteen-year-old knockabout comic. Unfortunately, the words of that rewrite have not survived.

Bert Williams was primarily a stage performer, but at the height of his Ziegfeld Follies stardom in the mid-1910s he also briefly branched out into film, making three short subjects with the Biograph Company. The second of these, A Natural Born Gambler, is the best place to see the kind of character he gained fame playing onstage during Buster's childhood. (In the first, 1914's Darktown Jubilee, Williams appeared in a stylish zoot suit rather than his usual clownish rags, and even got to flirt with a Black female character. The fear of a negative reaction from white audiences was so strong that the film was never released for fear of a boycott in the South.)

In A Natural Born Gambler he appears in his customary costume, playing a typical Williams character: a down-and-out member of a Black men's gambling club who charges his drinks on credit and does his best to hide the group's ongoing card game from a white vice cop. The movie, today easily found online, ends with the only filmed record of one of Williams's most celebrated stage routines: a poker game played solo and entirely in pantomime, with only Williams's expressions and gestures to suggest what cards he's drawn and how the other players are faring.

Whether or not Keaton ever saw A Natural Born Gambler, the card-game bit is one he must have seen on stage many times growing up.

Watching Williams's beautiful sparseness of movement as he enacts the miniature drama of a full hand of poker—trying to bluff, being forced to show his cards, suspecting his unseen table mates of cheating—it's impossible not to think of the scene in *The Cameraman* (1928) when Keaton, alone in an empty Yankee Stadium, mimes an entire inning of baseball, from pitching to hitting to signaling to an invisible catcher and threatening to tag a nonexistent baserunner.

Most of all, though, the transmission of performance styles between them is noticeable in Williams's signature walk. His feet turned out at duck-like angles, his shoulders hunched and his long arms hanging at his sides, Williams makes his way around the bar with a doleful, shambling gait. His walk is a slightly less stylized version of the "darkie shuffle" that Keaton would dust off a decade later in the *College* restaurant scene, five years after Williams—famously described by fellow vaudevillian W. C. Fields as "the funniest man I ever saw, and the saddest man I ever knew"[10]—had died of pneumonia at age forty-seven after collapsing during a performance.

The restaurant scene in *College* ends, none too soon, with a potential race riot: upon executing his "teacup roll," Buster/Ronald has accidentally rubbed off some of his black makeup on the carpeted floor. When the customers notice his exposed white cheek, he hightails it—still shambling Williams-style, but at a faster pace—back to the kitchen. There the flirtatious cook and her coworkers catch on to his ruse and arm themselves with the nearest weapons—knives and a cleaver—to chase him out. Terrified, Ronald dashes out of the restaurant and disappears down the street, having dropped the "darkie" act for good.

Keaton's homage to Williams in the blackface scene may well have been an unconscious one. To his mind, he was most likely simply imitating the movements of a standard comic minstrel—a character he may first have picked up as a child while admiring Williams's act from the wings, but one that was also ubiquitous in the entertainment culture of his youth. Still, whether it was intended or not, there is something about the narrative purpose this movement serves in the context of the *College* scene that strikes me as particularly Williams-esque. In the spirit of the older entertainer he had long admired, Keaton sometimes appears to deploy the familiar stereotypes of blackface minstrelsy (shuffling gait, excessive deference to whites) while also exploring how these tropes change meaning depending on who uses them, and why. By transforming into a stereotypical shuffling waiter when and only when his character's racial identity is called into question by a white customer, it is as if Keaton is acknowledging the performative nature of race in the segregated social world his characters, his audience, and he himself inhabit. His body understands, in a way it seems his conscious mind never did, that the "darkie shuffle" is by definition a put-on, and that donning blackface as a white man is an act of symbolic violence. The *College* restaurant episode concludes on the comic threat of real-world violence, as Keaton's feckless student flees the knife-wielding kitchen staff. It's a relief to the twenty-first-century viewer when this mercifully short sequence comes to an end, but there is also a certain satisfaction in seeing a white man in blackface experience something unusual in the long history of the form: consequences.

PART III

FALLING

"What do you think happened in your own career
   then?"
"Oh, everything happened. I got to the stage where
   I didn't give a darn whether school kept or not,
   and then I started drinking too much."

—Buster Keaton, from a 1958 interview
   with Robert and Joan Franklin

21

The Collapsing Façade

Production photo from the set of Steamboat Bill, Jr., *1927.*

In a way, Keaton's fall—the big, metaphorical one, the first he couldn't bounce right back from—began when that housefront collapsed over him in *Steamboat Bill, Jr.* In what is now his most famous stunt, Buster remains unharmed, framed in an open attic window just wide enough to clear his body by two inches on each side. Today this is probably the best known of Keaton's grand-scale set pieces, included in countless classic film montages and circulated online as a mesmerizing repeating gif.

The stunt is infinitely rewatchable, worth slowing down to advance frame by frame. You can choose to focus on Keaton's uncanny stillness as the weight of the wall rushes toward him and the neat timing of his delayed reaction as he rubs the back of his neck in confusion, processes his changed circumstances, then takes off at a run with a distrustful glance backward at the pile of wrecked lumber. Or you can try to spot the ropes, barely visible in the exposed cross section of house, that held the two-ton façade upright until the moment the camera rolled. Three men from the crew had been crouched on the roof out of sight, ready to cut the ropes whenever Buster's codirector, Charles Reisner, called action. The whole construction was rigged by Fred "Gabe" Gabourie, and it remains a mechanical marvel to this day.[1]

This shot is the culmination of a long-developing gag that began with a flimsy piece of stage scenery in the Arbuckle/Keaton short *Back Stage* and mutated into the revolving hinged wall in *One Week*, the one that lifts Sybil Seely up in the air while framing Buster in a window opening below. It is the window gag's logical end point, with suspense and the potential for mortal danger added on to the goofy prop comedy of the original joke. In that sense, it is the most quintessential of Keaton gags. Since childhood Buster had been getting this kind of double mileage out of his most daredevil stunts: he could risk his life and make it funny. This had been the whole premise of Joe Keaton's tall tale–filled marketing strategy: the "boy who couldn't be damaged" was happiest when he was both making audiences laugh and scaring the daylights out of them with the physical risks he took.

But the day the real-life wall fell, the Sunday of Labor Day weekend of 1927, must have felt to Buster not like a delivery from doom but the experience of being delivered up to it. The housefront, happily, failed to crush him, but something else just had. The day before the scene was to be filmed, Joe Schenck had informed him that the Buster Keaton Studio, along with the rest of Joe's production companies, was about to be shut down. *Steamboat Bill, Jr.* would be Keaton's last independently produced film.[2]

Joe was heading to United Artists, where he had already been on the board for the last three years, to become the company's president. The plan he proposed was to hand Buster over to Nick Schenck, his younger brother and former partner in amusement park management, now the president of both the Metro-Goldwyn-Mayer studio and its parent company, the Loews theater chain. Marcus Loew, the theater entrepreneur who had gone into business with the Schencks all those years ago, would die in the fall of 1927, but well before that the companies he had acquired over his years in the business—the Metro Picture corporation, the Samuel Goldwyn studio, and a small company owned by the young Canadian upstart Louis B. Mayer—had begun to combine their production wings into the giant corporate entity that would become Metro-Goldwyn-Mayer. It seemed only natural, with the Keaton/Talmadge/Schenck nexus having functioned for over a decade as a family business, that Nick would find a spot for Buster at what was certainly one of the cushiest landing places in a quickly changing film industry.

The consolidation of American film production into the "Big Five" studios of Golden Age Hollywood—MGM, 20th-Century Fox, Warner Bros., RKO Radio Pictures, Paramount—was essentially a done deal by late 1927, even if not all those companies had yet assumed their final form under those names. Joe Schenck had held on to the old independent model far longer than most producers of his ilk. Hollywood movies were a big enough business now to require economies of scale: not a handful of multipurpose crew members building sets on a studio lot the size of one square block but vast production complexes that were like miniature cities, staffed with departments of specialists who rotated from film to film: costumers, scriptwriters, electricians, carpenters, animal trainers.

The Hollywood economy was large enough that Wall Street, another institution that rose to new heights of power and cultural influence in the 1920s, had started to play a key role in the financial and creative decisions of the top movie moguls. After the freewheeling early days of independent production and distribution gave way to huge, vertically integrated companies like Paramount and MGM, the big banks of the East Coast, where the money side of the business was still based, got skittish about lending large sums to small studios with spotty box-office records. To get back their investment, they needed a reliable flow of commercial hits.

Keaton's obsession with authentic detail in period pieces like *The General*, and his prodigious imagination when it came to set pieces like the climactic *Steamboat Bill* hurricane, had certainly been busting his budgets and cutting into Schenck's box-office profits for the last few years. But in the context of the industry at large, Keaton's degree of profligacy was relatively unimpressive. Directors like Erich von Stroheim and F. W. Murnau—European émigrés with exacting artistic visions, who insisted on things like creating an eight-hour-long cut or building a different forced-perspective set for every camera setup—were burning through still more of their American producers' money.

Keaton had never had a head for business, but even he must have recognized well before his and Joe's Labor Day weekend talk that the film industry was changing. The box-office failure of *The General* and the middling performance of *College* had been on both his and Schenck's minds over the past year. And though the release of *The Jazz Singer* would not kick the sound revolution into high gear until that October, everyone in Hollywood was already well aware that talking pictures were the coming thing.

As early as the summer of 1926, Warner Bros. had released, with great fanfare, the first commercially distributed film with a synchronized music track and sound effects. *Don Juan* was a feature-length romantic adventure starring John Barrymore. The Hollywood historian Scott Eyman describes it as "an enjoyably baroque concoction featuring . . . sexual perversity, malevolent hunchbacks, torture on the racks, walled-up adulterers, flooded dungeons, and bad wigs."[3] The director was Alan Crosland, who the following year would direct Al Jolson in *The Jazz Singer*.

Don Juan may have been a mediocre movie, but the novelty of sound thrilled audiences much as the sight of flickering moving images had more than thirty years before. The day after the film premiered in New York alongside a series of Vitaphone shorts designed to showcase the system's ability to reproduce the human voice, the *New York Times* published a rave review less of the film than of the technology:

A marvelous device known as the Vitaphone, which synchronizes sound
with motion pictures, stirred a distinguished audience in Warners' Theatre
to unusual enthusiasm at its initial presentation last Thursday evening.
The natural reproduction of voices, the tonal qualities of musical instruments and the timing of the sound to the movements of the lips of singers
and the actions of musicians was almost uncanny.[4]

A few months later, in the fall of 1926, *Don Juan* had its West Coast
premiere at Grauman's Egyptian Theater in Los Angeles. Never one to
miss out on a technical novelty, Keaton was in the audience, as was his
old friend Roscoe Arbuckle. Also in attendance were Charlie Chaplin,
Harold Lloyd, Greta Garbo, Pola Negri, King Vidor, Allan Dwan, Victor
Fleming—the cream of mid-1920s silent stars and directors.[5] When the
final curtain fell on the evening's program, though, the crowd was the
opposite of silent. *Variety* reported the next day that "the house applauded,
cheered and stamped with its feet." One of the short films that played
in advance of the feature offered a sample of synched dialogue: a three-
and-a-half-minute-long speech from Will Hays, the Hollywood morals
czar who five years earlier had effectively run Arbuckle out of the film
business. Hays's dry direct-to-camera address praising the merits of the
new technology was said to have gotten a "deafening" ovation, though
one wonders if Buster and Roscoe joined in.

Like the hurricane that rips through the final act of *Steamboat Bill, Jr.*,
the storm of synchronized sound took its time to build. Not long after
that screening of *Don Juan* at the Egyptian, the financial heads of the
major studios traveled from New York to Hollywood for a meeting with
the industry's top creative brass. There is a photo of a group of these men,
powerful, white, mostly middle-aged and Jewish, standing in a row on a
sunlit lawn on the MGM campus, squinting into the lens. Present are both
Schenck brothers, MGM chief Louis B. Mayer and his startlingly young
protégé Irving Thalberg, William Fox of the company soon to become
20th-Century Fox, and a handful of other film business machers, among

them Keaton's former studio manager Lou Anger, by then working with Joe Schenck at United Artists.

The subject of this summit was how to survive the massive changes about to rock the industry, starting with the suddenly urgent need to wire movie theaters around the country for sound. It was already clear that the public's interest in talking pictures was about to expand much faster than the studios' capacity to produce, distribute, and project them. The executives would need to convince Wall Street banks to loan them the sums necessary to overhaul and equip not just the studios but the nationwide theater chains that, in many cases, still remained under their control.[6] To secure those funds, the studios would have to prove they could rake in profits that would be unthinkable for mom-and-pop (or husband- and brother-in-law) businesses like Keaton's or the Talmadge sisters'. The business of making movies was no longer analogous with running a theater company at the turn of the century. It had more in common with a mass-production system like the Ford assembly line, where input and output needed to be quantifiable and profit margins both reliable and large enough to satisfy stockholders.

In early 1927 the Fox Picture corporation debuted its own sound technology, Movietone, at first by adding synchronized scores to their already-released silent successes *What Price Glory?* and *Seventh Heaven*. These experiments sparked some audience interest. But in May of that year, Fox pulled off the publicity coup of getting synchronized-sound footage of Charles Lindbergh's departure for his transatlantic flight onto theater screens the evening of the same day he took off.[7]

The public excitement surrounding the Lindbergh stunt made this debut especially memorable, but in those early months of sound Fox newsreels went on to thrill audiences with such unhistoric subjects as (in the words of the official Movietone News site) "goats chewing laundry, gurgling streams and girls riding fire engines." Just as would happen in the next few years with early sound comedies, the mere presence of some kind of noise to accompany the action was, for a time, enough. The Movietone series eventually settled into a more sedate, goat-free format:

a brisk update on the political and cultural happenings of the week that would run for five decades and come to define the form of the theatrical newsreel. It is the Movietone News style that Orson Welles reproduces and lampoons in the "News on the March" sequence early in *Citizen Kane*.

All of this to say that by the summer of 1927, as Keaton and Gabourie were devising the collapsing housefront and the rest of the falling, flying, floating, and sinking sets that swirl through the dreamlike finale of *Steamboat Bill, Jr.*, the writing was on the wall for the end of silent pictures. But no one could have predicted how quickly and violently the industry that had produced them would transform, or how soon that change would be followed by the disaster of the Great Depression. In any case, Keaton had never been one for keeping up with the writing on Hollywood walls. He hadn't needed to. For ten years, with Schenck's protection, he had been working at a remove from the increasingly rigid laws of the movie marketplace. Schenck's initially hands-off approach allowed Keaton the freedom to try ambitious experiments that might or might not earn back their negative cost.

But as of that Labor Day weekend, Buster could no longer ignore the fact that his time as an independent filmmaker with a quasi-fraternal patron was over. He would continue for several more years as a rich and famous movie star; in fact, he was about to be handed the most lucrative job he had ever had. But never again in his life would he enjoy the freedom to conceive, shoot, edit, and star in a production like *Steamboat Bill, Jr.*, built from the ground up with a handpicked crew of trusted collaborators. The trajectory his career had followed from early childhood to early middle age, that smooth and steady upward arc, had hit its peak and was about to start a steep, perilous drop.

Later on, after the coming of his own private disaster—the blackout drinking, the profound if never-diagnosed depression, the protracted end of his marriage to Natalie and the brief blurry second one to Mae Scriven, his humiliating 1933 firing from MGM via a brusque personal memo from Mayer—Buster would speak of the day the housefront fell with an emotional candor that was rare for him. As early as 1930, while he was starring in a string of financially successful if artistically abysmal MGM comedies, he went out of his way to mention the *Steamboat Bill* stunt in an interview for a book of celebrity profiles called *Twinkle, Twinkle, Movie Star*. After describing the setup in some detail, he notes in a cryptic aside that "I was mad at the time, or I never would have done the thing."

There is no elaboration on what sense of "mad" is intended—angry? crazy? both?—or what might have happened to put him in such a state of mind. Withholding this information makes sense, given that *Twinkle, Twinkle* was a publicity platform for big stars like Keaton, Clara Bow, and Lon Chaney. Providing context about what had made him "mad" that day would have read as a criticism of his current employer, an acknowledgment that losing his independence still stung.

To a degree that is unusual in interviews from around the time of Keaton's greatest fame, the quotes in the *Twinkle, Twinkle* profile read like the subject's real voice: dry-humored and laconic, most animated when describing the material details of how certain effects were achieved. When he brings up the atmosphere of tension on the *Steamboat Bill* set that day, though, there is a different, more vulnerable tone: "Cameramen, electricians, and extras prayed as we shot that scene, and I don't mind saying I did a little praying myself. . . . Two extra women on the sidelines fainted, and the cameramen turned their backs as they ground out the film, and everybody on the set was frightened." I haven't seen the anecdote about the two fainting women anywhere else, and it may be meant as a joke, given that he goes on to observe that "I never had any reports that any women who saw the picture in motion picture houses fainted, so I guess the scene wasn't worth the risk."[8] But *Steamboat*'s codirector Charles Reisner (who in Buster's memory "stayed in his tent reading *Science and Health*" at the moment the cameras rolled) later told his son he had spent the day of the shoot "praying off in a corner" with a fellow practitioner of Christian Science.[9]

To simulate the effect of a hurricane, six Liberty-brand propeller engines built to power airplanes were trained on the set, placed with care so that the gale-force winds they created would not displace or warp the housefront in its descent.[10] The noise must have been deafening. In a much lower-tech piece of engineering, two nails had been driven into the ground to indicate the spot where Buster needed to place his heels to escape being crushed by the structure. The stunt, naturally, would have to be done in a single take. A set that elaborate, like a human body, could only be created and destroyed once. The line between laughter and danger that Buster had been toeing since early childhood was never finer than at that moment: he would pull off the stunt or die trying.

In later years, Keaton's third wife, Eleanor, a practical, plainspoken woman not given to dramatization or hyperbole, described her husband's state of mind that day as quasi-suicidal.[11] Whatever the outcome of the stunt, she implied, on that day he was indifferent to his own survival. Of course, Keaton could not have known back when he and Gabourie set out to devise the plan for the breakaway housefront that his studio would be taken away from him at the end of the shoot. It may be true that in the moment he half-wished for the falling set to crush him, but he had certainly not conceived the stunt with that in mind. Nonetheless, Eleanor's framing of the story touches on something evident to anyone who watches the scene today knowing its context in Keaton's life. There is a fateful rightness about the convergence of Steamboat Bill, Jr.'s hallucinatory finale, in which the falling façade is only one of many disintegrating shelters, and the storm that was about to rip through Keaton's professional and personal life.

Steamboat Bill, Jr. may be Keaton's most mature film, a fitting if too early farewell to the peak era of creative independence he had just lived through. Its relationship to the rest of its creator's work has been compared to that of Shakespeare's last play, The Tempest.[12] Keaton was only thirty-two at the time of Steamboat Bill's release, and he still had many films left to make (albeit only two more, The Cameraman and Spite Marriage, that could be said to be, for the most part, his). But his last independent production has a reflective, autumnal mood that sets it apart from mid-1920s masterworks like The Navigator and The General. For all their ingenuity and stunning displays of physical and technical prowess, both those films remain in some way boyish, the inventions of a grown child at play with impossibly outsized toys: the empty ocean liner, the pair of racing trains. In fact, it is this sense of play in *The General* that repelled *Life*'s Robert Sherwood, given the film's use of war as a historical backdrop.

I do not share Sherwood's moral horror at *The General*, but it's not my personal favorite of Keaton's films. *Steamboat Bill, Jr.* seems to me a richer and deeper piece of work than anything he had made up to that point in his life, making it all the sadder that soon thereafter he would find himself no longer in the position to make his own movies at all. Even if it had not turned out to be his last independent feature, *Steamboat Bill, Jr.* might have marked the end of a certain arc of his career. It revisits images and themes that had been central to his life since long before he started in film: the antagonistic relationship between a father and son, the seductive illusions of stagecraft, and the instability of "home."

"Steamboat Bill" was already a familiar pop culture property in 1927. It was both the title and the main character of a song that was first a hit in 1911 and continued to be performed, recorded, and—the most important popularity metric of the time—sold as sheet music for home use throughout the 1920s. The music was by a vaudeville act called the Leighton Brothers, who had just had a huge success the year before with a parodic version of the railroad ballad "Casey Jones," and the lyrics were by Ren Fields, author of Tin Pan Alley standards like "In the Good Old Summertime." (In 1949, that song too would lend its name to a movie: an MGM musical starring Judy Garland and Van Johnson, with an incongruously strawberry-blond-bewigged Keaton in a supporting role and as behind-the-scenes gag writer.) Keaton's film was not the last to recycle "Steamboat Bill" as a piece of what we would now call intellectual property. The following year Walt Disney's first cartoon with synchronized sound, *Steamboat Willie*, created a sensation and launched the one-hundred-plus-year reign of a previously little-known character called Mickey Mouse.

Like "Casey Jones," "Steamboat Bill" is a story song, a folk ballad about a hero who loses his life piloting a large vehicle to its destruction. But unlike Casey Jones, the real-life railroad engineer whose death in a

1900 crash inspired a folk legend, the Steamboat Bill of the song was a made-up character: a Mississippi River steamboat captain who dies in a boiler explosion while racing his boat against a rival craft, ending up as "a pilot on the ferry in that Promised Land."

Assuming the fiery death would have been written out of the story, a no-holds-barred race between two paddlewheel steamboats sounds like a natural Keaton property—but that's not the plot of *Steamboat Bill, Jr.* The story instead follows a fey Boston-educated youth, Willie Canfield (Keaton), who heads south to visit his estranged steamboat-piloting father, the Bill of the title (Ernest Torrence). Why have the two not seen each other since Willie was a baby? Why does his mother send him to meet his long-estranged parent only after he's finished his schooling? *Steamboat Bill, Jr.* offers no flashback or title card to explain this origin story. It simply deposits the feckless Willie in the fictional town of Riverboat Junction, where he must learn to serve on the boat with, and eventually earn the respect of, his macho, blustering father.

The figure of a hulking older man often recurred as a foil to Keaton's nebbishy if secretly athletic five-foot-five hero. Sometimes this character came in the form of a romantic rival (as played in the early shorts by the towering, barrel-chested vaudevillian Joe Roberts), or the forbidding father or brother of the Buster character's would-be sweetheart. Sometimes the antagonist in question was a policeman, or a whole city force of them chasing Buster down the street, as in *Cops*. In the 1920 short *Neighbors* the punishing paternal figure was the Buster character's actual father, played by none other than Joe Keaton, with some tricks drawn from their old familial knockabout.

But even when these films used material straight from the Three Keatons' playbook, none of them were directly *about* the relationship between a father and a son. Interpersonal connections of any kind—even the romantic courtships that drive nearly every Keaton plot—are rarely the subject of his movies. No matter that there is almost always a pretty young lady, sometimes complete with justice of the peace, awaiting him in the last frame; the Keaton hero's journey up to that point is typically a solitary one. Love is a static prize to be earned through personal valor, hard work, and feats of physical courage, not the result of a complex inter-personal struggle like the one between the grizzled William Canfield Sr. and his well-intentioned but hopelessly inept son.

Steamboat Bill, Jr. may resemble other Keaton movies in its setting — like *Our Hospitality* and *The General*, it takes place in a romanticized version of "the South," and like *The Boat* and *The Navigator* it takes place mainly aboard a boat — but the psychological space it explores has more to do with the old rivalry between Joe and Buster Keaton. There is the same comic juxtaposition of a large, short-tempered father with old-fashioned ideas about parental authority and a small, agile son seemingly put on earth to plague him. But by 1927, eleven years after the breakup of the act, the son's motivation is no longer the anti-authoritarian mischief of a clever boy. Willie Canfield — the second protagonist of a Keaton film to be designated a "junior," after the would-be detective hero of *Sherlock, Jr.* in 1924 — wants to earn his father's good opinion and ultimately his love. He does this in much the same way he goes about winning over the girl in earlier films: by struggling to overcome the obstacles the world puts in his way (tangled ropes, slippery decks, collapsing housefronts, gale-force winds) and by demonstrating his physical courage and problem-solving skill in a spectacular final rescue.

Along the way there are comic interludes that focus on the power struggle between father and son, with Willie usually in the role of an irritating thorn in his father's side. Chief among them is a wonderful short scene in a hat shop, where Bill Sr. tries to find a replacement for his son's hopelessly unmanly beret as the store owner places one ridiculous topper after another on the young man's head — including the classic Keaton porkpie, which Willie snatches off and hands back to the salesman before his father can see it. In multiple gags, Bill's attempts to show Willie the workings of his beloved boat result in embarrassing (if virtuosic) pratfalls, compounding the older man's shame at his miserable excuse for a son.

The peak of the father/son tension comes in a late scene when the hot-tempered Bill has been thrown in jail for punching out his rival in the street—a Joe Keaton situation if ever there was one. Buster's Willie arrives at the jailhouse with a plan: he has baked a set of tools into an enormous, hollowed-out loaf of bread to help his father escape. The problem is, Bill is so disgusted at the sight of his puny offspring that he refuses the gift. Willie, determined to set the old man free, waits till the guard is distracted, then embarks on a discreet but elaborate pantomime to communicate the plan to his father. Tapping his fingers idly as he hums a tune, he gradually transforms that gesture into a sawing motion, then a jail door swinging open, then a pair of legs walking their way down the loaf toward freedom. It is one of the best uses of pantomime in any Keaton film, because not only are his movements hilariously precise in their evocation of a jailbreak but the whole bit serves a larger dramatic purpose. By refusing to leave after his father's angry rejection, Willie demonstrates a different kind of valor than what he will soon display by diving into a flooded river to rescue his father, his girl, his girl's father, and, in a final gag, a handy minister. He sticks around, risking his own freedom to ensure his father's, because that's what a good son does. His insistence on setting his father free is motivated by love—not the abstract courtly love of a typical Keaton hero for his lady but the practical, problem-solving love of a rejected son for his emotionally remote father.

Though Bill Sr. remains unmoved by Willie's bread-based panto-mime, he does at last come around to recognizing his son's worth. Late in the film, after a hurricane tears through the town, Bill finds himself still locked in his cell as the whole jailhouse slides down a bank into the river. Willie, finally marshalling the nautical skills that have eluded him the whole movie, scrambles behind the wheel of his father's steamboat and plows head-on into the sinking prison in the nick of time, breaking the building to splinters and setting his grateful father free. It is the last in a long line of creatively destroyed dwellings over the course of Keaton's independent career, from the wonky kit home of *One Week* through the falling housefront of just a few minutes before.

Like Eleanor's interpretation of the collapsing façade as the enactment of a death wish, this may be a reading that the author never intended, but part of why I see *Steamboat Bill, Jr.* as a pinnacle of Keaton's art is because I sense, in that final reconciliation between father and son, something like a reckoning between the younger Buster and his own overbearing dad. Willie in *Steamboat Bill, Jr.* accomplishes what Joseph Keaton Jr. was never able to in seventeen years of basketball-twirling and broom-whacking: he triumphs over paternal authority, not by undermining or mocking it but by taking ownership of the parental role himself. In a rewrite of that fatal moment in 1916 when a fed-up Buster and his exhausted, abused mother left Joe Keaton drunk in Oakland without so much as a goodbye note, Willie Canfield saves his ornery father from drowning and thereby wins his admiration and love. This seems to me as frankly autobiographical a moment of wish fulfillment as Keaton ever put in a movie, and intended or not, there is symbolic power in the fact it turned out to be the last movie that was fully his own. The house known as the Buster Keaton Studio, where he had spent the past seven years far happier than in any of the real homes he had lived in during that time, was collapsing around his ears. But just like Willie Canfield stumbling dazed from the wreckage, Buster would only process the reality of what had just happened to him after a delay. In his case it would take not two seconds but around two years.

22

Grief Slipped In

MGM publicity photo, ca. 1927.

Louis B. Mayer tried to run his business like a family and his family like
a business, though he could never quite get either model to work. His
formidable personality dominated the company's culture for all thirty years
he served as the top executive at MGM. Perhaps more than any of the big
studio chiefs of Hollywood's golden age, Mayer insisted on imprinting his
own peculiar collection of traits on the glossy, high-toned products his
studio churned out. He was a sentimental autocrat who lost his temper
as easily as he cried; a cutthroat businessman who also held deep beliefs

about the wholesome values movies should espouse; a staunch political conservative in an era when much of Hollywood leaned leftward; and a meddlesome boss who was excessively preoccupied with both onscreen propriety and offscreen female purity.

Nineteen twenty-seven, the year Keaton signed his fateful contract with MGM, was a pivotal year for the company in ways that had nothing to do with the transition to sound that was about to roar through the industry. In fact, MGM was the last of the big studios to make that switch and would continue to put out successful silent films, including two with Keaton, until the end of the 1920s. But 1927 was the year MGM, formed by a corporate merger three years before, became the most financially successful film studio in the business, creating a net profit of $2.9 million for its parent company, the Loews theater chain.[1]

When Marcus Loew died suddenly of heart failure in September 1927 there was a power struggle between Mayer, who ruled over the studio's sprawling production lot in Culver City, California, and Nicholas Schenck, the New York–based financial head of the company. The two had long detested each other, with Mayer calling Schenck (whose name was pronounced "Skenk") "Skunk" behind his back. In contrast to the effusive Mayer—and unlike his brother Joe, known in the business for his menschy generosity—Nick was a chilly sort, a hardheaded businessman whom Mayer scorned as a bean counter.

Louise Brooks, ever the keen chronicler of early Hollywood's power elite, wrote a memorably blunt description of the Schenck brothers and Nick's wife, Pansy, in a personal letter to Keaton biographer Tom Dardis in the 1970s:

> Nick was a cold little man with a face like a slab of salt pork. Nick and Pansy could have been replaced by store dummies at any dinner party. Joe was a giant (5'11") among the tiny Jewish executives. He too had an unaccommodating face, looking as if it had been rolled out after composition leaving no expression at all.[2]

With Joe now installed as chairman of United Artists, the Schenck brothers headed up nominally competing companies. Yet they continued to do business in a larger-scale version of the old family style. Nicholas Schenck's daughter Nicola recalled years later how, though they lived on opposite coasts in a time when long-distance phone calls were an extravagance, the brothers spoke "three times a day at least. . . . I don't think either one of them ever made a deal without checking with the other one." They even, according to her, "invented their own languages, two of them, so that nobody could understand what they were saying. One was a variation on pig Latin."[3]

Among the schemes the brothers had floated in these coded conversations was a plan to merge the distribution wings of their two studios, flouting antitrust law by releasing all of UA's and MGM's output through the same nationwide network of film exchanges. That idea fell through in 1925 when Charlie Chaplin, one of the original founders of United Artists, nixed the plan, derisively referring to the Metro-Goldwyn-Mayer company as "the three weak sisters."[4] But it was only natural that two years later, as Joe was dissolving his independent companies to take charge of UA full-time, he would offer his top comedy star and brother-in-law of six years to his brother, promising Buster all the while that he would be taken care of like family.

At first Keaton put up what was, for him, an unaccustomed fight. Both Chaplin and Harold Lloyd advised him against the move. "They'll ruin you helping you," Chaplin cautioned him, as Buster remembered it to Rudi Blesh in the mid-1950s. "They'll warp your judgment. You'll get tired of arguing for things you know are right." And Lloyd put it more simply: "It's not your gang. You'll lose."[5] It's hard to imagine the circumstances of these conversations, given that none of the three top-earning silent-comedy stars were socially close. But at any rate, advice from self-produced stars like Lloyd and Chaplin would have been of minimal use, given that both men were in a financial position to take their time testing the waters of sound. Lloyd, made enormously wealthy by his movies' popularity and his own shrewd business instincts, held on to his independent studio well into the sound era. He also assembled a first-rate team, including longtime Keaton gagman Clyde Bruckman, to help rejigger his comedy for the sound era. And Chaplin, with the leisure afforded by his immense worldwide success, kept producing his own rapturously received silent films at widely spaced intervals throughout the 1930s and only released his first full talkie, *The Great Dictator*, in 1940. Keaton, however well paid, was still a salaried employee of Joe Schenck who did not even own stock in his own studio. His future success in the industry depended on finding another equally generous hands-off patron.

Within days Keaton was on a cross-country train to New York, where he first met with Paramount head Adolph Zukor. Upon asking point-blank if Zukor was interested in acquiring his whole operation, crew and all, he was told that Paramount had just signed Lloyd and that the presence of another comic star on its roster would be redundant. This made no sense to Keaton, since for the past few years his films and Chaplin's had both been distributed by United Artists with no apparent conflict, but as he put it to his first biographer, "There was no talking him out of it. I left by the same door I came in by: Keaton goes to MGM."[6]

What happened next reveals something about Keaton's style of conflict management that would serve him ill in the decade to come. In his words, he "went back to his hotel room to think it over and began brooding instead."

I got myself thoroughly mixed up, and then I made a mistake, just like in my comedies when I do just one little thing wrong and from then on I'm in the soup up to my neck. Here I decide to ride all my winnings on one throw of the dice—I went to see Nicholas Schenck! I was flustered. It was all too much like one of my own scripts. . . . This was before the stock-market crash. There was money everywhere. I should have gone out for some of it, found backing, kept my gang together, and gone about my business. . . . But instead, I went out, had three drinks, and called on Nick Schenck all softened up.[7]

It's striking that, in his retelling of this incident in the mid-1950s, Keaton sees the "mistake" of getting tipsy before an important business meeting as a real-life version of something his screen character might do: "it was all too much like one of my own scripts." The character he played in his movies was, quite to the contrary, a figure of courage, pluck, and constant forward motion. He was always getting in his own way, yes, but it's hard to imagine the fictional Buster withdrawing from a conflict to nurse his wounded pride with liquor.

Since his early twenties, drinking had played a prominent role in Keaton's daily life. In the context of Prohibition-era Hollywood, this was hardly unusual. The Talmadge sisters all drank (and would all three eventually become dependent on alcohol or drugs). Myra Keaton kept a bottle of bourbon close at hand as she played her endless games of pinochle. And though Joe Keaton became a teetotaler sometime in his mid-fifties after taking up with a woman who was a strict Christian Scientist, his alcoholic binges and the resulting bouts of violence had been an ever-worsening staple of Buster's youth and early adulthood. But as long as Buster's prodigious physical and mental energy had been channeled into turning out six shorts and then two features a year, drinking had been just one component of a busy life that involved long shooting days, fiercely competitive card games late into the night, and come-one-come-all Sunday barbecues around the Italian Villa's backyard pool.

By late 1927, though, unhappy in his physically and emotionally distant marriage to Natalie and unsure about his professional future, Buster began using alcohol as an escape, or, as in the case of that impromptu trip to Nick Schenck's office, a form of liquid courage. Keaton's drinking in the eight or so years to come would continue to display this passive, self-destructive quality. Joe Keaton had been a loud, brazen, social drunk, given to boasting and picking fights. Buster drank quietly and methodically, as an act of inwardly directed violence—and the moment when this habit began to accelerate to the point of affecting his life can be clocked in near-exact synchronization with his loss of creative independence.

Once he arrived in Schenck's office thus "softened up," there was little hope of striking a deal any different than the one the Schenck brothers had arrived at in his absence. Keaton had never been one for arguing, and in the hands of a practiced negotiator like Nick Schenck he was as pliable as clay. Nick assured him that there was no better place he could land than at the studio that was in the process of becoming Hollywood's richest. On the Culver City backlot, he told Buster, "Our big new plant will give you bigger production, relieve you of producing. You just have to be funny."[8] He also offered Keaton a weekly salary of $3,000, a full 50 percent more than he had been earning from Joe, plus a share of the profit from his films and even a living allowance for his father. Keaton did try to argue Nick up on the weekly amount—not that the most generous raise would have made a difference in the realm that most mattered to him, the freedom to make his own movies—but Nick held firm: "Three thousand a week is just right. And now we go to lunch."

Keaton had spent his entire life working with and for members of his immediate and extended family: first his parents, then his brother-in-law, and now, in a new twist on the familiar nepotistic theme, his brother-in-law's more powerful brother. Both Schencks assured him he would be well taken care of, appealing to that unworldly, almost childlike part of his nature that made him both a creative powerhouse and a supremely bad businessman. This paternalistic management style—combined, no doubt, with the three drinks—served to soothe Buster's qualms about his loss of independence. It was only with years of perspective on the deal that he would recognize the move to MGM as the worst mistake of his professional life. "They made a big deal of it," he would recall in the mid-1950s, "but actually, for Joe to hand me over to Nick was about like transferring change from one pocket to another."

That transaction was only one small part of a larger set of deals MGM brokered around that time to consolidate its new position as the wealthiest and most influential Hollywood studio. In 1927 Mayer also made an arrangement with William Randolph Hearst to distribute and cofinance the newsreels Hearst produced with his own company. Marion Davies, the actress who had been Hearst's mistress for a decade, was another MGM asset, and there was a tacit understanding that her less successful vehicles would be floated by the studio in exchange for positive coverage of MGM films in Hearst papers. (It was not at all the case, as some have assumed from the fictionalized version of the Hearst/Davies relationship in *Citizen Kane*, that Davies was without talent; she was a nimble comedienne who began to shine once she left behind the lugubrious historical dramas Hearst preferred. But her films, though well received, were rarely big moneymakers.) Mayer used his friendship with Hearst, as he would do later with President Herbert Hoover, to position his company in the public mind as the world's foremost film studio. For his part, Hearst treated the slightly younger Mayer as a personal protégé, writing him affectionate letters signed "Uncle William" and directing the staff at his nationwide chain of newspapers to "please send out good pictures and pleasant stories about [the Mayer family] to our papers, morning and evening, with instructions to print."[9]

MGM had one huge advantage over its competitors: an extensive physical plant that occupied over 180 acres, planted all over with willows and orange trees. (These gracious touches, along with the wide alleys separating the lots, would disappear from the studio grounds almost as soon as sound technology came along, requiring bulky equipment and huge enclosed stages rather than mobile cameras and open-air sets.) In addition to the established stars in their acting stable—Greta Garbo, John Gilbert, Marie Dressler, the Barrymore brothers—the studio was preparing to launch the careers of up-and-comers like Joan Crawford and Clark Gable. A distinct house style was emerging: lavish production values, elegant sets by the legendary in-house designer Cedric Gibbons, and stories that, whatever melodramatic depths they plumbed, always landed firmly on the side of motherhood, patriotism, and straight white monogamy. Mayer's political conservatism shows up in his preferred movies' studied refusal to engage with social issues or deal with the seamier side of life. Above all MGM set itself apart from the other major studios by its performer-centric approach to building a picture. It was around this time that the studio's publicity department came up with the slogan that would sum up the company's actor-focused philosophy: "The studio with more stars than there are in heaven."

Nineteen twenty-seven was also the year Louis Mayer began campaigning for the creation of a new industry-wide body, the Academy of Motion Picture Arts and Sciences. His original intent was less to honor the achievements of people working in the medium than to forestall the creation of organized labor unions by craft guilds like Actors' Equity. Thirty-six other members of the Hollywood elite joined Mayer in this effort, and the group spent most of its first year of existence settling disputes between studios and the heads of guilds. It was only the following year, once the shift to sound was well under way and the industry's labor situation had stabilized, that the Academy began to focus on giving out awards. In an interview decades later, Mayer gleefully admitted that the awards system had been created as a means of control: "The best way to handle [moviemakers] was to hang medals all over them. If I got them cups and awards they'd kill themselves to produce what I wanted."[10]

Once Keaton returned from his ill-fated trip to New York, he was installed at MGM with no small measure of fanfare. A publicity photo shows him arriving at the studio's famous arched entryway with a pair of overstuffed suitcases labeled "gags." For a dressing room, he was offered his own spacious bungalow on the studio's sprawling Culver City lot, but to Mayer's displeasure he insisted on renting a house just outside the studio gates. An item in the *Distributor*, a weekly newsletter published by Loews and sent to theater owners around the country, condescendingly claimed that Keaton had been overwhelmed by the demands of running his own studio and would be grateful for MGM's help: "No one man could carry all the responsibilities of picture making as Buster had to. So grief finally slipped in. . . . Now, under MGM supervision, with MGM gag men and title writers to help and MGM technicians to guide him, Buster will again assume his place at the top of the industry."[11]

Keaton's initial contact at the company was not with the volatile and imperious Mayer, who was no fan of either Keaton's work in particular or comedy in general. Rather, the executive charged with settling the studio's new star into his job was Irving Thalberg, the twenty-eight-year-old "boy wonder" producer who had begun his career as an assistant to Universal chief Carl Laemmle when he was only sixteen. By the time Keaton arrived at MGM in early 1928, Thalberg, four years his junior, had already been Mayer's right-hand man for five years. Slender, handsome, and frail, Thalberg was born with a congenital heart defect. His mother was told when he was a small child that he would not live far past the age of thirty (and, as a result, Henrietta Thalberg was never to be found far away from her only son, even after he married MGM's leading lady, Norma Shearer). In fact, Thalberg would make it to the age of thirty-six before dying of heart failure. But the knowledge that his time on earth would be short gave him a fierce, hyperfocused energy analogous to Keaton's own.

Keaton and Thalberg had a few other traits in common. Both had risen to the top of their fields at a startlingly young age; both were soft-spoken but immensely stubborn; both were modest, with Keaton often giving codirectors full credit on films he had actually helmed and Thalberg refusing any screen credit at all; and both were deeply invested in the quality of the movies they turned out, even if they differed in their notions of how to make them. Thalberg and Keaton had also been socially friendly for several years: Before he married Shearer in 1927, Thalberg had ardently and unsuccessfully pursued Keaton's sister-in-law Constance Talmadge.[12]

Thalberg was both fond of Keaton personally and an admirer of his work, and for a while it seemed as if he would keep his promise to protect MGM's new star from meddling by higher-ups. In a continuation of the family-style management that had defined Keaton's life up to then, Thalberg assigned his own brand-new brother-in-law, the producer Lawrence Weingarten, to manage the new star's unit. But despite Thalberg's and the Schenck brothers' promises, Keaton's freedom was contractually curtailed from the start. A clause in the agreement he signed in early 1928 specified that he could be "consulted as to story and direction, but the decision of the producer shall be final." The managerial oversight he had chafed at in his last few films for Joe Schenck was now codified into law. After seven years of having a handpicked crew on call to whip up whatever sets and props were needed in the course of shooting, he suddenly found himself working for a massive top-down bureaucracy where, in his words, "you had to requisition a toothpick in triplicate."[13]

Still, for his first two movies at MGM—the silent ones—Keaton retained some measure of creative control. For *The Cameraman* (1928) he was even able to retain several members of his old team, many working with him for the last time: Fred Gabourie as production designer, Elgin Lessley as cinematographer, and Clyde Bruckman as gag writer. Harold Goodwin, who played the villain in *College* and had developed a friendship with Keaton, returned in another incarnation of the Buster character's unscrupulous romantic rival. The director assigned to the project was Edward Sedgwick, a fellow former child vaudevillian who had grown up in a family act, the Five Sedgwicks, that used to cross paths with the Keatons on the touring circuit. Sedgwick would go on to direct all of Keaton's features at MGM and, many years later, share an office with him as a behind-the-scenes gag writer at the studio. After clashing initially on the set of *The Cameraman* the two men became good friends, with Sedgwick intervening, usually in vain, to save Keaton's ideas from being shot down by producers. In the 1930 talkie *Doughboys* they can be seen onscreen together harmonizing on a song with Cliff "Ukulele Ike" Edwards—one of the few moments in the gratingly cacophonous *Doughboys* that occasion actual pleasure on the viewer's part.

The story of *The Cameraman* follows a street tintype photographer who decides to reinvent himself as a newsreel cameraman after he falls in love with a secretary (Marceline Day) at the office of a newsreel company. In a neat bit of branding for the studio's newly hatched collaboration with the Hearst news empire, the office door is clearly marked "MGM News." It is Keaton's last great film, albeit one that in small moments betrays a sentimentality that would never have passed muster in a production from the Buster Keaton Studio. The film historian Imogen Sara Smith, one of the most astute observers of Keaton's comedy, has called this film "the last rose of summer," a phrase that captures the poignancy of witnessing the first and last time the talents of this unique filmmaker would manage to find full expression in the context of a big studio picture.[14]

In *The Cameraman* Keaton was working for the first time not from a skeletal story outlined on a postcard but from a fully fleshed-out script put together by, in his words, "too many cooks" in the MGM screenwriting department (only two writers are credited, but it was the studio's habit to sic entire teams of writers on a project, even if their names were left off the screen).[15] After repeatedly pleading his case to management, Keaton was able to strip away some of the extraneous story elements—as he put it years later, "Thalberg wanted me involved with gangsters, and get mixed up with this one and that one, and that was my fight, to eliminate those extra things."[16] But this remains one of his most heavily plotted silent features, with a love triangle, a professional coming-of-age story, and a big action set piece that takes place during a gang war in a heavily exoticized backlot version of New York's Chinatown.

The Cameraman is a good movie to use as an introductory stepping-stone to Keaton for newcomers, not because it is typical of his work but because it feels somehow cushioned from the sharp edges to be found in some of his earlier films, where romance is as likely to be sent up as swooned over. A pair of matched close-ups of the lovers' eyes as they gaze at each other over the top of his newly acquired movie camera has a tremulous sweetness that seems out of character for this pathos-averse director—but it is hard to resist an excuse to get closer to those wonderfully expressive eyes. And late in the film, when a betrayed and rejected Buster sinks to his knees on a sandy beach, it is both a step closer to melodrama than Keaton has ever ventured and a welcome chance to see him explore new territory as an actor.

The love story at the movie's center is, by Keaton standards, substantial. To call Marceline Day's Sally a well-rounded character would be a stretch, but at least she has a job, gets more screen time than the quasi-Victorian heroines of his earlier films, and seems to be won over by the Buster character's actual personality rather than by his courtly fulfillment of some arbitrary task. Sally is played with great verve and charm by Day, Buster's best onscreen love match since the Sybil Seely days. Joe Schenck had always believed in hiring whatever actress was handy, affordable, and easy on the eyes, but MGM was not a company to skimp on leading ladies, female stars being one of its most prized corporate assets.

At the time the lissome, doe-eyed Day, twenty years old, was a rising MGM contract player. She had been acting since the age of fifteen, first as one of Mack Sennett's Bathing Beauties and later opposite male performers as distinct from one another as the childlike comedian Harry Langdon, the comic western star Hoot Gibson, and the horror maestro Lon Chaney. The year before appearing in *The Cameraman*, Day was named one of the "WAMPAS Baby Stars," an annual selection of up-and-coming actresses by the Western Association of Motion Picture Advertisers that served as a launching pad for many major actresses: Clara Bow, Ginger Rogers, Joan Crawford, Lupe Vélez. Marceline Day's star never rose quite that high; she made a string of good films in the late 1920s, crossed over into talkies with some success, and won consistent critical raves even in her weaker pictures. But with the coming of sound she had trouble finding suitable vehicles. Her last film was a western for a Poverty Row studio in 1933. The next year she retired from acting, married a wealthy furrier, and stayed out of the public eye until she died in 2000, never in all those years granting a request for an interview.

Another reason *The Cameraman* stands out in Keaton's filmography is the New York City location filming. The Chinatown set was built on MGM's backlot, but principal photography had started in midtown Manhattan. The huge crowds the shoot attracted made filming difficult: a home movie taken by an observer on set shows what look like hundreds of people packed against barricades just to watch Keaton, in character, cross a street carrying his movie camera. The presence of so many gawkers disturbed the congenitally shy Buster, who after living for ten years in the small town that was the Hollywood movie colony hadn't yet grasped that he was now too famous to walk down Fifth Avenue incognito.

After only a few days of shooting, the production, then titled *Snap Shots*, was moved to the MGM backlot. But enough views had been captured of the busy streets of 1928 New York, with crisscrossing trolleys and double-decker buses barely missing Keaton's darting form as he sprinted through traffic, to make the rest of the movie hum with an energy that's more urban and modern than in any movie he had made over the previous decade in comparatively pastoral LA.

The most valuable footage from that scrapped location shoot was that solo baseball game acted out entirely in pantomime in an empty Yankee Stadium, with the unscriptable grace note of an elevated subway train crossing the screen in the background. Later on there is a scene in a tiny changing room at a public pool where Buster and a burly man try to change into bathing suits at the same time, getting hopelessly entangled in each other's limbs and garments. Both these sublimely funny scenes, and another in which Buster destroys the wall of his boardinghouse bedroom while trying to open a recalcitrant piggy bank, were wholly improvised on set. In fact the changing-room scene was so spontaneous that the unit manager, Ed Brophy, had to be called in to play the second bather.[17] By the time Keaton made his next movie at MGM, *Spite Marriage*, that kind of looseness on set would be an impossibility.

The Cameraman performed well at the box office and was almost universally praised by critics. Company lore had it that Thalberg would run the picture over and over in the screening room near his office, his slight frame doubled over in laughter; the dressing room scene was his favorite.

The widely acknowledged success of Keaton's first outing at MGM makes it all the more confounding why the studio's next move was not to relax but to tighten the producer Larry Weingarten's grip on the new star's production unit. In his memoir Keaton remembers, "I kept pleading: 'Give me Eddie Sedgwick to direct, two or three writers, my own prop man, electrician, wardrobe woman, and a few technicians, and I will guarantee to deliver pictures as good or better than *The Cameraman*.'"[18] In retrospect this was Keaton's last stand, a moment when, if anyone had listened, one small but important part of film history, and one man's whole life, might have turned out differently. But Thalberg, with his deep allegiance to the producer-centric ethos of the studio system, rejected this pitch for an independent unit, perhaps out of fear that if he granted it every star on the lot would start pushing for the same.

For decades after Louis Mayer fired Keaton, MGM used *The Camera-man* as a training film for new hires in the comedy department. The studio literally wore the print out using it for this purpose; the version that survives today has about three minutes missing because the original negative was damaged by striking too many prints off it.[19] Ironically, the missing scenes involved the Buster character's failed early attempts to capture news events on film: the launching of a battleship, a parade up Fifth Avenue. In a later scene that does survive, Buster sits in mortification in the screening room as the MGM newsreel staffers mock the double-exposed footage that makes it look as if the ship is sailing through the crowded parade grounds. In real life Keaton's relationship to MGM was just the reverse: the man they sent out in the streets with a camera was not an incompetent but a master, and the footage he returned with was not bungled but brilliant. What came next for the real Buster was also the opposite of what had happened to his fictional counterpart. Instead of "making good" by proving his worth after an early humiliating failure, he had carried through on his initial promise—that letting him do things his own way would result in a good and successful film—and was nevertheless punished by the outcome he had most feared. The cameraman was about to have his camera taken away.

23

Elmer

A *publicity photo for* Free and Easy, 1930.

With his second film at MGM, 1929's *Spite Marriage*, Keaton took on, or more accurately was assigned, a persona that would stick with him for the next four miserable years, until Louis Mayer sent him packing in 1933. The name of his character, a humble pants presser infatuated with a haughty stage actress, was Elmer Gantry—confusingly, no relation to the evangelizing antihero of the 1927 Sinclair Lewis novel of the same name. Over the course of the next four years Keaton's characters at MGM would be christened with such variations as Elmer Stuyvesant (in *Doughboys*, 1930), Elmer Tuttle (in *The Passionate Plumber*, 1932), and, in a few films including his last at the studio, *What? No Beer!* (1932), the extra-degrading Elmer Butts. Even when his MGM-era protagonists were named something other than Elmer, as in *Parlor, Bedroom and Bath* (1931) or *The Sidewalks of New York* (1931), they tended to share the same traits. They were clumsy, dimwitted, and gullible, mocked or disdained by the other characters. With a few exceptions, like the classics professor he played in *Speak Easily,* they were naïve, unsophisticated rubes, confused by the very existence of urban modernity and unsettled to the point of alarm by the presence of women.

Displaying a level of cluelessness that's still perplexing ninety years later, MGM's producers and writing staff failed to grasp that their new hire was uniquely qualified to solve the very problem they struggled with after his arrival: finding the right projects to cast him in. The persona he brought with him from his own films was simply inscrutable to them, or worse, they *thought* they understood it and chose new roles for him out of that deep misapprehension. In the translation from Buster to Elmer, Keaton's slightness of build became a pitiable lack of masculinity; his stoic reserve turned into dull incomprehension; and his characters' heroic struggle to master the material conditions of their world (technology, the laws of physics, the elemental forces of weather) was reduced to mere clumsiness. The name "Elmer" had been declining in popularity since the turn of the century, and by the late 1920s it struck the ear of the urbanized modern American as an old-fashioned country bumpkin name. It was, in itself, "funny," or at least the kind of verbal shorthand for humor that Keaton knew was wrong for his character well before he ever spoke a word on film.[1]

"Elmer" was also the name Keaton gave the pet Saint Bernard he acquired around the time he joined MGM. (Captain, the German shepherd Constance Talmadge gave the Keatons as a wedding gift, had been hit by a car and killed a few years earlier.) Elmer the dog became a studio fixture, accompanying Keaton to work every day and taking afternoon walks up and down the length of the lot with Greta Garbo. Keaton's namesake pet was the ostensible reason—or the flimsy excuse—for the cheeky sign he had made to hang over the front door of the bungalow dressing

room Mayer eventually forced him to move into on studio grounds: "Keaton's Kennel." The double meaning was clear: just as Keaton was keeping
a pet in his Mayer-approved quarters, so he himself was being kept by
studio management. Giving his dog the name that symbolized his own
professional domestication, and then going out of his way to underline
the connection by hanging that sign in full view of his employers, was a
form of passive—for Buster, everything was passive—resistance.

There would be many more Elmers, human and canine, throughout
Keaton's life. In a number of the low-budget quickie shorts he made for
Educational Pictures in the mid-1930s—*Grand Slam Opera*, *Allez Oop*,
Tars and Stripes, *Blue Blazes*, *One Run Elmer*—that would again be
his character's name. A few years later, making what he called "lousy"
two-reelers for Columbia, he revived the name for at least one outing,
1940's *Pardon My Berth Marks*. And in the late 1950s and early '60s, when
he and Eleanor raised Saint Bernards on their acre and a half of land in
the San Fernando Valley, one of their dogs would be called Elmer II. The
way this name kept recurring by Keaton's own choice suggests it came
to mean something more to him than a reminder of the trauma of his
MGM years. He seems to have grown attached to the moniker, maybe as
a dark joke about those times, or maybe simply because it reminded him
of that first Saint Bernard, whose sad fate we will learn in a later chapter.

At least by the final reel of *Spite Marriage*, the human Elmer's first
and last appearance in a silent film, he has transformed into a recogniz-
ably Keatonian hero. After the timid dry cleaner winds up married to his
actress crush for reasons explained by the title—she wanted to make the
actor she was really in love with jealous—he gradually proves his valor
through athletic feats of loyalty, culminating in a last act that takes place
in one of Keaton's old favorite settings, a ship at sea.

Still, the heavy hand of studio control is more in evidence in *Spite
Marriage* than in *The Cameraman*. The gangster subplot Keaton fought to
keep out of that film makes a third-act appearance in this one, as the boat
is invaded by rum-runners whom Elmer must fight off single-handedly
and with an unusual degree of violence (a vicious fistfight, multiple bottles

broken over heads). Moments where improvisation and pure comic action are allowed to take over are few and far between, but when they come they are memorable, like a four-minute-long scene in which the bride, having drunk too much on her wedding night, collapses into a boneless heap on the floor of the couple's hotel room. Buster/Elmer's task is to somehow transfer the dead weight of her body to the bed as she slides again and again out of his grasp, necessitating the use of various props and occasioning a series of complicated two-person falls. Like the dressing room scene in *The Cameraman*, it's an extended riff on the comic possibilities of two bodies in close proximity, but here there's the added frisson of the two characters being romantically linked, however unhappily.

There's nothing prurient about the putting-the-bride-to-bed routine, in keeping with Buster's lifelong distaste for "working blue." None of the awkward positions Trilby's body flops into is particularly revealing, and after he finally manages to hoist her onto the mattress, the besotted Elmer gives her no more than a chaste peck on the cheek before retiring to his own separate room. Nonetheless, producer Larry Weingarten objected strongly to the scene's inclusion, saying "I don't like that type of thing in my pictures." Keaton went over his producer's head to Thalberg and put up a fierce fight; in his words years later, "I talked like a Dutch uncle to save that scene."[2] It was one of the last times anyone at MGM would listen to him, but he was right: a write-up in the *Los Angeles Times* notes that, while the whole movie was a hit with the crowd, the hotel scene "had yesterday's matinee audience almost rolling on the floor in shouts of laughter."[3]

The putting-the-bride-to-bed routine, like the name "Elmer," would have a long afterlife. As a gag writer for Red Skelton in the 1940s, Keaton choreographed a similar routine for Skelton and MGM's star dancer Eleanor Powell. He himself revived the sketch with his third wife, Eleanor Keaton (also a former dancer at MGM), in the sack-of-potatoes role, for a series of bookings at European circuses and music halls in the 1940s and '50s. And Gregory Peck and Audrey Hepburn enacted an abbreviated version of it in 1953 near the beginning of William Wyler's *Roman Holiday*.

Spite Marriage's Trilby Drew (Dorothy Sebastian), the egocentric stage star who uses Elmer as a pawn in her scheme, is one of the most fully developed, if least likeable, of all Keaton heroines. A far cry from the sweet gingham-clad love objects of his early films, Trilby is a jaded sophisticate who's clearly more versed in the arts of both drinking and lovemaking than the socially awkward and sexually naïve Elmer. Her treatment of him is despicable right up to the final reel, when she finally begins to recognize his bravery and devotion as he rescues her from one shady gangster after another. But ill-tempered petulance and all, Trilby stands out amid Keaton's onscreen female foils as a real character whose decisions—usually terrible ones—are essential in moving the plot forward.

Like the cheerfully amoral pre-Code heroines who were about to enjoy a brief run of freedom in the early sound era, Trilby never gets a comeuppance for her calculating ways. Her relationship with Elmer, at least up until that last reel of seafaring adventures, has an almost sadomasochistic tinge; the more she spurns him, the more he pines for her, and although she finally takes him back after multiple displays of acrobatic valor, she never apologizes. Even more than Marceline Day's sympathetic secretary in *The Cameraman*, Trilby is a modern leading lady, a late-1920s example of the ever-evolving "New Woman." It's certainly hard to imagine any previous Keaton heroine, usually a virginal type watched over by a looming father or brother, marrying the hero on a selfish whim and then drinking herself unconscious.

However perverse their dynamic, Trilby and Elmer seem in the end to belong together, thanks to the tangible real-life chemistry between Sebastian and Keaton. Keaton had been sleeping with other women on and off since his official Talmadge-approved ejection from Natalie's bedroom five years earlier, but Dorothy Sebastian appears to have been the first one with whom he had an ongoing romantic affair, beginning sometime before the filming of *Spite Marriage*. They were involved on and off for the next year, until Sebastian married the western star William Boyd, best known for playing the clean-cut cowboy hero Hopalong Cassidy. She and

Keaton would rekindle their romance in 1936, after the breakup of both of their marriages and his second, successful stint in rehab.

Sebastian's background as a dancer made her an able scene partner for physical comedy; in the hotel room scene she was not merely a rag-doll prop but a skilled, if motionless, participant. Offscreen she was a throwback to the type of woman Keaton had dated during his first years in Hollywood, like the athletic comedienne Viola Dana: a free-spirited actress with a taste for practical jokes and a presence on the Hollywood social scene. She was an Alabama-born former showgirl who had befriended Louise Brooks when they were both thinly clad chorines in the racy Broadway revue *George White's Scandals*. (A review of the 1924 edition in which they appeared noted of the skimpy costumes that "decent women in the audience hid their faces until they could get used to the spectacle.")[4] Later, as a contract player at MGM, Sebastian had a role as a reformed flapper in the silent Joan Crawford vehicle *Our Dancing Daughters*. In real life she was also known as something of a party girl, if one with a low alcohol tolerance; her nickname around town was "Slambastian" for her habit of falling to the floor after only a few drinks.

It's not clear whether the drunk scene in *Spite Marriage* was based on Sebastian's fabled tendency to pass out cold, but there is some evidence that alcohol later became a problem in her life. In 1937 she was arrested for driving drunk on her way home from dinner at Keaton's house. Sebastian tried to convince a judge that it was her nephew, also a guest at the meal, who had been behind the wheel. This Trilby-like ruse was not successful, and she was sentenced to a year's suspension of her driver's license and a seventy-five-dollar fine. "Ex–Leading Lady Drunk" read one ungenerous headline about the incident. But Sebastian does not appear to have struggled with addiction to anything like the degree Keaton did, and her film career was far from over. She successfully navigated the transition to sound and continued working well into the 1940s. She had a small role in the 1939 George Cukor comedy *The Women* and was cast in Frank Capra's 1946 classic *It's a Wonderful Life*, though her part ended up on the cutting room floor.

The un-Keatonesque thread of pathos that ran through *The Camera-man* becomes a denser part of the weave of *Spite Marriage*. Trilby walks out on her husband the morning after their spur-of-the-moment wedding, advised by her lawyer and agent that her career will be ruined if word gets out that she's married a "cheap little pants presser." Meanwhile Elmer, still unaware that the marriage is a sham, knocks on her hotel room door with a bunch of flowers and a small stuffed dog. In a typical bit of MGM lily-gilding, the stuffed pet even has a teardrop embroidered under one eye. Trying to cheer up his hungover bride, Elmer opens the door a crack and makes the toy peek through, moving its head as if to make it speak. The joke is on him, as the only ones there to witness this ingratiating display are the members of Trilby's management team.

It's a small moment, and certainly less demeaning than many others he was about to endure in his new life as a contract player, but that heartstring-yanking stuffed dog is a prop it's impossible to imagine Keaton choosing on his own. *Spite Marriage* is full of such small tip-offs that the producers, not the star, were the ones in charge. But it remains recognizable as a Keaton film, with a story, a style, and a sense of humor largely in tune with his sensibilities.

Having realized before his producers did that sound was the future of the medium, Keaton had asked to make *Spite Marriage* his first talking picture, but the most Thalberg would offer was a synchronized music track with a few sound effects (blessedly few, as they are further examples of lily-gilding, emphasizing gags that are funnier on their own). MGM was the last major studio to adopt sound technology, and while they were producing some talkies by 1929, soundstage space on the lot was still at a premium. Mayer's conservatism extended to his approach to new technology, and Thalberg shared his belief that the talkie craze was merely a passing fad. The studio waited until 1930, three years after *The Jazz Singer* upended the industry, to debut the voices of several of its most valuable stars: Greta Garbo, Lon Chaney, and Buster Keaton.

Garbo became an even bigger star after she unveiled a husky Swedish-accented contralto voice in the drama *Anna Christie* with the line:

"Gimme a viskey. And don't be stingy, baby." She was one of only a handful of silent-era stars, along with Joan Crawford, William Powell, and Ronald Colman, to navigate the changeover to talkies with such ease that she increased her box-office drawing power. Chaney's story was much sadder. He had been an esteemed actor since the late teens, known as "the man of a thousand faces" for his ability to use makeup and body postures to transform himself into grotesque or monstrous characters: the Hunchback of Notre Dame, the Phantom of the Opera, the Wolfman. His first and only appearance in a sound film, a remake of his 1924 hit *The Unholy Three*, revealed that he had a rich voice to go with his marvelously expressive face and body. But only seven weeks after that movie's release, Chaney died suddenly of a throat hemorrhage at the age of forty-four.

As for Keaton, his introduction to talkies came in two stages. He had a nonspeaking dance sequence in *The Hollywood Revue of 1929*, MGM's attempt to capitalize on the early sound-era fad for revue-style musicals. The following year he took on his first real speaking role in *Free and Easy*, another musical set on the MGM backlot.

Career-wise, Keaton more than survived the transition to sound—he prospered under it, with every movie he made for MGM turning a tidy profit. Biographies and film histories have a tendency to skate quickly past Keaton's sound films at MGM or lump them into a single tragic category, when in fact, though all bad, they're bad in distinct and telling ways. They share the quality of being painful to sit through, especially the late ones in which the star's alcoholism and depression are plainly visible. But for viewers who care about his work and life, about the period of transition between silent and sound filmmaking, or about the changes in technology and popular taste that came with the first years of the Great Depression, the ten feature-length talkies he made between 1930 and 1933 are important documents. To watch them is to witness in real time the extinguishing of a singular artist's creative spark and the erosion of his professional confidence. It is also to see a long tradition of silent-comedy filmmaking—one that emerged from vaudeville, pantomime, magic shows, and other forms of live stage performance—in the process of being violently displaced by a new art form.

Aside from their misuse of their principal asset, the sound films Keaton made at MGM resemble each other in their uniform ugliness: they're harshly lit and stiffly staged, with soundtracks that veer between muffled and blaring. These characteristics were not uncommon in the very first talking pictures, given the vexing technical demands they posed. For the first time moviemaking required enclosed soundstages lit by bright, hot floodlights, with actors keeping close to a stationary microphone and the camera immobilized in a heavy soundproof box known as a "blimp." Still, not every sound film of the early 1930s was as statically framed and lumpily paced as, say, *Free and Easy*, Keaton's first talkie. Though, like every film he made at MGM, it was a box-office success, this frantically busy backstage musical might as well have been designed for the exclusive purpose of humiliating and misusing its star. Its ninety-two-minute running time feels interminable, with extended Buster-free stretches of dubbed operetta that portend Mayer's mid-1930s obsession with the warbling love duets of Jeanette McDonald and Nelson Eddy.

These singing scenes, like the dance sequences in which rows of identically dressed chorus girls execute unimaginative choreography with widely varying levels of skill, often involve Keaton's character only as a spectator, though he does get a chance to both sing and dance by the end of the movie. The screenwriters couldn't possibly have intended it, but the story is so stark an allegory about what was about to happen to him at MGM that, watching it with the knowledge of what came next, you want to shout "Run!" He plays Elmer (sigh) Butts, an accountant from Gopher City, Kansas, coming to Hollywood for the first time—not to become a star himself but to manage the acting career of his unrequited crush, local beauty queen Elvira Plunkett (Anita Page). Her pushy stage mother (Trixie Friganza) accompanies them on the train west, never missing a chance to express her contempt for the feckless Elmer.

What follows is, in essence, the story of a man being made into a movie star against his will. Trying to gain admission to the MGM lot, Elmer is accidentally swept up in a casting call and winds up playing a bit part so badly that he becomes an inadvertent comedy sensation. Elvira is courted by a caddish movie star (Robert Montgomery, at the start of an acting and directing career that would span five decades). Against all narrative and moral logic, she ends up choosing the cad—who in an earlier scene tried to foist himself on her by force—over the purehearted but slow-witted Elmer. Along the way there is much frenetic dashing between movie shoots in progress on the MGM lot, with cameos from studio directors and stars including Lionel Barrymore, Cecil B. DeMille, Jackie Coogan, and Dorothy Sebastian.

Free and Easy was originally titled *On the Set*. That would have been a more fitting title for what is in essence a promotional film for the studio, manifestly devoid of both freedom and ease. If nothing else this charmless backstage romance provides a glimpse at what the MGM lot looked like at the moment of transition from silent to sound. But though it departs from the premise that a movie studio is a magical place to be, the film somehow manages to make every moment spent there feel excruciating.

Elmer's audition for one role consists of little more than being throttled, thrown to the ground, and stepped on by a series of hefty character actresses, ending with Friganza, a matronly character comedienne. (She winds up getting cast as the queen to his king, making for a weird moment later on when he must sing a coyly suggestive duet with the mother of the girl he loves.) These repeated beatdowns offer Keaton the chance to show off a few nifty falls and to showcase his long-practiced skill at enduring physical punishment. But they serve no narrative function and fail to evolve from one repetition of the gag to the next; all that changes is the intonation of each successive battle-axe as she reads her line. Seen in this static, repetitive format, Keaton's still-impressive stunt work loses its connection with character and purpose.

The central joke of the old Three Keatons act had been the mobility and resourcefulness of the young Buster as he evaded his father's flying hands and feet. In his silent films, the adversaries multiplied and got harder to escape: an entire city's police force, an avalanche of giant boulders, hordes of stampeding cattle or would-be brides, a hurricane. But locked into that static frame as he's hurled to the ground by a half-dozen grumpy women, Elmer Butts becomes a pitiable victim rather than a nimble survivor. To laugh at his maltreatment at their hands—not that there is much temptation to—would feel sadistic.

The unseemly pathos reaches its apogee in *Free and Easy*'s final sequence. Here Elmer has been cast as the lead in a truly awful-looking film within the film, a sort of comic operetta where he plays a sad clown complete with *Pagliacci*-style makeup: a white face with painted-on eyebrows and a downturned mouth. He has become the human equivalent of *Spite Marriage*'s stuffed dog with a sewn-on teardrop: a toy engineered to provoke sympathy. The effect for anyone even passingly familiar with the somber dignity of Keaton's silent character is startling.

After a group dance whose rote choreography is no challenge—though he brings to it his own almost parodic flair, recalling the vaudeville burlesques of his youth—there comes a horrific scene in which Elmer-as-clown, suspended on wires, dances the part of a marionette. Surrounded by a semicircle of grass-skirt-clad chorus girls, he dangles and swoops over the stage. To perform boneless passivity as completely as he does requires no small measure of physical skill, but the metaphor for Keaton's subjugation by his new employers is so precise it hurts.

The team of writers Thalberg assigned to *Free and Easy* cannot have consciously intended this reading—if they had been that perceptive about their star's character and abilities, they would have written him a better part to begin with. But though Keaton would make worse movies in his time at MGM, he would never film a scene that was as perfectly emblematic of his status at the studio. Swinging back and forth on wires like a floppy doll, he is the inverse of everything his stage and screen persona had represented since childhood, stripped of agency, imagination, and even basic mobility.

At the end of the number, Elmer-as-marionette gets hauled up and out of frame by whatever invisible mechanism had been controlling it from above. The next scene has an ecstatic Elmer, still in costume, rushing to tell his beloved—who has been observing the shoot—that the producers were thrilled by his performance and plan to make him a big star. (Why exactly a shy small-town accountant with no show business aspirations *would* be a skilled dancer and comedian is a question the logic-free script never poses.) As he is on the brink of confessing his love, the oblivious Elvira gushes that she has just gotten engaged to the leading man, then sends Elmer back onto the soundstage with the same maddening phrase Martin Beck had launched at Joe Keaton from the wings of the Orpheum theater back in 1916: "Make me laugh!" The last shot of *Free and Easy* is a medium close-up of Elmer's face in full clown makeup, gazing tragically up into the flies.

The apotheosis of the tragic clown had been a recurring final image in popular movies of the 1920s, in particular at MGM. Just two years before *Free and Easy* was released, Lon Chaney had starred in the lurid melodrama *Laugh, Clown, Laugh*, where he played a similarly made-up circus clown who devises his own onstage death after he realizes to his horror that he is falling in love with the young woman he found abandoned as a child and raised as his own daughter. A few years before that Chaney had had even more success as a lovesick clown in the 1924 smash *He Who Gets Slapped*, the first film overseen by Thalberg at the then new Metro-Goldwyn-Mayer company. That character's brazen masochism—his world-famous circus act consists of nothing but being slapped over and over, in the reenactment of a traumatic memory from his pre-clown days—matched the performance style of its star. Chaney specialized in misfits, sympathetic monsters of the type that would soon be played by Boris Karloff and Bela Lugosi. The son of deaf and mute parents, he had developed his pantomime skills in part as a way of communicating with them, and was as emotionally intense and temperamentally "hot" as the silent Buster character was cool and reserved. Lon Chaney was an exceptional, irreplaceable talent; his death at the very beginning of the sound era is one of the great what-might-have-been moments in film history. But whoever at MGM decided it was a good idea to graft a Chaney-style ending onto a Buster Keaton musical comedy betrayed a profound misunderstanding of both actors.

In the final frames of the close-up that ends *Free and Easy*, Elmer shuts his eyes as if to escape the brightly lit soundstage where his private humiliation, unbeknownst to the crew training cameras and microphones on him, is being captured forever on film. A more perfect analogy for that precise moment in Keaton's own life would be hard to imagine.

24

The Road Through the Mountain

F. Scott Fitzgerald in Hollywood, 1937.

There's no evidence that Buster Keaton and F. Scott Fitzgerald ever crossed paths at MGM. Nor would there have been any reason for them to. As a comedy star and a screenwriter—or, in their later incarnations, a gag writer and in-house script doctor—they belonged to separate hierarchies within the studio, both subordinate to the all-powerful production wing headed up by Irving Thalberg. Their social circles would rarely if ever have overlapped: Fitzgerald spent his time with fellow writers like Anita Loos and Hollywood power players including Thalberg and his movie-star wife Norma Shearer, while Keaton preferred the company of other performers and, outside of the odd bridge game with Thalberg, seldom mixed with the studio brass. If Fitzgerald and Keaton did chance to be introduced at the studio commissary, it's hard to imagine any interaction between these two very different men going further than "Please pass the salt."

That's a shame, because if Buster and Scott had ever managed to strike up a conversation, they would have found they had quite a few things in common over the dozen or so years when their lives might have crisscrossed on the Culver City lot. Their professional stars had risen at almost exactly the same time, with Fitzgerald's bestselling first novel, *This Side of Paradise*, coming out in 1920, the same year as Keaton's hit directorial debut, *One Week*. Their fortunes would fall in rough synchrony as well: both struggled to find commercial success in the second half of the 1920s, even as they were creating some of the best work of their careers. Both would have a creatively unfulfilling but well-paid stretch of working for MGM in the late 1920s and early '30s, survive (barely) a patch of severe addiction and underemployment in the mid-'30s, and return to the same studio late in that decade to hold less glamorous jobs while living soberer and more stable lives.

Their wives in that first period of overlap—Natalie Talmadge Keaton and Zelda Sayre Fitzgerald, the retiring homebody and the manic extrovert—could not have been more different, but they both disappeared from their husbands' lives at around the same time, and with a similar agonizing slowness. In Natalie's case, the couple's long-running sexual and emotional estrangement ended in a bitter divorce in 1932, while Zelda's worsening mental illness eventually led to her institutionalization.

To wonder whether Fitzgerald and Keaton ever shook hands at one of the fake film shoots Mayer loved to stage for visiting VIPs or sat side by side at a lunch counter over bowls of the commissary's signature matzohball soup may seem like a trivial thought experiment. But when I try to picture Keaton's life at MGM in the 1930s it is through Fitzgerald's experience there that I'm able to imagine the details, if only because no one else then alive had the descriptive powers to evoke that world so well.

His final novel, *The Last Tycoon*, still less than half finished when he died, was a roman à clef about a driven, enigmatic film producer transparently based on Irving Thalberg. Along with the author's letters and notebooks from that time, the sixteen existing chapters of *The Last Tycoon* provide a glimpse of the inner workings of a never-named major studio in the early years of sound—years that coincide almost exactly with Keaton's time at MGM.

Fitzgerald's first experience in Hollywood came in 1927, the same year Keaton left independent production for MGM. Still in high demand then as an author of short fiction for commercial magazines, Scott signed with First National Pictures to write a flapper comedy entitled *Lipstick*—a vehicle for none other than Constance Talmadge, whom he had long admired.[1] Scott and Zelda spent two months living at the fashionable Ambassador Hotel, drinking and fighting while he struggled to produce a script. That task was made no easier by the fact Scott was also carrying on an unconsummated but indiscreet flirtation with the seventeen-year-old actress Lois Moran, causing Zelda to act out by setting fire to a bathtub full of clothes she herself had designed.

The alcohol-fueled hijinks that had given the Fitzgeralds an international reputation as party guests were distinctly unamusing to many denizens of the film colony. Correspondence between Fitzgerald and his agent suggests that "Dutch" Talmadge, herself no slacker in the flapping department, was among those put off by the tales of the couple's drunken pranks—for example, the time they raided the coat room at a dinner party, gathered up the guests' purses and other valuables, and plunged them into a vat of bubbling tomato sauce.[2]

At the end of a very messy month, Scott's movie treatment was deemed too literary to film, and *Lipstick* never advanced beyond the first phase of development. Nor did Fitzgerald ever collect the remainder of his fee; the Fitzgeralds left California poorer than when they arrived. But this failed foray into scriptwriting did result in one encounter that would stay with the author for the rest of his life. While in town, Fitzgerald had lunch with the twenty-six-year-old Irving Thalberg, then in his third year as head of production at the studio. The goal was not to discuss any specific project but simply to meet. Thalberg, unlike most studio executives, was an avid reader (in a 1924 profile, he cited his favorite authors as Bacon, Epictetus, and Kant), so it was no surprise he might seek out the acquaintance of one of the major novelists of his generation.

Fitzgerald retained a very clear memory of something Thalberg said at this lunch. Twelve years later he reconstructed the speech in his notes for *The Last Tycoon*, where it appears in highly condensed form in the first chapter. Ironically for a novelist who tried in vain for years to crack the code of Hollywood screenwriting, Fitzgerald reproduced the executive's musings in his notebook in language that sounds for all the world like the big speech in a movie:

> We sat in the old commissary at Metro and he said, "Scottie, supposing there's got to be a road through a mountain . . . and two or three survey-ors and people come to you and you believe some of them and some of them you don't believe, but all in all, there seem to be half a dozen possible roads through the mountain, each one of which, so far as you can determine, is as good as the other. . . . You say, 'Well, I think we will put the road there' and trace it with your finger and you know in your secret heart and no one else knows that you have no reason for putting the road there . . . and you've got to stick to that and you've got to pretend that you know and that you did it for specific reasons, even though you're utterly assailed by doubts at times as to the wisdom of your decision."[3]

Fitzgerald's note below this scrap of remembered conversation remarks on the "shrewdness" of Thalberg's mind but also, more notably, on its "largeness." The analogy between grand-scale filmmaking and civil engineering—a Keatonian connection if ever there was one!—opens the way, like a road through a mountain, to a more expansive view on the arbitrary nature of leadership. It can't have helped but add to Fitzgerald's fascination that Thalberg was also extraordinarily good-looking, slight-framed and serious-faced, with large, liquid brown eyes and wavy black hair—an appearance not unlike that of a certain slapstick comedian whose contract his company had just acquired.

Throughout his life, Fitzgerald was drawn to tales of professional success and failure. More than one critic has noted how many of his novels and stories are satirical Horatio Alger tales that exchange Alger's up-by-the-bootstraps happy endings for something much darker. But the author's lasting obsession with the memory of Thalberg's frail, pensive figure against the backdrop of the studio commissary points to a different kind of hero than the protagonists of Fitzgerald's earlier fiction. Monroe Stahr, the widowed young executive who is Thalberg's fictional stand-in, bears little resemblance to the self-deluded bootlegger of *The Great Gatsby* or the gifted and ambitious but ultimately failed heroes of novels like *Tender Is the Night* or *The Beautiful and Damned*. Stahr is an actual worldly success, an acknowledged innovator in his field, respected and admired by his employees and colleagues—with the exception of the treacherous Pat Brady, a studio head very loosely based on Mayer.

What fascinated Fitzgerald about the producer many in the industry regarded as a sort of show-business savant was his breadth of vision: an ability to hold in his head many projects in all stages of development, filming and post-production, and to give meaningful creative input on them all while also keeping an eye on larger forces at work in the industry and the country. In an interview conducted years after Thalberg's death, the screenwriter Ben Hecht marveled over his gift for oral storytelling in production meetings.[4] But Thalberg was neither a writer manqué nor a frustrated director. Rather, he was a born corporate impresario, one of the main architects of the studio system that ruled Hollywood for the next four decades.

The method Thalberg innovated at Universal and perfected at MGM had to do with the skillful husbanding and deployment of talent throughout the company: creating and recombining teams of writers on a project, installing and replacing cast members like moving parts in an engine, holding interminable story conferences where script problems were hashed out and power struggles adjudicated.[5] The movies that emerged from these clashes and compromises were always subject to Thalberg's soft-spoken but functionally despotic last word. By the time he began writing *The Last Tycoon* around 1938, Fitzgerald had come to marvel at the workings of the intricate machine that was Thalberg's MGM, but first he had had to be ground up in its gears a few times.

In 1931, with Zelda just out of a long stay at a Swiss mental clinic, their ten-year-old daughter Scottie away at boarding school, and the unpaid bills piling up, Fitzgerald made a second, solo visit to the movie capital. This time he would be working for the young executive whose mystique had intrigued him four years earlier. Thalberg had tasked the author with adapting a popular *Saturday Evening Post* serial, *Red-Headed Woman*, into a sex comedy that would be titillating to audiences while protecting MGM's high-class brand. As the author of his time most renowned for both his sexual frankness and his understanding of youth culture, Fitzgerald must have seemed like a natural choice to tackle the script.

For the length of his two-month stay, Fitzgerald threw himself into the task, keeping mostly sober (though the exceptions were disastrous) while he researched the dramatic structure of recent hit films and made notes on editing and camera placement that went far beyond what a standard script would specify. But in keeping with MGM style, he was assigned an in-house cowriter, and Fitzgerald loathed collaboration even more than he loathed Los Angeles—a town about which he once wrote to his agent, "I hate the place like poison with a sincere hatred."[6]

Fitzgerald's 1931 Hollywood stint sounds, if possible, even more humiliating than his first. One Sunday afternoon, he and a fellow screenwriter were invited to a party at the Thalbergs' posh Malibu home. There, after violating several of his ever-changing self-imposed rules about exactly how much and when he could drink, Fitzgerald horrified the assembled guests, all A-list stars and directors, by calling them to the piano to listen while he warbled a song about the hostess's pet poodle with the silent-film heartthrob Ramon Navarro accompanying on the piano. The hosts were gracious about this embarrassing incident: Thalberg quietly asked a sober guest to take Fitzgerald home, and the next day Norma Shearer sent a telegram to the writer's MGM office: "I thought you were one of the most agreeable persons at our tea."[7] The following year Fitzgerald would write a short story, "Crazy Sunday," based on this event. Its tone is self-lacerating, even if the fictionalized version of the author comes off with rather more dignity than the real-life version did.

In the end the *Red-Headed Woman* script was also deemed impossible to film. As Anita Loos remembered it in her memoir, *Kiss Hollywood Good-By*, Thalberg handed the whole thing over to her for a rewrite, saying that "Scott tried to turn the silly book into a tone poem!"[8] This news was leaked to Fitzgerald by his cowriter as he was preparing to depart for the East Coast, believing that he had made good on his five-week contract and was about to see his name onscreen for the first time. He was so crushed by this second Hollywood rejection that, according to one executive at the company, "Fitzgerald didn't draw a nonalcoholic breath for a month."[9]

While Scott struggled in vain to produce a script that would both please his producers and advance his own literary fortunes, Buster was also dealing with the loss of a coveted project. Thalberg's big idea in 1931 had been to draw in shrinking Depression-era audiences with an all-star ensemble cast—a fresh idea in an industry long driven by films that tended to be, like Keaton's, built around a single strong personality.

As Thalberg envisioned it in one of his endless story conferences, these productions would be lush backdrops for Hollywood pageantry, "a painted carpet upon which the figures walk." The German novel *Grand Hotel* seemed like the perfect vehicle for adaptation: the year before it had been an international bestseller that MGM then acquired the rights to and bankrolled as a hit Broadway play. Thalberg was not particularly fond of the property, calling it "lousy," but he correctly sensed that with a star-packed cast and a generous production budget *Grand Hotel* would be an irresistible box-office draw.[10]

The story recounts the crisscrossing fates of a group of colorful types at a Berlin hotel: an over-the-hill ballerina, a crass business tycoon and his sexually harassed stenographer, a fallen aristocrat turned jewel thief, and a dying accountant who decides to spend his life savings on a stay at the luxury establishment. In the project's original conception, the ballerina was to be played by Greta Garbo, the stenographer by Joan Crawford, the industrialist by Clark Gable, the thief by the silent-era star John Gilbert (a former lover of Garbo's both onscreen and in real life, adding to the film's audience appeal), and the accountant—a mousy type named Kringelein—by Buster Keaton. The director, Edmund Goulding, had a hunch that the studio's top comedian might make a splash in a straight dramatic role, and Keaton was thrilled at the chance to test his range and appear in a prestige project alongside so many of the studio's biggest stars. But less than a month after the cast list was announced in the trade press, all of the male parts were recast.

Gable's star was rapidly rising, and it was decided that rather than playing supporting heavies he should be given romantic leads, so he was cast opposite another hot MGM property, Jean Harlow, in *Red Dust*. Gable's *Grand Hotel* part went to the veteran character actor Wallace Beery. Gilbert's career, on the other hand, was in steep and rapid decline from his days as the screen's most ardent lover. His offscreen behavior, including flagrant public drunkenness and gun-toting paranoia, had made him a special enemy of Mayer, whose sense of propriety was offended by the louche, profanity-spewing star. So the part of the urbane jewel thief went to John Barrymore—also a noted drunk, but in 1931 not yet a low-functioning one. Finally, after observing the chemistry of the Barrymore brothers on the set of the MGM detective comedy *Arsene Lupin*, Thalberg decided to replace Keaton with John's brother Lionel, the eldest child of the storied theatrical family and a stage star, film actor, and occasional director since the 1910s.

Thalberg at first preferred Keaton for the Kringelein role, but over the long course of story conferences that preceded a project the size of *Grand Hotel*, he was persuaded that a cast boasting not one but two Barrymores would add to the novelty value of a star-stuffed ensemble picture. Some sources suggest that Mayer put his thumb on the scale against Keaton, persuading Thalberg and Goulding that the comedian's growing reputation for drinking and absenteeism would make him unreliable on set. Certainly Mayer had no love for Keaton, or vice versa. But in the end the decision was Thalberg's to make. Despite his admiration for Keaton's style of comedy, the intuitive producer chose to cast the film based on what he felt would deliver *Grand Hotel* as a total, glossy package: Lionel Barrymore it would be.

Keaton was never informed of this change by the studio. He learned he had lost the part from a headline in *Variety*, and his response was the same as that of Scott Fitzgerald upon learning, only weeks before, that his script was about to be scrapped and rewritten: he soothed his disappointment by going on a lengthy drinking binge. It must have added to the sting for both Fitzgerald and Keaton that the properties offered to and then taken away from them went on to be industry-changing hits.

On its release in 1932, *Red-Headed Woman* was a box-office smash. Its star, Jean Harlow, had already appeared in a few big movies, but never in a part that allowed her to develop what would become her signature screen persona: a brash flirt with a smart mouth and a shameless awareness of her own sexual power. Audiences immediately demanded more Harlow, and in the five years that remained before her sudden death of kidney disease at age twenty-six, she made thirteen more films. *Red-Headed Woman* was unusually racy for an MGM release, with overtly sexual situations and teasing moments of suggested nudity. The moral panic it caused at the Hays Office and at church pulpits across the land helped lead to the stricter enforcement of the production code the following year, as the reins of the organization passed from Will Hays to the devout Catholic Joseph Breen.

Grand Hotel, released a week earlier than *Red-Headed Woman*, had even more success. Though reliable box-office statistics from the time are hard to pin down, it was by some accounts the top-grossing movie of 1932, the year often cited as Thalberg's creative peak. The next year it won the Academy Award for best picture and kicked off a genre of star-packed single-location films that lives on to this day, from *Airport* to *Clue* to *The Grand Budapest Hotel*. When John Ford's *Stagecoach* was released in 1939, its publicity campaign used the slogan "*Grand Hotel* on wheels." In a riff on this formula, the 1940 college picture *Winter Carnival* — scripted in part by an uncredited F. Scott Fitzgerald — was described by one critic as "*Grand Hotel* on skis."[11]

The first glimpse of *Grand Hotel*'s circular silver-and-black lobby desk, created by MGM production design guru Cedric Gibbons and photographed from a then-unusual bird's-eye angle by the studio's top cinematographer, William Daniels, provoked waves of applause from the audiences who flocked to the film on its yearlong roadshow tour. Ninety years after its release *Grand Hotel* remains an early triumph of the design style now known as Art Deco (in its day, it was simply called "modern"). Like many big successes of the very early sound era, the movie now plays as stiff and stagey in parts, more a well-crafted artifact than an engaging piece of storytelling. But it's fascinating to watch as an example of what the studio system was just starting to figure out it could do.

Grand Hotel is also a showcase for big performances that playfully burlesque the stars' public images. Garbo later dismissed her own turn as the faded dancer Grusinskaya, a figure so floridly tragic she verges on camp. It's in this role that the actress spoke the line that would follow her throughout her later life as a reclusive retired celebrity: "I just want to be alone." But Garbo's best moments come early on in her doomed romance with the count, when her somber mask gives way to an infectious smile as she all but skips through the hotel's lacquered halls.

John Barrymore feared he was too old for his role as the love-smitten baron. At fifty, he was twenty-three years older than his leading lady and would permit his world-famous profile to be photographed only from its better side. But he matches Garbo clinch for clinch in a performance that pokes wry fun at his long career as a swashbuckling rake. Garbo and Barrymore were great admirers of each other's work, and though they did not have an on-set affair (as both had done before with costars), their mutual adoration for the camera is on full and dazzling display. It returned their love: ninety years after the film's release, their scenes, including a discreet fadeout that leaves little doubt as to how the dancer and the nobleman end their first night together, are the high point of *Grand Hotel*.

The second plot, with Wallace Beery as the businessman and Joan Crawford as his traveling secretary and, it is implied, kept mistress, has held up less well. Beery had been a star since the 1910s and was one of MGM's most popular character actors. Crawford was an up-and-coming talent at the studio, having gained fame as a wayward flapper in silent melodramas like *Our Dancing Daughters* (costarring Keaton's longtime mistress Dorothy Sebastian). But their acting styles clashed: Where he was broadly gestural in communicating his character's grasping crudity, her understated emotional directness looked toward a new era of Hollywood. Beery was a temperamental man with a big ego who at one point stormed off the set saying he would come back when his scene partner learned to act. What he didn't see was that Crawford was acting for the close-ups—and very flattering close-ups they were, shot through a special box fitted with five layers of white silk by Daniels, the only cameraman Garbo would allow to light her.[12]

As Kringelein, the fifty-three-year-old Lionel Barrymore, stout and gray-haired, was a contrasting physical and temperamental type to his rakish younger brother John. Unlike Keaton, the eldest Barrymore sibling was then at a sweet spot in his career. When *Grand Hotel* premiered in the spring of 1932, he had just won the Academy Award for best actor, playing an alcoholic lawyer in the courtroom drama *A Free Soul*. He remained a popular star for decades afterward, specializing in bumbling-but-kindly roles in the Kringelein mode, but is probably best known to twenty-first-century audiences as the miserly Mr. Potter, Jimmy Stewart's banker nemesis in the 1946 classic *It's a Wonderful Life*.

Lionel's performance in *Grand Hotel* was widely praised. *Variety* wrote that "first honors again go to Lionel Barrymore for an inspired performance as the soon-to-die bookkeeper, a character drawn with bold outlines and etched in with a multitude of niceties of detail . . . a performance that goes the gamut of human comedy to half-expressed tragedy."[13] Nearly thirty years later, talking to Charles Samuels for his as-told-to autobiography, Keaton also admired Barrymore's performance, saying, "Lionel, as usual, handled himself masterfully," while noting that "I would have played the part differently. I do not say better, mind you, just differently."[14] He didn't elaborate on his vision for the character, but he had more to say about the experience of losing out on *Grand Hotel* than about any of the films he himself made at MGM.

If the decision had gone the other way in one of those Thalberg-led production meetings, what might Keaton have done with the role of Kringelein? It would certainly have been a unique role in his film career up to that point: a straight and even tearjerking supporting part with few chances for physical comedy, though he would no doubt have found places to work in gags and stunts. Kringelein's first big solo scene is almost dialogue-free, as the mild-mannered clerk stumbles up to his hotel suite tipsy from a night of carousing and feels his way through the darkened rooms into bed. Barrymore gets a few laughs bumping into the walls and furniture as he searches for a hidden flask, but it's easy to imagine Keaton turning the same scenario into a delirious cascade of falls.

Barrymore's performance as Kringelein is warm and endearing, even twinkly, played in an emotional register foreign to the more temperamentally cool Keaton. On the other hand, the comedian's constitutional reserve might have given his interpretation of the dying accountant a different, lonelier quality, compounded by the fact that, like Kringelein, Keaton was at that moment living through a kind of existential crisis. And though Keaton's voice, a froggy bass with an unmistakable midwestern twang, would have made Kringelein sound more rustic than the polished stage voice of Barrymore, the cast already offers up a grab bag of vocal styles: Garbo is a Swede playing a Russian, the Barrymores have the round mid-Atlantic vowels of stage-trained American actors of their generation, and Beery alone, confusingly, attempts a less-than-consistent German accent. (The chance to do an accent had been the bait Thalberg used to get Beery to take the part, which the actor had at first resisted, not wanting to play a villain.)

Keaton's presence in the film would also have changed the tenor of the ending, when Crawford's character Flaemmchen agrees to travel the world as the accountant's companion in his remaining days. In the existing version of *Grand Hotel* this relationship is framed as avuncular, not sexual: implied in the verbal contract between the two is that, unlike her former boss, Flaemmchen's new benefactor has no intentions toward her. If Keaton, still matinee-idol handsome at age thirty-six, had been paired with Crawford instead, the possibility of a romantic connection between the two characters would have been harder to overlook.

When *Grand Hotel* proved to be a smash, Keaton pitched Thalberg the idea of a burlesque takeoff with himself in the role of the clerk (this time afflicted not with a fatal disease but with incurable hiccups), Laurel and Hardy as the industrialist and his rival in button-manufacturing, Jimmy Durante as the romantic baron, and the middle-aged female comedy team of Marie Dressler and Polly Moran as the tragic ballerina and the put-upon stenographer. He described this never-realized project at length to Samuels, still sounding amused at the image of Dressler's "battleship of a figure" in a slapstick version of Garbo's costume: a white tutu, a floor-length fur coat, and "slippers about a foot and a half long."[15]

Spoofing more self-serious forms of entertainment was territory where Keaton felt at home. He had been doing it all his life, from his child-hood impressions of well-known stage stars through movies like *The Frozen North* and *Three Ages*, which parodied, respectively, Bill S. Hart's melodramatic westerns and the pseudohistorical epics of D. W. Griffith. Though the *Grand Hotel* spoof idea was little more than a clothesline from which to hang a story, Keaton had made successful comedies out of far flimsier premises. If the cast he proposed could have been assembled, the movie might well have been a hit; after all, Keaton's movies at the studio thus far, regardless of quality, had all turned a tidy profit.

But Thalberg chose another road through the mountain, and the *Grand Hotel* parody (the proposed title was *Grand Mills Hotel*, after an infamous Bowery flophouse called the Mills) was never made. It was Warner Bros. that not long after churned out a mediocre Vitaphone short called *Nothing Ever Happens*, a broad burlesque of the MGM hit with Greta Garbo's lighting double playing the role of the unlucky ballerina.

Whether or not Keaton would have made a good Kringelein, it's sad to consider how getting the role, or even getting the chance to spoof it later in a movie he actually wanted to make, might have changed his path at MGM by renewing his confidence in his own judgment. He said as much nearly thirty years later, in an unusual might-have-been moment for a man who seldom expressed regret or bitterness: "Doing a picture I was so eager to do might have enabled me to stop drinking and re-establish myself as a man whose only business was making people laugh."[16]

Keaton also misremembered the timing of the *Grand Hotel* events in a telling way. As he recounted the story to his ghostwriter Charles Samuels, after Keaton was fired from MGM in early 1933 Thalberg reconsidered and sent Buster's friend and frequent MGM director Eddie Sedgwick to invite him to come back and make the *Grand Hotel* parody. Keaton, still furious at Mayer, refused—for which, his late-fifties self admitted, "I was a fool."[17] In reality, almost a year and a half passed between the pitch and the firing, and Thalberg had dismissed the pitch out of hand. It is true that at some point after his dismissal Keaton angrily rejected an olive branch extended by Thalberg, but the *Grand Mills Hotel* project was long out of the picture by then. However much he liked both Keaton's comedy and the man himself, Thalberg was not about to hand over the production reins to an ever-less-dependable employee.

Maybe Keaton collapsed this chronology in his memory because losing out, twice in a row, on the chance to work on a creatively satisfying project at MGM seemed to him to exist on a single continuum with the humiliation of being fired just over a year later via an impersonal memo from the office of Louis B. Mayer, hand-delivered to his studio bungalow by messenger. After all, everything between those points had been a blur of bad movies and worse domestic relations, made blurrier by a soaring alcohol intake. As for the triumphant but false detail of the pitch being belatedly accepted, tacking that on might have been Buster's unconscious way of restoring some dignity to the ignominious memory of what he calls in the same chapter the worst years of his life. (It's also possible that Charles Samuels, who made no recordings of their interviews and often massaged his subject's anecdotes into a more conventional narrative shape, had a hand in the retelling.)

In the year and a half or so after Buster lost out on *Grand Hotel*—for reasons having nothing to do with that loss, though it can't have helped—his life went into free fall. His breakdown was never as public as the meticulously self-documented "crack-up" of the author of *The Great Gatsby*, but Keaton, who had been a stickler for commitment from both cast and crew on the sets of his own films, was suddenly getting a reputation for drinking and unreliability. Still, he remained MGM's top comedy star, and his movies, no matter how bad they got, kept making money.

His last film before the *Grand Hotel* near miss had been *The Sidewalks of New York*, the maudlin tale of a sheltered millionaire who takes on the project of reforming a gang of street kids in order to win the heart of one youth's sister. For the first time since his arrival at MGM, Keaton was paired with a director other than his friend Eddie Sedgwick. This time around he had been assigned Zion Myers and Jules White, a team up till then associated with a series of all-canine comedies called "the barkies." White would direct Keaton again in some of the cheap two-reelers he made for Columbia in the mid-1930s, and later work with the Three Stooges on some of their most successful features.

Keaton was annoyed at being made the first human subject for a pair of dog directors. Most of all he resisted White's overbearing style of direction: the former canine wrangler insisted on telling the veteran comic how to move. More infuriatingly for Keaton, he told him how *not* to, since the studio discouraged any stunts that might put their expensive property in physical peril. Whether because of this degrading work, his ever more distant marriage, or his deepening addiction, Keaton's behavior during the *Sidewalks* shoot pushed boundaries he had never tested before.

He persisted in his longtime tradition of after-lunch baseball games on the set, but now that he was an employee rather than the boss, these went from collaborative brainstorming sessions to an expensive delaying tactic. They also divided the cast and crew into the Keaton-supporting rebels and the loyal company types. Mayer, furious at both the defiance and the expense, threatened to insert a no-baseball clause in Keaton's contract. But afternoon batting practice aside, Buster was exploring more dramatic and costly ways to act out. Filming a scene that involved a dive off a boat, he evaded the waiting pickup craft, swam all the way to shore, and disappeared for a week of carousing.[19]

Sidewalks of New York was Keaton's least favorite of his own MGM talkies; he would recall it decades later as "godawful."[20] Even by the low standards of his early 1930s output, this film is among the worst, a limply paced and all but laugh-free attempt to transplant a version of the rich milquetoast character he had played on and off since *The Saphead* in 1920 into the setting of a thoroughly unconvincing backlot Lower East Side. But turkey though it was, *Sidewalks* was anything but a bomb at the box office. In fact, thanks to the clout of the studio's marketing arm it was the most financially successful of the eight features he made at MGM, and easily outgrossed every one of his independent films of the 1920s.[21]

His next film after *Sidewalks* was *The Passionate Plumber*, a leaden adaptation of a French stage farce that is most notable for being Keaton's first pairing with the popular stage and radio comic Jimmy Durante. Durante was two years older than Keaton, a ragtime pianist who had started in vaudeville in his teens. By the early 1930s he was starting to find work in the movies, where he never quite seemed to belong, though he would appear in a dozen or so over the next two decades before finding a place in the new medium of television.

Durante had gotten famous for doing everything that Keaton, not so much on principle as by disposition, would never do. The persona of the entertainer already nicknamed "Schnozzola" was a prolific talker, given to mugging, malapropisms, fourth-wall-breaking, and catchphrases like "Hot-cha-cha!" Though the two were friendly offscreen, Keaton admitted years later that Durante's constant rain of chummy punches in the arm actually hurt. Onscreen, they make for a gruesomely ill-matched pair. Durante's gonzo energy washes Keaton out, making his stillness look like inertia and his diffidence like passivity. Durante's relentless bonhomie can feel almost violent, though he was by all accounts a genuinely warmhearted man. In his presence Keaton's normally hyperexpressive body seems to stiffen and shrink, as if trying to burrow into the screen.

Since breaking up the family act Keaton had always preferred to perform, essentially, alone. Even during his years of apprenticeship with Arbuckle, the two had only rarely functioned as a two-man comedy team in the style of Laurel and Hardy. But Thalberg was looking to build a new star in Durante and still floundering for the right way to use Keaton, so it was decreed that these two comics so opposed in appeal and demeanor should make a series of movies together: *The Passionate Plumber*, *Speak Easily*, and *What! No Beer?* They were set to make another, *Buddies*, with the child star Jackie Coogan as third wheel, at the time of Keaton's firing in early 1933.

Speak Easily, together with *Doughboys*, is often called the best of Keaton's MGM pictures, but that only shows how low a bar a movie had to clear to earn that title. At least this wan backstage romance, directed once more by his original MGM collaborator Eddie Sedgwick, lets Keaton play someone nominally smarter than his stock "Elmer" character. Here he is a naïve classics professor who falls for a dancer and, falsely believing he has inherited a fortune, agrees to bankroll the lackluster traveling show she works with. Durante is the show's pianist, which gives him plenty of chances to do his signature bit: seated at the keyboard, he interrupts his playing to tell a joke directly to the audience, then laughs at it himself with a little head shake that seems to say "Ain't we havin' fun?" One participant who clearly ain't is Keaton. Though he has not lost his athleticism or his timing, he has little chance to use either in this loud, talky, and mostly static comedy.

Speak Easily does have one pratfall-rich scene between Buster and Thelma Todd, a tart-tongued comedienne sometimes billed as "the Ice Cream Blonde." In contrast to nearly all of Keaton's previous female costars, Todd was an experienced comic and a proven box-office draw by the time they worked together. She had already played opposite Charley Chase, Harry Langdon, the Marx Brothers, and Laurel and Hardy, and the comedy producer Hal Roach had teamed her with ZaSu Pitts, a comic and dramatic star since the silent era, in their own series of slapstick shorts about two working girls sharing a New York flat.

In *Speak Easily* Todd plays the gold-digging rival of Buster's pure-hearted but dull love interest. She tries to get the professor drunk and seduce him so that, by his own Victorian-era standards, he will be obliged to marry her, but in the process gets too trashed herself to follow through. The next morning, in one of the racier moments ever to occur in a Keaton film, the two of them wake up side by side—but in separate beds, with dialogue inserted to reassure the audience that, as per MGM standards, their night together was chaste. Todd's pre-Code cheekiness makes for a nice contrast with the professor's old-fashioned prudery, and in a welcome break from the cacophony of the scenes with Durante, much of the humor between them is physical rather than verbal. As with the *Grand Hotel* might-have-been, it's impossible not to imagine what might have happened if Keaton and Todd had gotten a chance to team up again.[22]

What! No Beer?, Keaton's last film at MGM, was made and released at his personal and professional nadir: when its release date came in February 1933, he had just been fired eight days before. Half a year before that, Natalie had finally sued him for divorce, and while the movie was being made Keaton was drinking, by his own estimate decades later, a bottle of whisky a day. He had essentially moved out of the Italian Villa and was living between his bungalow dressing room on the studio grounds and a tricked-out custom-built bus he had bought from a Pennsylvania Railroad tycoon and dubbed his "land yacht."[23]

To Mayer's intense annoyance, this thirty-eight-foot-long vehicle became a party magnet for disenchanted employees. Sam Marx, a producer in Thalberg's unit, remembered it as "a revolutionary headquarters, a center for employee dissent."[24] Keaton liked to park the land yacht on studio grounds, where it drew an around-the-clock crowd of drinking, card-playing comedy writers and actors, along with whatever female company they could find. Even Eddie Mannix, the head of studio security who served as Mayer's eyes, ears, and, when necessary, fists, sometimes showed up for a drink and a game. One often-repeated anecdote has Mayer bursting onto the land yacht to tell the revelers to pipe down and Keaton unceremoniously ordering him off the bus. Whether or not this story is true, the conflict it points to was real: Mayer's longtime distrust of Keaton's quest for independence was resolving into an active desire to oust this troublesome and ungovernable employee from the lot. Thalberg continued to stand up for Keaton, whether out of personal sympathy or because his comedies continued to turn a reliable, if not *Grand Hotel–*sized, profit for the company.

In a 1932 promotional short made for the "MGM on Parade" series, Keaton and his friend Lew Cody—a fellow star since the silent era, a fellow alcoholic, and since the death of his wife Mabel Normand two years earlier, a fellow bachelor—can be seen playing cards inside the vehicle in full naval costume: Keaton is styled as a Napoleonic admiral in a plumed hat, with Cody as his captain. A still photo taken around the same time shows Durante joining them in a sailor's uniform to pose outside the bus. Most of the publicity photos Keaton had posed for in his years at MGM were posed studio portraits that framed him as a smoldering matinee idol, in stark contrast to the dopey "Elmer" type he appeared as onscreen. But these deliberately goofy shoots taken in and around the land yacht are a strained attempt at behind-the-scenes comedy. The studio's powerful public relations arm was working overtime to frame this chaotic phase of their star's new bachelorhood as a devil-may-care good time.

What! No Beer? may not be the worst movie Keaton ever appeared in, but it's without question the hardest to watch. The director, once again, was Sedgwick, and the script was by Thalberg's usual successive teams of writers. Production began at the height of Buster's miserable "land yacht" period in late 1932, and filming had to be stopped several times on account of his absences. Sometimes he would disappear on days-long benders, then get sent by management to an expensive drying-out facility in Arrowhead Springs while the cast and crew tried to shoot around his absence.

In the end the shoot took more than six weeks to complete, even though the resulting film lasts barely over an hour. The sixty-five-minute running time is a mercy given how hard it is to see Keaton, still only thirty-seven years old, visibly ravaged by drink and depression. His appearance has altered shockingly since *Speak Easily*, filmed just half a year before. In that film he might be said to look tired and a little drawn, older than his boyish persona in the silent years, but not worryingly unwell. In *What! No Beer?* his face appears gaunt, his eyes puffy, and his speech in some scenes markedly slurred. On the rare occasions when the story called on him to outrun an adversary or turn a flip over a piece of furniture, Keaton's body was still agile enough to do it—those basic stunts were embedded in his muscle memory. But his every look, gesture, and line delivery communicates a sense of dazed entrapment, and the surrounding movie has a slapdash, listless quality that seems to mirror his chaotic inner state.

In some scenes the distinction between Keaton and his character, maybe the most passive and pushed-around of all the abject Elmers he played, seems to collapse. Both have given up on trying to get a word in edgewise, much less offer any resistance to the blows that rain down on them from all sides. In an extra twist of irony, Durante plays a character whose first name is Jimmy. It's as if the screenwriters were going out of their way to help establish the public persona of their new comedy star— which may well have been the case, given how tenuous Buster's hold on the top spot was at the time the script was being written.

The extra-humiliatingly named Elmer J. Butts, like the professor in *Speak Easily*, is an unworldly patsy, easily conned out of the cash he has saved up and hidden in the stuffed specimens around his taxidermy shop. *What! No Beer?* is a topical comedy set against the coming end of Prohibition, a subject just then being debated by "wet" and "dry" factions in Congress after the landslide victory of Franklin Delano Roosevelt in the 1932 presidential election: the official repeal of the Eighteenth Amendment would not come until December 1933, ten months after the movie's release.

Keaton and Durante play a pair of buddies who run afoul of bootleggers when they decide to make their fortune by opening a brewery just as the national vote is about to pass. What follows is a blur of double-crossings and gangster-related hijinks, with an energy level at once frantic and inert.

There's a long scene in a flooded brewery where Durante, Keaton, and a crowd of extras do variations on the old "human mop" routine from Three Keatons days, with Buster's limp body being dragged and flung through a roomful of suds.

Every one of the dreary talkies Keaton made at MGM had at least one good scene, a moment when he managed to break free from the prison of Elmer and become the performer he still knew how to be. These moments point toward a different path his career might have taken in the age of sound. In *Doughboys* there's the scene when, for no reason provided by the story, he engages in a three-man jam session with Ed Sedgwick and Cliff "Ukulele Ike" Edwards, Buster picking a uke of his own as they harmonize on an old vaudeville tune. In *The Passionate Plumber* there is Keaton's pistol duel with Gilbert Roland, an extended riff on the comic possibilities of an affair of honor. (Keaton would re-create this act as a pantomime during his successful engagements at the Medrano circus in Paris in 1947.)

What! No Beer?'s one good scene comes near the end of the movie and is completely dialogue-free. The much-put-upon Elmer Butts finds himself driving a truckload of beer barrels across town, pursued by a pack of gangsters. He parks the truck on an upward incline and, inevitably, the barrels break free and roll down the hill, seeming to chase Elmer as he scrambles out of their way. It's a small-scale reinvention of the breathtaking finale of *Seven Chances* (1925), which had Keaton's bachelor protagonist being chased by a pack of would-be brides into a perilously steep chasm. On the way down, he sets off an avalanche and must outrun dozens of hurtling rocks, from tiny pebbles to giant boulders (the stones were papier-mâché props, but the heaviest ones weighed up to four hundred pounds).

The beer-barrel scene is filmed in a nicely framed series of long shots that allow space for the visual geometry of the joke: the steep drop, the careening cylinders, the lone figure just managing to scramble out of their way. For once in the cramped, clammy universe of the MGM talkies, it matters where the camera is placed, and for approximately two minutes it is exactly where it needs to be. It's hard to imagine that Keaton, even in the rough shape he was in, didn't consult with Sedgwick over the setup and timing of this scene. In the last fifteen minutes of the last feature film he would ever star in for a major studio, there is a moment that feels purely his, and knowing that he was still capable of staging such moments is almost as sad as seeing him in the condition he appears in for the rest of the movie.

Apart from the painful irony of seeing a man in the throes of alcoholism being literally chased by containers of beer, there is one more detail in the barrel scene that seems to comment with unintended cruelty on the star's life circumstances during filming. At the bottom of the hill sits a T-shaped intersection with a row of shops—a set built specifically for the scene so that, as a capper, one of the cars swerving away from the barrel avalanche could crash through the window of a grocery store.[25] Next door to that market stands a prominently featured billboard for a movie: none other than MGM's *Grand Hotel*.

It makes sense that the studio would take advantage of an opportunity to promote its biggest prestige picture of the year, then still in the midst of an extended roadshow tour. But the sight of that billboard in the distance as Keaton dashes down the hill is a reminder of what *Grand Hotel*'s wild success must have represented to him in late 1932. The opportunity to play Kringelein, or to spoof him in the *Grand Mills Hotel* project, represented the last shot he had gotten at a role that might have excited and challenged him before a miserable year spent churning out awful—and, even more depressingly, successful—buddy comedies with Durante.

Though MGM was headed up by a trio of Jewish executives—Mayer, Thalberg, and the New York–based moneyman Nick Schenck—the studio was renowned for its prodigal festivities at Christmastime. Every year hundreds of gift baskets were given away to needy families who lined up inside the studio gates. Employees were then invited to a sit-down turkey dinner with all the trimmings. Mayer would attend, at some point standing up to deliver one of his trademark weepy speeches to the stable of employees he loved to call a "family." But after the studio patriarch left to spend the evening with his actual family—a wife and two grown daughters whose lives he ran almost as autocratically—the backlot would break out into merrymaking of a less wholesome sort.

The celebrations on Christmas Eve of 1932 were especially wild. MGM was the only one of the five major studios in Hollywood to come out of the worst year of the Great Depression in better financial shape than it began, thanks to big hits like *Grand Hotel* and *Red-Headed Woman*, mid-budget successes like the Keaton-Durante comedies or the Norma Shearer melodrama *Smilin' Through* (a remake of an old Norma Talmadge silent), and the first installment of the popular *Tarzan the Ape Man* series, starring the swimming champion Johnny Weissmuller. The company was flush with money and riding high; a photo from that day shows Marion Davies in full Christmas-elf regalia, overseeing the distribution of bundles of food, candy, and toys. In his after-dinner speech Mayer proudly, if prematurely, announced: "I say the country has emerged from the depression, and so we have!"

In his memoir, *Mayer and Thalberg: The Make-Believe Saints*, the producer and screenwriter Samuel Marx vividly evokes the bacchanalia that followed:

> It was as if [Mayer] had signaled for the celebration to explode, though he would not participate. When he left the studio, work officially ended and suddenly bacchanalia reigned. . . . Every desk spilled over with its profusion of bootleg Scotch, bathtub gin and questionable beer. No man dared be seen without a smear of lipstick on his face. If he wiped it off, a girl would soon replace it. . . . In the music department, back-to-back pianists played different tunes. In the portrait department, anyone could have his picture taken. Couples engaged in amorous and sometimes erotic poses that fortunately would not haunt them when they soberly remembered: the photographer, drink in hand, neglected to load his camera. . . . In the projection rooms stag films ran without stop, playing to standing room only, except for those unable to stand.[26]

A script clerk at the party later recalled finding Jean Harlow unconscious on the ground outside and helping her back in. (Harlow's desire
to blot out the world that night is understandable, given that her husband of only two months, MGM producer Paul Bern, had been found
dead under mysterious circumstances earlier that year.) Another guest
having trouble staying on his feet was Buster Keaton. Attempting a tricky
acrobatic stunt while no doubt highly intoxicated, he hit his head on the
floor, lost consciousness, and spent the rest of the night on the sofa in a
director's bungalow.

Irving Thalberg was generally a light drinker, but that night, buoyed
by his biggest year yet of financial and artistic success, he too had more
than what Marx recalled as "his customary scotch and soda." He received
a long line of congratulatory employees in his office, "girls with kisses,
men with handshakes," then ventured out into the party to hug the women
he had missed.[27] The next morning he woke feeling under the weather,
and Shearer, always anxious for his health, insisted he stay home from
work till he recovered. A few days later Thalberg had a heart attack at
their beachfront Santa Monica mansion. He would live another three
years before dying in 1936 at age thirty-seven—more time than the thirty
years doctors had given him when he was born a cyanotic "blue baby."
But his health, and the history of the studio he helped to build, were
never the same.

During Thalberg's eight-month leave from the studio, Mayer hired
his son-in-law David O. Selznick as a replacement. Selznick did not stay
in the job long, both because he recognized the impossibility of filling
Thalberg's shoes and because he feared being seen as a beneficiary of
nepotism. But by the time Thalberg returned to work the balance of
power at MGM had changed. Mayer's taste, always more sentimental
and conservative than Thalberg's, began to dominate the studio's output.
The Thalberg method of top-down production was there to stay, but
Thalberg himself had been maneuvered into a less powerful position by
the man who had once treated him as a surrogate son. This is the period
of their relationship Fitzgerald sought to dramatize in The Last Tycoon,

making Mayer's fictional stand-in, the blustering mogul Pat Brady, not only disloyal but murderous.

That 1932 Christmas party was exactly the sort of shindig at which Fitzgerald would likely have made a "Crazy Sunday"–style fool of himself. If nothing else, it would have provided valuable research for the Hollywood novel he would one day write. But he spent that Christmas far from Hollywood, living with the emotionally fragile Zelda in a rented Maryland mansion called La Paix and drinking steadily but not (yet) disastrously while he worked to finish his semi-autobiographical novel *Tender Is the Night*. Its publication and lukewarm reception in 1934 would mark the beginning of the low point of the author's life, a two-and-a-half-year stretch of creative stasis and intermittent binge drinking, with Zelda in and out of institutions and even his most "commercial" stories no longer reliably selling.[28]

Fitzgerald attempted suicide in 1936 after the publication of a cruel profile in the *New York Post* painted him as a pitiful has-been, spending his fortieth birthday bargaining with his "sobriety nurse" over when it was time for his allotted ounce of gin. (By that time, as we'll see in the next chapter, Keaton had already married and divorced *his* sobriety nurse.) Later that same year Fitzgerald published three essays in *Esquire* that chronicled his experience at rock bottom, later bundled together as "The Crack-Up" in the posthumous collection of that title. Fitzgerald rediscovered the distinctive voice that had made him a sensation ten years before: the "Crack-Up" essays are as vivid and perceptive as his best fiction. But their raw honesty was perceived by most of Fitzgerald's contemporaries as a lapse in taste and a humiliating sign of weakness. The essays also gave editors and studio executives pause about hiring an author who seemed like such a risky bet.

After coming closer than either liked to acknowledge to drinking themselves to death, Scott and Buster, living on opposite coasts, clambered their way back to (relative) sobriety and domestic contentment as the Depression decade drew to a close. Their paths would not converge again until the summer of 1937, half a year after Thalberg's death, when they both returned to work at MGM within the same week.[29] Five years after flaming out spectacularly, they were back on the Culver City lot as behind-the-scenes consultants, drawing on their long-honed professional skills—gag writing for Keaton, dialogue punch-up for Fitzgerald—to function as small but significant cogs in what was by then a very well-oiled moviemaking machine. By then both were also living mostly sober lives, in Scott's case with periodic and usually disastrous slips off the wagon.

Their offices would almost certainly have been in the same building, the one that housed the studio's writing staff in the late 1930s, only steps from the main commissary. It's hard to imagine that they would not at some point have crossed paths in the hallways or elsewhere on the studio's sprawling campus, which now included an artificial lake and standing sets for locations as varied as a New York City streetscape, a quaint European village, and a Victorian girls' school.[30] Keaton shared a two-room office suite with his former director and good friend Edward Sedgwick; the underemployed comedian used his spare time to build Rube Goldberg–style machines, like a device that moved an unshelled nut through an elaborate series of ramps and slides before cracking it with a tiny hammer. His job involved such tasks as writing gags for the Marx Brothers (an act he later criticized for what he saw as the brothers' lax work ethic) and revising his own old routines for the up-and-coming comic Red Skelton, who would eventually star in remakes of three Keaton silents. Keaton rarely received onscreen credit for his contributions; in a period of his life that was mostly about keeping his head down and making enough money to support his parents and siblings, that was just fine by him.

Fitzgerald worked on many scripts over the remaining three and a half years of his life, but only ever received onscreen credit for one film: 1938's *Three Comrades*, an adaptation of an Erich Maria Remarque novel about post–World War I Germany. The screenplay, to Fitzgerald's dismay, was substantially rewritten by the up-and-coming writer and future director Joseph Mankiewicz. ("Oh, Joe, can't producers ever be wrong?"

Fitzgerald pleaded in a draft of a letter to Mankiewicz that may never have been sent. "I'm a good writer, honest.")[31] Scott never really got the hang of screenwriting, though he had at least one pass at the scripts of several major MGM productions, including, at one point, *Gone with the Wind*. But his writing time in Los Angeles was far from wasted: it was in those years that he was able to produce what exists of *The Last Tycoon*, a book that, even less than halfway completed, stands among his most ambitious and accomplished works.

The women Keaton and Fitzgerald rebuilt their lives with in the late 1930s after a long dive into the abyss of alcoholism and depression had much more in common than Natalie and Zelda had. Both were working women, independently employed in an industry related to their partner's: Eleanor Norris, who would become Eleanor Keaton in 1940, was a contract dancer at MGM, while Sheilah Graham, Fitzgerald's companion from 1937 until his sudden death of a heart attack in her apartment in 1940, was a magazine writer and syndicated celebrity columnist. Eleanor and Sheilah were also both pragmatic caretakers, invested in their partners' physical and psychic well-being and in the creative work that made it possible. And both outlived their partners by decades and became, among other things, guardians of their legacies: after Keaton's death in 1966 Eleanor threw herself into helping to locate, preserve, and promote his films, while Graham wrote no fewer than three books about her time with Fitzgerald.

The popular misconception about Keaton's and Fitzgerald's late careers is that after a period of youthful glory they declined into a life of penury, personal misery, and creative barrenness. In fact, both their life stories show an enormous capacity for resilience and self-reinvention. As creators with strong individual visions, used to having the final say about what their work should look like, they had at first been miserable in the confines of the Hollywood studio system, then unable to function within it at all. Neither was able to find a comfortable professional perch at MGM until he had passed through what Fitzgerald's essay "Handle with Care,"

the last in the Crack-Up series, named the "real dark night of the soul."
And that dark night included, for both of them, more than one stint in
an alcohol rehab facility. Back when Thalberg was devising his own road
through the mountain, he had chosen to leave Fitzgerald and Keaton
behind. But by the time they started work in the writers' building in the
summer of 1937, they had come out the other side.

25

Not a Drinker, a Drunk

Keaton with his second wife, Mae Scriven, at the premiere
of *King Kong* at Grauman's Chinese Theater, 1933.

Keaton once characterized his status in the early 1930s as being "on top
of the world—on a toboggan."[1] The image is a comedic one; it's easy
to embroider a whole movie around it, a winter-sports-centric Keaton
feature that never was. But it also evokes with precision the anxiety and
dread of that moment, the sense of teetering on top of a steep descent and
sensing for the first time the merciless pull of gravity. When the momentum that had borne him upward his whole life started to slow, the drop
was more vertical than any cliff he had ever leapt over, and suddenly his

fabled resistance to harm—his lifelong billing as "the boy who couldn't be damaged"—was no longer working the way it used to.

At some point in the early 1930s Keaton's fast-tracked trajectory through history came to a sharp halt. Suddenly he found himself entirely congruent with his times: a depressed person at the height of the Great Depression, an alcoholic facing the end of Prohibition, an unemployed divorcé taking whatever work he could get to support his large dependent family. In a few years—at least until his career was revitalized in the early 1950s with the coming of television and the rediscovery of silent comedy—Keaton would even start to seem behind the times, a relic of Hollywood's early days.

He was not as much a victim of Depression-era shifts in cultural taste as were silent-era stars like Lillian Gish, John Gilbert, or the Talmadge sisters. (Norma's first two talkies flopped, ending her career; Constance chose never to make a sound picture at all, retiring from the screen for good in 1929.) Had he dealt with his drinking problem sooner and/or been cast in more suitable projects, it's easy to imagine Keaton reviving his career in the talkie era, whether as an actor, a director, or both. Instead, the woeful *What! No Beer?* marked the last time he ever starred in a feature film for an American studio.[2] Though he would devise and stage comic business for movie stars from Clark Gable to Judy Garland to Esther Williams in his twelve-year stint as an uncredited MGM gag writer, he never got another shot at directing a feature film.

The period in American history just following the 1929 stock market crash has often been compared to a hangover. (One of the first to suggest the analogy was none other than F. Scott Fitzgerald in his 1931 essay "Echoes of the Jazz Age," a rueful portrait of the decade he called "the most expensive orgy in history.")[3] There is a reason the Depression years were a time of radical changes in cultural taste, with leftist polemics on the Broadway stage, socially conscious bestselling novels, and the rise of the moralizing (if also glamorizing) gangster picture: in every domain, the 1930s were keen to put the 1920s behind them. That decade-long blur of wild stock market growth and wilder partying seemed callow and frivolous in the harsh light of a new decade, with the economy in ruins. This hangover quality is even tangible in the look of many Depression-era movies, not because cinematographers were nursing headaches from their last bender (though some surely were) but because the closed studios required for sound recording were windowless, thick-walled boxes that required banks of lights so hot one sound engineer of the time recalled the actors' hair pomade starting to smoke.[4]

For Buster Keaton the 1930s were the hangover years not just culturally but physiologically. The period from around mid-1932 to late 1935, when he was at his lowest and drinking the hardest, constitutes one of the rare moments in his life when being ahead of his time put him at a distinct *dis*advantage: he was born just a few years too soon to benefit from the historic shift in the treatment of addiction that took place starting on June 10, 1935, traditionally celebrated as the Founders' Day of Alcoholics Anonymous.

Whatever Keaton was doing on that date, and for several months after, it almost certainly involved heavy drinking. He would not "get sober" — a concept that, as we'll see, meant something very different for him than it did for the founders and members of AA — until his release from the Sawtelle Veterans' Hospital on Halloween Day of that year, after a harrowing two-week stay that at one point involved restraint by straitjacket. In the veiled language typical of both the Hollywood publicity machine and the stigmatization of alcoholism at the time, Keaton's physician made a statement to the press that the actor was "suffering from a nervous breakdown brought on by family and financial worries," adding that "his condition is very grave."[5]

Historians of the movement now suspect the traditionally observed date may be off by a week or so, but it was sometime in mid-June of 1935 that Bill Wilson, a New York City–based stock analyst who had been sober for just over six months, handed Robert Smith, a proctological surgeon in Akron, Ohio, a bottle of beer to steady his shaking hands before an operation. The surgery, thankfully, was a success, and the patient recovered. More significant, the doctor never touched another drink. Nor did the man who gave him his last beer ever waver from the sobriety he had achieved the year before in a Manhattan rehab hospital.

There, pleading with a God he had never believed in to show himself if he existed, Wilson had experienced what he later referred to as a "hot flash": a burst of bright light accompanied by a sudden rush of exaltation and clarity, "as though the great clean wind of a mountaintop blew through and through."[6] He asked his attending physician, Dr. William "Silkie" Silkworth, if this experience should be interpreted as a divine epiphany or merely a hallucination induced by the belladonna elixir he had been given during detox. Silkworth, a pioneer in the treatment of problem drinkers, told his patient that since his case was grave enough to require a miracle, he might as well proceed on the theory that he really had been visited by some supernatural force. "Whatever it is you've got now," Wilson recalled him as saying, "hang on to it. Hang on to it, boy. It is so much better than what you had only a couple of hours ago."[7]

"Silkie" was right: there was no alcoholism treatment modality with anything like a reliable success rate in the mid-1930s, so a bolt of white light from the beyond was as good a way out as any. Silkworth was familiar, as Wilson would soon become, with the work of the Swiss psychoanalyst Carl Jung, who had written that the only hope he had seen for turning around severe cases of alcoholism lay in some version of a spiritual experience. This need not be a religious conversion per se; it could be one of many variations on the phenomenon Wilson later came to call "deflation at depth," the surrender of one's own ego to a higher power upon recognizing that one's addiction has become unmanageable.

This experience would become one of the central pillars of Alcoholics Anonymous. Yet it was not Bill Wilson's solitary revelation in late 1934 that the founders chose to mark the origin of the program. It was that day the following summer when, after working unsuccessfully with other alcoholics for the past six months, he finally managed to pass his own still-shaky practice of sobriety on to another struggling drunk. This act of person-to-person transmission, Wilson soon realized, was the key not only to his friend's continued sobriety but to his own. The self-sustaining mutual-aid model that emerged through the partnership of Bill W. and Dr. Bob, as they would be publicly identified until after their deaths, was transformative. It was not for nothing that Aldous Huxley, who befriended Bill in the 1960s (and on several occasions took LSD with him to explore its value as a psychotherapeutic tool), called him "the greatest social architect of the century."[8]

The framing of alcoholism as an illness rather than as a sin or character flaw did not begin with AA; researchers into the intractable social problem of addiction had first floated the idea in the mid-nineteenth century. But it was the widespread success of the program that began to change the way Americans, and eventually people around the world, understood their own and their loved ones' relationship to substance abuse. The term "alcoholic" in the sense of a person dependent on liquor was not in wide usage when Bill W. and Dr. Bob first met in that summer of 1935, introduced through members of the Akron chapter of a religious movement, the Oxford Group. When Bill, in town on what turned out to be a failed business venture, called up a non-alcoholic member of the group asking her to put him in touch with any local drunk he could meet with to head off a relapse, he identified himself more colloquially as a "rum hound."[9]

Treatment for alcoholism and drug addiction in the mid-1930s had not changed much from the end of the last century, when Joe and Myra Keaton worked as entertainers in one of the countless traveling medicine shows that often sold, among their remedies, elixirs promising a cure for the "demon rum"—concoctions that as often as not contained alcohol themselves. Bill W., like Buster, was born in 1895 (that year again!), at a time when the temperance movement was taking a more radical turn. They had both just turned five when Carrie Nation, the infamous hatchet-wielding temperance crusader, smashed up her first saloon, a hotel bar in Wichita, Kansas. Nation and her followers immediately became the subject of countless newspaper caricatures and barroom jokes. There was even a 1901 film about her movement, *The Saloon Smashers*, an Edison Company comedy directed by Edwin S. Porter, which shows a group of bartenders being chased from their place of work by an invading pack of hatchet-swinging women. It's more than likely that both Bill and Buster, whether or not they ever saw *The Saloon Smashers* as six-year-olds, spent their childhood surrounded by images of temperance activists as meddling female moralizers who made it their business to impinge on masculine freedom and fun.

The world Keaton and Wilson grew up in, with its ongoing cultural and political battles between "wet" and "dry" factions, was not a place hospitable to the idea that alcoholism was a physical ailment whose sufferers deserved compassion and treatment rather than punishment and reformation. If you were a chronic and incorrigible drinker in those years, chances were you ended up either in the drunk tank at the city jail (as Joe Keaton did on more than one occasion), at a grim public inebriate asylum, or, if you had the means, at one of the more upscale drying-out spots known as "jitter joints" or "dip shops." It was at such an institution, the Charles B. Towns Hospital in Manhattan, that Bill W., a former stock speculator who had not quite yet drunk up all the money he made during the 1920s financial boom, had his white-light experience.[10]

Bill and Dr. Bob's encounter in June 1935 may have marked the beginning of what would become Alcoholics Anonymous, but the group's membership grew slowly at first. The founders' resistance to advertising and other forms of publicity and their agreed-upon commitment to "corporate poverty"—no membership dues, no affiliations with any political party or religious organization, no accepting of large donations from companies, institutions, or even individual philanthropists—gave the organization great structural and reputational integrity. But those same principles made it hard to get out the word about this simple yet revolutionary new method.

For the first few years, new groups sprang up only when people who had attended one of the two original meetings, at Dr. Bob's home in Akron or Bill's in Brooklyn, carried the idea back with them to their home city. Strong word of mouth among alcoholics and their families, combined with Bill's quasi-evangelical zeal for finding and helping fellow drunks, took the program a long way. But four years into its existence the movement could only claim to have kept about one hundred people around the country sober. Still, however modest the absolute numbers, AA's success rate at keeping drunks from relapsing was better than any other method going could claim.

AA's momentum picked up only a little when a book with the group's new official name as its title was privately published in 1939 and sold via direct mail order—a risky business venture that eventually turned out to be key to the group's financial self-reliance. But on March 1, 1941, the *Saturday Evening Post*, one of the nation's most-read weekly magazines, ran a long, thoroughly reported, and very enthusiastic cover story about the program. The author was careful to guard the anonymity of all the subjects interviewed, who included Bill and Dr. Bob. Requests for more information poured in, and sales of what came to be called "the Big Book"—an outsized, brightly colored volume printed on extra-heavy paper stock, the better to be easily located and paged through by a desperate "rum hound"—started to skyrocket.

In short order AA began to grow exponentially: by the end of 1941, only ten months after the article's publication, membership in the program had quadrupled.[11] The group resisted the urge to professionalize by keeping its financial and ideological distance from the medical establishment, but some doctors began recommending that alcoholic patients look for local AA meetings to attend in combination with more conventional forms of treatment.

The publication of this specific article is often cited in histories of the movement and in AA's own literature as a crucial turning point. The *Post* piece's success in expanding the reach of the program was such that six years later Bill convinced the author, Jack Alexander, to write a follow-up documenting the group's growth from around two thousand members—a number arrived at, in Alexander's words, only "by scraping hard, and some of these were still giving off residual fumes"[12]—to something close to ninety thousand, with local meetings being held across the continental United States, as well as in the United Kingdom, Australia, South Africa, several Scandinavian countries, and even a leper colony in Hawaii.

If Keaton happened to glance at that first article in the *Saturday Evening Post*, he would likely have seen the story about a promising new method for reforming drunks as having nothing to do with him. After all, by the spring of 1941 he was more than five years out from his successful "drying-out" at Sawtelle Veterans' Hospital, a year into his marriage to Eleanor, and living an ordered and pleasant life in the small Cheviot Hills bungalow he had bought for himself after his divorce from Natalie nine years before.[13] Every weekday morning Buster and Eleanor drove together to MGM, where she had a job as a contract dancer and he spent the days in the office he shared with Ed Sedgwick, consulting on comic business for other actors, chatting with studio pals (including his favorite comedy protégée, the contract player Lucille Ball), and tinkering with his homemade mechanical devices, which were ingenious enough that people from around the studio dropped in to see them in action. His life was much smaller-scaled and less creatively engaging than it had been in the days of the Buster Keaton Studio, but it was infinitely more peaceful and less chaotic than what he had lived through in the past decade.

But if Keaton did leaf through that issue of the *Saturday Evening Post* one spring morning while waiting for a haircut at the MGM barbershop, and if he was in an uncharacteristically self-reflective mood at the time, his eyes might have lingered on a paragraph that seems to describe to a T what we know of his personality when drinking:

> By nature touchy and suspicious, the alcoholic likes to be left alone to work out his puzzle, and he has a convenient way of ignoring the tragedy which he inflicts meanwhile upon those who are close to him. He holds desperately to a conviction that, although he has not been able to handle alcohol in the past, he will ultimately succeed in becoming a controlled drinker. One of medicine's queerest animals, he is, as often as not, an acutely intelligent person. He fences with professional men and relatives who attempt to aid him and he gets a perverse satisfaction out of tripping them up in argument.[14]

Every story about Keaton's drinking problem as it overlapped with his professional and personal life displays just this quality of evasive defiance. Even though he had seen his own father go through a similar crisis when he was a teenager, and even though a few close friends tried to reach out to him during his most self-destructive phase in the mid-1930s, he seems to have met all such expressions of concern with brusque and sometimes vehement denial.

The actor William Collier Jr.—also nicknamed "Buster," though he did not use the name professionally—was a popular leading man at Columbia, a good friend of Keaton's, and a frequent guest at the Italian Villa in the late 1920s with his on-and-off lover Louise Brooks. Talking to Keaton biographer Tom Dardis in the 1970s, Collier recalled a disastrous duck-hunting trip he took with Buster sometime in the early 1930s. Constance Talmadge had come to him on the family's behalf to see if "he couldn't do something about Buster's drinking," and he decided to take advantage of Buster's love for the outdoors to set the stage for a one-man intervention.

The two Busters spent an unpleasant weekend near Bakersfield, camping out in the well-appointed "land yacht." Keaton not only drank steadily all weekend but brought along an unnamed female companion who, though she remained nearly silent the whole trip, nonetheless made heart-to-heart conversation between the two friends difficult. In what sounds like a sordid variation on a gag from a Keaton silent, the comedian at one point cut off the circulation in his own feet by groggily pulling on the girl's boots in place of his own when the men rose before dawn to go hunting; the whisky he had drunk before bed numbed the pain enough that he only noticed his mistake after they had already set out on their hunt.

The tight boots proved impossible to remove and eventually had to be cut off Keaton's legs with a knife. But when Collier, finally crouched with a properly shod and relatively sobered-up Keaton behind a duck blind, found a moment to broach the subject of his friend's escalating habit, the response made it plain that no further conversation on the topic would be forthcoming: "Listen! If you were sent up here to me to have this big thing out with me, and tell me how I'm doin' wrong, you're just wastin' your time. I know the only person in the world that can cure me of that is me! So listen, I know what I'm doin'."[15]

This quote comes to us only secondhand, but it nails the blunt, homely cadence of Keaton's speech in recorded interviews; Collier, a gifted light comedian, may well have been doing his best impression of his old friend into Dardis's tape recorder. It's no surprise that someone as fiercely private as Keaton would have shut down any and all attempts to meddle in his personal behavior. But there were moments in those years when he almost seemed to be sending out a call for help in his own way—silently, with his body. Buster Collier was also there on the night when, as Louise Brooks put it in a 1977 letter to Dardis, Keaton "took a baseball bat to the glass doors of the built-in bookcases of his bungalow at MGM."[16]

The incident has become a staple of Keaton lore, a biopic scene waiting to be filmed: After a small dinner party at the Italian Villa, Keaton suddenly asked Collier and Brooks, who were then in the midst of rekindling an old on-set affair, to drive him to the Kennel. When they got to the bungalow he calmly fixed them each a drink, then went into the next room, returned with a bat, and smashed every pane of glass in the bookshelves that lined the walls. There were a lot of individual panels, MGM star dressing rooms of the day being nothing if not handsomely appointed, and the job took a while. When it was done Keaton sat back down and resumed the conversation with no acknowledgment of what had just happened.

In its way, this gesture was a precise reenactment of the "furniture massacre" that a drunk Joe Keaton had visited on a Providence, Rhode Island, theater all those years before: an act whose sole purpose was to deliberately and publicly show contempt for the boss's property, docked salary or professional reputation be damned. It was Joe's systematic destruction of those chairs and that fancy French sofa that had directly led to the Keaton family act's demotion from the top vaudeville houses to the shin-bruising three-show-a-day Pantages circuit, where they lasted one unhappy season before Buster broke up the act and fled by cross-country train with his mother, his father left behind at the stage door drunk and alone. This painful memory may not have been consciously present to Buster's mind the night he covered his bungalow floor in shards of glass, but like the impact of every fall he had taken since childhood, it resided somewhere in his body.

To its reluctant tenant, "Keaton's Kennel" must have felt like just what its name suggests: a cage, a place to be kept while awaiting his next call to a closed-in soundstage on a lot walled in by the locked and guarded gates of MGM. It's no wonder that a man whose whole life to that point had revolved around movement, action, and the freedom to improvise would act out by destroying the most immediate symbol of his own captivity. Keaton's disposition toward the open expression of anger, or of any strong negative emotion, was what we would today call "avoidant."

All his life Keaton simply steered out of the way of interpersonal conflict. When Natalie's star lawyer, who would later successfully defend the swashbuckling star Errol Flynn against two credible allegations of statutory rape, served Keaton divorce papers in 1932, the comedian's response was to ignore them, effectively handing his wife the bulk of their shared estate.[17] This deep-rooted unwillingness to face confrontation of any kind—including, presumably, with himself—served him very poorly in the years between his firing from MGM and his sobering up in the fall of 1935.

Keaton's increasing alcohol intake in this period also led him to make some dubious business decisions, like the calamitous nine weeks he spent in St. Petersburg, Florida, in the spring and summer of 1933, only a few months after his ignominious firing from MGM. Kennedy Productions, a company newly founded by a mix of local developers, carpetbagging investors, and Hollywood refugees, was optimistically if chaotically attempting to turn St. Petersburg into what the local press was calling "Hollywood East." The company was already wrapping production on its first film, *Chloe*, a low-budget melodrama set in the Louisiana bayou.

But by landing a star as big as Keaton, the Kennedy group was significantly expanding its ambitions. The St. Petersburg *Independent* boasted
a few weeks before the comedian's arrival that "with the coming to
St. Petersburg of Keaton, St. Petersburg becomes second only to Hollywood in the importance of the moving picture business." The day before
he arrived the headline of the same paper, in large type, was KEATON
PRODUCTION MOVES HERE.[18]

The deal was that Keaton would make six features over the next
two years with an option to renew for three more years, all at the same
rate of pay he had been getting at MGM: $3,000 a week. His first film,
The Fisherman, was to be written by his old collaborator Lew Lipton, a
cowriter of Keaton's last two silents and the last movies he made that could
be considered truly his: *The Cameraman* and *Spite Marriage*. Lipton's
involvement in the Florida project must have been a draw for Keaton at
this low point in his life: here was a colleague who knew his preferred
way of working and had even helped him find a way to make the movies
he wanted in the top-down corporate atmosphere of MGM. As Keaton
told the local papers soon after they arrived, "We came here to make our
kind of pictures."[19]

The proposed director of *The Fisherman*, Marshall "Mickey" Neilan,
was a less reassuring prospect, though he and Keaton were personally
friendly. He had been a major figure since the early silent era, first acting
opposite Mary Pickford in the 1910s and later directing her in some of her
most critically praised performances. But Neilan's career had been on
the skids for longer than Keaton's because of chronic drinking. In some
of his later collaborations with Pickford, it was said, he had been so out
of commission that she had basically directed the films herself.[20]

St. Petersburg enthusiastically welcomed Keaton. He was presented
the key to the city and, to judge by the steady stream of local news stories
about his presence there, all but followed down the street by curious
reporters: even his choice to take a swim at the local Surf Club with
Neilan was covered as an item in "Beach News." But that summer in
Florida was an indisputable bust, almost comical in its thoroughgoing

wrongness. The promised twenty-one-thousand-square-foot soundstage was soon downscaled to ten thousand square feet (and at any rate was nowhere near finished), and the outdoor locations were too swarmed by mosquitoes to frame a decent shot. There was no infrastructure whatsoever in place to make feature films in Florida: costumes and equipment would have to be shipped by boxcar from New York or California at the company's expense, a fact Keaton had to point out to his disorganized collaborators after planning for the shoot was already underway.

The heat and humidity melted the emulsion off the film and the makeup off the face of leading lady Molly O'Day, another silent-era star fallen on hard times. In 1928 she had sought out painful and humiliatingly well-publicized weight-reduction surgery when her studio, First National, told her to fit back into her costume from a film made the year before or risk losing her star contract. The operation was "successful" in that, combined with strenuous dieting, it did eventually reduce O'Day's dress size, but it also left her with seams of scars running up both sides of her body. The studio reneged on its promise to give her work if she lost weight, and by 1930 she had declared bankruptcy.[21] When she signed with Kennedy Productions three years later, still only twenty-three years old, she must, like Keaton, have been willing to overlook a lot of red flags in her excitement about getting back her career.

Molly O'Day would make six more films before retiring from the screen in 1935, but *The Fisherman* was never completed or, by all appearances, even started. There is no surviving footage, and the film seems to have gone no farther than a lot of production meetings and a publicity shoot with Keaton in a sombrero and O'Day in a señorita costume; according to the *Independent*, Keaton was thrown from his horse, a white gelding named Man in the Moon. Still, his time in St. Petersburg was not entirely idle; while there he played baseball to a packed stadium with the city league team the Coca-Cola Bottlers (Coca-Cola being a major local industry and one of the investors in Kennedy Productions). The team lost, but Keaton, playing third base—always his favorite position, the action-packed "hot corner" of the baseball diamond—"kept the grounds in an uproar."[22] Many years later, a St. Petersburg newspaper editor recalled him providing less wholesome entertainment: "He did most of his work in a local bar where, from time to time, he entertained the customers by taking off his pants and sweeping the floor with them."[23]

As plastered as he may have been over much of those nine weeks, it was neither Keaton's drinking nor any lack of commitment on his part that made the Florida deal fall through. Kennedy Productions was a sinking ship—they would only manage to turn out two more films before being bought out in 1935—and after their new star candidly told them he believed they were throwing their money away, he was allowed to leave with his full fee of $27,000 and no hard feelings on either side. As he puts it in his memoir, "they listened, paid off and I was out of another job. The project had been widely publicized, so what I got out of it was a couple of weeks' pay and another failure on my record."[24]

The Florida project turned out to be a humiliating misfire. But the most consequential bad decision Keaton made in those blackout years was his marriage to Mae Scriven, the live-in nurse who had been hired to keep him sober enough to be functional during the filming of *What! No Beer?* and who had slipped, as blurrily as everything that happened that year, into the role of girlfriend and then wife. Around New Year's Eve of 1932—one week after the MGM Christmas party where he cracked his head on the floor attempting a stunt—Keaton took a notion to travel with Scriven to Tijuana. This town a few miles south of the Baja California border had recently become a fashionable pleasure destination, the Las Vegas of its day, with casinos, horse racing, plentiful legal booze, and a strip of high-end hotels.

The place Buster and Mae stayed that week was the Agua Caliente resort, a minaret-topped, quasi-Moorish fantasia especially popular with the Hollywood crowd: Jean Harlow, Clark Gable, Gary Cooper, and the Marx Brothers were all photographed cavorting on the golf course or around the vibrantly tiled swimming pool. The evening floor show at Agua Caliente in the early 1930s featured a father-daughter act with a teenage dancer named Margarita Carmen Cansino, who in a few years would have her black hair dyed red, her "ethnic"-looking hairline (she was half-Spanish) raised by electrolysis, and her image refashioned into that of a Hollywood star named Rita Hayworth.

It appears that Mae Scriven's duties as a sobriety nurse ended where her intimate relationship with her client began. She made no effort to steer him out of this particular bender, seeming in fact to have joined in the revelry, and when they returned from Mexico at the turn of the new year they were married, though not yet in a legally binding manner. After Buster's divorce from Natalie was finalized later that year, he and Mae stood before a judge and said their vows again. They would remain together for two more years, until she in turn sued him for divorce in the summer of 1935, only a few months before he "got sober" (exactly what that meant to Keaton, as opposed to the likes of Bill W. and Dr. Bob, is a question we'll get to in a moment).

Mae Scriven remains a shadowy figure in Keaton's life story. In speaking of her to his first biographer he seems to refer to her mainly as "the nurse," perhaps out of fear that anything more specific would bring his litigious ex back into his life. In his memoir he dispatches the whole relationship in a sentence, saying "that second marriage of mine did not last long, which is the nicest thing about it I remember."[25] Even Mae's name seems to waver in and out of focus. In news items and public records from the time it appears indiscriminately as Scriven, Scrivens, Scribben, or Scribbens, and later in life, after two more marriages and divorces, she would go by some half a dozen other names: Mae Gassert, Mae Zengel, Jewel Mae Keaton, and finally, when attempting to reinvent herself as a stage producer and playwright in the mid-1950s, Jewel Steven (though she still sometimes billed herself as "the former Mrs. Buster Keaton").

Likewise, Mae's image in photographs is hard to pin down. She was attractive but not movie-star beautiful, with wavy dark hair and slightly hawklike features, standing a shade taller than her husband when wearing heels. She dressed stylishly but not extravagantly: in a photo of the two of them attending the premiere of King Kong at Grauman's Chinese Theater in 1933, she has an almost bohemian air in a matching white cloche hat and shawl, while he is natty, if dazed-looking, in top hat, tails, and cane (an accessory that, in that unsteady year, might have come in handy for balance). Mae's gaze at the camera is often severe, but in some pictures she seems to look at her husband with an expression of real warmth. How he looks at her is harder to read, given that in most photos from that period he seems either drunk or unwell.

Mae grew up in a farming family in central California, where she was an outstanding student and dreamt of going on the stage before choosing the more practical route of becoming a registered nurse. By the time she met Keaton she was twenty-seven years old, had already been married and divorced, and had worked both in doctor's offices and for private clients for ten years. She had cared for at least one other high-profile entertainer dealing with addiction: Joe E. Brown, a rubber-faced comedian and former child acrobat who was a friend of Keaton's and played alongside him on the MGM Lions company baseball team.[26] Brown is most familiar to moviegoers today as Osgood Fielding III, the unflappable millionaire in Billy Wilder's *Some Like It Hot* who responds to the revelation that his love object, Jack Lemmon's Josephine, is not a woman but a man in a dress with the immortal closing line "Nobody's perfect."

Mae was certainly far from it. But though she tends to come off as a villain in accounts of her second husband's life, her motives in marrying Buster, however dubious, were at least not of the conventional gold-digging variety. He was fired from his job at MGM just weeks into their not-yet-legal Tijuana marriage; had she been looking for a way out when his funds and prestige ran low, that would have been the ideal moment to make her exit. Yet she stuck by him through the Florida fiasco and for two years after that, as his income shrank and his Hollywood hireability waned.

In 1934 Keaton got a contract to star in a series of shorts for Educational Pictures, a low-budget outfit that billed its two-reelers as "the spice of the program." He would star in sixteen shorts for Educational over the next three years, contributing as a cowriter on only one and directing none. The Educationals were shot on flimsy sets in the space of a few days, a far cry from the four to six weeks he used to spend crafting his own two-reelers in the 1920s. Only a few hold up as solid beginning-to-end entertainments, but they all contain at least one flight of Keatonian invention, and even the worst among them is more watchable than nearly every one of his MGM talkies, where his misery and sense of entrapment are on full display. By the time he signed with Educational, he had come around to accepting suboptimal working conditions in exchange for job security—anything was better than uncertainty and eventual disappointment of speculative projects like the Florida mess.

Keaton seems to have approached the new gig as an honest if modest-paying job in which—as long as he could white-knuckle it through the workday without drinking—he could use his skills as a performer and contribute the odd comic idea. It's no accident that the only Educational short he cowrote and the best of the lot, *Grand Slam Opera* (1936), is the first one he made after emerging from the Sawtelle stay. It features a pair of inspired solo dance scenes, including a moment when Keaton pastiches Fred Astaire's soft-shoe dance from *Top Hat* the year before. There is also the wordless encounter with a waitress flipping pancakes that harks back to Keaton's 1917 visit to Childs Restaurant. Many of the Educational shorts continue to rely on some version of the dimwit "Elmer" character, sometimes complete with the name, but for all their weak dialogue and uneven pacing, they demonstrate a better understanding of Keaton's basic comic persona than did the MGM debacles.

The Educational job paid well enough for Mae and Buster to get by while Buster continued to support his mother and siblings, but Mae took it upon herself to supplement the household income in ways both legal and less so. There was a furniture-selling scheme she ran a few times that involved charging expensive items to Keaton's line of credit, then reselling them at slashed prices for handy cash. Late in their marriage she opened a short-lived beauty parlor with the name "Buster Keaton's Beauty Shop," adding a small-print "Mrs." before the "Buster" when he objected to the use of his name.[27] And according to some accounts, Mae was also known to exchange sex for money when household finances were tight.

In an interview given a decade after her brother's death, Louise Keaton described accompanying Mae to the Biltmore Hotel and waiting in
the lobby while her sister-in-law "entertained" seven or eight men in an
afternoon, customers Louise characterized as some of her own "good
men friends"—which suggests that members of the Keaton family, possibly including Buster, were not only aware of this alleged side hustle of
Mae's but game to recruit clients for it.[28] The Keatons were, after all, stage
people who had spent decades traveling the country, living in theatrical
boardinghouses and subsisting in an entertainment economy that often
intersected with the world of sex work. One of Buster's own early sexual
memories, recounted with cheerful candor to his biographer in the 1950s,
was of contracting what was probably gonorrhea in his teenage years after
visiting a brothel near the Muskegon actors' colony. It's plausible that
Buster was too out of it during his marriage to Mae to notice that she
was turning tricks to help pay the bills. It's also plausible that he looked
the other way, ignoring that unpleasant reality just as he ignored his own
addiction.

The two-plus years Buster spent married to Mae and drinking heavily
were without doubt the darkest time of his life; in his memoir, they appear
in a section titled "The Chapter I Hate to Write." Reading about their
relationship, it's hard to drum up much sympathy for Mae, who seems
to have been an unstable and attention-hungry woman less interested
in the health of her partner than in her own nearness to fame. But an
argument could nonetheless be made that without her he might not have
survived those years at all.

His whole life Keaton had entrusted the practical details of day-to-
day life, including and especially the handling of money, to women.
When he was a child it was Myra who had carried beneath her skirts
what in vaudeville slang was called the "grouch bag," a hidden pouch
containing the act's weekly earnings. After he married Natalie Talmadge,
his paychecks from Joe Schenck went directly to her; the Italian Villa
and the yacht he christened the *Natalie* were entirely in her name. And
once Eleanor Norris became his wife in 1940 she spent the remaining

twenty-six years of his life performing the roles of, in the words of one Keaton biographer, "a combination valet, cook, housekeeper, bill payer, and constant reminder."[29]

As unhappy as their time together was, Mae Scriven also fulfilled this crucial role of caretaker and domestic helpmate without which the already dependent Buster, then at his physical and emotional low point, would have been hopelessly lost. In an interview given to the *St. Louis Post-Dispatch* in the fall of 1933 to promote a weeklong vaudeville engagement in that city, Keaton acknowledged as much when he said of his wife (identified by the reporter as the former "Miss May Scribbed") that she "sews the buttons, mends the holes and keeps me in control."[30]

Mae's skill as a seamstress has been lost to history, but at that last task, keeping Buster in control, she cannot be said to have succeeded, not that anyone could. Throughout their marriage he continued to go on regular binges, and in a pattern typical of both addiction treatment and gender relations at the time, Mae seems to have seen it as her wifely role to nurse him back to health after each crisis, rather than to help him find a way to live alcohol-free. In fact, her motivation to be his caretaker was strong enough that even months after she had sued him for divorce in mid-1935, Mae tried to rush back to Buster's side when the headlines blared that he had been taken to the hospital at Sawtelle in a straitjacket. (Other versions of the story say he was taken there unconscious and the straitjacket was required to keep him from escaping the next morning. In the embroidered retelling of his first biographer, Keaton slips the restraints using a method picked up from Houdini.) At any rate, by that point Buster was done with the marriage and refused to see his recently estranged second wife.

Mae insisted to an Associated Press wire reporter that "I know I can help him. I nursed him through a similar collapse three years ago and I can do it again." She even let them publish the gushing note she sent to the hospital, which if Buster was in any shape to read the papers must have mortified him: "Darling, please tell the nurse when you feel like seeing me. Elmer and I are waiting. Oodles of love, Mae."[31]

The note went unanswered, and in fact Buster would never again lay eyes on Elmer, the Saint Bernard who had been his companion at home and at work since the late twenties. By the time he came home from the hospital on Halloween Day, Mae had sold the dog out of spite and moved out of the Cheviot Hills house for good, taking exactly half of everything, down to the silverware. Buster hired a private detective to track down Elmer's new owner, sending him as far as Mae's hometown near Fresno, but the pet he had named after his own sound-era persona was never recovered.[32]

It's unclear what it was about this particular hospital stay that reversed Buster's downward trajectory. Why did October 1935 constitute what in AA language would be called his "rock bottom" moment, when there had already been so many comparable low points? It doesn't seem to have had much to do with the treatment offered, a form of intensive aversion therapy that had already failed to work on him once before. In his stomach-churning description, "it starts with three days during which the nurses and doctors do nothing but pour liquor into you, giving you a drink every hour on the half hour . . . they start you off on whiskey and on succeeding rounds give you gin, rum, beer, brandy, wine—before they get around to the whiskey again. . . . When you plead, 'Oh no! Take it away, *please!*' all you get from your barmaids and bartenders in white coats is a friendly smile."[33]

This nightmarish vision of negative reinforcement through enforced drunkenness, combined with involuntary hospitalization and the use of a straitjacket, would today be regarded as a form of medical torture, but in the mid-1930s it was what passed for the vanguard of alcoholism treatment. Another common therapy that had failed to get Buster sober in the past was a version of the nineteenth-century "water cure": in his hazy last year at MGM he had been sent to periodic drying-out sessions in the sulfur caves at Arrowhead Springs in California's San Bernardino Mountains, where the natural hot springs were thought to have healing properties. But the sulfur caves and the straitjacket had one thing in common: they had not been freely chosen by the patient himself. Until sometime during that involuntary internment in October 1935, Keaton was by the definition of any modern addiction treatment program a hopeless case: he simply had no desire to get better.

As Buster Collier's hunting trip story and Louise Brooks's account of the glass-smashing incident at the MGM bungalow make plain, Keaton on a drinking spree was a very hard person to reach, a man with immense reserves of anger and next to no capacity to express it. Whatever happened to him during that stay at Sawtelle, it had nothing to do with the extended helping hand of a fellow problem drinker, much less a white-light epiphany. All his life Keaton remained completely indifferent to religion or metaphysics of any kind. His films stand as proof of his belief in the immanence of the material world, a place where the only higher powers are the laws of physics: speed, weight, force, gravity.

Keaton's second biographer, Tom Dardis, himself a sober alcoholic who returned throughout his career to the complex relationship between creativity and addiction, writes that the staff at Sawtelle, led by Keaton's longtime personal physician John Shuman, must have "finally got it into his head that he simply *couldn't* drink anymore, that he'd reached a stage when he'd soon kill himself."[34] This strategy of rational persuasion, though Shuman could not have known it, was exactly the one Dr. Silkworth had suggested the year before to Bill W. in the wake of his "hot flash" revelation, when Bill was unsuccessfully preaching to other drunks about the necessity to submit to a higher power. In Keaton's case, his private admission of his own powerlessness over alcohol may have come along with another humbling recognition: that the relationship with Mae, like his marriage to Natalie, was definitively over and that he would have no one to depend on but himself when he got out. He seems to have made the decision to stop drinking out of sheer determination to survive.

Still, Dardis's version of Keaton's sobering-up experience at Sawtelle is not entirely accurate. As Keaton himself told the story in multiple places years later, the first thing he did upon release was to walk across all eighteen holes of the golf course that bordered his house, enter the clubhouse, and order two double Manhattans. "They not only tasted great, they stayed down," he boasts in his memoir, seeming to relish the memory.[35] In some tellings he specifically links this moment to a personal victory over liquor: by freely deciding to drink exactly what, and how much, he wanted, he was proving to himself that he now had a handle on his drinking.

Needless to say, downing four shots of hard liquor immediately upon release from a rehab facility was hardly what Alcoholics Anonymous, then or now, would consider sobriety. In fact, drinking on the way home from the hospital after treatment was one of the signs specifically mentioned in the "Big Book" as a symptom of what Bill W. classified as a fourth-stage alcoholic, the level of drinker most difficult to help. Another sign he provided of this stage, the set of extreme withdrawal symptoms collectively known as delirium tremens, was also something Keaton had experienced.

Later on, Keaton was able to speak of his history as a blackout drinker with the matter-of-fact honesty that AA fellowship encourages with its introductory formula at meetings: "I'm [name] and I'm an alcoholic." James Karen, a younger actor who worked with Keaton beginning in the 1950s and grew very close to him in his final years, recalled him summing up his relationship to alcohol with the words "I'm not a drinker, I'm a drunk"[36]—a distinction that might have come straight from the mouth of a member at a meeting. At some point during that involuntary two-week stay at Sawtelle, Keaton seems to have felt his way toward at least the first of what would eventually become known as the twelve steps of recovery: the ability to admit to himself that he had lost his power over alcohol.

But without the crucial element of an ongoing mutual aid network—the one-drunk-helping-another formula that Bill W. and Dr. Bob had hit upon in Akron that June—the sobriety Keaton found in October 1935 proved unstable in the long term. For the rest of his life he would have periodic slips, at least two of them serious enough to result in hospitalization. And though from 1940 onward he had the support of a loving partner, his relationship to the bottle continued to be something he dealt with essentially alone.

In 1941, a year into their marriage, Buster and Eleanor spent a summer touring the East Coast with the revival of an old Broadway comedy-mystery called *The Gorilla*. The play was a hit, with Keaton as the canny lead detective getting especially good notices. "Keaton keeps his audience in breathless suspense and gales of laughter," noted the *Connecticut Record-Journal*, while the *Brooklyn Daily Eagle*, partial to Buster since his vaudeville days and one of the few papers to have appreciated *The General* on its release, wrote that "Mr. Keaton makes himself a favorite of the audience with little effort. . . . His gift is for underacting, always has been."[37] After nearly a decade making a living off behind-the-scenes gag writing and the low-budget shorts he dismissed as "cheaters," working in front of live audiences again was energizing for Buster, and the idea of returning to his office job at MGM must have been a letdown.

Driving home, Buster and Eleanor made a short stopover in Muskegon. There Buster got to introduce his new bride to the cornmeal-battered lake perch that was the specialty at Bullhead Pascoe's Tavern, the bar across the street from the baseball field where he had spent eight summers playing ball with local kids and other juvenile performers on holiday (and where Joe Keaton had no doubt tied on many a drinking spree). But Jingles' Jungle had long ago been sold, and the summer actors' colony had vanished in tandem with vaudeville itself.

Whether Buster washed down his perch with a mug of beer is unknown, but the nostalgia stirred up by this visit seems to have broken his fragile hold on sobriety. On returning to the Cheviot Hills house and his MGM job, he went on his first bender since the stay at Sawtelle nearly six years before. Eleanor had never seen him so much as take a drink, and she was scared enough to call his doctor, who sent her husband back to the hospital, this time with no straitjacket needed and for only a week's stay.

After her husband's death, Eleanor Keaton sometimes expressed annoyance with accounts of his life that focused too much on his time as a heavy drinker. She especially disliked Tom Dardis's 1979 biography, for which she had provided hours of interviews and research help. She felt Dardis wallowed in the relatively few years Buster spent as a severe alcoholic and gave short shrift to the thirty years he lived afterward in relative sobriety as a working entertainer, content in his marriage and fully capable of supporting his still-dependent family of origin. And it's true that, in the vast scope of everything Keaton experienced and achieved in his seventy-year life span, being an out-of-control drunk over the course of two and a half to three years in early middle age played a numerically small part. But in telling the story of those seventy years, there's no way around the painful fact that his career was derailed in large part because of his struggle with alcohol, a struggle that returned sporadically for the rest of his life.

Harold Goodwin, the tall, handsome actor who had played the villain in *College* back in 1927 and become a good friend and regular costar over the ensuing decades, told a story about something that happened in 1949 on the set of *The Buster Keaton Show*. That was the title of a comedy sketch program taped before a live studio audience that aired for one season on KTTV, a CBS affiliate station in Los Angeles. In the early days of television such local-only programming was common, since most cities still lacked the technology to pick up nationwide broadcasts.[38]

Keaton's first solo foray into television may have had a limited viewing audience, but it was no small-time production. *Variety* wrote that its $3,000 budget was "the largest sustaining television nut on any local station,"[39] and it quickly became popular enough that one night executives from CBS came to watch a live taping with an eye toward giving him a series with national reach.

According to Goodwin, a supporting player and cowriter on the show, there were bigwigs in the audience when Keaton missed a stunt along the lines of the one that had knocked him out at that MGM Christmas party back in 1932: "He had a little too much to drink, cut his head, and there was blood."[40] It's impossible to know whether Keaton was sabotaging himself out of nerves or if drinking was simply his way of dealing with the pressure of producing a half hour a week of new material, something not even the most strenuous three-a-day vaudeville circuit had demanded. But despite enraptured reviews—*Life* magazine said that "at the age of

54 he is taking pratfalls on a bare floor that other comics wouldn't try on a pile of marshmallows"[41] — *The Buster Keaton Show* never went national.

The 1950s was a decade of career resurgence for Keaton, with small but high-profile roles in major Hollywood films and regular work in television and on the stage. But in moments of high stress, his sobriety could still get shaky. While he was in London working on a series that never made it past the pilot stage, Buster learned that Myra had died at age seventy-eight. Eleanor later described how, after reading the telegram from his brother, Buster had disappeared for four or five hours, leaving her certain he must have gone on a binge. But when he returned to their hotel he was sober, his eyes red from weeping; he had been walking the streets of the city all that time, mourning his mother in privacy.[42]

Back at the house where they had lived with Myra for the past fifteen years, Buster started to drink again, and by late that fall he was back at Sawtelle Veterans' Hospital in critical condition; he had begun hemorrhaging after a coughing fit ruptured veins in his esophagus. Newspapers reported him as being near death, though most tiptoed around the cause, calling it a "gastrointestinal ailment." The doctors told Eleanor to gather his loved ones at his bedside. But after five days Buster's condition had begun to improve, and when he left the hospital three weeks later his doctor, impressed by his physical resilience, gave him a good prognosis, with one harsh caveat: he had to stop drinking if he wanted to stay alive.[43]

Eleanor would later say that she wished the doctor had included a smoking ban as well, since it was lung cancer that eventually killed her chain-smoking husband. But either way, Buster would likely have found a way to cheat on the rule. Once again, as he had twenty years before, he listened closely to the doctor's warnings and took them seriously . . . for a time. Not long after his release from the hospital an interviewer came to his house to discuss the career achievement award he had recently received from the George Eastman House in the company of a select group of silent-film pioneers. As the conversation got under way, the subject of Buster's recent medical close shave came up (though without any reference to the role played by alcohol) and he confessed, in what for him constituted a moment of vulnerability, that "it kind of scared me a bit."[44]

By the 1960s Buster and Eleanor had come to an agreement that he could have one or two glasses of beer a day before dinner, a civilized "cocktail hour" that friends from that time remember him observing with no apparent ill effects. Two years before he died, Keaton was visited by Kevin Brownlow, then a young film historian collecting oral histories from silent film stars for what would become his seminal book *The Parade's Gone By*. Near the end of their long and animated conversation Keaton enthusiastically showed off his tiny home "saloon" setup, complete with old-fashioned brass footrail and spittoon, and offered the interviewer a glass of ice-cold draft beer from a chilled aluminum barrel: "If you like beer," he said proudly, "this is the best in town."[45]

In essence, for the thirty years between his first sobering-up late in 1935 and his death in early 1966, Keaton lived life as what AA literature of the time called a "dry drunk," someone who was capable of "putting the cork in the bottle" for months or even years at a time but who had not profoundly transformed his life by surrendering his will to a higher power or reaching out to help other alcoholics. Between his lifelong atheism, his characterological stubbornness, and his aversion to confrontation in any form, it seems hard to imagine a world where any such thing could have happened.

By 1955, the year of Buster's last serious alcohol-related health crisis, Alcoholics Anonymous was a worldwide phenomenon. In fact, that year the program celebrated its twentieth anniversary by releasing an expanded second edition of the "Big Book" to widespread press coverage, a far cry from the group's early days pitching self-published books by mail order. The concept of alcoholism as a sickness rather than a vice had even started to penetrate popular culture. In 1945, Billy Wilder's *The Lost Weekend*, an adaptation of a bestselling novel about an alcoholic writer's experience at rock bottom, had become a smash hit and swept the Oscars with four major awards, including best picture. Wilder and his cowriter Charles Brackett consulted with members of the group on the script, though in accordance with the tradition of anonymity AA was never credited or explicitly mentioned.[46] *The Lost Weekend*'s success led to a streak of well-received films that showed the problem of alcohol dependency in a more honest and compassionate light than Hollywood had previously shined on the subject, among them *A Tree Grows in Brooklyn* (1945), *The Country Girl* (1954), and *A Star Is Born* (1954).

At the time of Keaton's last Sawtelle hospital stay, the use of AA as an effective aid to medical treatment for alcoholism would almost certainly have been familiar to his doctors, if not to the patient himself. Yet no one seems to have encouraged Keaton to seek support from his fellow drunks — maybe because his doctors knew their patient's temperament too well by then, maybe because Keaton's worldwide celebrity would have made it hard for him to do much of anything anonymously. Still, in the hard-to-imagine circumstance that he had sought out a weekly meeting, he would not have been the first Hollywood star to be associated with the group. In 1953, Lillian Roth, a singer and actress since the silent era, spoke openly and in detail about her voyage to rock bottom and recovery through AA on a groundbreaking episode of the TV show *This Is Your Life*. The following year she published a bestselling memoir, *I'll Cry Tomorrow*, which was made into an acclaimed film with Susan Hayward in the lead.[47]

Buster's experience of sobriety might have been very different, with no or fewer relapses and more clarity about how to live as an addict in recovery, had he been able or willing to integrate the practice of AA into his life. And there was one figure in Buster's life who, at the moment when he most needed help, might have been able to reach out to him as a fellow alcoholic transformed by sobriety: his father. Since sometime in the mid-1920s Joe Keaton had been living a sober life, thanks to his relationship with a woman his children later recalled only as "the Christian Science lady."[48] Like the product of the nineteenth century he was, he had finally been won over neither by rational persuasion nor by the fellowship of other drunks but by a Christian woman preaching temperance.

Though Joe and Myra never officially divorced, she was not only fine with this new relationship but seems to have welcomed it. When he wasn't

drinking, in Eleanor's words, Joe was "a darling man," and he and his absti-
nent lady friend were sometimes invited to the house on Victoria Avenue
for family birthdays or holidays.[49] To be sure, Joe played a far smaller part
in his son's adult life than did Myra, but during the years when Buster's
drinking was most out of control, his father had many opportunities to
take him aside and talk with him about the self-destructive behavior that
in so many ways resembled his own rock-bottom period some twenty years
before. He does not appear ever to have done so, no doubt for some of the
same reasons that kept Buster from confronting his own problem for so
long. Both Joseph Keatons were avoidant, proud and stubborn to a fault;
rather than acknowledge their shared demons in each other's presence,
they chose to grapple with them for years on their own.

For most of his last few decades Joe lived in a series of Los Angeles
residential hotels preferred by show-business old-timers, the monthly tab
paid for by Buster. The 1940 census lists his occupation as "motion picture
actor," a somehow touching designation for the vaudevillian stalwart who
had once disdained the trendy "flickers" and only relented to play bit parts
in the films of his son. Until the end of his life he hung on to clippings
and posters for the Three Keatons' old act, with images of Buster in the
just-like-Dad "Irish" getup he wore in early childhood.

For all his failings as a father, Joe Keaton does seem to have loved his
son. That he was never able, or inclined, to pass on whatever wisdom
he had gained from his own struggle with alcohol is a tragic missed
opportunity, made more cruelly ironic by the fact that both the founders
and most early members of AA shared a similar profile to Joe and Buster
at their respective rock bottoms. Until the group's membership began
to diversify as word about the movement spread, most attendees at AA
meetings were once-successful white men somewhere in middle age who
had damaged their own careers, reputations, and families by refusing to
face up to their problem with drinking.

At the end of his life Joe suffered from age-related dementia and was
put in a care home, a fact that made Buster too uncomfortable even to
talk about. He told his first biographer that his father had died after being

hit by a car, when in fact, though Joe Keaton did sustain minor injuries in a 1944 accident, his 1946 death certificate says he died of pneumonia due to "senile psychosis."[50] There were plenty of times in interviews throughout his life when Buster went along with a show business myth (like the story, probably started by his publicist Harry Brand, that it was Houdini who first nicknamed the indomitable baby "Buster" after seeing him fall down a flight of stairs) or conflated timelines or incidents from his past so as to put his spin on a story, but it was unusual for him to make up a lie out of whole cloth. Joe's senility seems to have been a demonstration of his father's frailty that Buster felt the need to cover up for, as if to protect Joe from being seen as anything less than competent, manly, and strong. James Karen—among the most psychologically astute of Keaton's friends, to judge by his sharply observed stories about him—believed that Buster secretly disliked Joe, "but he would never admit it because he thought it was un-American to dislike your father."[51] Until his own final days on earth Buster refused to hear a word against the man who, by sheer dint of throwing him, had taught him to fly, to fall and somehow, miraculously, to land.

PART IV

LANDING

Hell, the way I feel, I might just live forever.

—Buster Keaton in 1965,

three months before his death

on February 1, 1966

26

Old Times

With Charlie Chaplin in a scene from Limelight, *1952.*

"If anybody else says it's like old times," grumbles Buster Keaton's never-named character in Charlie Chaplin's 1952 backstage melodrama, *Limelight*, "I'll jump out the window." (A more accurate transcription would be *winda*; even in a movie set in Edwardian-era London, Keaton keeps his customary flat midwestern drawl.) We first meet this un-nostalgic fellow seated at a dressing room mirror, pasting on a droopy mustache: he is a faded music hall comedian preparing for a one-night-only gala performance with his long-ago stage partner. In the foreground, powdering his grease-paint, sits Chaplin's Calvero, a washed-up clown with a drinking problem. The two show business veterans are about to face an audience together for the first time in many years. In real life, it would be the first and only time.

It's strange to think that, though their careers on stage and film over-lapped over a period of five decades, Keaton's sole appearance along-side Chaplin comes in these few, mostly silent scenes in the last fifteen minutes of *Limelight*. The rest of the movie focuses not on the rela-tionship between their characters but on the considerably less palatable one between Calvero and Tereza (Claire Bloom), a suicidally depressed young ballerina who falls in love with the aging clown after his belief in her talent helps her recover from a state of hysterical paralysis. If that sounds like a dramatic premise so extreme it must have been intended as camp, you have clearly underestimated the self-seriousness of *Limelight*.

Shot on a meticulous backlot re-creation of the London music hall milieu Chaplin remembered from early childhood, *Limelight* stands at a turning point in the careers and lives of both Chaplin and Keaton, though in both cases the reasons for the change have little to do with the movie itself. After nearly two decades out of the spotlight, Keaton, in the early 1950s, was in the midst of a version of the late-life comeback Chaplin's alter ego in the movie so desperately seeks. Meanwhile, Chap-lin's career was about to enter its long final chapter of exile and artistic decline. He would direct only two more films, *A King in New York* in 1957 and *A Countess from Hong Kong* in 1967, before his death in 1977. Both were shot in Europe and were poorly received, sometimes to the point of derision, by critics and audiences alike. Their similar titles are a hint at how Chaplin perceived himself in that last phase of his life: as a kind of banished royalty.

Opinions about *Limelight* were and remain divided, but it is the last film Chaplin made that can reasonably be defended as a major entry in his filmography. If it had been his last one, it would have made for a fitting if flawed goodbye to an extraordinary career. But watched today it has more power as an unflatteringly precise portrait of its creator's lifelong artistic and personal fixations than as a piece of entertainment. Seventy years after its debut, with its creator's life arc in the rearview mirror, *Limelight* seems at once so confessional and so equivocatingly self-serving that it's hard to get past its autobiographical elements and judge it purely as a work of art.

For decades Chaplin had been making tabloid headlines because of his troubled relations with women—or more accurately, girls. He had a nasty habit of impregnating the young actresses he met at casting calls, then marrying them out of a sense of duty (or for fear of scandal) and neglecting them to the point that they sued him for divorce. The first time around, with the sixteen-year-old Mildred Harris in 1918, her initial claim of pregnancy had turned out to be a false alarm, but their union soon resulted in a child, a son born with serious birth defects who lived just three days. The baby's name was Norman Spencer Chaplin, but Harris insisted that his gravestone read only "The Little Mouse."[1]

Grief over that loss is often cited as the inspiration for the tender father-son relationship at the center of Chaplin's first feature-length film, *The Kid* (1921). That film went into preproduction ten days after the loss of his first child, and the first task he undertook was to find an infant to cast in the role of his foundling son, played for most of the movie by the extraordinary five-year-old actor Jackie Coogan. But Chaplin had no tenderness to spare for his own child's newly bereaved teenage mother, and Harris found herself all but abandoned as he threw himself more obsessively than ever into his work. Within a few months of their son's death they were living separately, and the following year she sued him for divorce on the grounds of desertion and cruelty. Years later Harris told an interviewer, "That's the only thing I can remember about Charlie . . . he cried when the baby died."[2]

Five years after that marriage's well-publicized dissolution, Chaplin repeated the same scenario with another sixteen-year-old, Lita Grey. This time the relationship had a disturbing backstory: Grey had played a flirtatious angel in a dream sequence in *The Kid*, "vamping" the Tramp and another male character when she was no more than twelve. This second marriage lasted two years and produced two children before Grey too sued for divorce in an even more widely covered scandal. In the mid-1930s there was yet another May-December marriage, this time to Chaplin's *Modern Times* costar Paulette Goddard. By the time of their secret wedding on a trip to China, the bride was in her mid-twenties, which made her the oldest of his four wives at the time of their marriage, though their relationship had started years earlier. After Goddard appeared opposite him one more time in *The Dictator*, they too divorced, this time amicably and with no children.

Concerns about Chaplin's "morals"—a euphemistic framing for the systematic grooming and abuse of very young women—had already started to turn popular opinion against him well before 1943, when his sex life made headlines again after a paternity suit from the actress Joan Barry.[3] His image did not improve when, only two weeks after Barry's suit came before the court, he revealed his fourth and final marriage to the New York debutante and aspiring actress Oona O'Neill, then eighteen to Chaplin's fifty-four. Oona's father, the celebrated playwright Eugene O'Neill, had only played a small part in her life since her early childhood, but on learning she had eloped with a man only six months his junior he publicly disowned her.[4]

Tereza "Terry" Ambrose, the dancer played by Claire Bloom in *Limelight*, is an evident stand-in for this recurring figure in Chaplin's life: the much-younger muse turned potential romantic partner. (In fact, in two long shots Bloom is doubled by O'Neill, who resembled her strongly.) But the movie lets Chaplin's character off the hook by reversing the roles of pursuer and pursued. In his fictional recasting of the old man–young girl dynamic (Chaplin was sixty-two at the time of filming, Bloom twenty), it is Terry who insists their mentor/mentee relationship should become something more and pleads with Calvero to marry her, while he resists. Instead, he encourages her to pursue a romance with a man nearer her own age—an earnest young composer played, in an inadvertently creepy bit of casting, by Chaplin's twenty-six-year-old son, Sydney (the second of his two children with Lita Grey). One plot thread involves Calvero and Terry pretending to be man and wife in order to appease their landlady, but the implication is that their relationship remains chaste. The most suggestive moment in the movie has nothing to do with Terry at all; it comes when Calvero presents a pantomime sketch about the proprietor of a flea circus whose wayward flea Phyllis goes on a long and ticklish journey through his trousers.

Limelight can be unsparing in its honesty about the narcissism inherent in being a performer. There is a painful dream sequence where the trained-flea sketch flops, leaving Calvero to face an empty theater, and another scene, not a dream, where he is jeered offstage before his act is over. Chaplin was not only willing to confront his own craving for applause and acclaim but driven to do so, and *Limelight* as a whole can be seen as both a deliberate analysis and an unconscious symptom of that compulsion.

But when it comes to Chaplin's lifelong obsession with young women as unformed vessels in need of his artistic and emotional tutelage, the film's gaze is decidedly more sparing. Calvero may refrain from having sex with Terry; in fact, except for one dream sequence where he imagines them flirting in a sketch onstage, he shows no sign of being attracted to her. But the movie nonetheless presents him as her combination mentor, father figure, and idealized love object. His power over her is such that, when he tries to hand her off to his young rival (played, again, by Chaplin's own son), she eventually assents to the relationship despite her protests that Calvero remains her true love. By the end of the film Terry has become a world-famous ballerina; she has achieved the artistic apotheosis Calvero foresaw for her and sought in vain for himself. But the idea that she might pirouette off into the limelight alone, choosing neither of the two men, seems not to have been a possibility.

Terry can be seen as an idealized amalgam of all the women in Chaplin's life. Like his mother, she is an English music hall dancer whose ability to perform has been hampered by mental illness (at least until Calvero comes to her rescue, as Chaplin was never able to do for his mother). Like the girls and very young women he seduced and sometimes married later on, she is a beautiful blank canvas waiting for him to paint. Like Oona, her literal stand-in, she is a doting wifely type who looks out for Calvero's health, tolerates his moods, and darns his socks. Chaplin filmed a few flashback scenes about Terry's destitute childhood, but for the final cut he removed this background material. We first meet the character at the lowest point of her life: sprawled on her bed in an angelic white nightgown, clutching a bottle of pills after a suicide attempt. All we know about her is that she is a lovely victim in need of saving, an office that Calvero almost immediately appears on the scene to fulfill.

Bloom's radiant performance makes Terry's devotion to Calvero moving, even if we learn little about what drove her to try to kill herself or what motivates her to dance. But as a vision of the feminine ideal seen through the eyes of a man known for his serial maltreatment of women, Terry is an unsettling figure: a "true artist" (in Calvero's words) who realizes her potential only after she has been rescued, transformed, romantically rejected, and endlessly lectured by a wise older man.

Chaplin's political convictions presented a different kind of public relations problem from his many sex-related scandals, but the two strands interwove in his press coverage, as well as in his FBI file. Columnists at right-leaning papers tended to present him as indefinably shady, a figure of both sexual and political perversity who was generally not to be trusted. (Given the ambient anti-Semitism of the time, the case against him sometimes also included conspiracy theories that he was hiding a Jewish origin.) His vocal support for a variety of left-wing causes and open statements of sympathy for communist Russia meant that J. Edgar Hoover's FBI had been keeping an eye on him since the first "Red Scare" of the early 1920s. Still, despite his undeniable (and undenied) sympathy with the left, no amount of scrutiny had succeeded in linking Chaplin to Communist Party membership, much less to any espionage-related activity.[5]

By the time Chaplin got around to making *Limelight* in the early 1950s, the country was in the midst of its second Red Scare. The era of Senator Joseph McCarthy and the House Un-American Activities Committee was in full swing, and a group of conservative politicians, including the up-and-coming young senator Richard Nixon, were making it their business to either hound Chaplin out of the country or get him to testify in front of a congressional committee.

As a direct result of these pressures, *Limelight* turned out to be the last film Chaplin made before his self-exile from the United States, even though the film's story had nothing to do with politics. While on a trans-atlantic ocean voyage with his family to promote the world premiere in London, Chaplin learned via radio news bulletin that the US attorney general had rescinded his permit for reentry. If he wished to return to the country where he had resided since early adulthood without ever giving up his British citizenship—another reason, in some quarters, to question his patriotism—he would have to first sit for an interview about his political beliefs and associations. CHARLIE CHAPLIN BANNED FROM U.S. PENDING QUIZ, read the headline in the *Los Angeles Times*. As a result of the controversy, *Limelight* was shown at only a few theaters in the United States at the time of its release, though it was a well-received success abroad.

This threat was little more than bullying on the part of the Justice Department. The FBI had nothing on Chaplin, and if he had submitted to the symbolic humiliation of a reentry "quiz" he would likely have been let back in. But a deeply offended Chaplin took the United States government at its word and vowed never to set foot in his adopted homeland again. A dozen years later, installed at the remote Swiss villa where he, Oona, and their eight children lived for the last quarter century of his life, he wrote in his autobiography that "whether I re-entered that unhappy country or not was of little consequence to me. I would like to have told them that the sooner I was rid of that hate-beleaguered atmosphere the better, that I was fed up of America's insults and moral pomposity."[6]

He broke his vow only once, when in 1972 he flew to Los Angeles to accept an honorary lifetime achievement Oscar. Popular opinion toward him had softened as the excesses of the McCarthy era waned, and his sex scandals had faded from public memory, as the sex scandals of powerful men so often do. Later that same year *Limelight* finally saw its first wide release in the United States, two full decades after it was made. The year after that it would win Chaplin his only competitive Oscar, for the exquisitely melodic score he had composed himself (as he had for all his movies since *City Lights*) by humming the themes over and over to the film's music director. The second time around Chaplin, bitter about the two-month time limit that had been placed on his last entry visa, did not return to accept the trophy. Four years later he would die in his Swiss home at the age of eighty-eight.

The years since the coming of sound had been rough on Chaplin's career in a completely different way than they had for Keaton's. Unlike Calvero in *Limelight*, who believes he can only be funny when drunk, Chaplin had no personal struggles with addiction, even though his father had died of acute alcoholism at age thirty-eight. And his troubles were certainly not financial: after surviving a childhood of dire poverty in the London slums, he found himself rich enough by the late 1920s to weather the transition to sound with his artistic freedom intact. In fact, his immense wealth had for some time given him the leisure to make exactly the movies he wanted to at the pace he preferred, which since the advent of sound in particular had meant very, very slowly. Chaplin's struggle in the talkie era (aside from the myriad personal failings chronicled above) was to figure out how his exacting and intuitive style of filmmaking could work in the context of an increasingly efficiency-minded film industry.

Stories of Chaplin's perfectionism, his willingness to halt filming for days or even weeks while he reworked a gag or a piece of business, his vast ratios of film exposed to footage used, are legend. But with the coming of sound this already unusual way of working became harder to sustain. Even for a filmmaker wealthy enough to produce his own films, sound-stage space was limited and in high demand, and crews were starting to unionize. As Keaton had learned at MGM during those same years, the changes wrought by sound meant that shooting schedules had to be observed for the machine to function. Certainly, in Chaplin's case, pro-duction could no longer be held up indefinitely while the director, star, producer, composer, and all-around auteur agonized over a creative block.

For the whole of the 1930s Chaplin made only two films, *City Lights* (1931) and *Modern Times* (1936). Both were silent or near-silent[7] movies at a time when nothing could have been more out of style, yet both were hailed as masterpieces and flocked to by audiences—even if some critics found the anti-industrialization message of *Modern Times* to be overly didactic. As silent features made well into the sound era, *City Lights* and *Modern Times* are, by their mere existence, protest films; their form as much as their content is a critique of modernity in all its mass-produced alienation.

Over the next decade Chaplin made only two more movies. In 1940, as the Roosevelt administration dithered over whether and when to enter the war in Europe, came *The Great Dictator*, his first true talkie thirteen full years into the age of sound. *The Great Dictator* was an antifascist satire that turned the didacticism up several notches by ending with a six-minute direct-to-camera speech about world peace and universal brotherhood, delivered by a fourth-wall-breaking Chaplin still in costume as an ersatz Adolf Hitler. In his autobiography he recalled the resistance he encountered from his own studio, United Artists, and from the censorship office, which warned that the movie might not be allowed to be shown in England. "But I was determined to go ahead," Chaplin wrote, "for Hitler must be laughed at."[8] By the time the film was released, England and Germany were at war, and *The Great Dictator* not only was shown in the United Kingdom but served as a morale-boosting piece of propaganda.

The Great Dictator was the biggest moneymaking hit of Chaplin's career, but its preachy ending was divisive. A reviewer for the conservative Hearst paper chain wrote that the film was "at its best when Chaplin devotes himself to comedy,"[9] and the critic at the *New York Post* uncharitably if accurately observed that "the speech is so completely out of key with all that has preceded it that it makes you squirm."[10]

For the most part, even audiences who had long distrusted Chaplin's left-wing politics responded positively to his latest ripped-from-the-headlines satire, and he was invited to make the same impassioned if vague speech at various public events over the course of the war. But that same vagueness gave ammunition to those already keen to label Chaplin an unpatriotic coward who had dodged service in World War I (in fact, he said, he had registered for the US draft but never been called). *The Great Dictator* became the highest-grossing feature of Chaplin's career at the time of its release, and was nominated for five Oscars. It won none—maybe an early sign that for all the reverence he was still held in at that time, Hollywood's patience for Chaplin's political speechifying had its limits.

In 1947 Chaplin upped the ante by releasing the pitch-black comedy *Monsieur Verdoux*, a movie that asked audiences to replace their cherished memories of the Little Tramp with an icy antihero who serially courts, marries, and murders rich widows; the idea, based on a true story, had first been suggested to Chaplin by Orson Welles. *Verdoux* also threw in explicit critiques of both capitalism and the Cold War arms race, two unpopular stances to adopt in the patriotic and fervently anti-Communist atmosphere of post–World War II America.

"Chaplin Changes. Can You?" asked the movie's poster. Audiences decided they could not, and the borderline nihilistic *Verdoux* bombed at the box office and with most critics, though a few hailed it as the filmmaker's greatest work to date. Regardless, the net effect of its failure was to further turn public sentiment against its once adored star. After *Verdoux* Chaplin entered into another long fallow period. Over the next few years he would take up and discard multiple long-simmering ideas before settling on the most autobiographical among them: *Limelight*.

During his dizzying rise to fame in the mid-1910s, Chaplin had been the first movie star to be anointed with the title of "artist" by the likes of his theatrical champion Minnie Maddern Fiske. But as the century reached its midpoint, the cultural valuation of silent comedy was starting to shift: in September 1949, "Comedy's Greatest Era," a multipart *Life* cover story by the writer James Agee, made the kind of impact it seems impossible to imagine any one piece of film criticism having now.

Agee was a singular figure in the media landscape of his time in something like the way Robert Sherwood had been in his, though with an added sheen of movie-star glamour. He was an essayist turned movie critic turned screenwriter whose lyrical prose and immoderate love for cinema had made him both a household name and a darling of the intellectual elite, even for some who still scoffed at the medium itself. The poet W. H. Auden wrote a letter to the *Nation* to say that, though "I do not care for movies very much and I never see them . . . in my opinion his column is the most remarkable regular event in American journalism today."[11]

Agee first became known in the 1930s for writing the soaring if occasionally impenetrable text that accompanied Walker Evans's bestselling collection of Depression-era photographs, *Let Us Now Praise Famous Men*. After overlapping stints as a weekly critic at *Time* and the *Nation* during the 1940s, he went on to collaborate on the scripts of now-classic films like John Huston's *The African Queen* and Charles Laughton's *Night of the Hunter*. A *Death in the Family*, an unfinished autobiographical novel published only after his death, won him a Pulitzer Prize for fiction.

Agee was a literary celebrity of a sort: a man of intense friendships and self-destructive habits, a thrice-married chain-smoker and unreformed alcoholic with the roughly handsome features of the actor John Garfield. Like the equally multifaceted Sherwood, Agee was a weekly movie critic who wrote from the perspective of someone thinking about much more than movies, without ever losing touch with the primal pleasures the medium had to offer. "Comedy's Greatest Era" is still anthologized in collections of essential writing on film; it's a playful but pointed manifesto on behalf of the rediscovery of the movies the author remembered from his youth, with their "beauties of comic motion which are hopelessly beyond reach of words."

Agee was only forty when he wrote "Comedy's Greatest Era." (He would die five years later, of a heart attack in a taxicab, after a life spent burning the candle at a ruinous pace.) But in 1949 most of the silents he recalled with such fondness had been all but impossible to see for at least twenty years. They were either left to molder in forgotten storage vaults, as was happening to more than one of Keaton's features at that very moment, or, more often, unceremoniously disposed of.

The Museum of Modern Art in New York did have an important, if incomplete, collection of silent comedies that Agee used in his research, and as he notes, there were a few hundred prints of popular titles in circulation to rent if you happened to own a home movie projector. But for the ordinary viewer silent comedy had become a quaint relic known mainly through spoofs that reduced the form to a few inaccurate clichés. These were movies like *Hollywood Cavalcade*, a 1939 comedy set in the silent days in which Keaton appeared in a cameo as "himself," hurling cream pies with deadly accuracy at the pretty face of star Alice Faye. Never mind that not one of his own comedies had ever featured a single airborne pastry, let alone a grand-scale pie fight.

Chaplin, unsurprisingly, comes first in the *Life* article's four-part roundup of individual silent comics, billed in an old-timey typeface as "The Tramp." As far as Agee was concerned, he wrote, the close-ups of that character's face in the final shots of *City Lights* constituted "the greatest piece of acting and the highest moment in movies." But the reader gets the feeling that Agee saved the section on Keaton, titled "The Great Stone Face," until the end, after affectionate tributes to Harold Lloyd ("The Boy") and Harry Langdon ("The Baby"), not because he ranked Keaton lowest among the four but because the author felt a special attachment to the man who "carried a face as still and sad as a daguerreotype through some of the most preposterously ingenious and visually satisfying comedy ever made." Keaton himself opened his memoir, published eleven years after "Comedy's Greatest Era," with a quote from the piece, noting with pleased pride that "that kindly critic, the late James Agee . . . has described my face as ranking 'almost with Lincoln's as an early American archetype: haunting, handsome, almost beautiful.'"[12]

"Comedy's Greatest Era" is a love song to a lost art form, but also, implicitly, a call to arms for the preservation and rediscovery of a vanishing cultural patrimony.[13] The article got one of the biggest responses in the magazine's history. Readers of Agee's generation were reminded with a pang of the films of their youth, while the coming crop of moviegoers, too young to remember the days before sound, was suddenly motivated to seek out these hard-to-find treasures. The film historian Tom Stempel has written that he "fell in love with the silent comedies before [he] ever saw any" when, as a small child, he became fascinated by a photo in the *Life* article that showed Keaton sitting alone on a pew in an empty church;

twenty years went by before he discovered the source of the image, the 1925 feature *Seven Chances*.[14]

Thanks to Agee's vociferous championing of the widely maligned *Monsieur Verdoux*—he devoted no fewer than three columns to it in the *Nation*, calling it "one of the best movies ever made"[15]—the critic struck up a friendship with Chaplin and spent considerable time with him in 1951 while in Los Angeles for the release of *The African Queen*. As it happened, Agee's presence there overlapped with the filming of Chaplin and Keaton's big comic scene in *Limelight*. The critic and his wife, Mia, were invited to be in the audience, along with the cast, crew, and a group of journalists brought in to generate advance publicity for the movie that was being positioned, ironically as it would turn out, as Chaplin's grand return after a decade slipping from public favor.[16] Press coverage was not the only motivation for filling out the audience on the days the sequence was shot: as stage veterans since childhood, Keaton and Chaplin surely knew that in front of a live crowd they would time their gags better and find laughs more effectively.

Their near-silent sequence takes place on and around a variety theater stage. (Filming took place on a working stage owned by RKO Studios, dressed by production designer Eugene Lourié to look exactly like the Empire Theater in London circa 1914.) The sketch is a near-wordless musical duet for a one-night-only gala performance: Calvero is a maniacal violinist whose mood shifts to match whatever melody he's playing, while Keaton, as his somber-faced partner, accompanies on piano. Or tries to: as he plays, the loose pages of the score keep sliding off his music stand in a never-ending cascade. While the pianist contends with this Niagara Falls of paper, Calvero, sawing at his violin till the strings pop, does an odd bit that has first one leg, then the other mysteriously shortening itself until it disappears up his pant cuff and must be shaken back down to its normal length.

Once this curious ailment sorts itself out, Calvero decides that his stage mate's grand piano is in need of tuning. He opens the lid, whacking his partner in the face, and together they rummage through the instrument's innards with pliers in hand, cutting and pulling out great tangled masses of wire. When the pianist finally sits down again to play, they both realize (with exquisitely synchronized timing) that he has stepped on his partner's violin and is now wearing it as a kind of wooden snowshoe. Unfazed, Calvero produces a spare violin from his back pocket, and their musical duet proceeds at breakneck speed until, as the crescendo reaches its peak, he falls into the orchestra pit and lands in a bass drum.

Calvero's plunge into the pit is a planned part of the act, but the fatal heart attack he sustains in the pratfall is not. Still stuck in the drum, he is carried back to his dressing room amid waves of applause. He even asks to be brought back out for a curtain call. But the movie viewer, unlike the fictional ones in the theater, recognizes that the old clown is dying. In the film's last moments Calvero is seen from afar, lying on a prop couch in the wings while, in the extreme foreground, his protégée spins past him onto the stage, her career as a world-famous ballerina now fully under way. Standing around Calvero's makeshift deathbed are a few of their theatrical colleagues, among them the nameless pianist, now out of stage makeup and in his shirtsleeves. He looks on in respectful silence as a doctor arrives to pronounce Calvero dead. Suddenly his solemn face, so comically incongruous in the clowning scene, is exactly what the moment requires.

Keaton's whole part in the filming took about three weeks, including rehearsals. While everyone who was present agreed that the two veteran comics seemed to enjoy the work and treated each other with mutual respect, accounts of their collaboration differ. Lourié recalled the two engaging in a "friendly rivalry" to upstage each other, with Chaplin occasionally objecting to Keaton's contributions: "Chaplin would grumble. . . . He would say, 'No, this is *my* scene.'" Claire Bloom told Chaplin biographer David Robinson that she thought "some of his [Keaton's] gags may have been a little too incandescent for Chaplin because, laugh as he did at the rushes in the screening room, Chaplin didn't see fit to allow them all into the final version of the film."[17]

The Agees, too, recalled onlookers being dazzled at the inventiveness of the business Keaton improvised onstage; when they saw the finished film, both felt that most of the best gags had been cut. Eleanor Keaton spent only one day on the set of *Limelight*, but she always dismissed these accounts as rumors cooked up to fuel a supposed rivalry between the two filmmakers that in reality had never existed. "As I remember," she said of her husband's experience, "he had a wonderful time. I don't know whether Chaplin did or not."[18]

Eleanor's memory that the Chaplin/Keaton collaboration proceeded without incidents of competition or professional jealousy was supported and amplified by the character actor Norman Lloyd, a film-industry fixture from the silent era until his death in 2021 at the age of 106 and an invaluable trove of old Hollywood lore. Lloyd was a member of Orson Welles's Mercury Theater ensemble and worked with Alfred Hitchcock and Jean Renoir. He also had a small but significant role as a sympathetic stage manager in *Limelight*, and more than sixty years later he still called the experience of being in the audience during the filming of the Keaton-Chaplin clown act "one of the great events in my life."[19]

Above all, what struck Lloyd was how Chaplin's directing style changed on the days he and Keaton spent working up the details of their act. Chaplin was known for being the most hands-on director imaginable, acting out whole scenes for his cast members, down to the last gesture and line reading. Even Bloom, who had nothing but glowing words about her experience making her film debut under Chaplin's direction, admitted that the more self-confident actor she later became would have resented his constant micromanagement. But in preparing the silent scene with Keaton, Lloyd recalled, "They had almost a shorthand. They just did it . . . very objective, and minimal conversation. They just went at it, and Charlie said 'we print that.' It was the top of professionalism." It's notable that this rhythm of shooting—print the first take if possible, to keep the action fresh—was much more typical of Keaton's directorial philosophy than Chaplin's. His presence on set as a fellow master of improvisation seems to have changed the typical environment on a Chaplin shoot (slow, exacting, and constantly subject to the director's imposition of his own vision) into something closer to Keaton's own, more laid-back "way of workin'."

However well their scene may have gone at the time of shooting, the onscreen result of the Chaplin-Keaton collaboration in *Limelight* has always struck me as a maddeningly incomplete record of their one time performing together. Gag for gag the scene is still probably the funniest one in the movie, with each comic getting ample opportunity to explore the things he does best: pantomime and emotional expressiveness for Chaplin, prop comedy and falls for Keaton. Both of them seem to be in the zone, comfortable with the material and with each other as partners. Yet there is little sense of build or flow in the interaction between them, mainly because of a directorial choice that has nothing to do with what might or might not have ended up on the cutting room floor.

Except for the suite of gags involving the tuning of the piano, the two comedians almost never share the frame in a shot wide enough to show them both head-to-toe at the same time. Without an establishing master shot to return to, the film audience loses the chance to witness what the fictional stage audience is presumably seeing: the two clowns' growing frustration with their instruments and with each other. For example, Keaton's myopic pianist seems eager to get started on their duet, yet we get no reaction shot of his response to the inexplicable leg-shortening problem that is delaying his partner. Nor does Calvero appear to be aware of his friend's ongoing struggle with the slippery music score.

This interchange was precisely the kind of character-based sketch comedy in which both comedians had gotten their start, and which by all accounts they executed to perfection at the time of filming. But the effect Keaton strove for in his own films—to prove by means of camera placement and editing that everything the audience saw was happening to real bodies in real space and time—is mostly lost in this scene's oddly isolating editing and framing. For all the film audience knows, the two could be performing the majority of the sketch in different times and places.

It remains a mystery exactly why Chaplin chose to frame and cut this scene the way he did, given that he showed elsewhere in the same movie (in the ballet and solo comedy numbers, for example) that he knew how to frame onstage action so as to see as much of the space around the performers as possible. Was the decision to present the sketch with Keaton as two loosely connected bits of comedy business motivated, consciously or not, by a fear of being upstaged? Or, in a film that makes much of Calvero's sense of isolation from his audience, was this scene's chopped-up rhythm and sense of just-missed comic opportunities somehow deliberate? If so, why is the sketch presented as having been a huge hit? Edited and framed as it is, the scene still makes audiences laugh. But there is a certain melancholy in knowing that the real-life audience at the shoot had a perspective on the collaboration of these two towering talents that moviegoers for the rest of time will never get to see.[20]

If it isn't clear from all that's come so far, I am not the biggest fan of *Limelight*, however important its place in film history. Setting aside the fundamental ickiness of the central love triangle—an element now impossible to separate from what we know about Chaplin's own predilections—it seems to me an airless and fussed-over work, given to sententious maxims about art and mortality. Most of these come straight from the mouth of Calvero, who is presented with insufficient irony as a font of hard-won wisdom. His dying words to Tereza—"The heart and mind. What an enigma!"—give a sense of some of the more painfully unsubtle passages of dialogue, adapted by Chaplin from his own never-published novella.

Sometimes on purpose and sometimes despite its best intentions, *Limelight* is maybe the purest example in Chaplin's work of what the critic Andrew Sarris called his fundamental "solipsism as an artist."[21] The walls of Calvero's flat are covered in posters from his old performances and a photograph of his younger self, a man the audience instantly recognizes as the Chaplin of silent days: the Tramp out of costume. When the jilted Terry protests that she still loves Calvero, his jarringly smug reply—"Of course you do. You always will"—might as well be addressed directly to the movie audience of 1952. That was the true love object Chaplin was hoping to win back with his mid-century turn away from political satire and toward confessional autobiography.

The criticism often levied against Chaplin is that his attempts at mixing drama and comedy can turn mawkish. That seems to me an unfair judgment of movies like *The Kid* or *City Lights*, movies whose heartstring-tugging moments spring from the same pantomimic font of expression as their deliriously silly gags. *Limelight* is something else: a wearyingly verbose treatise on performance that tells us rather than shows us how to feel about its hero, and a career-culminating tour de force that is still somehow not a great movie.

Still, like it or not, *Limelight* should be seen by anyone trying to understand the life and work of Charlie Chaplin, who was—like him or not—among the most significant public figures of the twentieth century. And for all its maudlin passages, the film has a strange, solemn majesty, especially when the talking stops for a bout of wordless pantomime or a swell of that achingly romantic score. Every time I watch *Limelight* I'm more mystified by its dense weave of introspection and obliviousness, the parts of himself Chaplin ruthlessly confronts and the parts he refuses to see. In the moral slack it cuts its hero, its romantic gaze on events that could be interpreted as anything but, and its insistence on female youth and beauty as eternal principles that give life meaning, it reminds me of no other film so much as Woody Allen's *Manhattan*—if *Limelight* had ended with Calvero not dying backstage but racing to Terry's side to pledge his love to her, age gap and power differential be damned.

Still, *Limelight* remains invaluable as a record both of individual performances—Chaplin's, Keaton's, Bloom's—and of vanishing performance traditions. The action takes place in 1914, the year England entered the Great War and Chaplin got started in pictures. But Calvero, a has-been music hall clown, represents a style that dates back even earlier, to the late nineteenth century. Just as James Agee's 1949 tribute to silent comedy was also a call for its preservation and reevaluation, *Limelight*'s nostalgia conceals a pointed argument that the popular art of the past still matters. In the end Calvero dies, but his passion for the music hall stage lives on in Tereza—who as a ballerina represents an even older tradition, though her youth and vitality link her to the future.

The Chaplin who made *Limelight*, however big his blind spots, was invested in looking forward as well as backward: The movie's love for the popular culture of the past is nothing if not modern. It's impossible not to wonder what kind of movies he might have gone on to make next, had he not retreated into self-exile and what Calvero calls "a feeling of sad dignity"—a state of mind, he tells Tereza, that spells the death knell of funniness for a clown.

Like Keaton, Chaplin was a living bridge between the stage-based entertainment of the nineteenth century and the mass-produced technology of the twentieth. It seems fitting that as the new century passed its midpoint, their performing lives would finally converge. But when those three weeks' shooting on *Limelight* ended their paths diverged again for good, with Chaplin mostly withdrawing into domestic life and fatherhood while Keaton entered a new period of success and visibility as a working actor on the big and small screen.

Keaton's resurgence was not the result of *Limelight*. His comeback had begun at least two years earlier, with a supporting role in the 1949 Judy Garland musical *The Good Old Summertime* (for which he also choreographed the comic business), two successful if short-lived weekly TV series in 1949 and 1950, and a memorable two-line cameo in Billy Wilder's 1950 Hollywood satire, *Sunset Boulevard*. At any rate, almost no one in the United States would be able to see *Limelight* until Keaton had been dead for six years, so the legends that have grown up around his brief appearance in the film, apocryphal or not, came too late to have any effect on his career.

Keaton jokingly describes in his memoir how Chaplin seemed surprised when he showed up for their first meeting in advance of the *Limelight* shoot looking neither ravaged nor broke: "Apparently he had expected to see a physical and emotional wreck. But I was in fine fettle. I'd just been in New York for four months doing an average of two TV guest shots a week. So I was prosperous and looked it."[22] Still, until the end of his life Chaplin remained convinced that in casting Keaton in 1951 he had offered him a job at a time when he was down and out.

Chaplin and Oona O'Neill's eldest daughter, Geraldine—herself an acting legend in American and Spanish cinema since the 1960s—told the story of bringing home a boyfriend who, after paying due respect to the by-then-elderly Chaplin, expressed enthusiasm for Keaton's comedy. At dinner the young man pressed his girlfriend's famous father for stories of what it had been like to work with the Great Stone Face. Geraldine's father, as she recalled it, "just got smaller and smaller and he shrunk, and he was so hurt, it was like someone had stabbed him . . . and after dinner he was thinking and he was looking into the fire, and suddenly he peeped in a little voice. He looked my friend in the eye and he said: 'But I was an artist.' And no one knew what he was talking about. And then he said, 'You know, I gave him work.'"[23]

"Artist," that title bestowed on the creator of the Little Tramp by the theatrical elite back in the mid-1910s, still held meaning for Chaplin all those decades later. Not only did he still care about the designation, he wanted to make sure it would remain exclusively his in perpetuity. In contrast, on the rare occasions late in his life when such high-toned accolades were thrown his way, Keaton dismissed them, saying that "no man can be a genius in slapshoes and a flat hat." Eleanor later recalled how he would recoil from prospective interlocutors who tried to break the ice with "that genius bullshit."[24]

The only exception Keaton allowed to his no-genius-in-slapshoes rule was Charlie Chaplin. Though he could wax sardonic at times about the English comic's slow working methods or love for ideological grandstanding, he always placed Chaplin at the pinnacle of film comedy, telling his agent he would have taken the *Limelight* role if it paid nothing at all. From the early 1920s on, Keaton notes in his memoir, critics "said [Chaplin] was a genius, something I would be the last to deny" — though in the same paragraph Keaton admits that "the avalanche of praise for Charlie's brilliant direction also turned his head, I am afraid." Keaton was hardly the first to note that Chaplin's enormous early acclaim, along with the isolating effects of fame, later interfered with his ability to spontaneously connect with his audience. *Limelight* is an exploration of that same phenomenon by the man who felt it more keenly than anyone.

Chaplin's 1964 autobiography is a very different enterprise from the casual as-told-to memoir Keaton had essentially dictated to Charles Samuels four years earlier. Over the course of nearly five hundred pages written exclusively and often eccentrically by the comedian himself, Chaplin recalls his early years in the London slums and the celebrity-packed dinner parties of his later life at a level of detail worthy of Marcel Proust, while entire marriages and long stretches of his film career get skimmed over in a sentence or less.

In his introduction to this bricklike tome, Chaplin biographer David Robinson astutely pinpoints the decisive shift that occurs at the end of the eleventh chapter, when the twenty-six-year-old Chaplin vaults to a historically unprecedented level of worldwide fame. From that point onward the style of the book suddenly and irrevocably changes. Florid descriptions of precise if fleeting memories give way to a reserved tone of "sad dignity" worthy of Calvero himself. "Till now," Robinson writes, "we have followed the adventures of a young man, struggling, striving, experimenting and finally rocketed to success by his talents. Now we are presented with the self-portrait of a world celebrity, contentedly courted by princes and presidents." Chaplin's autobiography, in its curious split between meticulously re-created sense memory and complacent abstraction, resembles no film of his so much as *Limelight*—and evokes, in this reader/viewer at least, a similar chilly antipathy.

You can also scour the Chaplin autobiography's pages in vain for a mention of Buster Keaton. This omission in itself implies no particular enmity on the author's part. There are far more important figures in his life who go unreferenced, including Roland "Rollie" Totheroh, his loyal and patient cinematographer over the course of four decades, and Lita Grey, the mother of two of his children, who is never mentioned by name.[25] Just as Keaton's unnamed character in *Limelight* is left standing silently off to the side during Calvero's dying curtain call, Chaplin's hefty farewell to the world includes no mention of their time working together. In fact, the whole experience of making *Limelight* is dispatched in a few paragraphs, though the controversy surrounding its release and the Chaplin family's subsequent self-exile takes up many pages.

It wasn't until decades after the making of *Limelight* that the "Chaplin or Keaton?" question emerged as a parlor game for film lovers and film critics. It's not a game I love playing: the urge to list, rank, and pit one kind of art or artist against another (including the bestowing of prizes) has always struck me as playing to the worst aspects of human nature, our instinctive and probably inescapable drive to align ourselves with systems of power, authority, and status. Not only is there room enough for both of these two incomparable figures and many others in the silent-comedy pantheon, there's an excellent argument to be made for blowing up the pantheon altogether, especially given how many movies from that time have been lost. When I first undertook this project, a friend who is a devotee of silent comedy confessed that, in his own lovely formulation, he wore "the red rose of Chaplin" and not "the white rose of Keaton." As critics go I've never been one for ranking, but the color of the rose on my lapel can be guessed by which of the two I've nearly written a book about.

Chaplin's artistry as an actor and pantomimist, his ability to convey shadings of character through gesture, facial expression, and movement, was unsurpassed. His sophisticated fusion of the music hall traditions of his childhood with the new medium of film was unique in its time, even if it was never as a director that he shone the brightest. In life he could be cold and arrogant; as an entertainer, he created a more direct emotional bond with more people around the world at once than anyone had done in history. In *Limelight* Chaplin tries, not always in the best of faith, to explore these contradictions in himself, as well as the gulf between his youthful clown persona and the "sad dignity" of his older self.

Norman Lloyd's stage manager character is one of the attendants at Calvero's deathbed, standing alongside Keaton, Sydney Chaplin, and others in a composition that recalls a Baroque religious painting. Lloyd's memory of filming this scene was that as the camera dollied out to take a wider view of the wings and the stage together, Keaton was continually murmuring under his breath to Chaplin, advising him to "keep still,

Charlie, you're in the center of the shot."[26] In his way—and in the style of silent dramatic directors who often talked their lead actors through scenes while the camera rolled—Keaton was codirecting this final scene, or at least keeping an eye on aspects of the production that the famously control-obsessed Chaplin could hardly monitor while a sheet was being pulled over his head.

When *Limelight* ends on Calvero's death in the wings, with Keaton's character silently standing behind him and the real Keaton not-so-silently providing updates on the position of the camera, there is a symbolic rightness to the composition. Like the dancer who pirouettes by into the spotlight, the dying clown's stage partner is still on his feet; having managed to stay in the business all these years, he will presumably go on to perform again. Chaplin would have twenty-five more years to live after the movie's release and Keaton only fourteen. But the former spent the next quarter century essentially retired, while the latter never stopped working. For the second time in his life, getting in on the ground floor of a new entertainment technology would allow Keaton to reinvent himself and start his career afresh. A whole generation of Americans, those born more or less around the time of *Limelight*, grew up knowing him only as the guy who was always on television.

27

The Coming Thing in Entertainment

On the set of Ten Girls Ago, 1962.
(Photo courtesy of Chris Seguin.)

When Chaplin and Keaton met for the first time in decades in advance of the *Limelight* shoot, the first thing they talked about was TV. As they exchanged pleasantries, the sixty-three-year-old Englishman marveled at how fit the fifty-six-year-old American was looking. "Charlie, do you look at television?" came the unexpected reply. "Good heavens, no," said Chaplin, explaining that like many a high-minded parent in the decades to follow, he did not permit his children to so much as look at the "lousy, stinking little screen." He then again observed what fine form Keaton was in and asked what he did to stay in shape. "Television," answered Keaton, his career then in the midst of a revival thanks to the rise of the new medium. This teasing exchange, recounted in a tone of playful malice in Keaton's memoir, neatly sums up the differences between the two:

the populist and the aesthete, the mechanically minded futurist and the nostalgic technophobe, the pragmatic craftsman and the idealistic artist.[1]

Keaton liked everything about television: appearing on it, watching it, talking about advances in TV technology or the future of the medium to whomever would listen. In 1948 his son Jim, by then a twenty-six-year-old Coast Guard veteran with young children of his own, got a TV set as a gift from his aunt Norma (neither of the two acting Talmadge sisters had children, and they never tired of showering their nephews with lavish gifts). It was the first set anyone in his neighborhood had owned, a GE with a ten-inch screen that, as Jim remembered it, "weighed a ton. My dad came over the first weekend we had it. All afternoon he sat mesmerized in front of this thing. . . . At dinner I remember him saying, 'This is the coming thing in entertainment.'"[2]

A question in a late-life interview about the cost of TV production set Keaton off on an unrelated tangent comparing the picture quality of American and European TVs: "Their sets are beautiful, and the French have the number one, the best television. I believe we have, what is it, five hundred lines in our picture? There's 750 in the French. They got a much finer grain on their picture than we do." In another interview from the same era, he seemed to foresee the coming world of cable TV and on-demand streaming services, though he imagined an economic benefit to the consumer that has failed to materialize in our age of proliferating subscriptions:

> I'm anxious to see the day when television and the motion picture industry marry and set out a system, because it can't continue the way it is. I see only one solution to it: There should be paid television, and they could keep the costs so low that the poorest man in the world could have a television, they can keep the entertainment that low-priced. And in that way you'd make pictures exactly the way you used to make them before television.[3]

Soon after encountering TV for the first time, Keaton bought a set for the home he and Eleanor then still shared with his mother and siblings.

Thereafter, to visit the Keatons was to hear the TV in the background, always at high volume to compensate for the hearing loss he had suffered since an ear infection during his service in World War I. In between jobs he would sit in front of it for hours, playing solitaire, smoking and offering a running critique of whatever was on to whoever passed through. James Karen recalled him watching a show while shouting instructions at the screen as if he were directing it: "Cut! Now move that camera!" Visitors to the San Fernando Valley house he bought with Eleanor in 1956 recalled him in the converted garage he called his "den," keeping one eye on a tiny black-and-white screen while he held up his typically laconic end of the conversation. "The man never left his den," one of his grandsons recalled in an interview. "He *loved* television. And he watched everything."[4]

Though he never mentioned it by name, among his favorite watches during the 1950s must surely have been the pioneering sitcom *I Love Lucy*, starring his old friend and onetime MGM protégée Lucille Ball. When asked to name the best comedians of the up-and-coming generation he would often cite Ball as one of his "pets," calling her timing "impeccable." In fact, Keaton had had a behind-the-scenes role in getting *I Love Lucy* on the air. In 1950, when CBS was trying to convince Ball to star in a sitcom based on her successful radio series *My Favorite Husband*, she agreed to sign on only if the show could costar her real-life husband, the Cuban-American bandleader Desi Arnaz. The network balked at the idea of a domestic comedy centered around a couple of mixed race, so the two worked up a live vaudeville routine to be filmed as an experimental pilot.

Keaton coached Ball in the big physical comedy scene, an act borrowed from the Spanish clown Pepito that involved Ball as a dimwitted but resourceful cellist auditioning for a spot in Arnaz's orchestra. This pilot never aired at the time (and was thought to be lost until 1989, when it was finally discovered and aired on CBS as part of a Lucille Ball tribute special). But it was funny enough to convince CBS to give Ball and Arnaz their own prime-time series, which would run for 180 episodes and become perhaps the most influential of all early situation comedies. A pared-down version of the cello sketch found its way into a first-season episode, so although Keaton never guest-starred on *I Love Lucy*, he is nonetheless there as a behind-the-scenes presence.[5]

As had happened before with both vaudeville and silent film, Keaton's career on the small screen happened to coincide with the medium's golden age. His long association with MGM ended around 1949, when he found that he was getting enough work as a performer for hire not to need the comedy-doctor day job he had held at the studio for thirteen years. Though Buster was nowhere near as unhappy at this second MGM gig as he had been at the first, he was unquestionably underemployed, and severing ties with a place where he had so much painful history must have come as a relief.

A short promotional film made for the studio's twenty-fifth anniversary in 1949, easily viewable on YouTube, offers a glimpse into Keaton's relationship to the institution where he had worked in some capacity for most of the past two decades. Just before a typically fulsome speech from Louis B. Mayer, the camera pans across table after table of stars seated for a formal luncheon, some still in costume from whatever movie they were shooting. At the end of one long table sits Keaton, between the juvenile actor Claude Jarman Jr. and—at a small separate booth with her own dish—Lassie. These deliberately comic seating arrangements can't help but evoke the bad old days of "Keaton's Kennel" and the overbearing canine-comedy director Jules White. The comedian's place at the studio had always been akin to that of a mascot.

Most of the celebrities on view in this ten-minute short seem engrossed in eating or conversation; they are either unaware of the moment the camera passes by them or acknowledge it with a quick fourth-wall-breaking smile. Ava Gardner and Clark Gable share a laugh with Keaton's old screen partner Jimmy Durante, while Judy Garland, seated next to Fred Astaire, leans over the back of her chair to chat with someone at the table behind her. But the moment the camera comes to a stop at Keaton's end of the table, he is not only "on," his face professionally blank as it always was when he knew he was being filmed, but already engaged in an improvised bit of prop comedy. He takes a bite of celery, appears to dislike the taste, makes a move as if to spit it out in his hand, and then — playing on his and our awareness of the camera's presence — reconsiders the rude gesture, his eyes darting away from the all-seeing lens in mock shame. It's over in seconds, a micro-performance in a context that didn't require one. Is he doing the bit for his own amusement, or fulfilling his longtime MGM mandate to supply bits of comedy business wherever he can? Either way, the subtext of the celery gag is clear: he is out of place at this stuffy studio function, he knows it, and he knows we know it, too.

In his first role in a talkie, MGM's all-star roundup The Hollywood Revue of 1929, Keaton had appeared, silent and unsmiling, at the end of a long line of MGM contract players. Everyone wore identical yellow rain slickers and hats, and everyone but him was belting the latest hit song from the MGM musical unit, "Singin' in the Rain." The message conveyed by Keaton's body language in those few seconds of screen time was itself a joke about his odd-man-out status at the studio: his dubious face and darting eyes seemed to ask, "What am I doing here?" Twenty years later at the anniversary luncheon, his relationship to the studio with "more stars than there are in heaven" was about the same. He was still the guy at the end of the line, comically out of place in Mayer's preferred atmosphere of glamorous uniformity but doing his best to get a laugh from that very fact.

By the early 1950s Keaton had started to get small but highly visible roles in big-budget films like In the Good Old Summertime and Sunset Boulevard. But as he had foreseen in his son's living room, appearances on the big screen no longer represented the pinnacle, much less the cutting edge, of recorded entertainment. In fact, by the time Keaton began starring in his own weekly TV series in late 1949 the motion-picture business was in a full-blown panic. The following year, alongside a review of that show's second incarnation, The Buster Keaton Comedy Hour, Variety ran a story with this typically alarmist headline: "MUST REVIVE WANT-TO-SEE HABIT." The unnamed author goes on to fret that "with the national B.O. suffering another sinking spell, industry execs are concerned that 'going to the movies' has become increasingly less routine to the American family and is rapidly moving into the category of 'something special.' How to combat that tendency—and whether it can be successfully combated at all—is seen as the problem facing the industry."[6]

A few forces converged to make the late 1940s and early '50s the moment TV took off and movie attendance began to decline. In 1948 the Supreme Court case *United States v. Paramount* put an end to the monopolies of the six major film studios by forbidding them to own their own theater chains or engage in the practice of block booking (making films available to distributors only in compulsory bundled "blocks"). In 1952 the Federal Communications Commission ended a five-year freeze on licenses for new television stations, put in place after a nationwide run on licenses had created difficulties with signal interference. Up until then the United States had had only a handful of "television cities," urban centers with the infrastructure to support a mix of national and local programming.[7]

In 1949, the year the first television set appeared for sale in the Sears, Roebuck catalog, fourteen states in the union were still without television service entirely.[8] As the century passed its midpoint, only 9 percent of American households owned a TV; the primary home entertainment device remained, as it had since the 1930s, the family radio. In many places people intrigued by the new technology gathered to watch in whatever local saloon had splurged for a set.[9]

Owning a television in the late 1940s, as Jim Keaton and his father did, was akin to owning a personal computer in the early 1980s: it was a luxury product for early adopters, a technology recognizable to almost everyone but affordable (or even useful) to relatively few. But with the increased availability of manufacturing materials, advances in function and design, and the ramping up of the consumer economy after World War II, the home TV screen soon became the "electronic hearth" it would remain for the rest of the century and well into our own.

By the late 1950s something like 90 percent of American households owned a TV set, and the medium was becoming associated with consumerism and conformity—the "boob tube" image that would cling to it until the arrival of prestige television around the turn of the twenty-first century. But in that short span of time when its future was still uncertain, television had the chance to experiment with new forms, some avant-garde, some so retro they harked back to a time before the invention of motion pictures.

The overlap between early television and vaudeville was so marked that a new term, "vaudeo," was coined to describe the phenomenon. The young medium's first offerings were dominated by variety programs, many imported direct from years of success on radio, so that the trajectory of successful comics often went from stage to radio to television, skipping the movies entirely. *Texaco Star Theater*, hosted after late 1948 by the former vaudevillian and Borscht Belt comic Milton Berle, was one of the first radio shows to successfully make the jump to TV. Berle's volatile, borderline aggressive hosting style was so popular that some restaurants and nightclubs started closing on Tuesdays, seeing how much business fell off when "Uncle Miltie" was on the air.

By the time *Texaco Star Theater*, by then called *The Milton Berle Show*, ended in 1956, Berle's nickname had become "Mr. Television" and variations on the live variety show were everywhere. Many were hosted by former stage clowns: Martha Raye, Ed Wynn, even Keaton's former screen partner Jimmy Durante. But the most durable (and most truly vaudevillian) of the lot, providing a stage for animal acts, plate-jugglers, and rising pop sensations alike until 1971, belonged to Ed Sullivan, an entertainment columnist whose awkward stage presence became a running joke and a part of the show's appeal.

Keaton appeared on Sullivan's show many times—he loved to tell the story of how he once stumped the host with an old theatrical illusion that had also appeared in *Sherlock, Jr.*—as well as on countless other variety shows throughout the decade. Often, but not always, the act he presented was a variation on a routine from his silent films. His first appearance on TV came in 1949 as a guest star on *The Ed Wynn Show*, the first live-broadcast series to be taped on the West Coast (in the early days of television, most shows were produced in New York). The sketch he performed with Wynn, a fellow old-time vaudevillian, was an elaboration on the molasses-in-a-hat routine he had done with Arbuckle in his first film, *The Butcher Boy*, thirty-two years before. The outdatedness of silent film became a part of the joke, with the actors holding up cue cards to simulate intertitles.

It was the appreciative response to that guest spot that led to *The Buster Keaton Show* later that same year. This half-hour-long series ran for a season on the local Los Angeles station KTLA; only one episode has survived.[10] To judge by that sample, the show fell somewhere in between a situation comedy and a sketch series: after a hasty narrative setup (his character, also named Buster, needs to be trained for a prizefight), Keaton is left mostly alone in a gym full of props: free weights, a jump rope, a rowing machine, and that long-ago favorite Three Keatons prop, a basketball.

The dialogue and story setups are weak, maybe because one of the show's two writers, Buster's longtime gag man (and credited codirector on *The General*) Clyde Bruckman, was often too drunk to deliver his weekly script material on time.[11] But once Keaton gets down to the business of physical comedy there is no need for sound, except for the live audience's laughter, applause, and occasional gasps. The high point is a bit where Keaton, alone on camera, sinks half a dozen or more baskets from a succession of unlikely angles—overhead from behind, lying flat on the ground, as a casual flourish at the end of a dance—without ever glancing at the hoop.

The idea of Buster having his own nationally syndicated TV series never went anywhere after 1950, to his eventual relief. "It's the quickest way to Forest Lawn that I know of," he would say years later, "trying to dig up material for that weekly show." But those early experiments at least showed Keaton how he wanted to work in TV: if not live, then to a live studio audience. He laid out his thinking on this matter to the oral historian Studs Terkel in a radio interview years later:

When I first tried a television show, when it was a young business, we were working to an audience. Then later on they talked me into doing 'em just to a silent motion picture camera. Well, it didn't work, because no matter what you did it looked like something that had been shot thirty years ago. It didn't look up to date. . . . And the canned laughs are absolutely no good at all. They don't ring true at all.

Up until the mid-1950s one of the new medium's most popular formats was the "anthology drama": freestanding mini-teleplays that featured different writers, directors, and stars every week. Among other things, this was a way for young talent to find a platform. Shows like *Kraft Television Theater*, *Goodyear Television Playhouse*, *Studio One*, and *Playhouse 90* became a testing ground for rising movie stars (Paul Newman, Joanne Woodward, Sidney Poitier, Rod Steiger) and soon-to-be-famous writers, directors, and TV personalities: Paddy Chayefsky, John Frankenheimer, Arthur Penn, Rod Serling.

In 1954, for the anthology drama series *Douglas Fairbanks Presents*, Keaton played the lead in a half-hour teleplay that was a loose adaptation of Nikolai Gogol's short story *The Overcoat*. Titled *The Awakening*, it was a vaguely Orwellian allegory about a timid clerk in a bureaucratic dystopia who scrimps and saves to replace his shabby coat with an expensive custom-made one. *The Awakening* is written and directed in a style typical of television drama in the mid-1950s: the script is overbaked, with a climactic speech that lays out the story's themes with un-Keatonian obviousness. Still, the show is notable for providing the only straight dramatic lead he had played since his season as a stock-company Little Lord Fauntleroy at age eleven. Playing a cipher turned rebel who finally rises up against the cruelty of the system he has long upheld, Keaton is not only credible and sympathetic but startlingly modern. He seems to understand the genre he's performing in, even though starkly symbolic two-act dramas written for the small screen were a new form that bore little relation to his stage or film experience.

There was hardly a television trend of the 1950s or early '60s that Keaton didn't get in on at some point. Continuing his long run as a family-friendly entertainer, he appeared twice on the domestic sitcom *The Donna Reed Show* and did a slapstick bit with Eleanor on the children's program *Circus Time*. On *Candid Camera*, he pranked onlookers at a lunch counter with a routine involving an ill-fitting toupee and a bowl of soup. In a comic episode of *The Twilight Zone*, he played a time-traveling janitor from 1890 who, after some mishaps in the present day, decides to go back to his own era.

More than one of his TV roles shared this theme of a desire to return to days gone by. In the 1955 teleplay *The Silent Partner* he was a forgotten silent comedian named "Kelsey Dutton," clearly modeled on the real Keaton, who watches quietly from a bar stool while his former director accepts a lifetime achievement Oscar. In flashbacks he appears as his fictional younger self, his only de-aging makeup a ludicrous black wig—an odd choice until you consider that, even at age sixty, Keaton was the only one who could do the falls. Somehow these backward-looking TV roles never came off as a bid to rest on his laurels, maybe because they were projects others cast him in rather than stories he created for himself. When asked he was happy to play the part of a pie-throwing old-timer, but in real life he was turned toward the future, a time traveler who had arrived from 1895 and decided to stick around.

He was the coming thing in entertainment, always. As a juvenile star on the stage he had sometimes been mistaken for, or passed off as, a small-statured adult; as an older man, he brought a youthful energy to his experiments in a new medium. But some of his most creatively and personally rewarding work in middle age happened in one of the most ancient of all entertainment formats: the circus. Between 1947 and 1954 Keaton traveled to Paris three times for a season-long engagement at the Cirque Medrano, often performing with Eleanor as a partner in the act.

Some accounts of Keaton's late life—the ones that want to frame him as a tragic figure permanently destroyed by Hollywood—present his time performing with the circus as some sort of comedown, as if he had been reduced to sweeping up after the elephants while honking a red nose. In fact, he held the prize second-act slot at one of Europe's most prestigious and innovative circuses, at a time and in a place when clowns were among the most valued of live performers.

The Cirque Medrano, sometimes called the "Temple of Clowns" or the "pink circus" (for its peach-painted vaulted ceiling), was not a traveling tent show like the one that tours France today under that name but a permanent building in the bohemian neighborhood of Montmartre. It had been a working circus of some kind since its construction as the Cirque Fernando in 1875. In surviving photos — the building was torn down in 1973, replaced by a Carrefour supermarket — it is a rounded structure with a conical top that suggests a circus tent.

The place had long been a haunt for painters, given its location just blocks from the Bateau-Lavoir, a ramshackle building that served as a low-cost boardinghouse for artists. In the late nineteenth century acts at the Cirque Fernando were painted and sketched by Auguste Renoir, Edgar Degas, Georges Seurat, and Henri Toulouse-Lautrec. These artists became fascinated by the venue's clowns, dancers, equestrian acts, and, in Degas's case, a celebrated mixed-race aerialist who went by the name "Miss La La" and performed feats of strength while hanging by her teeth from a bar suspended from the ceiling.

The Spanish-born clown Geronimo "Boum Boum" Medrano, the Cirque Fernando's biggest star and top box-office draw, took over management of the circus in 1897, and the Cirque Fernando became the Cirque Medrano. In the decade that followed it attracted a new generation of artists including Fernand Leger and Pablo Picasso, both residents at the Bateau-Lavoir. Leger published a book of sketches made backstage at the Medrano; Picasso's transformative "rose period" centered on portraits of the circus's pink-clad acrobats and diamond-patterned harlequins against stark, desert-like backgrounds. One of the Medrano's unusual features was a backstage bar where fans could mingle with their favorite performers. Picasso attended the circus three or four times a week and loved to carouse with the clowns after the show.

In 1912 Boum Boum died unexpectedly, and his only child, Jérôme Medrano, inherited the circus at age five. At age twenty-one, after having been sent away to the country's best schools, Medrano the younger announced his plans to take over management of the circus, with big ideas about how to modernize the show while keeping its traditions alive. Over the next few decades he became part of a generation of early twentieth-century circus owners—another was John Ringling North, the business-whiz nephew of the Ringling Brothers—who reinvented the venerable form by mixing traditional circus acts with entertainers from the worlds of film, television, and pop music.

For Jérôme Medrano, a passionate cinephile, that meant pulling in talent from Hollywood. Before World War II closed down the circus in 1940 (during this period, Jérôme went into hiding to work for the French Resistance), Laurel and Hardy had been set to guest-star for a season. Landing Keaton to open the fall season in 1947 was a way of showing Parisians that the Medrano was back with a vengeance from its wartime lull.[12]

For the first half of the twentieth century, the circus in Paris was both an esteemed art and a thriving business, with competing venues all around the city. The Medrano's steeply tilted theater-in-the-round style arena had a seating capacity of around two thousand, too small for the big animal acts that were the specialty of its main rival, the Cirque d'Hiver. But that scale made it an ideal venue for the clown acts that became its claim to fame. Arthur Moss, editor of the Parisian expatriate journal *The Quill*, described the unique atmosphere of the Medrano in a 1924 dispatch:

> The *cirque intime* has many and obvious advantages. There is never more than one act in the ring at a time, though as the acts are changing half a dozen minor clowns rush noisily about. . . . As all the action is visible from every point in the house, it must of necessity be entertainment of a calibre that will bear such close scrutiny. This is particularly true of the clown acts. Instead of the confused antics and tumblings of bespangled figures lost in the kaleidoscope of three rings and five stages, the single

small arena produces definite individualistic *comiques* of the class of Charlie Chaplin.[13]

To be compared to Chaplin in 1924 was about as lavish a compliment as a "minor clown" could get. But in France Keaton was nearly as highly esteemed, and remained so even when his career in the United States was at its lowest ebb. By 1947, when he first headlined at the Medrano, he had not had a role in a major Hollywood movie in nearly fifteen years. But the French still gave their beloved "Malec," as his silent persona was called there, a king's reception. A poster outside the circus advertised him as *"le comique numéro un du cinéma américain."* His Medrano debut was a hit, packing the house every night while his fellow clowns clustered in the entrances around the ring to watch. The Cinémathèque Française quickly organized a retrospective of his silent films; one night he attended, and was photographed inspecting an old-fashioned movie camera.

Buster seems to have enjoyed these intermittent gigs in Paris. A publicity shot from his 1947 debut shows him surrounded by onlookers as he crouches down to leave his hand- and shoe-prints in wet cement in the circus lobby, something he was never invited to do at Grauman's Chinese Theater in Hollywood. In another photo he poses, looking bemused, in front of a ten-foot high mural of his own face on the building's exterior wall. A gag photo taken backstage shows him engrossed in a card game with three chimpanzees; Eleanor laughingly recalled that one of the chimps from the act that year formed a desperate attachment to him and an equal and opposite dislike to her.

Keaton had worked in Europe a few times in the 1930s and '40s, starring in low-budget films like *Le Roi des Champs-Elysées* and *An Old Spanish Custom*, quickie jobs where he had had little creative input. But the Medrano trips must have felt very different. Here at last was the experience he had longed for at age thirteen, when the Three Keatons crossed the ocean for their first gig abroad, at the Palace Theater in London. Joe had sabotaged that trip with his quick temper and irrational xenophobia; he was affronted by the notion of an Old World with different customs to adjust to, just as he had felt personally attacked by the invention of motion pictures, and when the weeklong engagement was up, he fled with his family back to the familiarity of the US vaudeville circuit.

But by the time of the Medrano engagements almost forty years later, Joe Keaton had been dead for a year, and his son, after a decade spent as an on-call comedy doctor for other people's movies, was finally given the chance to develop just the live act he wanted, with the circus owner's blessing and ample onstage support from both Eleanor and the circus's skilled troupe of clowns. He could refine the same sketch over the course of a run rather than scramble to find new gags every week, he gave only one performance a night rather than the two-a-day norm of his child-hood, and he was rapturously received by an audience that ranged from middle-class Parisian families to highbrow connoisseurs of the circus arts to a smattering of his former Hollywood colleagues. In the five-minute clip of a Medrano performance that survives, Wallace Beery and Chico Marx can be seen laughing in the stands.

For his first Medrano engagement Keaton re-created and expanded on the comic duel he had staged with his friend Gilbert Roland in *The Passionate Plumber*, an otherwise lamentably cloddish MGM talkie. The next time around, in 1951, he restaged the "putting the drunk bride to bed" scene from *Spite Marriage*, with Eleanor in the sack-of-potatoes role once played by Dorothy Sebastian. And for his last Medrano season in 1954 he created a series of sketches, some solo and some with Eleanor as his partner, about his hapless character trying and failing to complete simple daily tasks, getting himself hauled off after every scene by a clown dressed as a cop. The novelist and sportswriter Paul Gallico, who befriended the Keatons on one of their ocean crossings to Paris, attended one of those 1954 performances and wrote about it for *Esquire* magazine:

> I went to the Medrano, of course, to catch the turn of the star clown billed there. He came on, a sad-faced little fellow wearing a flat, pork-pie hat, string tie, too-big clothes, flap shoes, carrying a moldy dress suit

on a hanger, obviously looking for a cleaner's. Before he had done, the suit was a wreck on the arena floor and the audience was in hysterics.

The Medrano act as Gallico described it seems to weave in material from both the Three Keatons act and the silent films: at one point Buster's character provokes the ringmaster by interrupting his song, just as he used to rouse Joe's comic ire by interrupting his improvised ballads. By the end the hapless Buster is "chased all over the arena, not only by the cops but a file of ushers and attendants." The idea of the act bursting the bounds of the stage to spill into the surrounding theater recalls Buster's flights into the orchestra pit or the audience as a child. And Gallico recognized in the delighted shrieks of the children in attendance an updated version of his own joy watching Keaton films in his youth:

> This was my deadpan boy, hero of a hundred movies, frustration's mime, pursued, put upon, persecuted by humans as well as by objects. . . . When, during the chase, he vanished through an exit, to appear a moment later high up in the arena entangled with the orchestra and the minions converged on him anew, I could hear the undertone of the ecstatic children's laughter — "poor little man" — and listen happily to their renewed delight when he got away again. That world every child and child-in-man understands and Keaton has always been one of its greatest interpreters.[14]

At least one child in the audience at that same 1954 engagement experienced not only delight but transformation. Dominique Jando, today a circus historian and former clown who has been working in the circus profession for over fifty years, was nine years old when his father took him to see Keaton at the Medrano. By age fourteen, Jando was volunteering at the Medrano circus; at eighteen he was performing there as a clown. Speaking sixty-seven years later about the impact of that performance on his life, he says, "He came into my inside world. It was not something I had to speak of. For me, clowning was what Buster Keaton did."[15]

Though the Medrano engagements paid well, they were not hugely profitable for the Keatons, because French law only allowed foreigners to take a limited amount of cash out of the country. So Eleanor and Buster spent their Paris trips living much higher on the hog than usual, staying at the five-star Georges V hotel and frequenting a restaurant, Chez Joseph, that served a rich lobster dish Keaton later re-created at home for guests. Eleanor retained a fond memory of those trips, telling an interviewer more than forty years later that "they were fun, they were wonderful."[16]

The Medrano engagements came to an end in 1954 after Jérôme Medrano and the Keatons had a dispute about whether they could perform at other European circuses or music halls once the Paris gig was over, given that it was Jérôme who had paid for their round-trip travel to the continent. Buster and Eleanor shrugged at what they saw as an arbitrary restriction and continued to accept other engagements while abroad, but Medrano's desire to keep such a name-brand act exclusive to his circus was understandable.

The circus was by then on the wane as a popular art in Europe, and by the early 1960s the Medrano would be bought out by its rival Cirque d'Hiver and lose its unique, clown-focused character. But Jérôme Medrano never stopped finding ways to adapt the circus to the times; in 1956 he helped start a weekly TV program filmed at circuses around Paris, called *La Piste aux Etoiles* ("The Runway of the Stars"). It became one of the longest-running TV shows in French history, playing on one network or another until 1978.

The mid-1950s were a time of change, loss, and self-reinvention for Keaton, both in his personal and professional life. After Myra's death in 1955 and the subsequent drinking-related health crisis that landed him in the hospital with a near-fatal throat hemorrhage, he seems to have rethought how he wanted to spend the years left to him. His guest spots on TV variety shows became less frequent. Instead, he took walk-on movie parts in the all-star mega-productions that became the fashion until the middle of the next decade: *Around the World in 80 Days, It's a Mad Mad Mad Mad World, A Funny Thing Happened on the Way to the*

Forum—movies with comically long titles and overstuffed casts to match. These were often shot in international locations, a perk both Buster and Eleanor enjoyed, and they paid well for less work than scrambling to create a twenty-minute-long comedy sketch for a single TV guest shot.

In the early 1960s Keaton also signed on for a series of cameos in a string of "beach musicals" produced by the B-movie outfit American International Pictures: *Beach Blanket Bingo, Pajama Party, How to Stuff a Wild Bikini*. These were unapologetic schlock for the youth market, movies about which, when questioned by an interviewer, Keaton could only summon a "contemptuous noise."[17] Some of the projects he signed up for may have occasioned an under-the-breath scoff, but Keaton liked to work.

The parts he took on in his last fifteen years of life made use of the stoic mask of his face more than of his still-agile body, though he seldom missed the chance to throw in a fall or stunt whenever he could. A series of stills taken in the mid-fifties, when he was nearing sixty, shows him casually turning a backflip. By the time he appeared in a minor role in *A Funny Thing Happened on the Way to the Forum* at age seventy, only a few months away from his death from lung cancer, he finally accepted the use of a stunt double for long shots of his character running. But when it came time to film Keaton's medium-shot inserts, the stuntman who doubled him recalled the toga-clad comedian startling the crew by running facefirst into a tree branch.[18] Just as he had done when he was a kid being thrown across the stage, Buster was still eliciting laughs and gasps at the same time; where he had once seemed too young to be subjected to such punishment, now he seemed too old. But at both extremes of his life, as at all points in between, his equanimity in the face of disaster remained at the heart of the joke.

In 1955 Keaton brokered a deal between future and past when he took advantage of the decade's fad for show business biopics—especially those involving dramatic slides into addiction—and sold the rights to his life story to Paramount for $50,000. The result was a woefully inaccurate and worse, unfunny movie starring a game but miscast Donald O'Connor. Keaton attended preproduction meetings, served as technical adviser on how to re-create scenes from his old films, was present on set to oversee the comedy scenes, and even helped the star, thirty years his junior, learn a few of his old stunts: a photo spread in *Life* magazine showed them in matching gray sweatsuits rehearsing the "teacup roll" from *College*, a trick O'Connor admitted he never mastered.

Keaton and O'Connor quickly bonded; the younger man had also grown up in a family vaudeville act and a few years before had played an ex-vaudeville musician in *Singin' in the Rain*. As Eleanor recalled, "He adored Buster . . . it was like brothers, they knew each other immediately."[19] But the director's standing invitation to view the daily rushes was politely ignored. Keaton could tell from observing the shoot exactly what the resulting film would look like, and, remembering how pointless his creative battles at MGM had been, he kept his distance.

The Buster Keaton Story was a by-the-numbers backstage melodrama that wallowed in Keaton's alcoholic years, made it look as though his struggles in the sound era were a result of an inability to handle spoken dialogue, and ended on the jarringly un-Keatonian image of his fictionalized alter ego grinning widely as he waved at an appreciative audience. At least the script's thoroughgoing inaccuracy meant that neither of his two ex-wives had reasonable grounds to object to their portrayal, since neither the social-climbing showgirl played by Rhonda Fleming nor the preternaturally supportive casting agent-turned-wife played by Ann Blyth bore any resemblance to women in Keaton's real life (or in the real world). This did not stop Mae Scriven, then working as a beautician in New York under the name Jewel Steven, from filing a $5 million libel lawsuit against Paramount, but the suit went nowhere.

Buster and Eleanor privately regarded the biopic as mortifying hokum. "We went to the first preview at a theater over in Glendale," she remembered, "and we practically crawled on our hands and knees to get away, and just got away as quick as we possibly could, almost before the thing ended, it was so horrible."[20] Given the film's inaccuracies, the fact it was also a stinker probably came as a relief: they knew it would soon sink from sight, and they had already collected their $50,000, which they spent on the first home they bought together and the last place Buster would live: a two-bedroom ranch house on an acre and half of land in the San Fernando Valley community of Woodland Hills.

In 1957, on the movie's release, the Keatons gritted their teeth and made the rounds on TV to plug *The Buster Keaton Story*. One day, believing he was headed for a business meeting at NBC, Keaton found himself ambushed into a guest appearance on *This Is Your Life*, with surprise visits from major figures in his life that had been arranged in advance by Eleanor in an experience she dryly described as "hell." His evident misery at hearing his life story recapped in the maudlin tones of host Ralph Edwards gives way to glimpses of real emotion at only a few points. When the actress Louise Dresser, an old friend of his parents from vaudeville days, comes out of the wings to embrace him, his eyes fill with tears, which she gently wipes away, saying "Don't cry, you'll make me cry too." When Dresser's namesake, Keaton's younger sister Louise, makes an entrance, he affectionately mock-strangles her, evident sibling code for "how could you do this to me?"[21] And when Eleanor finally shows up as the last member of the guest lineup, his relief at her presence is palpable. As she sits down beside him for the interview portion of the show, he shoots her a look and asks, "Did you rehearse this?"

In the late fifties and early sixties Keaton began supplementing the income he was earning from walk-on movie roles by appearing in TV commercials, an emerging market now that small-screen advertising was moving away from the old model by which a single company would sponsor an entire show (the *Texaco Star Theater*, the *Kraft Television Theatre*) in exchange for personal on-air endorsements from the hosts. As TV moved away from the customs of radio, ads became small freestanding spots interspersed throughout a program, and these mini-movies turned out to be well suited to Keaton's gifts.

His unsmiling visage, by then deeply etched with lines, became the face at various times of Alka-Seltzer, Simon Pure beer, Ford Econoline vans, Shamrock motor oil, Milky Way candy bars, and Levy's rye bread. He seldom turned down an offer for a well-paid commercial job, telling an interviewer, "It's easy work for me. Do 'em quick and stay home here and enjoy life."[22] Enjoy life he certainly did in those years, but the "stay home" part was not strictly accurate; Eleanor estimated that in his later years she and her husband spent an average of six months a year on the road, making out-of-town TV or stage appearances, shooting movies abroad or touring in summer-stock plays.[23]

Part of the motivation for doing ads, no doubt, was to put away money for Eleanor to live on after his death. But commercials also gave Keaton the chance to dream up stunts and gags again: an elaborate car chase for a Ford ad, a series of silent pantomime sketches for Simon Pure beer, or an elaborate swan dive from a high board for a Jeep commercial. His ads tended to have a clean visual style, with the camera placed far back enough to show his whole body in the frame and no cuts to interrupt the action. The companies that hired him as their spokesperson got a seasoned director into the bargain, and most of them seem to have taken advantage of that fact by letting him take charge of both conception and execution.

Between TV commercials and small movie roles, Keaton wasn't hurting for work when, in the spring of 1964, he was approached by a young theater director named Alan Schneider about starring in a short art house film called simply *Film*, the first and, as it would turn out, last movie to be scripted by the Irish modernist playwright Samuel Beckett. Schneider, like Beckett, had no practical experience in filmmaking. He had made his name directing the first American productions of many of Beckett's plays, including the American debut of *Waiting for Godot* in 1956 at, of all places, the Coconut Grove Playhouse in Miami—essentially an out-of-town tryout for an eventual Broadway production that Schneider would not direct.[24] At that time, Keaton had been offered the role of Lucky, an enslaved character who shows up midway through the first act and never speaks a word until near the play's end. Prodded to make a speech by his master, Pozzo, who has been leading him around the stage on a rope, Lucky delivers a single three-page-long monologue that is a parody of theological gibberish, devolving as it goes along into delirious stammered nonsense.

It's easy to see why Beckett might have envisioned Keaton as a potential Lucky, and why eight years later the playwright chose to cast the comedian in his sole venture into filmmaking.[25] As a teenager in the Dublin suburb of Foxrock, Beckett had been a passionate fan of silent comedy, from Chaplin to Keaton to Laurel and Hardy. The trappings of that era's screen clowns—baggy hobo clothes, worn-out shoes, and battered hats—show up over and over in the detailed costume descriptions Beckett supplied for many of his plays: the donning, doffing, and swapping of bowler hats is a significant running joke in *Godot*. And among all the silent film comedians it is clearly Keaton, with his stoic acceptance of an implacably hostile universe, whose sensibility meshes closely with Beckett's. A Keaton hero might, as in *The Frozen North*, step out of the New York subway and find himself in the icy Arctic Circle; a Beckett character might, as in *Endgame*, begin a play buried up to her waist for no discernible reason. The only recourse, in both scenarios, was to accept the incomprehensible circumstances one found oneself in and proceed with the business of life, in all its cosmic and comic absurdity.

As a onetime "human mop" whose comedy had always derived from his placid acceptance of extreme physical circumstances, Keaton would likely have made a sublime Lucky, and the part of him that shunned pretension would surely have grasped the deeper sense, if not the exact meaning, of Lucky's torrent of quasi-erudition. He would also have had the chance to work with his old vaudeville compatriot Bert Lahr, *The Wizard of Oz*'s cowardly lion, who played one of the two principals in the Coconut Grove preview. But Eleanor Keaton habitually prescreened the scripts her husband was sent, and upon reading the play she told him that "I can't make any sense of this thing. I have no idea what it's about."[26] Buster took her at her word and turned down the job without reading a single line of the play that would become one of the landmarks of twentieth-century drama.

Years after Buster's passing, Eleanor stuck to her guns, telling an interviewer that "when they get super-intellectual and artistic with me, they lose me." And it's likely that if he had read the *Godot* script, as Eleanor urged him to, Buster would have been equally puzzled. Among many traits the couple shared was a lack of and general indifference toward formal education. Eleanor's father, an electrician at Warner Bros. studios, had died in a work accident when she was ten, and at fifteen she dropped out of school to help support her mother and younger sister as a dancer, much as Buster's stage prowess had supported the Keatons from his early childhood on. Both grew up on the old-school ethos that an entertainer's job was to amuse and impress audiences; in Buster's words, "the audience's duty ended when they paid to get in."[27] The idea of a two-and-a-half-hour-long play about the emptiness of existence must have struck them as simply silly. Yet when he played the lead in Beckett's *Film* eight years later, Keaton was able to deliver a performance of haunting power that far outstrips the quality of the film itself—even if he did later tell a journalist, "Heck, I'd be the last one to comment, because I didn't know what those guys were doing half the time."[28]

Contradictory stories abound about the making of *Film*, which took place in lower Manhattan over eleven broiling-hot days in the summer of 1964. An essay Schneider wrote to accompany the published screenplay suggested that the director, actor, and playwright had next to nothing to say to each other, describing an awkward three-way meeting in a New York hotel room during which Keaton's eyes remain glued to a Yankees game while he answered their questions in monosyllables. But a *New Yorker* item reported on the *Film* set observed a "wordless conversation" between the playwright and the comedian between setups: as Beckett watched, Keaton performed a mini-pantomime that involved searching for change in his pocket, finding none, then continuing to dig through an imaginary hole in the pocket all the way down to his pant cuff. "Upon reaching the cuff," the author writes, "he produced a quarter, held it up triumphantly, and handed it to Beckett. Beckett threw back his head and laughed."[29]

Precious little of that skill for improvisation found its way into *Film*. This twenty-minute-long black-and-white short, silent but for one whispered "Shhhh!" is a dour cinematic exploration of the philosophical principle that, in the Latin phrase that opens the published script, *esse est percipi* — to be is to be perceived. What story there is involves Keaton's nameless character (in the script he is called "O," though this name never appears in the film) trying to escape the eye of the camera (personified in the script as "E") as it chases him through rubble-filled streets.

Pursued by this unseen tormentor, O runs into a building, up a staircase, and eventually into a very Beckettian room, run-down and bare but for a bed, a rocking chair, a goldfish bowl, a parrot cage, and what the script describes as a "large cat and small dog" who both have an "unreal quality." Keaton is shot only from behind until the film's final moments, when the camera, as if possessed of its own consciousness, sneaks up on him as he falls asleep in the rocker. The ending shows his face in extreme close-up, one eye covered with a patch, as he awakes to regard the camera with an expression of abject horror, then buries his face in his hands.

There is one bit of business involving the ejection of the dog and cat — each time he puts one outside the door, the other runs back in — that is as close as *Film* ever gets to physical comedy. Before the shoot Keaton had offered to contribute ideas to this cat-and-dog routine, the only part of the script he liked or understood. Schneider rebuffed this offer with the chilly reply that interpreters of Beckett "didn't normally pad [his] material."[30] When it came time to shoot the scene, though, Schneider had to concede that "some of the outtakes, with Buster making faces at the animals and breaking up, were funnier than anything in the film."[31]

Then again, there have been wakes that are funnier than anything in *Film*. In his prose and his writing for the stage, Beckett could be riotously, scabrously hilarious in a way that made comedy indissoluble from tragedy; *Godot* is nothing if not an illustration of his ability to write great material for clowns. But his sole venture into cinema came with such a heavy conceptual apparatus — essentially, the idea that the camera's gaze is a terrifying and even violent threat — that no one present on set, not even the legendary Russian cinematographer Boris Kaufman, had a clue how to translate the cerebral Irish playwright's vision onto celluloid. The deepest irony in regard to *Film*'s failure to pull off its creators' tricky visual premise is that the most knowledgeable and intuitive cinematic mind on the set, Keaton's, was never consulted at all.

By everyone's account—Schneider's, Beckett's, Eleanor's, and that of James Karen, who played a small role in *Film*—the shoot was a grueling experience. The sixty-eight-and-a-half-year-old Keaton, clad in his traditional porkpie hat and one of the long heavy overcoats Beckett loved to dress his characters in, did take after take at a full run in ninety-degree heat while Schneider learned on the fly how to match shots and expose footage properly. The fact that Keaton had no understanding of the project as a whole made him the ideal Beckettian actor: the playwright had long been up front about preferring interpreters of his work who made no inquiries into its meaning. Schneider had had doubts about casting Keaton in the role, but once on set both he and Beckett were thrilled with the comedian's performance and awed by his capacity to endure physical discomfort. In Beckett's recollection, "while I was staggering in the humidity, Keaton was galloping up and down and doing whatever we asked of him."[32]

The location, a construction site near a soon-to-be-demolished wall in lower Manhattan, was soon overrun with gawkers. Allen Ginsberg dropped by to observe the filming with his longtime partner Peter Orlovsky, and later wrote a poem about the experience of seeing Keaton "under the Brooklyn Bridge / By a vast red-brick wall still deadpan alive in red suspenders."[33] A thirteen-year-old film buff named Leonard Maltin came to the set with a school friend, spotted Keaton reading a newspaper in the backseat of his car, and shyly approached to introduce himself.[34] The project's intellectual cachet also attracted a contingent of European admirers. The French director Alain Resnais showed up to observe the filming with actress Delphine Seyrig, and took a stark black-and-white snapshot of Keaton standing alone against the crumbling brick wall that could easily have been a still from *Hiroshima Mon Amour*, Resnais's influential art house hit from five years before.

Film had its world premiere at the Venice Film Festival in September 1965. As Schneider had feared might happen, it was received by audiences more as a Keaton project than a Beckett one. Buster, by then nearly seventy and, though he didn't know it, dying of the lung cancer that would put an end to his life less than five months later, attended the festival and was met after the screening with a five-minute-long standing ovation. Addressing the crowd with tears in his eyes, he made a brief speech: "This is the first time I've ever been invited to a film festival, but I hope it won't be the last."[35] (It was nineteen words longer than the speech he had given when accepting his only Oscar, for career achievement in 1960: "Thank you.")

Most audiences greeted *Film* with befuddlement. When it played at the New York Film Festival a few weeks later some critics even took offense at what they saw as its deliberate obscurantism. The *New York Times's* Bosley Crowther called the short "a miserable and morbid exercise" and suggested that the way it used Keaton's familiar persona disrespected a cinematic legend: "It is a cruel bit of obvious symbolism in which to involve an old star who has given a lot of pleasure to millions of people."

Film never found distribution outside the festival circuit, and was seldom seen until its restoration and rerelease, alongside the fascinating experimental documentary *Notfilm*, in 2015. For some, though, the could-have-been mystery of this collaboration between two towering twentieth-century artists has remained a subject of fascination. The French philosopher Gilles Deleuze, writing his last book in 1993, named *Film*, then mostly regarded as a hard-to-find art house curio, as "the greatest Irish film"[36]—a strange honor, given Beckett's profound alienation from the homeland he once called "the place of my failed abortion."[37]

Beckett himself told Schneider he regarded their collaboration as an "interesting failure." "In some strange way," he wrote in a letter to the film's editor soon after the shoot was done, "it gains by its deviations from the strict intention, from the big crazy idea to a strangeness and beauty of pure image."[38] Keaton insisted in interviews that the playwright's unlikely venture into cinema was nothing but "a wild daydream he had," but his guess as to *Film*'s possible meaning is essentially a reformulation of *esse est percipi*: "A man may keep away from everybody, but he can't get away from himself."[39]

Film's success or failure was a matter of little concern to its star. The project came along at a time in his life when, as far as he was concerned, there were more interesting things going on. His own films were starting to be restored and rediscovered at festivals and retrospectives around the world thanks to his work with Raymond Rohauer, an obsessive collector of silent movie prints and the manager of the Coronet Theater in Hollywood. After Buster and Eleanor attended a screening of *The General* there in 1954, Rohauer approached them and, despite Buster's reticence, struck up a conversation. Over the next few years the two men became unlikely business partners on a quest to track down as many as possible of Buster's independent features and shorts, transfer them from decaying nitrate film to fire-resistant safety stock, and secure the rights so that the Keatons could profit from the movies' distribution around the world. Some of these prints were being kept in the Keatons' garage, where to Rohauer's horror Buster casually inspected the highly flammable reels with a lit cigarette in his mouth. Other prints were found moldering in a tool shed on the grounds of the Italian Villa, which by then belonged to the actor James Mason and his family.[40]

Rohauer had a penchant for promotion, including self-promotion. Unlike Keaton, he was a shameless credit hog who enjoyed slapping his name onto the opening titles of every film he acquired in the largest type possible, and his ethically dubious copyright lawsuits rubbed many in Hollywood the wrong way. His freewheeling approach to securing movie rights was often seen as a form of piracy, with one associate calling him "the carrion crow of Beverly Hills."[41] The Keatons were not fond of Rohauer personally, and Eleanor made a point of telling interviewers to take anything he said about her husband or his work with a grain of salt. But Rohauer's ruthless dedication to tracking down and restoring lost silents is the reason many of Keaton's films—along with Harry Langdon's, the German Expressionist actor Conrad Veidt's, and a warehouse full of outtakes from Chaplin's silents—have survived to be watched and studied into the present day. Because of Rohauer's efforts, by the time Keaton took that bow at the Venice Film Festival he was in the midst of a full-on career resurgence, one that continued after his death as more lost films were recovered and restored.

Amid all the showbiz pies Keaton had a finger in during the 1960s — commercials, bit parts in American and foreign films, summer-stock tours in Broadway revivals, appearances at state fairs with Eleanor, a stint in Las Vegas — there was one late-life project that reflected his own creative sensibilities better than anything he had done on film since the arrival of sound. That was *The Railrodder,* a comedy short commissioned by the National Film Board of Canada in 1964 to promote tourism in the country. Only a few months after the muggy and uninspiring *Film* shoot ended, Buster and Eleanor found themselves living for six weeks in a comfortably appointed private railroad car as they crossed the whole of Canada, from Nova Scotia to Vancouver, filming *The Railrodder.* The director, a young British-Canadian named Gerald Potterton, was a longtime Keaton fan who not only listened to his star's suggestions but virtually allowed him to codirect the movie.

The result is, in a way, the twentieth and final silent Buster Keaton short, made over forty years after his last one before going into features (*The Love Nest,* in 1923). It was not the last film Keaton would appear in — in the remaining fifteen months of his life after its completion, despite worsening health, he traveled to Italy to appear in the low-budget farce *Due Marine e un Generale* (released in English-speaking countries as *War Italian Style*), to Spain to film his bit part in *A Funny Thing Happened on the Way to the Forum,* and to Canada once again to star in *The Scribe,* an industrial film about construction site safety. But *The Railrodder* might legitimately be considered Keaton's personal farewell to cinema, the last time he was involved in a project that made use of the full range of his gifts (or most of them; left to his own devices he might have come up with a slightly more substantial story).

The Railrodder's premise is so simple as to barely constitute a plot: Keaton's nameless and never-speaking character responds to a newspaper ad's invitation to "SEE CANADA NOW!" by traversing the country alone in a one-man railway speeder. In this conflict-free reenvisioning of

The General, Buster encounters the occasional train-related setback, but given the lack of a pursuing enemy or any real goal other than to enjoy the journey, most of the action revolves around the daily tasks he struggles to complete on the tiny moving vehicle. As the backdrop changes from pine forests to open plains and the skylines of various Canadian cities, the imperturbable voyager hangs his laundry out to dry, knits a sweater to protect against the chill, hunts for duck behind a leaf-covered blind, and pulls an entire tea set from an impossibly roomy onboard storage box for a dainty afternoon pick-me-up. The point is as much to showcase the surrounding scenery as to stage comedic action, but the nuance of Keaton's work with props and the stillness of his presence as his trusty railcar chugs over high trestle bridges and past steep cliffs lend the film an unhurried sense of majesty. Unlike the 1920s silents, *The Railrodder* is filmed in rich color, with long takes of the solo traveler seen from afar, a lone figure traversing the landscape in his cheery red-and-yellow open-air vehicle.

The real-life Keaton loved the outdoors—his and Eleanor's honeymoon back in 1940 had been a weeklong camping trip—and in *The Railrodder* it's easy to sense the freedom he must have felt on a long-distance railway journey not unlike the countless ones he had made growing up on the vaudeville circuit. In the course of the unusual shoot, with the small crew living in a string of railroad cars as the filming moved westward, Potterton and the Keatons grew close. Decades after Buster's death, the director continued to visit Eleanor whenever he came through Los Angeles; today in his nineties, after five decades as a director and animator, Potterton remembers the making of *The Railrodder* as one of the high points of his career.

Another Canadian filmmaker, a documentarian named John Spotton, tagged along on the shoot to make a behind-the-scenes documentary called *Buster Keaton Rides Again*, also financed by the National Film Board. Keaton wasn't thrilled with the presence of this secondary crew, fearing that being filmed in offscreen moments would violate his long-standing personal rule about staying in character on camera. But the result of Spotton's labors, a fifty-five-minute black-and-white companion to *The Railrodder*, is priceless viewing to anyone interested in what Keaton was like as a performer, a director, and a private person.

Except for the odd still photo and the testimony of a few silent-era colleagues, there are few records of what he was like on set, but *Buster Keaton Rides Again* captures Keaton and Potterton in the act of debating camera setups and solving problems as they arise. Discussing a moment involving a nonprofessional bit player, Keaton agrees with the younger director that, above all, the man should not be instructed to "act." Codirecting a scene in which a group of railway workers, all native Italian speakers, come running out of a tunnel, he physically places each extra where he needs him to be in relation to the camera, communicating his intentions with movement rather than words. (Two French clowns who worked with him at the Medrano circus remembered a similar method of nonverbal communication.)[42]

In his time off work, too, Keaton is fascinating to watch; without the stoic mask he usually hid behind when a camera was present, he is quick to laugh, tell a story, or get up from his seat and act out an idea. He launches into a spontaneous impression of Louis B. Mayer's histrionics, coaches a novice bridge player in the game's basic strategy, blows out the candles on his sixty-ninth birthday cake (it would be his second to last), and underneath the charming final credits, strums a ukulele as he sings a slightly racy variation on the old railroad ballad "Casey Jones." There are also glimpses of Buster's affectionate and teasing relationship with Eleanor, whom we see joining him for a game of cards and badgering him to lie down for a nap after a long day of shooting ("I think I'll sell her," he confides to the offscreen cameraman).

In the documentary's most revealing scene, the usually amenable Keaton clashes with Potterton over how to shoot a potentially dangerous gag. As the railcar crosses a high trestle bridge over a river, the plan is for the character's unfolded map to blow into his face, enveloping his whole upper body in a flapping sheet of paper as he struggles to free himself—a higher-stakes version of the old newspaper gag from *The High Sign*.

Understandably, Potterton fears the situation is too risky to film the way Keaton has devised it: a sixty-nine-year-old man, moving at a fast clip over a high drop-off, standing up in an open one-man vehicle with his vision completely obscured. But Keaton vehemently insists that he is perfectly capable of executing the gag as planned. Grumbling about it to Eleanor in their train car dressing room, he says, "That's not dangerous. It's child's play, for the love of Mike. I do worse things in my sleep." Eleanor, who would be in a position to know, doesn't disagree but advises him to take his complaints to the director, not her. In the end, the scene was filmed the way Keaton wanted it, and the result looks perfect: funny and frightening at the same time, the same combination of thrills he had been delivering to audiences since early childhood.

Coda

Eleanor

Eleanor and Buster Keaton on the set of The Railrodder.
(Photo courtesy of David de Volpi.)

Previously [Eleanor] had done no acting, had worked only as a
dancer. But she did so well in those first appearances [at the Cirque
Medrano] that I have never needed another woman partner.

— Buster Keaton,
My Wonderful World of Slapstick

A question that hangs over Keaton's late years the way "was he abused?"
hangs over stories of his childhood is this: was he disappointed at
how his career had turned out? In both instances, the question seems as
impossible to answer as it is beside the point. Just as he had always scoffed
at the notion that his onstage upbringing had been unduly violent, Keaton
dismissed any suggestion that he spent the last half of his life haunted

by a sense of professional unfulfillment. In fact, he often insisted how fortunate he was to have had exactly the career and life he did. "I think I have had the happiest and luckiest of lives," he told the cowriter of his memoir. "It would be ridiculous of me to complain. . . . I count the years of defeat and grief and disappointment, and their percentage is so minute that it continually surprises and delights me."

In his personal life, certainly, Keaton found a degree of domestic happiness in his last decade that he had never enjoyed before as an adult. He was sixty by the time he and Eleanor moved into their ivy-hung ranch house on the poetically named Sylvan Street in Woodland Hills. For the next ten years they lived there in a state of domestic contentment he had never known in his eleven years of marriage to Natalie (or certainly in his two grim ones with Mae Scriven). On the acre and a quarter of land where their house stood, Keaton planted fruit trees—lemon, peach, plum, apricot—near the stand of walnuts that were already there when they moved in, and kept a vegetable garden where he grew radishes, tomatoes, turnips, and lettuce. Every year for Christmas, his granddaughter remembers, her family would receive a ten-pound bag of unshelled walnuts.

The Keatons, who shared a lifelong love for animals, owned two successive Saint Bernard dogs in Woodland Hills; the first was named Elmer II, after Buster's long-lost pet of the 1930s, but Eleanor, grumbling that "not every St. Bernard needs to be called Elmer," insisted on calling his successor Junior rather than Elmer III. They also had a cat, Jenny, and a dozen Rhode Island Red hens in a henhouse Buster built to look like an old-fashioned schoolhouse, with a miniature flag that he raised every morning and lowered at night.

The Sylvan Street house had other whimsical features, some recalling the tricked-out dwellings from Keaton silents like *The Electric House* or *One Week*: a model train circled from Buster's garage workshop to the kitchen and out to the backyard, with train cars sized perfectly for ferrying hot dogs, popcorn, and Coca-Cola to visiting friends and grandchildren. With the earnings from his commercial work, Buster put in a swimming pool that the Keatons surrounded with colored stones they collected on their travels. They played bridge—the card game they had met over in the late 1930s and that occupied much of their leisure time for the rest of their lives together—nearly every day, whether they were at home or in one of the countless hotel rooms and railway cars they occupied during their travels around the world for work.

I don't pretend to understand the rules of contract bridge, a relatively new form of the game that was at the peak of its popularity around 1938 when Eleanor, looking to learn how to play, began dropping by the ongoing game at Buster's house without any sense of who the quiet man behind the cards was, other than that he was a gag writer she sometimes saw around the MGM commissary. But I know bridge is what enthusiasts call a "deep game." Like chess, it offers infinite potential for variation, and can never be completely mastered in the short space of a human lifetime. Unlike chess, it is also a game of partnership in which the highest skill level can only be reached when a player finds someone who can tune in, without words, to her own style of playing and thinking. A game of bridge is an intimate act, even and especially for those who, like the Keatons did, play mostly in silence.

When Eleanor and Buster were flying back from their long stretch of foreign engagements in the fall of 1965—the presentation of *Film* at the Venice Film Festival, followed by the filming of *War, Italian Style* in Italy, *A Funny Thing Happened on the Way to the Forum* in Spain, and *The Scribe* in Toronto—he was taken ill on the plane and had to be given oxygen. The next day in Los Angeles the deep cough that had been bothering him on and off for years, diagnosed just before the trip as a bad case of bronchitis, was found to be lung cancer. In what might now be regarded as a violation of medical ethics but in 1965 was simply spousal consideration, Eleanor never told Buster the truth. He was given three months to live by the doctors who diagnosed him, and the prediction turned out to be almost precisely correct. Keaton, who had always moved faster than he was expected or needed to, ended his life right on time, clocking in just a few months past the biblical allotment of threescore and ten.

Those last months were spent at home, playing bridge with friends, minding the chickens (whom Buster had named after midcentury screen goddesses: Ava, Marilyn, Zsa Zsa), and enjoying the peace of being back at the home he had taken sixty years to find. He spent only one night in a hospital, the night before his final day; soon after he was sent back home the next morning, the cancer metastasized to his brain. He spent the last full day of his life, January 31, 1966, in a highly uncharacteristic state for Buster Keaton: anger. The man who detested conflict, whose whole comic persona sprang from a kind of sublime passivity, raged mightily against the dying of the light. As Eleanor remembered it, "You've always heard the old saying about going out kicking and screaming, well he did. He didn't wanna go. . . . He didn't pay any attention to who was anywheres near him except to keep them away. He did not want any help."[1] Finally, with the help of sleeping pills, he was persuaded to lie down; by the next morning he was gone.

An aide had come from the hospital to help Eleanor, a man named Chick, and the question Buster asked him over and over on that last, mercifully short day is especially haunting in the context of the life he had just lived: "Why don't I just give up? Why don't I?" He seems, always, to have been someone for whom giving up was an unthinkable option, whether the foe he was facing was Joe Keaton's onstage wrath or any one of the implacable forces Buster was forever setting against himself in his movies: tornadoes, raging rivers, hordes of pursuing cops, avalanches of papier-mâché boulders, or whatever else fate provided.

By the time Keaton died in 1966, the medium he spent much of his late life both watching and appearing on was undergoing another sea change. If he had lived another three years, he would have witnessed the most-watched live event on television up to that time, the *Apollo 11* moon landing in the summer of 1969. Given another half decade and the will to keep performing (which it's hard to imagine him ever losing), he could have done guest spots on any of the next wave of TV variety shows that came along starting in the late 1960s: *The Carol Burnett Show, The Smothers Brothers Comedy Hour, The Sonny and Cher Show, Laugh-In.* A whole decade more of life, and he could have hosted an episode of the first season of *Saturday Night Live*. One more year after that and he might have been an all-time great guest on *The Muppet Show*. If he had made it to age eighty-eight, as Charlie Chaplin did, he would have been around for the introduction of the Macintosh home computer in 1984—a device that, like the early TV sets of the late 1940s, would surely have stimulated his technophile curiosity. And if he had lived a full century, all the way to 1995, his life span would have overlapped with the beginnings of what was then called the "world wide web" and is now so ubiquitous as to not need a name. Even at one hundred years old, it's hard to imagine Buster not being an early adopter.

As for movies . . . what would have happened if Keaton had been alive to witness the definitive demise of the studio system that had stifled his creative freedom when it arose in the late 1920s? What might he have made of the industry-changing violence of *Bonnie and Clyde*, released just a year and a half after his death, or of the art house film explosion of the mid to late 1960s: Bergman and Kubrick and Cassavetes? Would he have laughed at the show business satire of Mel Brooks's *The Producers*? When the Hays Code was finally officially retired in 1968, forty-seven years after Will Hays had arrived in Hollywood and gone out of his way to wreck Roscoe Arbuckle's career, would the seventy-two-year-old Buster have felt a private, quiet satisfaction?

Eleanor Keaton outlived her husband by thirty-two years and became, among other things, a dedicated advocate and promoter of his work, traveling to speak at screenings and festivals of Keaton silents. She also kept working herself, often with animals: she bred and trained Saint Bernard dogs, including several of the canine stars of the 1990s family movie franchise *Beethoven*. She had a job for a time at a pet shop and volunteered as a docent at the Los Angeles Zoo.

Eleanor sold the Woodland Hills ranch house not long after Buster's death and lived in a series of modest condominiums around Los Angeles, where she had a wide circle of friends both in and out of the entertainment industry. She loved *Barney Miller* and *M*A*S*H*; she cooked pot roast for her friends and went with them to movies and hockey games; in short, she had the simple, happy life Buster would have wanted for her.[2]

She never remarried, and doesn't seem to have kept playing bridge with anything like the same frequency. After all, she had lost her ideal partner.

Eleanor died in 1998 at age eighty, having lived long enough to celebrate her husband's one hundredth birthday at film festivals and screenings in his honor. Now, over 125 years since he was hurled into it, the world records his memory in new mediums he never could have anticipated but would no doubt have welcomed. Online, his wild stunts and mute expressions circulate as YouTube montages, GIFs, and memes. The movie screen he once tried to climb into in *Sherlock, Jr.* has given way to the countless private portals of home and mobile screens. He is a language everyone speaks, the language of film itself.

At the end of a research trip to Los Angeles for this book, I decided to visit Keaton's grave at the Forest Lawn Memorial Park, in the Hollywood Hills. I bought a bunch of sunflowers—a simple, unpretentious flower that seemed somehow appropriately midwestern—and called a car service to drive me to the site. The driver, a young Armenian immigrant, respectfully asked whose grave I was on my way to visit, and when I told him the name his face lit up. Buster Keaton! The whole drive we talked about moments the driver remembered from Keaton films, which apparently had been inescapable on Soviet-era television throughout his childhood. When we reached the cemetery, he helped me find the grave and stood there while we continued to talk, our mood somehow not sad but animated—even six feet under, Keaton was making us laugh.

Only when we were getting ready to leave did the driver confide that he knew his way around Forest Lawn for a reason: his own father, who had died not long before, was buried there. We decided to take one sunflower from Buster's bouquet and walk it over to his father's grave, and as we did, the driver promised that the next time he and his mother came to Forest Lawn, he would make a detour to see Buster. A few months later he sent me a text: a photo of a single rose on Keaton's grave.

It would be an easy, if inexhaustible, job to end on a catalog of all the places Keaton's influence can be seen today in the world: citations of his gags in the films of Jackie Chan or Edgar Wright, a glimpse of his speeding figure projected on the side of a building at the beginning of *John Wick 2*, the countless websites and Twitter feeds and attempted bicycle stunts he has inspired. But my most lasting memories from the experience of writing this book are the conversations with individual people, often strangers, whose faces light up when they hear Keaton's name, or who—like a teenage girl who sold me a Subway sandwich across the street from a Muskegon, Michigan, theater about to show *The General*—furrow their brows in nonrecognition but declare themselves intrigued enough to look him up later. His life, with miraculous elegance, happened to coincide with the invention of a technology that records the very thing he was unsurpassed at: movement. And so he is out there to be seen, streaming past us on every conceivable platform, still and always ahead of his time.

Acknowledgments

To write a book about someone with a legacy as huge and a public record as extensive as Buster Keaton is to enter a labyrinth of interconnected texts, films, and images. A succession of vastly overqualified research assistants helped with archive-diving before moving on to pursue their own brilliant projects: Abbey Bender, LeeAnna Bowman-Carpio, Ethan de Seife, Jo Livingstone, and Lisa Sims.

Kevin Brownlow, the dean of silent film scholars (though *dean* is too solemn a word for the energy and delight he brings to his work) generously sat for an interview in the noisy upstairs lobby of the Castro Theater during the San Francisco Silent Film Festival in 2019. If not for the work he has done over the past five decades to study, preserve, and promulgate the legacy of silent movies, the rest of us who care about them would have a lot less to watch and to write about.

John Bengtson, an expert on silent film locations, provided help not only via his indispensable books on the topic but by talking to me on the phone about the places Keaton lived and worked over the course of his life. John also brought his sharp eye and buoyant curiosity to a read of the final draft.

Dominique Jando, Greg DeSanto, Gregory May, and Steve Smith, all professional clowns and/or teachers and historians of clowning, kindly spoke to me about the influence of Keaton on their careers and on the circus profession.

Peter Labuza was always on hand with reading suggestions; every time I went to the Margaret Herrick Library in Los Angeles—which, because of Covid, was not nearly as many times as I would have liked—he was there at a table, working. Louise Hilton, a research specialist at the Herrick, was knowledgeable and responsive to my queries and understood why, even though it has been beautifully digitized on the library's site, I needed to hold Myra Keaton's scrapbook in my hands. Paul Friedman from the General Research Division of the New York Public Library came through with links to hard-to-find archives. Lauren Redniss, Karen Tongson, and David Copenhafer helped me locate and navigate academic databases while motivating me to think as rigorously and write as shimmeringly as they do.

Polly Rose was kind enough to do a "Buster read" of an early draft. Her prompt and astute responses saved me from some embarrassing errors, and she never failed to dazzle me with her truly Talmudic knowledge of silent film lore.

Bob and Minako Borgen drove me around Los Angeles to visit silent film locations, talked to me about their twenty-five-year friendship with Eleanor Keaton, and shared everything from dinner at Musso and Frank's to movies, books, photos, and hard-to-find film clips. I understand why they meant so much to Eleanor and I hope, like her, to always have them in my life.

Many members of the International Buster Keaton Society, aptly nicknamed the Damfinos, offered their knowledge, insight, and curiosity about silent film and film history. The names that come to mind are Binnie Brennan, Chris Seguin, Don McHoull, Eryn Leedale-Merwart, Gabriella Oldham, Jack Dragga, Patricia Eliot Tobias, Ron Pesch, Ruth Sharman, Trish Walters, and Vicki Smith, but many others shared ideas and enthusiasm at the three Keaton conventions I was fortunate to attend and present research at in the course of writing. Keaton's granddaughter Melissa Talmadge Cox attended two of them and graciously shared stories of her Grandpa Buster, both at the podium and over dinner. I hope we'll be able to gather again, in Muskegon or elsewhere, soon.

A small group of people existed in that rare overlap between close friend and close reader. They read parts of the draft in progress, sometimes still in a chaotic state, and offered comments or just a much-needed "Keep going": Alek Lev, Anne Gatschet, Bob Borgen, Caleb Hunt, Summer Brennan, Rachel Syme, and Zoe Rosenfeld. David Franklin descended on angel's wings at a crucial moment and brought his mighty intellect to bear on a crash read of the full manuscript.

Other friends had no direct involvement with this book, but I could never have become the person who wrote it without their conversation, friendship, and love over many years. I was writing in dialogue with them all the time, even when they didn't know it: Aamir Cheema, Ali Bahrampour, David Foreman, Elsa Davidson, Heather Caldwell, Jessica Burstein, João Camillo Penna, Jody Rosen, John Swansburg, Kevin Attell, Prudence Tippins, Romney O'Connell, Saleta Gomez, Sherrill Tippins, Sidney Bob Dietz II, Sirietta Simoncini, Timothy Noah, and—to keep this list from getting truly unwieldy—everyone in the group who gathers for fall weekends in Worthington.

My most excellent colleagues at *Slate* and on *Slate* podcasts were almost comically tolerant of my on-and-off disappearances for book leaves of various lengths. They include but are not limited to: Cameron Drews, Chau Tu, Dan Kois, Forrest Wickman, Julia Turner, June Thomas, K. Austin Collins, and Stephen Metcalf.

Writers I admire sometimes made my day by dropping me notes of encouragement out of the blue: Adam Gopnik, James Sanders, Josh Levin, Kathryn Schulz, Phyllis Nagy, and Samuel Anderson. Others were invaluable resources for their knowledge of film and theater history: Anne Helen Petersen, Farran Nehme, Fritzi Kramer, Isaac Butler, James L. Neibaur, Karina Longworth, Mark Harris, Richard Brody, Sarah Ganske, and Trav S. D.

Two complete strangers to me, Bruce Levinson and Leigh Bunton, went out of their way to lend me out-of-print books I couldn't find anywhere else. And countless people I know only through Twitter sent me down research paths I would never have thought to pursue.

The sisters at St. Gertrude's Monastery in Cottonwood, Idaho, hosted me for a five-week-long writing retreat in the summer of 2019. I can't express how much their hospitality, kindness, and respect for silence meant to me as a writer and a person. In particular, Sr. Teresa Jackson, Sr. Corinne Forsman, and my cowriting fellow Heather King made my time there peaceful, productive, and fun.

The one person without whom this book would not exist—other than Buster Keaton—is Rakesh Satyal, who convinced me over coffee not only that I had a book in me but that it was this one. In the process of shepherding it through the first three-quarters of the editing process, he became a valued friend and the most trusted of readers. My agents, Elyse Cheney and Adam Eaglin, were unfailingly patient and enthusiastic about the book even when the pandemic put a crimp in my writing plans, and Adam and his assistant Isabel Mendía went beyond the call of duty to do an eleventh-hour read of the manuscript. Jade Hui ably shepherded the project through the last stage of production, Benjamin Holmes copyedited it with Buster-worthy speed and skill, and James Iacobelli designed a fantastic book jacket from exactly the photo I chose. Nicole DiMella helped me secure rights to the images I wanted and helped me discover even better ones I would never have found on my own.

I missed out on way too much time with three wonderful families while this folly of a book came into being. My parents, Joe and Diane Stevens, gave me and my siblings Scott and Tracy a love for words and ideas and a sense of adventure that I hope we will pass down to our own kids. My in-law family—Bennett and Judie Weinstock, Nancy and Michael Yecies, and their children—put up with my extended absences with unstinting generosity. Above all, the two weird and wonderful individuals with whom I live, Robert Weinstock and Pearl Zeldin, endured an inconceivable number of hours in which I disappeared beneath piles of movies and books. I thank them for giving me the time and space to pursue what I love, though not nearly as much as I love them.

Notes

Preface 1895

1 Marion Meade, *Buster Keaton: Cut to the Chase* (New York: HarperCollins, 1995), 14.
2 Tom Gunning, "Primitive Cinema—A Frame-up? or The Trick's on Us," *Cinema Journal* 28, no. 2 (Winter 1989): 5.
3 Eileen Bowser, *The Transformation of Cinema, 1907–1915* (Berkeley and Los Angeles: University of California Press, 1990), 4.
4 Louis Tanca, "Les frères Lumière proches du régime de Vichy, ou la tache sur un symbole patrimonial de Lyon," Rue89lyon.fr, October 13, 2017, https://www.memoires-deguerre.com/2017/10/les-freres-lumiere-proches-du-regime-de-vichy-ou-la-tache-sur-un-symbole-patrimonial-de-lyon.html.

PART I THROWN

1 Rudi Blesh, *Keaton* (New York: Macmillan, 1966), 27.

1 They Were Calling It the Twentieth Century

1 Meade, *Cut to the Chase*, 25.
2 Blesh, *Keaton*, 31.
3 Meade, *Cut to the Chase*, 27.

2 "She Is a Little Animal, Surely"

1 Mary Renck Jalongo, "The Story of Mary Ellen Wilson: Tracing the Origins of Child Protection in America," *Early Childhood Education Journal* 34, no. 1 (August 2006): 1.
2 Stephen Lazoritz and Eric A. Shelman, *Out of the Darkness: The Story of Mary Ellen Wilson* (Lake Forest, CA: Dolphin Moon Publications, 1998), 325.

3 Sallie A. Watkins, "The Mary Ellen Myth: Correcting Child Welfare History," *Social Work* 35, no. 6 (November 1990), 500–503.

4 Lazoritz and Shelman, *Out of the Darkness*, 229.

5 Ibid., 325.

3 "He's My Son, and I'll Break His Neck Any Way I Want To"

1 Joe Keaton, playing the father of Buster's character in the 1920 two-reeler *Neighbors*.

2 "Laws of the State of New York, and of the United States, Relating to Children," New York Society for the Prevention of Cruelty to Children, November 1876, https://www .loc.gov/item/17018283.

3 Buster Keaton, interview with Studs Terkel, 1960; collected in Kevin W. Sweeney, ed., *Buster Keaton: Interviews* (Jackson: University Press of Mississippi: 2007), 112.

4 Buster Keaton with Charles Samuels, *My Wonderful World of Slapstick* (New York: Da Capo Press, 1982), 33.

5 Viviana Zelizer, *Pricing the Priceless Child: The Changing Social Value of Children* (Princeton, NJ: Princeton University Press, 1985), 85.

6 Benjamin Barr Lindsey, "Children on the Colorado Stage," *Survey*, October 14, 1912.

7 Elbridge T. Gerry, "Children of the Stage," *North American Review* 151 (July 1890): 18.

5 A Little Hell-Raising Huck Finn

1 M. Alison Kibler, *Rank Ladies: Gender and Cultural Hierarchy in American Vaudeville* (Chapel Hill and London: University of North Carolina Press, 1999), 120.

2 Robin Bernstein, *Racial Innocence: Performing American Childhood from Slavery to Civil Rights* (New York: New York University Press, 2011), 20.

6 The Boy Who Couldn't Be Damaged

1 The item from the Kinsley, Kansas, *Graphic* about the toddler Buster's clothes-wringer accident comes from the Pinterest account of Sarah Zittel, and was brought to my attention by Polly Rose.

2 Myra Keaton scrapbook, Margaret Herrick Library, Academy of Motion Picture Arts and Sciences, Beverly Hills, California.

3 Meade, *Cut to the Chase*, 45.

4 Tom Dardis, *Keaton: The Man Who Wouldn't Lie Down* (London: Andre Deutsch Limited, 1996), 19.

5 Meade, *Cut to the Chase*, 53.

6 "'"Buster" Is a Big Boy Now,' Mourns Daddy Keaton at New Palace," *Fort Wayne Journal-Gazette*, February 25, 1915.

7 "Make *Me* Laugh, Keaton"

1 Meade, *Cut to the Chase*, 48.
2 Blesh, *Keaton*, 82.
3 Meade, *Cut to the Chase*, 44.
4 Blesh, *Keaton*, 82.
5 Ibid., 80–81.
6 Ibid., 81.

PART II FLYING

1 Buster Keaton, interview with Fletcher Markle, *Telescope*, aired April 17, 1964, Canadian Broadcasting Company.

8 Speed Mania in the Kingdom of Shadows

1 Nellie Revell, "Speed Mania Afflicts Vaudeville," *Theatre Magazine*, October 1917, 216.
2 Jay Leyda, *Kino: A History of the Russian and Soviet Film* (London: George Allen & Unwin, 1960), 407–9.
3 Vachel Lindsay, *The Art of the Moving Picture* (New York: Macmillan, 1916), 12.
4 Lucy France Pierce, "The Nickelodeon," *World Today*, October 1908, quoted in Gerald Mast, ed., *The Movies in Our Midst: Documents of the Cultural History of Film in America* (Chicago: University of Chicago Press, 1982), 52–53.
5 Chicago Vice Commission, "Cheap Theaters," 1911, quoted in Mast, *The Movies in Our Midst*, 62.

9 Pancakes at Childs

1 Keaton and Samuels, *My Wonderful World of Slapstick*, 90.
2 Blesh, *Keaton*, 84.
3 "Remaining Childs Restaurants," *Forgotten New York*, July 25, 2015, https://forgotten-ny.com/2015/07/remaining-childs-restaurants/.
4 "Business: Childs' War," *Time*, February 11, 1929.
5 "Lost Washington: Childs Fast Food Restaurants," Greater Greater Washington, Nov. 30, 2010, https://ggwash.org/view/7454/lost-washington-childs-fast-food-restaurants.
6 E. B. White, "Spain in Fifty-Ninth Street," *New Yorker*, June 15, 1935.

10 Comique

1 Geoffrey Nowell-Smith, *The Oxford History of World Cinema* (New York: Oxford University Press, 1996), 49.
2 Adela Rogers St. Johns, "The Lady of the Vase," *Photoplay*, June 1923.

3 James L. Neibaur, *Arbuckle and Keaton: Their 14 Film Collaborations* (Jefferson, NC: McFarland & Company, Inc., 2007), 17.

4 Lisle Foote, *Buster Keaton's Crew: The Team Behind His Silent Films* (Jefferson, NC: McFarland & Company, Inc., 2014), 185.

5 Sweeney, *Interviews*, 18.

II Roscoe

1 Mack Sennett, *King of Comedy* (Lincoln, NE: Lively Arts, 2000), 45.

2 David Yallop, *The Day the Laughter Stopped* (New York: St Martin's Press, 1976), 60.

12 Brooms

1 Neibaur, *Arbuckle and Keaton*, 58.

2 Ibid., 96–97.

3 Sweeney, *Interviews*, 193.

13 Mabel at the Wheel

1 Brian Duryea, "The Necessity of Thrills," *Green Book Magazine* 15, no. 4 (1916).

2 Julian Johnson, "Impressions," *Photoplay*, July 1918.

3 Julian Johnson, "Mary Pickford," *Photoplay*, February 1916.

4 Delight Evans, "Mary Pickford, the Girl," *Photoplay*, July 1918.

5 Zanny Love, "Hollywood's Leading Ladies: Mary Pickford," New York Public Library, April 11, 2018, https://www.nypl.org/blog/2018/04/11/mary-pickford-women-hollywood.

6 Joanna E. Rapf, "Fay Tincher," in Jane Gaines, Radha Vatsal, and Monica Dall'Asta, eds., *Women Pioneers Film Project* (New York: Columbia University Libraries, 2013), https://wfpp.columbia.edu/pioneer/ccp-fay-tincher/.

7 Betty Harper Fussell, *Mabel: Hollywood's First I-Don't-Care Girl* (New Haven, CT: Ticknor & Fields, 1982), 34–35.

8 Ibid., 81.

9 Greg Merritt, *Room 1219: The Life of Fatty Arbuckle, the Mysterious Death of Virginia Rappe, and the Scandal that Changed Hollywood* (Chicago: Chicago Review Press Incorporated, 2013), 67.

10 Julian Johnson, "Impressions," *Photoplay*, June 1915.

11 Fussell, *Mabel*, 44.

12 Ibid., 53.

13 Ibid., 174.

14 George D. Proctor, "Oh, It's an Interesting Life!" *Motion Picture News*, December 13, 1913.

15 "Oh, Those Eyes," *Biograph Bulletins*, April 1, 1914.

16 Will Rex, "Behind the Scenes with Fatty and Mabel," *Picture Play*, April 1916.

17 Charlie Chaplin, *My Autobiography* (London: Bodley Head, 1964), 148.

18 Sweeney, *Interviews*, 67.

19 Ibid., 96.

20 Chaplin, *My Autobiography*, 149–52.

21 Rex, "Behind the Scenes with Fatty and Mabel."

22 Mack Sennett and Cameron Shipp, *King of Comedy* (Garden City, NY: Doubleday, 1954), 179.

23 Chaplin, *My Autobiography*, 152.

24 Sidney Sutherland, "Madcap Mabel Normand—The True Story of a Great Comedian," *Liberty*, September 6, 1930.

25 Chaplin, *My Autobiography*, 150.

26 Fussell, *Mabel*, 95.

27 Minta Durfee, interview by Don Schneider and Stephen Normand, July 21, 1974, https://www.angelfire.com/mn/hp/minta1.html.

28 Adela Rogers St. Johns, *Love, Laughter and Tears: My Hollywood Story* (Garden City, NY: Doubleday, 1978), 67.

29 "Mabel Normand Fighting Death," *Los Angeles Herald*, September 20, 1915.

30 "Octopus Seizes Mabel Normand," *Photoplayers Weekly*, September 4, 1915.

31 Steve Massa, *Slapstick Divas: The Women of Silent Comedy* (Albany, GA: Bear Manor Media, 2017), 40.

32 Randolph Bartlett, "Why Aren't We Killed," *Photoplay*, April 1916.

33 Karen Ward Mahar, *Women Filmmakers in Early Hollywood* (Baltimore: Johns Hopkins University Press, 2006), 123.

34 Fussell, *Mabel*, 234.

35 Ibid., 114–15.

36 Ibid., 231.

37 Sutherland, "Madcap Mabel Normand."

14 Famous Players in Famous Plays

1 Frederick Lewis Allen, *Only Yesterday* (New York: Bantam Books, 1931), 1–2.

2 F. Scott Fitzgerald, *This Side of Paradise* (New York: Alfred A. Knopf, 1920), 59.

3 Matt Kelly, "The Father of Black Baseball," Major League Baseball, https://www.mlb.com/history/negro-leagues/players/rube-foster.

4 David and Julia Bart, "The Centennial of KDKA's Historic 1920 Broadcasts," *Antique Wireless Association Review* 33 (2020): 25–32.

5 "The Bombing of Wall Street," *American Experience*, PBS, aired February 13, 2018, https://www.pbs.org/wgbh/americanexperience/films/bombing-wall-street/.

6 Ann Douglas, *Terrible Honesty: Mongrel Manhattan in the 1920s* (New York: Farrar, Straus and Giroux, 1995), 8.

7 Keaton had seen no action in the war; by the time he arrived in France the hostilities had ended, and he spent his months of service putting on shows to entertain the troops

waiting to be shipped home. Two of his early sound films at MGM, *The Hollywood Revue of 1929* and *Doughboys*, would incorporate elements of the acts he performed with his unit, the Sunshine Players.

8 Meade, *Cut to the Chase*, 309.

9 Neal Gabler, *An Empire of Their Own: How the Jews Invented Hollywood* (New York: Anchor Books, 1988), 31–32.

10 Dardis, *The Man Who Wouldn't Lie Down*, 65.

15 Home, Made

1 Philip Stewart, "Henry Ford: Movie Mogul?" *Prologue*, Winter 2014, https://www.archives.gov/files/publications/prologue/2014/winter/ford.pdf.

2 Katherine Cole Stevenson and H. Ward Jandl, *Houses by Mail: A Guide to Houses from Sears, Roebuck and Company* (New York: Preservation Press, 1986), 19–32.

3 Sweeney, *Interviews*, 125.

4 Lea Stans, "Sibyl Seely, Buster's Most Charming Leading Lady," *Silent-ology*, July 21, 2015, https://silentology.wordpress.com/2015/07/21/sybil-seely-busters-most-charming-leading-lady/.

5 Sybil Seely has historically been credited as Buster's wife in *The Frozen North*, though that character appears to be played by an unknown actress who resembles her.

16 Rice, Shoes, and Real Estate

1 Margaret L. Talmadge, *The Talmadge Sisters* (Philadelphia: J. B. Lippincott Co., 1924), 174–75.

2 Meade, *Cut to the Chase*, 144.

3 Keaton and Samuels, *My Wonderful World of Slapstick*, 135.

4 John Bengtson, "Greenacres, Pickfair, Chaplin's Breakaway Home, and Keaton's Italian Villa," *Silent Locations*, March 5, 2019, https://silentlocations.com/tag/buster-keatons-italian-villa/.

17 The Shadow Stage

1 F.P.A., "Plutarch Lights of History no. 3: Charles Chaplin," *Harper's Weekly*, March 25, 1916.

2 Minnie Maddern Fiske, "The Art of Charles Chaplin," *Harper's Weekly*, May 6, 1916.

3 Charles Grau, "Charlie Chaplin," *Harper's Weekly*, May 6, 1916.

4 Sime Silverman, "The Life of a Cowboy," *Variety*, January 19, 1907.

5 Anthony Slide, *Inside the Hollywood Fan Magazine* (Jackson: University Press of Mississippi), 3–21.

6 Barbara Hall, "Gladys Hall," in Jane Gaines, Radha Vatsal, and Monica Dall'Asta, eds., *Women Pioneers Film Project* (New York: Columbia University Libraries, 2013), https://wfpp.columbia.edu/pioneer/gladys-hall/.

7 Frank R. Adams, "The Stuffed Shirt," *Photoplay*, October 1923.

18 Battle-Scarred Risibilities

1 Harriet Hyman Alonso, *Robert Sherwood: The Playwright in Peace and War* (Amherst: University of Massachusetts Press, 2007), 12–20.

2 Robert Sherwood, Silent Drama, *Life*, March 3, 1921.

3 Ibid., December 29, 1921.

4 Ibid., October 25, 1923.

5 Ibid., March 3, 1921.

6 Ibid., October 6, 1921.

7 Ibid., February 24, 1927.

8 Howard Wolf, "Buster Keaton Needs Stuffed Club, Pies," *Akron Beacon-Journal*, December 19, 1927.

9 Robert Sherwood, Movies, "The Cameraman," *Life*, October 5, 1928.

10 Ibid.

11 Robert Sherwood, "Screen Comedian Out of His Element." *Film Daily*, May 14, 1930.

19 One for You, One for Me

1 Mordaunt Hall, "A Civil War Farce," *New York Times*, February 8, 1927.

2 "The General," *Variety*, February 9, 1927.

3 Martin Dickson, "The General," *Brooklyn Daily Eagle*, February 7, 1927.

4 Katherine Lipke, "Comedy Is Lost in War Incidents," *Los Angeles Times*, March 12, 1927.

5 Dardis, *The Man Who Wouldn't Lie Down*, 144.

6 Meade, *Cut to the Chase*, 172.

7 Ibid., 165.

8 Blesh, *Keaton*, 149.

9 Sweeney, *Interviews*, 46.

10 "City Deserted for Filming Big Scene of Keaton's Picture," *Cottage Grove Sentinel*, July 26, 1926, reprinted by the Cottage Grove Historical Society in *The Day Buster Smiled* (Cottage Grove, OR: Eugene Print, Inc., 1998), 27.

11 Charles Dorn, *For the Common Good: A History of Higher Education in America* (Ithaca, NY: Cornell University Press, 2017.)

12 Sweeney, *Interviews*, 210.

13 Ibid., 175.

20 The "Darkie Shuffle"

1 Daniel Moews, *Keaton: The Silent Features Close Up* (Berkeley: University of California Press, 1977), 261.
2 The cook, who goes uncredited, was played by the pioneering Black actress Madame Sul-Te-Wan (née Nellie Crawford), who in 1915 became the first African American, male or female, to sign a film contract when she accepted a part in D. W. Griffith's *The Birth of a Nation*. She played small roles in landmark Hollywood films into the 1950s, appearing in *King Kong*, *The Maid of Salem*, and *Carmen Jones*.
3 Glenn Dixon, "The Makeup of a True Pioneer," *Washington Post*, August 22, 2004.
4 Both of these names were associated with stock minstrel types that long preceded Williams and Walker's incarnations of them. Before "Jim Crow" became shorthand for the segregationist policies of Reconstruction-age America, it was the name of a popular character (as well as a song and a dance craze) originated in the 1830s by the first major blackface entertainer, a white New Yorker known as Thomas "Daddy" Rice. "Zip Coon" was a standard type that emerged soon after, a flashy, womanizing dandy who spoke in pretentious malapropisms, underlining his tendency to talk "above his station."
5 Camille F. Forbes, *Introducing Bert Williams* (New York: Basic Books, 2008), 35.
6 Sweeney, *Interviews*, 132.
7 Forbes, *Introducing Bert Williams*, 289.
8 Ibid., 115.
9 Keaton and Samuels, *My Wonderful World of Slapstick*, 78–79.
10 Michael Feingold, "The Sad Funny Man," *Village Voice*, February 5, 2008.

21 The Collapsing Façade

1 This detail of the stunt's construction comes from the research of the Keaton collector and filmmaker Jack Dragga, who managed to find and interview one of the three crew members who cut the ropes. Based on this interview, Dragga re-creates the stunt with plastic miniatures in his short film *The Great BK Mystery 2*.
2 Meade, *Cut to the Chase*, 179.
3 Scott Eyman, *The Speed of Sound: Hollywood and the Talkie Revolution 1926–1930* (New York: Simon & Schuster, 1997), 99.
4 Mordaunt Hall, "Vitaphone Stirs as Talking Movie," *New York Times*, August 7, 1926.
5 Eyman, *The Speed of Sound*, 103.
6 *United States v. Paramount*, the Supreme Court ruling that outlawed vertical monopolies in the picture business, was still eleven years away.
7 Eyman, *The Speed of Sound*, 113.
8 Harry T. Brundidge, *Twinkle, Twinkle, Movie Star!* (New York: E. P. Dutton & Co., Inc., 1930), 209.
9 Interview with Charles Reisner's son Dean Reisner, quoted in Oliver Lindsey Scott, ed., *Buster Keaton: The Little Iron Man* (Christchurch, NZ: Buster Books, 1995), 235.

10 Sweeney, *Interviews*, 61.

11 Scott, *The Little Iron Man*, 233.

12 Dardis, *The Man Who Wouldn't Lie Down*, 154.

22 Grief Slipped In

1 Tino Balio, *MGM* (New York: Routledge, 2018), 54.

2 Louise Brooks to Tom Dardis, March 25, 1977, Louise Brooks papers, Margaret Herrick Library, Beverly Hills, California.

3 Scott Eyman, *The Lion of Hollywood: The Life and Legend of Louis B. Mayer* (New York: Simon & Schuster, 2012), 128.

4 Joyce Milton, *Tramp: The Life of Charlie Chaplin* (New York: HarperCollins, 1996), 268.

5 Blesh, *Keaton*, 297–98.

6 Ibid., 298.

7 Ibid., 299.

8 Ibid., 300.

9 Eyman, *The Lion of Hollywood*, 116.

10 Ibid., 117.

11 Dardis, *The Man Who Wouldn't Lie Down*, 161.

12 Mark A. Vieira, *Irving Thalberg: Boy Wonder to Producer Prince* (Berkeley: University of California Press, 2010), 40.

13 Blesh, *Keaton*, 303–4.

14 Imogen Sara Smith, *Buster Keaton: The Persistence of Comedy* (Chicago: Gambit Publishing, 2008), 176.

15 Sweeney, *Interviews*, 143.

16 Ibid., 144.

17 Brophy had appeared in some bit parts before this ad-libbed scene, but afterward his career took off, and he played character roles at MGM throughout the 1930s. He plays the drill sergeant who makes the Buster character's life miserable in *Doughboys*.

18 Keaton and Samuels, *My Wonderful World of Slapstick*, 212.

19 Smith, *The Persistence of Comedy*, 181.

23 Elmer

1 My late grandfather's given name was Elmer. He was a dashing, cosmopolitan, thoroughly modern man, and after their marriage in the mid-1930s my even more modern grandmother rechristened him "Mike," a name they both felt suited him much better and that he went by for the rest of his life.

2 Blesh, *Keaton*, 311.

3 "Keaton Silent and Funny," *Los Angeles Times*, June 1, 1929.

4 "Scandals of 1924," *Indianapolis Times*, July 12, 1924.

24 The Road Through the Mountain

1 In a 1921 profile Fitzgerald mentioned that "Personally, when I go to the pictures, I like to see a pleasant flapper like Constance Talmadge or I want to see comedies like those of Chaplin's or Lloyd's. I'm not strong for the uplift stuff. It simply isn't life to me." The omission of Keaton from this list of favorites is unsurprising, given that at the time of this interview he had only released a few two-reel shorts as a solo director. But it seems likely that Keaton's uplift-free comedy would also have been to Fitzgerald's taste. See "Fitzgerald, Flappers and Fame: An Interview with F. Scott Fitzgerald," *Shadowland* 3, no. 5 (January 1921).

2 Aaron Latham, *Crazy Sundays* (New York: Viking Press, 1972), 42.

3 Matthew Bruccoli, *Some Sort of Epic Grandeur: The Life of F. Scott Fitzgerald* (Columbia: University of South Carolina Press, 1981), 257.

4 Vieira, *Irving Thalberg*, 173.

5 Thalberg's appetite for story conferences was insatiable. The director King Vidor tells a story in his memoir about showing up at the producer's office to discuss a script and being asked to take the meeting in a chauffeured car. He and his cowriter had just begun laying out their vision for a western about Billy the Kid when they realized they were being driven to a funeral home. Without knowing who was being buried, they filed in and took seats next to Thalberg, who continued to whisper his thoughts about the script as the eulogies got underway. As it turned out, the funeral was for Mabel Normand, dead of tuberculosis at age thirty-seven. The silent-era legends Vidor spotted around the room included Normand's widower Lew Cody, Marie Dressler, Charlie Chaplin, Mack Sennett, Harry Langdon, and Buster Keaton, all of them crying. "I was fascinated by their faces," Vidor wrote. "These funny faces had made people roar with laughter the world over. Now they were distorted by grief into another, equally ridiculous grimace." See King Vidor, *A Tree Is a Tree*, quoted in Christopher Silvester, ed., *The Penguin Book of Hollywood* (London: Penguin Books, 1998), 144–47.

6 Arthur Krystal, "Slow Fade: F. Scott Fitzgerald in Hollywood," *New Yorker*, November 8, 2009.

7 Vieira, *Irving Thalberg*, 166.

8 Anita Loos, *Kiss Hollywood Good-By* (New York: Viking Press, 1947), 34.

9 Samuel Marx, *Mayer and Thalberg: The Make-Believe Saints* (New York: Warner Books, 1975), 231.

10 Vieira, *Irving Thalberg*, 176.

11 David Bordwell, "1932: MGM Invents the Future, Part 2," *Observations on Film Art* (blog), March 22, 2015, http://www.davidbordwell.net/blog/2015/03/22/1932-mgm-invents-the-future-part-2/.

12 Jeffrey Vance and Mark A. Vieira, "Commentary," *Grand Hotel*, directed by Edmund Goulding, Blu-ray, Warner Bros., 2013.

13 Alfred Rushford Gleason, "Grand Hotel," *Variety*, April 19, 1932.

14 Keaton and Samuels, *My Wonderful World of Slapstick*, 242.

15 Ibid.

16 Ibid., 244.

17 Ibid., 243.

18 Dardis, *The Man Who Wouldn't Lie Down*, 225.

19 Meade, *Cut to the Chase*, 205.

20 Keaton and Samuels, *My Wonderful World of Slapstick*, 240.

21 Meade, *Cut to the Chase*, 205.

22 This could-have-been is especially sad to consider, given that Todd would live only three more years after the filming of *Speak Easily*. She died at just twenty-nine, under circumstances mysterious enough that they are better remembered now than her excellent work in comedy: she suffocated in her car while parked in a garage at the home of her married lover's ex-wife, a retired actress named Jewel Carmen. Theories have persisted for decades that Todd either killed herself or was murdered by Carmen, but after an extended investigation her death was ruled to be an accidental case of carbon monoxide poisoning.

23 Meade, *Cut to the Chase*, 211.

24 Marx, *Mayer and Thalberg*, 158.

25 For an informative investigation into the location shoot of this scene, see John Bengtson, "Keaton's 'What, No Beer?' Barrel Avalanche," Chaplin-Keaton-Lloyd Film Locations (and More), September 23, 2017, http://silentlocations.com/2017/09/23/keatons-what-no-beer-barrel-avalanche.

26 Marx, *Mayer and Thalberg*, 253.

27 Ibid.

28 Bruccoli, *Some Sort of Epic Grandeur*, 340–45.

29 Dardis, *The Man Who Wouldn't Lie Down*, 246.

30 Steven Bingen, Stephen X. Sylvester, and Michael Troyan, *MGM: Hollywood's Greatest Backlot* (Solana Beach, CA: Santa Monica Press, 2011).

31 Bruccoli, *Some Sort of Epic Grandeur*, 430.

25 Not a Drinker, a Drunk

1 Blesh, *Keaton*, 314.

2 He did get top billing in a few low-budget international films in the 1930s and '40s. Only one of these, *Le Roi des Champs-Elysées*, is worth watching except for the most masochistic Keaton completist; another, the seldom-seen 1938 British flop *The Invader*, has been named by film historian Kevin Brownlow as one of the worst movies ever made.

3 F. Scott Fitzgerald, "Echoes of the Jazz Age," in *The Crack-Up* (New York: New Directions Books, 1956), 21.

4 Eyman, *The Speed of Sound*, 200.

5 "Frozen Face Film Star Collapses Under Load of Family Difficulties," *Chippewa Herald-Telegram*, October 22, 1935.

6 Ernest Kurtz, *Not God: A History of Alcoholics Anonymous*, (Center City, MN: Hazelden Educational Services, 1991).

7 Francis Hartigan, *Bill W.: A Biography of Alcoholics Anonymous Cofounder Bill Wilson* (New York: Thomas Dunne Books, 2000), 4.

8 Susan Cheever, "Bill W.: The Healer," *Time*, June 14, 1999, http://content.time.com /time/subscriber/article/0,33009,991266,00.html.

9 Henrietta Sieberling, quoted in John Sieberling, "Congressman Sieberling's Remarks about Bill Wilson's Visit to the Sieberling Estate" (speech, Founders' Day meeting, Alcoholics Anonymous, Akron, Ohio, 1971), https://silkworth.net/alcoholics-anonymous /congressman-seiberlings-remarks-about-bill-wilsons-visit-to-the-seiberling-estate/.

10 Hartigan, *Bill W.*, 60.

11 Ibid., 143.

12 Jack Alexander, "The Drunkard's Best Friend," *Saturday Evening Post*, April 1, 1950.

13 When the US entered the Second World War in late 1941, Louise and Harry Keaton both got temporary jobs in a munitions factory in Las Vegas. Buster, not wanting to leave his mother alone in the house he had bought for her and his siblings back in the early 1920s, sold the Cheviot Hills place and he and Eleanor moved in with Myra on Victoria Avenue. They would live there, at times with Louise, Harry, and Harry's wife and young son crammed in, until Eleanor and Buster finally moved into their own house in June 1956.

14 Jack Alexander, "Alcoholics Anonymous," *Saturday Evening Post*, March 1, 1941. The fact that this hypothetical drunkard and all the professionals who might help him are men echoes much of early AA writing in its blinkered sexism (one of the proposed titles for the book *Alcoholics Anonymous* was *One Hundred Men*). AA did have some influential female members early on, especially Marty Mann, who became an active advocate for the destigmatization of alcoholism and was a founding member of the National Committee for Education on Alcoholism, which later became the National Council on Alcoholism and Drug Dependence.

15 Dardis, *The Man Who Wouldn't Lie Down*, 192–93.

16 Louise Brooks to Tom Dardis, March 24, 1977, Tom Dardis papers, Margaret Herrick Library, Beverly Hills, California.

17 Meade, *Cut to the Chase*, 212.

18 "Keaton Production Moves Here," *St. Petersburg Evening Independent*, May 29, 1933.

19 Christopher Carmen, "The Florida Fiasco," in *The Best of the Keaton Chronicle*, vol. 1 (International Buster Keaton Society, 2002), 10.

20 Tricia Welsch, *Gloria Swanson: Ready for Her Close-Up* (Jackson: University Press of Mississippi, 2013), 87.

21 Megan Koester, "Hollywood's First Weight-Loss Surgery: Molly O'Day," January 20, 2020, Make Me Over series episode 1, in *You Must Remember This*, produced by Karina Longworth, podcast, http://www.youmustrememberthispodcast.com/episodes/2020/1/13 /hollywoods-first-weight-loss-surgery-molly-oday-make-me-over-episode-1.

22 DeYoung, "Making Movies on Weedon Island."

23 Ibid.

24 Keaton and Samuels, *My Wonderful World of Slapstick*, 245.

25 Ibid., 246.

26 Meade, *Cut to the Chase*, 213.

27 Ibid., 216.

28 Dardis, *The Man Who Wouldn't Lie Down*, 232.

29 Ibid., 252.

30 "He Knows How to Smile," *St. Louis Post-Dispatch*, October 2, 1933.

31 "Breakdown Proves Love Has Not Died for Ex-Mrs. Buster Keaton," *Iola (Kansas) Register*, October 23, 1933.

32 Scott, *The Little Iron Man*, 300.

33 Keaton and Samuels, *My Wonderful World of Slapstick*, 246.

34 Dardis, *The Man Who Wouldn't Lie Down*, 244.

35 Keaton and Samuels, *My Wonderful World of Slapstick*, 247.

36 Smith, *The Persistence of Comedy*, 196.

37 "Buster Keaton Comes Back to the Brighton as a Star," *Brooklyn Daily Eagle*, July 9, 1941.

38 Only one episode of this live-taped show has survived, because the only way to preserve television at that time was to use a kinescope, a primitive recording technology whose poor image quality Keaton disdained. *The Buster Keaton Show* of 1949 is often confused with the similarly titled *Buster Keaton Comedy Show* of the following year, which was nationally broadcast, taped to film without a live audience, and lasted only thirteen weeks before being canceled.

39 "3G Budget put on Keaton Teleshow," *Variety*, December 16, 1949.

40 Meade, *Cut to the Chase*, 241.

41 James L. Neibaur, *The Fall of Buster Keaton* (Lanham, MD: Rowman and Littlefield, 2010), 183.

42 Dardis, *The Man Who Wouldn't Lie Down*, 264.

43 Ibid.

44 Sweeney, *Interviews*, 12.

45 Ibid., 214.

46 Kurtz, *Not God*.

47 Some AA members weren't happy about Roth's violation of the anonymity principle, especially after she slipped back into drinking when her third marriage (to her AA sponsor) fell apart. But her public acknowledgment of her own alcoholism broke an important taboo. After her *This Is Your Life* appearance, the program received forty thousand letters from viewers asking for help with their own or their loved ones' drinking. In 1957 Keaton was a guest on the same program; his lost years were vaguely summed up as a time when "you tried to fight things within yourself, in a way," showing that the stigma around public admission of alcoholism was still firmly in place.

48 Dardis, *The Man Who Wouldn't Lie Down*, 119.

49 Scott, *The Little Iron Man*, 335.

50 Meade, *Cut to the Chase*, 238.
51 Ibid., 55.

26 Old Times

1   David Robinson, *Chaplin: His Life and Art* (London: Grafton Books, 1985), 252.
2   Lita Grey Chaplin, *My Life with Chaplin* (New York: Grove Press, 1966), 264.
3   A blood test indicated that Chaplin was not the baby's father, though he didn't dispute that he and Barry had had an extended affair. But the test wasn't allowed as evidence in court, and Chaplin eventually agreed to pay for the child's support until adulthood, though he played no part in her life. See Robinson, *Chaplin*, 525–28.
4   Robinson, *Chaplin*, 529.
5   Charles J. Maland, *Chaplin and American Culture: The Evolution of a Star Image* (Princeton, NJ: Princeton University Press, 1989), 264–73.
6   Chaplin, *My Autobiography*, 455.
7   Both used synchronized music scores based on themes composed by Chaplin, while *Modern Times* also incorporated a nonsense song.
8   Chaplin, *My Autobiography*, 387.
9   Maland, *Chaplin and American Culture*, 180.
10 Ibid.
11 John Wranovics, *Chaplin and Agee: The Untold Story of the Tramp, the Writer and the Lost Screenplay* (New York: Palgrave Macmillan, 2005), 22.
12 Keaton and Samuels, *My Wonderful World of Slapstick*, 11.
13 The Keaton tribute that closes the Agee article kicks off with a few factual inaccuracies, but it's a marvel of insight and wit, containing perhaps the most perceptive sentence ever written about the "Great Stone Face": "Beneath his lack of emotion he was also uninsistently sardonic; deep below that, giving a disturbing tension to the foolishness, for those who sensed it, there was in his comedy a freezing whisper not of pathos but of melancholia." See James Agee, "Comedy's Greatest Era," in *Agee on Film*, vol. 1 (New York: Perigee Books, 1941), 2–19.
14 Tom Stempel, *American Audiences on Movies and Moviegoing* (Lexington: University Press of Kentucky, 2001), 12.
15 Agee, *Agee on Film*, vol. 1, 250.
16 Tom Dardis, *Some Time in the Sun* (New York: Charles Scribner's Sons, 1976), 214–15.
17 Robinson, *Chaplin*, 568.
18 Scott, *The Little Iron Man*, 357.
19 "Interview with Norman Lloyd," *Limelight*, directed by Charles Chaplin, Blu-ray, 2015, Criterion Collection.
20 Five years after *Limelight*, Keaton re-created a version of the musical duet sketch on *The Martha Raye Show*, with Raye, a comedienne who had appeared with Chaplin in *Monsieur Verdoux*, in the role of the violinist. The TV version adds in many more gags focused on the pianist, and also frames more shots to show both performers at

once. Given that the purpose of the TV sketch was to showcase Keaton as Raye's guest star for the week and not to advance a story about her own character, this shift in focus doesn't necessarily indicate that all the added material was originally included in the *Limelight* version.

21 Andrew Sarris, "*Monsieur Verdoux*," in Richard Schickel, ed., *The Essential Chaplin* (Chicago: Ivan R. Dee, 2006), 262.

22 Keaton and Samuels, *My Wonderful World of Slapstick*, 271.

23 Geraldine Chaplin interview, in *The Life and Art of Charles Chaplin*, directed by Richard Schickel, 2003.

24 Meade, *Cut to the Chase*, 259.

25 Harold Lloyd is mentioned once, in the entirely neutral context of Chaplin having once rented a space previously used by Lloyd's production company. Though he waxes poetic in his admiration for some of the stage clowns who preceded him in the business, Chaplin is almost silent on his contemporaries.

26 "Interview with Norman Lloyd," *Limelight*.

27 The Coming Thing in Entertainment

1 Keaton and Samuels, *My Wonderful World of Slapstick*, 271.

2 Meade, *Cut to the Chase*, 240.

3 Sweeney, *Interviews*, 55.

4 Meade, *Cut to the Chase*, 276.

5 Brenda Neece, "A Cello Helped Launch One of the Most Popular TV Shows of All Time," Cello Museum, September 15, 2020, https://cellomuseum.org/a-cello-helped-launch-one-of-the-most-popular-tv-shows-of-all-time/.

6 "Must Revive Want-to-See Habit," *Variety*, March 1, 1950.

7 Erik Barnouw, *Tube of Plenty: The Evolution of American Television* (New York: Oxford University Press, 1982), 110–15.

8 J. Fred MacDonald, *One Nation Under Television* (New York: Pantheon Books, 1990), 60.

9 Robert J. Thompson, "Television in the United States," *Encyclopedia Britannica*, https://www.britannica.com/art/television-in-the-United-States/The-late-Golden-Age.

10 Because so little early TV has been preserved, this first series is often confused with the similarly titled *Buster Keaton Comedy Show* from the following year, and not much is known about either one. Two episodes of the second show were cut together and released overseas as a feature titled *The Misadventures of Buster Keaton*; otherwise, the second series appears to be entirely lost.

11 Matthew Dessem, *The Gag Man: Clyde Bruckman and the Birth of Film Comedy* (Raleigh, NC: Critical Press, 2015), 214–15. In 1955, Bruckman, unable to hold down a job or to manage his alcoholism, borrowed a gun belonging to Keaton, telling him he wanted it for protection on an upcoming road trip, and shot himself in the bathroom of a Los Angeles restaurant.

12 Dominique Jando, "Cirque Medrano (Paris)," *Circopedia*, http://www.circopedia.org /Cirque_Medrano_(Paris).

13 Arthur Moss, "Letters from Abroad: Cirque Intime," *Freeman* 8 (January 2, 1925): 399–400.

14 Paul Gallico, "Circus in Paris," *Esquire*, August 1, 1954.

15 Author interview with Dominique Jando, June 8, 2021.

16 Scott, *The Little Iron Man*, 342.

17 Sweeney, *Interviews*, 215.

18 Meade, *Cut to the Chase*, 302.

19 Scott, *The Little Iron Man*, 370.

20 Ibid.

21 Harry Keaton, by contrast, gets only a stiff handshake in their *This Is Your Life* encounter. Their relationship had cooled as it became clear that Harry had no intention of working toward financial independence from his brother, and in 1956, the sale of the house where he had lived on and off for decades with his siblings and their mother left him with no job and no place to go. Harry eventually moved to the California border town of San Ysidro, where he managed a hotel for a time, bet on dog and horse races, and died after a fall in the street in 1983, at age seventy-eight. See Meade, *Cut to the Chase*, 307.

22 Caryn James, "How Keaton Commanded His Life's Last Stage," *New York Times*, October 6, 1996.

23 Author interview with Bob and Minako Borgen, longtime friends of Eleanor Keaton, May 20, 2021.

24 The Coconut Grove *Godot*, a production that stayed painstakingly true to Beckett's exacting vision for the play, was a notorious flop. After confusing advance publicity billed the show as "the laugh sensation of two continents," its bleak vision of life as a perpetually extended death sentence sent the audience, largely well-heeled tourists looking for after-dinner amusement, out of the theater in droves. See Alan Schneider, "No More Waiting!" *New York Times*, January 31, 1971.

25 Keaton wasn't the first casting choice for *Film*; other names discussed included Charlie Chaplin, Zero Mostel, and the Irish actor Jack MacGowran. See Alan Schneider, "On Directing *Film*," in *Film by Samuel Beckett* (New York: Grove Press, 1969), 66.

26 Scott, *The Little Iron Man*, 300.

27 Keaton and Samuels, *My Wonderful World of Slapstick*, 280.

28 Sweeney, *Interviews*, 234.

29 Jane Kramer, "Beckett," *New Yorker*, August 6, 1964.

30 Schneider, "On Directing *Film*," 68.

31 Ibid., 81.

32 Samuel Beckett, interview by Kevin Brownlow, quoted by Brownlow in *Notfilm*, a 2015 essay film about the making of *Film* directed by Ross Lipman.

33 Allen Ginsberg, "Today," in *Collected Poems 1947–1997* (New York: HarperCollins, 2006), 353.

NOTES 415

34 Leonard Maltin, interview in *Notfilm*, directed by Ross Lipman, 2015.

35 Sweeney, *Interviews*, 232.

36 Gilles Deleuze, "The Greatest Irish Film," *Essays Critical and Clinical*, trans. Daniel W. Smith and Michael A. Greco (Minneapolis: University of Minnesota Press, 1997), 23.

37 Samuel Beckett, *The Letters of Samuel Beckett*, vol. 1: *1929–1940*, Martha Drew Fehsenfeld and Lois More Overbeck, eds. (Cambridge, UK: Cambridge University Press, 2009), 647.

38 Samuel Beckett, *The Letters of Samuel Beckett*, vol. 3: *1957–1965*, George Craig, Martha Drew Fehsenfeld, Dan Gunn, and Lois More Overbeck, eds. (Cambridge, UK: Cambridge University Press, 2014), 629–31.

39 Dardis, *The Man Who Wouldn't Lie Down*, 270.

40 Meade, *Cut to the Chase*, 250–55.

41 Michael Binder, *A Light Affliction: A History of Film Preservation and Restoration* (London: Lulu.com, 2015), 88.

42 Buster Keaton, interview in *Buster Keaton: A Hard Act to Follow*, directed by Kevin Brownlow and David Gill, Thames Television, 1987.

Coda Eleanor

1 Scott, *The Little Iron Man*, 415.

2 Author interview with Bob and Minako Borgen.

About the Author

Dana Stevens has been *Slate*'s chief film critic since 2006. She is also a cohost of the magazine's long-running weekly culture podcast, the *Slate Culture Gabfest*, and has written for the *New York Times*, the *Washington Post*, the *Atlantic*, and *Bookforum*. Stevens lives with her family in New York. You can follow her on Twitter @thehighsign.